By Force of Will

By Force of Will

The Life and Art of Ernest Hemingway

Scott Donaldson

THE VIKING PRESS   NEW YORK

Copyright © Scott Donaldson, 1977
All rights reserved
First published in 1977 by The Viking Press
625 Madison Avenue, New York, N.Y. 10022
Published simultaneously in Canada by
The Macmillan Company of Canada Limited

LIBRARY OF CONGRESS CATALOGING IN PUBLICATION DATA
Donaldson, Scott.
By force of will.
Includes index.
1. Hemingway, Ernest, 1899–1961. I. Title.
PS3515.E37Z5857   813'.5'2 [B]   76–18306
ISBN 0–670–19824–2

Printed in the United States of America
Set in Linotype Times Roman

Acknowledgment is made to the following for permission to use material:

HARVARD UNIVERSITY PRESS: Lines from *The Poems of Emily Dickinson*, edited by Thomas H. Johnson. Cambridge, Mass.: The Belknap Press of Harvard University Press. © 1951, 1955 by the President and Fellows of Harvard College. Reprinted by permission of the publishers and the Trustees of Amherst College.

HOUGHTON MIFFLIN COMPANY: Lines from "Poet" from *Songs for Eve* by Archibald MacLeish. Copyright 1954 by Archibald MacLeish. Reprinted by permission of Houghton Mifflin Company.

CHARLES SCRIBNER'S SONS: Passages from the published works of Ernest Hemingway are protected by copyright and were reprinted by permission of Charles Scribner's Sons.

"Hemingway's Morality of Compensation" originally appeared in *American Literature*, XLIII (November 1971), in somewhat different form.

To Stephen

CONTENTS

INTRODUCTION

In this book, I set out to discover and record what Ernest Hemingway thought on a variety of subjects, including love and money, religion and politics, sports and war, and then, from these disparate fragments, to construct a mosaic of his mind and personality, of the sort of man he was.

The primary place to look for Hemingway's ideas is in the fiction. As he himself put it:

Q: In your novels are you writing about yourself?

A: Does a writer know anyone better?

The beliefs of his fictional protagonists do not, of course, necessarily square with those of their creator; still, his stories and novels yield up many of the answers. "I do not believe," his friend Evan Shipman commented, "that I ever heard him express a serious opinion that I did not find later in his work."

The nonfiction is also revealing: the books, magazine articles, and newspaper dispatches in which he held forth on a myriad of topics without the gauze of the storyteller shrouding his thought. His letters constitute another valuable trove. Other information has been gleaned from interviews, from written memoirs and reminiscences of those who knew Hemingway well (I did not know him at all), and, finally, from the mountain of critical and biographical material whose proliferation testifies to his continuing hold on the contemporary imagination. The sources, in short, include virtually everything written by or about Ernest Hemingway.

Some may challenge the validity of this undertaking, on the ground that Hemingway's writing was flawed by a "deficiency of conscious mind" or "lack(ed) all mentality" and therefore does not deserve study. But it is wrong to dismiss him casually as a writer of limited intellectual equipment, however much the façades of his art and life may seem to support such a view. As Wright Morris has observed, Hemingway's famous style suggested a far simpler man than was actually the case. With its clarity, brevity, and concreteness, it was a style which militated against philosophical discourse. His plots often centered around violent confrontations leading to serious injury or death, and many of his characters were uneducated and ignorant people: boxers and bullfighters, sportsmen and sporting women. On the basis of his early fiction, Wyndham Lewis characterized the Hemingway protagonist as a dumb ox, and later critics have taken up the lead. But Jake Barnes is a newspaperman who has been around, Frederic Henry a student of architecture in Rome, Robert Jordan a college professor on leave, and Thomas Hudson a professional artist. None of these protagonists, obviously, is unlettered or stupid.

What *is* true of them all, to a greater or lesser degree, is that they share a disinclination to philosophize, much. They learn from experience, and distrust abstract generalizations. They also keep warning themselves not to think, but the warning isn't against rational thought. In Hemingway's lexicon, *to think* means to worry, to suffer sorrow, to revisit in memory the site of a trauma. In "Big Two-Hearted River," Nick immerses himself in the world of his senses: the ache of his pack, the chill of the trout stream, the taste of the beans and spaghetti. But he does not do so—as the Hemingway hero has been accused of doing—out of voluptuary tendencies or out of mindless stupor; the fishing trip is a therapeutic ritual of escape from his memories of the war. Keep busy, keep active, and you might get tired enough to stop thinking, stop remembering.

His image as an anti-intellectual was one that Hemingway himself encouraged through his rugged appearance, his adventurous outdoor life, and his open contempt for any language that smacked of the pretentious. A writer, he believed, always got in trouble when he started thinking on the page, and in Big Trouble when he went in for Big Thinking. "The essential of big writing," he commented in 1930, "is to use words like the West, the East, Civilization, etc." He'd discovered, to bring the abstractions down to earth, that "when you stand with your nose toward the north, if your head is held still, what is on your right will be east and what is on your left will be west," and though you could write "very big" putting those words in capitals, it was "very liable not to mean anything."

The easy mistake to make about Hemingway, and about his writing, is to take both at surface value alone. Margaret Anderson, who knew Ernest during his expatriate days in Paris, concluded that the one adjective to describe him was "simple." Malcolm Cowley, on the other hand, chose "complicated" as the one word which best summed him up, and Cowley, who knew Ernest for many years, came far nearer the mark, for Hemingway *was* a complicated man, with a difficult, a quirky, and frequently a contradictory mind.

Like that of most canonical American writers, his thinking both reflected and repudiated its native origins. In predicting the imminent demise of Hemingway's reputation, a critic argued in 1971 that though he had exerted an enormous influence "on the taste, and even the thinking, of the young" in his time, the writer now seemed "less a product of our tradition than a titan of ego and energy existing in a world all his own." Certainly Hemingway possessed unusual stores of energy, but he was not a creature from another planet. His ideas came originally from the American middle class in the American Midwest at the turn of the century, and were altered or discarded or, surprisingly often, reaffirmed under the stress of his tremendously wide-ranging and active life. He owes much of his staying power, in fact, to the sense of communion which his writing generates. He came from the same culture as most middle-class Americans of his time, and his "mind of great subtlety and enormous powers of selective observation" (as Allen Tate described it) mirrored and helped to shape the thinking of that culture. In a poem about Hemingway, Archibald MacLeish summed up his gift of perception through a wonderfully apt metaphor:

> There must be
> Moments when we see right through
> Although we say we can't. I knew

A fisher who could lean and look
Blind into dazzle on the sea
And strike into that fire his hook,

.   .   .   .

And with a fumbling hand that shook
Boat, all bloody from the gaff,
A shivering fish.

By Force of Will

i

Fame

The Writer as Celebrity

Ernest Hemingway died one of the most famous men in the world, with a reputation that transcended political and geographical boundaries. As Philip Young has pointed out, his suicide on the morning of July 2, 1961, called forth official statements of regret not only from the White House but from the Vatican and the Kremlin as well. Furthermore, he was one of the rare writers whose fiction appealed both to the general public, which made him rich, and to the gatekeepers of the academy, who made him respectable. On the ultimate value of his work, as on that of his contemporaries, posterity may withhold final judgment, but the auspices fairly gleam. Perhaps no writer who currently "is taught" in high school and college is so widely read as Hemingway, and he is exhaustively written about as well.

Most of what has been written about him, however, concentrates on his life, for whatever his reputation as an author may come to be, during the last half of his sixty-odd years Ernest Miller Hemingway was a notoriously well-known man. People knew who he was, they knew his nickname, and they knew what he looked like. Knowing so much, they sought to know more. Like Marilyn Monroe or Dwight David Eisenhower, he became, in his own time, an authentic celebrity, whose every

1

minor adventure was newsworthy. Still more remarkably, he remains a celebrity, so that his very name touches with glamour the careers of two of his granddaughters, one a writer and the other an internationally famous model.

About Hemingway's fame this side of Olympus, there can be no doubt. But two questions persist. To what degree did he cultivate his celebrity? What effect did his fame have on his art?

To a certain extent, Hemingway could hardly help becoming a public personality. According to Archibald MacLeish, he possessed the "tremendous physical presence" characteristic of leading performers on the stage or in the halls of government. "The only [other] person I have ever known," MacLeish said, "who could exhaust the oxygen in a room the way Ernest could just by coming into it was Franklin Delano Roosevelt." Malcolm Cowley was also exposed to this same quality of Hemingway's—now fashionably called charisma and applied to a good many people who do not and never will have it. Even the earliest photographs of Hemingway, Cowley maintains, reveal his extraordinary power of projecting himself, so that others in the picture fade into the background. Certainly, this was true at the Oak Park, Illinois, high school, where he spent an ordinary four years without distinguishing himself as athlete, scholar, or class officer. Yet during the last eighteen months of this period Hemingway was mentioned by name fifty-nine times—not including his own written contributions—in the pages of *The Trapeze*, the school newspaper. During his Paris days, Hemingway almost immediately gained an underground reputation as a writer to watch, though he had published very little. As Morley Callaghan wrote, he "had a peculiar and, for him, I think, fatal quality. He made men want to talk about him." They talked about him then, and they haven't stopped.

In fact, as John Raeburn's article on Hemingway's popularity points out, he qualified as the *first* genuine celebrity among American authors, though there were public writers before him who were "known to and honored by far more people" than those who read their books. When Longfellow visited England, Queen Victoria's household staff peeped from behind doors for a glimpse of the Fireside Poet. Twain succeeded Longfellow as the "beloved" public writer of his generation, and there have been others since. But only with the development of mass communication has it been possible for the public writer to be transformed into the celebrity. Raeburn describes the relationship between the mass media and the celebrity as symbiotic: in return for the fame the media "bestow upon him, the celebrity allows his private life—his character, his tastes, and his attitudes—to become a commodity to be consumed by the mass audience." In his opinion, Hemingway willingly entered into this symbiotic web, advertising himself in ways which predicted the emergence of Norman Mailer. But Raeburn ignores the point that when an artist becomes a celebrity, he will be written about willy-nilly.

Take Hemingway's treatment by Hollywood, for example. Fourteen times between 1932 and 1972 his stories or novels were converted into films. In the process, the moviemakers not only distorted much of the fiction beyond recognition but they also tried to cash in on their author's reputation. Unlike other writers, as producer David O. Selznick recognized, "Hemingway [was] himself a star. He [had] box office." So the press agents went to work exploiting their star. They understood that his mass appeal derived largely from the contradiction he apparently embodied between the rugged man of action and the effete man of letters—a contradiction nicely summed up in the *New Yorker* drawing of a muscular, hairy-armed Ernest gentling a rose in his hand. Not since Byron had a famous writer drawn so much of his literary material from his own experiences in the world out there, a dangerous world of wars and amours and gigantic animals. As the press release for Selznick's version of *A Farewell to Arms* asserted, Hemingway represented "a sort of demi-god of American manhood."

Taking their cue from this tough-guy image, Hollywood publicity releases transformed his stories into sadistic tales of adventure and sex. They spoke of the "Brutal Fascination" which awaited the moviegoer. They characterized "that Hemingway kind of love" as "vicious," "ruthless," "primitive," "LOVE LIKE THE LASH OF A WHIP, HEMINGWAY STYLE," although nothing remotely resembling the work of the Marquis de Sade appeared in his fiction, or in the movies based on his fiction, for that matter. The publicists also circulated apocryphal yarns about the author, including this one about his skill as a pugilist: "At a middleweight boxing championship bout in Paris a few years ago . . . he became incensed when the champion struck one foul after another at his opponent. Abandoning his ringside seat, Hemingway climbed into the ring, took a single sock at the champion, and knocked him out cold." To this extravagance, Ernest objected that anyone but a fool knew that "writers do not knock out middle-weight champions, unless the writer's name happens to be Gene Tunney" and concluded: "While Mr. Hemingway appreciates the publicity attempts to build him into a glamorous personality like Floyd Gibbons or Tom Mix's horse, Tony, he deprecates it and asks the motion picture people to leave his private life alone." That, however, the press agents were not prepared to do, for it was precisely his private life which stirred public interest in films based on his work. And, to do them justice, they were only slightly more guilty of propagating legends which would not bear close examination than was Hemingway himself.

For the truth is that—although his natural charismatic quality and the hungry engines of publicity helped make him a celebrity—the writer himself, or rather one side of him, also participated to the process. Ben Finney writes of lunching with Hemingway at "21" in 1935, and emerging from that Manhattan restaurant to find a group of autograph seekers on hand. They immediately surrounded Finney, whom they mistook for the actor Pat O'Brien. "You don't want my autograph," Ben told them, and suggested they ask his companion instead. "Who's he?" they asked. "Ernest Hemingway," Finney replied. "Who's he?" they asked again. The incident, Finney reported, sent Ernest into a funk that lasted through several highballs. As if to prevent recurrences, after that time Hemingway was rarely out of the news. His adventures in the Spanish Civil War and World War II kept his name before the public. When he came to New York, he either brawled in public, or it was reported that he did. His divorces and marriages were gossiped about in print, and the very social *Town and Country* magazine discoursed upon his sporting activities and his recipe for tropical coolers.

At mid-century, two long magazine profiles served to pique rather than to satisfy public curiosity. The first, by Cowley in *Life* (January 1949), presented an intimate "Portrait of Mister Papa" against the background of his earlier life and his present existence at Finca Vigia, his home outside Havana complete with swimming pool and a yacht moored nearby. The other, Lillian Ross's profile for *The New Yorker* (May 1950), recorded in full comic detail the gruff and belligerent talk of Hemingway on holiday in New York. Feinting and covering up against imaginary opponents, Ernest drank enormously, recounted in pidgin English a number of improbable adventures, and measured himself, in seemingly maniacal confusion of the fighter and the artist, against competition from the past: "I started out very quiet and I beat Mr. Turgenev. Then I trained hard and I beat Mr. de Maupassant. I've fought two draws with Mr. Stendhal, and I think I had an edge in the last one. But nobody's going to get me in any ring with Mr. Tolstoy unless I'm crazy or I keep getting better." The talk was of artistic accomplishment, the manner that of a tough.

When in January 1954 he survived two African plane crashes in the space of two days, Ernest seemed to defy mortality. Though the accidents had a ruinous effect on his health, they did provide him with the pleasure of reading his own obituaries, and of inspecting the reminiscences of a number of columnists who used the occasion of Hemingway's rumored death as an opportunity to call attention to their intimacy with him. As Richard Watts observed at the time, "I seem to be the only columnist who isn't an intimate friend of Ernest Hemingway's"; in fact, Hemingway *did* keep in touch with several of the columnists, including Leonard Lyons and Earl Wilson, during the last fifteen years of his life. As a result, John O'Hara, who in 1950 had called Hemingway the greatest writer since Shakespeare, chided him in print after the crashes for exposing "himself to overfamiliar gestures on the part of his inferiors who include not only the chatterers but restaurateurs, Hollywood producers, society folk, college professors, theatrical agents, dilettantes, punchy pugs, politicians and the Lord only knows what all." Top dog Hemingway, he wrote, had attracted more than his share of ticks, and now was the time to get rid of them. "Listen," Ernest told O'Hara, "maybe I wouldn't like your friends either."

In the summers of 1959 and 1960 Hemingway traveled from fiesta to fiesta in Spain, where he was lionized by the Spaniards as an adopted countryman, an expert on the bullfight, and an international celebrity whose very presence helped to draw crowds. John Crosby, who had lunch with him at Aranjuez in 1960, observed that a few tables away "a couple of American girls were staring hard at Papa, who—even in a Spanish town in fiestatime—was pretty picturesque," with his white beard and his hair combed down over his forehead "like the beatniks in Montparnasse." Papa enjoyed all the attention, Crosby felt sure. "He was a big lovable ham about being stared at, was Mr. Hemingway." But if he savored such moments, Hemingway understood, too, that the famous had to pay certain penalties.

The Penalties of Fame

His renown had three distinct harmful effects on the way his writing was received. In the first place, overfamiliarity with Hemingway's appearance and exploits tended to breed a measure of contempt for his fiction. To the mass media, he was primarily a lover or a fighter or a sportsman or, in his Papa role, a Nestor handing down oracular pronouncements on every subject under the sun—and only secondarily a writer in whose fiction the public discovered the reassuring illusion, as Emilio Cecchi expressed it, "of having finally hit upon a literature which has nothing to do with literature, which is not spoiled or weakened by literature."

The vast public fame and flourishing financial success also led to a second handicap: the occasional malice of the green-eyed critic who resented Hemingway's popularity. Nearly all his life, Hemingway kept up a running battle with the critical establishment, which, he was sure, was out to destroy him. Just wait, he warned the young editor of *Esquire* magazine, Arnold Gingrich, as early as 1934, wait until you become a success and make a lot of money—*then* you'll get a panning.

But the most pernicious danger of Hemingway's celebrity lay in the overpowering temptation to assess the writing in terms of the writer's life and legend. As Earl Rovit observes in his book on Hemingway, "in the case of no other serious American writer except Mark Twain and Walt Whitman [has] the writer's personality become such an intrusive and confusing factor in the judgment and reception of his works." He has been widely condemned, for example, for the callous attitude toward women supposedly exhibited in his fiction. In fact certain of his heroines are idealized, and none qualify as the helpless second-class citizens they are widely presumed to be by many contemporary readers. Often, indeed, Hemingway's fictional women emerge as more admirable than his men: braver, more faithful and loving, more responsible. Here the powerful public image of Hemingway as a much-married male chauvinist—a fairly accurate image, as it applied to the man himself—has effectively blurred the vision which readers bring to his books.

Hemingway's celebrity also had unfortunate consequences on his creative output, since the demands of fame inevitably interfered with his work schedule. The part of him which housed the private artist knew that to practice his craft he needed seclusion, isolation, respite from attention. That had been true even for Charles Baudelaire, who—Ernest informed the readers of the Toronto *Star Weekly* in 1922—used to parade through the Latin Quarter with a purple lobster on a leash. "I suspect," Hemingway wrote, "that Baudelaire parked the lobster with the concierge down on the first floor, put the chloroform bottle corked on the washstand and sweated and carved at the *Fleurs du mal* as all artists have worked before or since." Hemingway was wrong about Baudelaire; the man with the lobster was Gérard de Nerval, but the error hardly obscures his point. The job of the writer was to write, not to strike poses.

In the early stages of his career Ernest seemed to be truly "press-shy." In 1931, for example, he consented to an interview during a bibulous evening with Eric Knight, but the next day sent a note begging out of the engagement and explaining why. He had never yet talked for publication, he told Knight, and didn't want to start now, since as an old newspaperman he knew that when a writer talked, nine times out of ten he made a horse's ass of himself. It was, Hemingway said, "damned important" to him not to give the interview because talking about his work would destroy any pleasure he took in it, and once you started you couldn't stop.

Lamentably, that prediction began to come true not long after his encounter with Knight. In books like *Death in the Afternoon* (1932) and *Green Hills of Africa* (1935), and in the series of articles he wrote for *Esquire* in the mid-1930s, Hemingway elaborated on his expertise in the manly sports of bullfighting, hunting, and fishing, and interviewed himself on such profound subjects as life, love, art, war, and politics. By the time he returned from the Spanish war he had become a legendary figure, sought out by true admirers and celebrity collectors alike. Hemingway took certain steps to discourage the more flagrant invasions of his privacy—he avoided cameras and telephones, disguised his name on passenger lists, posted a sign at Finca Vigia reading "Mr. Hemingway does not receive visitors," refused to read aloud from his works, and repeatedly turned down invitations for public appearances. But by 1940, at the latest, the Hemingway myth had been established, and both in private conversations and in correspondence—notably in some tall tales concerned with his experiences in World War II—and finally in his fiction, he began to contribute his own embellishments to the legend of the vastly experienced Papa Hemingway whom Edmund Wilson called his "worst invented character."

In *Across the River and into the Trees* (1950), Hemingway constructed an unfortunate parody of this public legend. Colonel Richard Cantwell, the fifty-year-old protagonist of that novel, emerges as the least believable and dullest of Hemingway heroes. Implausibly strong despite a terminal heart condition, the colonel easily wins a fight with two young sailors who make slurring remarks about his nineteen-year-old Venetian mistress, Renata. Incredibly virile despite his age, he has intercourse with her three times during one gondola ride. But Cantwell's most disturbing quality is his virtual omniscience. Not only does he, as a veteran soldier, expound at length upon combat and the stupidity of most generals but he goes on—prompted by the adoring Renata—to deplore the ineffectuality of politicians and to indulge in literary criticism. He also demonstrates superior know-how on more trivial subjects. He has long ago "checked out" on elevators. He takes a corner table in restaurants to keep his flanks covered. He makes certain that all his pockets have flaps and buttons. He cuts clams closer to the shell than even the clam-seller does. He reaches "accurately and well" for the champagne on ice. He is entirely too expert. As the colonel says of himself, he "knows too much."

Though Hemingway and his hero are of an age, and though he was enamored of a young Venetian when he wrote the book, he was right in insisting that Colonel Cantwell should not be taken as his direct counterpart. The trouble with the novel is not that Cantwell equals Hemingway; it is that Cantwell equals Hemingway's impossible public persona—tough as nails, sensitive as hell, and wise as Jove. In *Across the River and into the Trees*, Ernest clothed his hero in the trappings of the Hemingway legend, and so compromised his art; furthermore, there are traces of the regrettable Cantwellesque manner in Santiago and Thomas Hudson, the two fictional protagonists who succeed him.

Even aside from its effect on his writing, Hemingway's notoriety took a considerable toll. His distinctive appearance and style of life offered an irresistible lure to impostors. As early as the mid-1930s, a presumed sportsman who usually stayed at the Explorers Club in New York began to pose as Hemingway in order to lure young men to his rooms. On the road, this impersonator went so far as to sign Hemingway books in bookstores and to lecture on his (Ernest's) writing. In

1952 another phony turned up in Paris trailing a string of bad debts, and yet a third pretender surfaced in Hawaii in 1956. The most persistent and successful impostor was a bullfight *aficionado* and retired oil man with a Ph.D. in Spanish, who came to Spain in the late 1950s sporting a Hemingway-like beard and doing nothing to disabuse those who took him for the author. He sometimes enjoyed hospitality in his role as substitute Hemingway and boldly signed autographs, taking care to write comments in Spanish if the request was made in English and vice versa. Even after Hemingway's death, the impostor continued to pen autographs bearing such messages as "The man you think I am is gone to glory, and so cannot sign . . . Ernest Hemingway."

At least once, Ernest's celebrity put his life in danger. Shortly after the twin plane crashes of 1954, he stopped in the Italian town of Cuneo to purchase a bottle of scotch, and in his weakened condition was nearly crushed by a crowd of admirers when the salesgirl recognized him and spread the word. At the next stop, he had his beard shaved off as a disguise; and still later, philosophizing on the close call, he concluded that the only thing that mattered was writing books that would last and "to hell with" publicity. He didn't want to be on exhibition, like an elephant in a zoo, or to settle for fame "over a weekend."

When such moods struck, he rededicated himself to his work. In September 1956, for example, he wrote a "situation report" for *Look* magazine in which he lamented that he had interrupted his writing in order to spend four months filming *The Old Man and the Sea*. "Never again," he promised, would he interrupt the work that he was "born and trained to do" until he died. It was a promise he could not keep, and one the readers of *Look* did not want him to keep. For Hemingway the writer, the work was everything; for Hemingway the celebrated man of action who loved fishing and hunting and drinking and brawling and basking in the limelight, it was not enough. Finally, he became a folk hero, an international legend, and—at his worst—something of a public fool. As Gertrude Stein observed, when the public gets involved "you are not the same you." Still, Hemingway the writer left a legacy whose significance makes his public image unimportant. What he discovered about Dante, following a trip to Italy in 1949, was that the great Italian was probably one of the "worst jerks" who ever lived, but how he could write! Perhaps, he suggested in a letter to John Dos Passos, there was a lesson in that for all of us.

ii

Money

Preoccupation with the Dollar

In a catalogue of subjects worth writing about, Ernest Hemingway included not only such predictable topics as love and death but also, rather more surprisingly, money. Of course he was right. A number of excellent novels are woven around the struggle to acquire money. Normally, though, such books have been written in America either by a social realist like William Dean Howells or by a politically oriented author like John Dos Passos in the 1930s, and in either company Hemingway seems out of place. Yet money fascinated him, and his writing—both fiction and nonfiction—is permeated with observations about, analogies drawn from, and pronouncements upon what Henry James called the world of "sordid gain."

Nowhere is Hemingway's preoccupation with the subject more evident than in his newspaper writing. In his first newspaper job, seven months as a cub reporter for the Kansas City *Star* in 1917, he was in no position to choose his subjects. He did general assignment work, covered the "short stop run" consisting of the railroad station, general hospital, and police station number four, and eagerly abandoned the post to join the ambulance service in World War I.

Following a period of recuperation from his war wounds, however, he caught on as a space-rate feature writer with the Toronto *Daily*

Star (and later as a European correspondent for the *Daily Star* and its weekend edition, the *Star Weekly*), and in that role was assigned no regular beat at all. Allowed to write about anything that interested him and that might interest the paper's readers, he chose for his first article a piece on how young Canadians cultivated the arts and saved money by circulating rented paintings from house to house. His second publication dealt humorously with the availability of free shaves at the local barber college, his fourth scornfully with a war profiteer trying to masquerade as a veteran. Other pieces, for which he was paid from half a cent to a cent a word (if and when they were printed), focused on cheap dental care from trainee dentists, the selling of outworn clothing to unsuspecting country cousins, the unmarketability of war medals, and the superiority of checks to traveling clocks (which tick away while "the young man is starving") as wedding presents.

This last, a first-person account, clearly lay close to Ernest's heart, for it appeared shortly after his marriage to Hadley Richardson. By late 1921 the American scene began to pall for both the Hemingways, and they embarked for Paris, whence Ernest would send back dispatches as a fledgling foreign correspondent. Here the problems of domestic budgets yielded to a concentration on the effects of runaway inflation. In Toronto, he had seen a barker attempt to peddle a 250,000 ruble note for 25¢, but now, in postwar Europe, he saw, and vividly wrote about, what it meant to live in a country whose money was not worth the paper it was printed on.

The country was Germany, where the mark plummeted in value from about 100 to the dollar in early 1922 to nearly 3 million to the dollar in mid-August 1923. Traveling through the defeated country in the late summer of 1922, the young correspondent found, to his middlewestern chagrin, that he had spent "something over a million marks" in only ten days (a year later, he could easily have spent over a million at luncheon). Furthermore, since the mark kept dropping in value daily, Hemingway actually had more money at the end of his spending spree than he had when he started out. If he could stay in Germany long enough, he wrote back home to Oak Park, he might eventually be able to live entirely free. For tourists and speculators, then, the inflationary spiral provided private windfalls. Those who lived on the French side of the border between the two countries, for example, could convert their francs into marks and buy food and drink for practically nothing in Germany. With disgust, Hemingway reported on the "swinish spectacle" of young people from Strasbourg crossing the Rhine to Kehl in order to gorge themselves on "fluffy cream-filled slices of German cake. . . ."

But to people on fixed incomes, to the retired, to the businessmen aiming to plow profits back into expansion, inflation spelled disaster. A widow with a family of three boys had once been considered "very well-to-do," but by 1923, her annual income could support her family for only two weeks. A married couple, each sixty-four years old and both blind, received "from their capital, which they earned by hard work, an income of 3400 marks," before inflation enough to live on, now "half a week's wages of an unskilled laborer." Fresh from his busiest season ever ("We had people sleeping in the billiard room on cots"), a German hotelkeeper in Triberg reported that "all the money we had taken in all summer was not enough to buy our preserves and jelly for next season. . . . The proprietor of the big hotel on the hill there committed suicide last week." The bitterest tragedies, Hemingway learned from those trips to Germany, were money tragedies.

In his dispatches to Toronto, Hemingway also displayed a grasp of the complexities of international finance. He understood that the German government was debasing its currency to improve its balance of trade. He saw what inflation in Germany and Austria meant to the tourist business in Switzerland, a land of hotelkeepers unable, because of the stability of the Swiss franc, to attract any customers. In a series of articles he criticized the French policy of exacting reparations from Germany by occupation of the Ruhr, a policy by which the French government aimed to ruin the defeated nation's industry while simultaneously "biting off its own nose."

On a more personal level, his newspaper accounts demonstrate Hemingway's conviction that the desire for money corrupted almost everyone. Greed led to crime, and so he wrote about devices to foil bank robbers, about a store manager's conviction that there were no such beings as kleptomaniacs (only thieves), about the smuggling of Canadian whisky into the United States at steep prohibition prices, about gunmen who could be hired for $400 to commit murders, about policemen in Chicago paid to nod while the law was broken before their eyes, about American tourists rolled in Paris after they had already been cheated of most of their money at sleazy night clubs.

Avarice produced corruption in high places as well as low. The French government sold banner space to *apéritif* manufacturers during the Bastille Day street celebrations, just as the French press sold its news space ("it is not considered very chic to advertise" in a French daily). In Italy, the bankers and manufacturers bought the services of the Fascisti to subdue the communists, and then tried to hire other mercenaries to fight the monster they had created. The way to go fishing in Germany was not to buy a license, a process involving yards of red tape, but simply to bribe a warden if caught. Upon presentation of a handsome tip, a Spanish postman would present the letters he brought for you. Madame Marie, an innkeeper in Adrianople, overcharged for her accommodations, which the guest had to share with the lice. She admitted that 100 drachmas was too much, but she ran the only hotel, and "It is better than the street? Eh?"

Through these articles runs a strongly moralistic tone and a deep suspicion of the motives of almost everyone where money is concerned. In a dispatch about the Genoa Economic Conference of 1922, Hemingway vented his scorn on Marcel Cachin, the leader of the French Communist Party, in a sketch which portrayed his "drooping face, frayed red mustache and his black tortoise-shell spectacles . . . constantly on the point of sliding off the tip of his nose." Cachin, he explained, had a very rich wife and could afford to be a communist.

This combination of high-mindedness, as to his own standards about money, and cynicism, as to the standards of others, forms but one of several contradictions in Hemingway's economic attitudes. On the one hand, he gained something of a reputation in the expatriate colony as a sponger; on the other, once he had the money to dispense, he became a more-or-less-famous soft touch. At the beginning of his career, he occasionally turned down profitable offers for his work; yet after he became a famous artist he set out to market his product for the highest possible return. In looking back on his youth, he invested poverty with an almost holy aura, and he consistently attacked "the rich" as a class in his writing, while as the years wore on he spent more and more time in their company. To find an explanation for these apparent contradictions, one must go back to his boyhood in Oak Park, during the first two decades of this century.

Ernest Hemingway's parents were solid middle-class citizens living in the eminently respectable Chicago suburb of Oak Park, the place where the saloons stopped and the churches began. His father, Dr. Clarence Edmonds Hemingway, conducted a general practice successful enough to support comfortably his wife and their family of six children. The youngsters lacked for none of the essentials of life, but in the matter of spending money, Dr. Hemingway exercised a strict frugality. Convinced, as Ernest's much younger brother Leicester put it, that "the path to hell was paved with easy money," their father issued his children an allowance of a penny per week for each year of age. The five-year-old got a nickel a week, the fifteen-year-old fifteen cents. The children were expected to contribute to Sunday school out of this beneficence, rather spartan even for the time, and particularly so in prosperous Oak Park, where the young Frank Lloyd Wright was receiving some of his first architectural commissions. They were further required to keep accounts of their expenditures and show the ledgers to their father weekly—a duty Ernest observed by lumping nearly everything under "miscellaneous." To supplement his allowance, Ernest mowed lawns, shoveled snow, and delivered the local paper, *Oak Leaves*. Around the house and at Windemere, the Hemingways' summer place at Walloon Lake, in one of the loveliest reaches of northern Michigan, he also performed other tasks for payment on a piecework basis. Nonetheless, he was often short of cash during his high-school years, a circumstance that amounted to something of a social handicap.

But there was no basic disagreement about finances until 1920, when—some eighteen months after his return from Italy—his parents grew restive about their son's apparent lack of interest in making his own way in the world. The conflict came to a head in the summer of that year, when Ernest and his friend Ted Brumback, who had been a fellow reporter on the Kansas City *Star*, were whiling away the time fishing at Windemere. Except for a brief two-week period, Dr. Hemingway spent the summer in Oak Park taking care of his practice. At the cabin, Mrs. Hemingway assigned Ernest and Brummy to dishwashing and painting and digging holes for garbage disposal until the youths finally rebelled and were ordered off the premises, shortly after Ernest's twenty-first birthday celebration. Importuned by his wife, Dr. Hemingway first wrote his son stern letters about his living up to responsibilities, and then relented in an attempt to heal the rift. Presumably he and Ernest were reconciled, but mother and son were not. She had treated him, Ernest felt, like a hired man.

During the last ten days in July, Dr. Hemingway reported to his wife every other day on his correspondence with their erring son. "I advised [Ernest] to go with Ted down Traverse City way and work at good wages and at least cut down his living expenses," he observed. "I have written him that I wanted him to get busy and be more self-supporting and respectful." And later, "It is a great insult that he and Ted Brumback should take it for granted that they can lay down on the family as they have been doing. . . . I so wish Ernest would show some decent loyalty to you and not keep on the sponge game." Then, "If those big boys had gumption at all they would have volunteered all the paint work and had it done long ago. . . . We have done too much. He must get busy and make his own way, and suffering alone will be the means of softening his Iron Heart of selfishness." Directly to his son, Dr. Hemingway wrote that he should "try and not be a sponger," that he should "pack up and try elsewhere until you are again invited . . . to Windemere."

Harsh as these communications seem, they hardly rival the dressing down that Grace Hall Hemingway visited upon her son in a letter comparing her mother's love with a bank account on which Ernest had made excessive withdrawals: "Unless you, my son Ernest, come to yourself; cease your lazy loafing and pleasure seeking; borrowing with no thought of returning; stop trying to graft a living off anybody and everybody; spending all your earnings lavishly and wastefully on luxuries for yourself . . . unless, in other words, you come into your manhood, there is nothing before you but bankruptcy—you have overdrawn. . . ."

It was a message Ernest Hemingway could neither forgive nor forget.

Offers Refused and Accepted

From his parents' point of view, their son had stalled long enough—doing odd jobs, but nothing steady—after his return from the wars. It was time for him to settle down, to work full time, at the very least to go to college. But Ernest could ill abide such disapproval, especially since in his upbringing he had assimilated the same Protestant work ethic which motivated their criticism. Besides, he knew (as his parents seem not to have known) that he had already rejected a most appealing opportunity to subsist on another man's generosity.

The offer had come while Ernest was still in Italy, recuperating from wounds inflicted by mortar and machine-gun fire at Fossalta. During this period Ernest fell in love with and hoped to marry Agnes von Kurowsky, one of his American Red Cross nurses. Agnes, more than seven years older than her handsome nineteen-year-old patient, seems not to have taken his proposal very seriously. Nonetheless, she tentatively agreed to follow him back to the States, less out of any commitment to their relationship than out of the conviction that it was in Ernest's best interests. If he stayed in Europe, she felt, he would be making a very bad mistake, one which involved a man named James Gamble.

A wealthy man in his mid-thirties (he was related to the Gambles of Procter and Gamble), Gamble served in the summer of 1918 as Inspector of Rolling Canteens for the Red Cross in Italy. In June he came to Schio, where Ernest was driving ambulances, seeking volunteers to distribute cigarettes and chocolate to the Italian troops on the Piave. Along with a number of his friends, Ernest held up his hand, and on about July 1, Captain Gamble drove Hemingway, Bill Horne, and Warren Pease from Schio to the Piave, dropping off Horne and Pease at San Pedro Norello, but taking Hemingway on to Fossalta, where, a week later, he suffered the injury that cured him of any feelings of immortality.

After a successful operation in Milan to remove *scaggia* fragments from his legs, Ernest received a succession of visitors at the hospital. As the first American *wounded* in Italy (though another Red Cross volunteer, Lieutenant Edward M. McKey, had been killed on June 16), he qualified as something of a celebrity and, besides, as Agnes remembers, "men loved him," he "could keep them entertained with his tales as they sat around his bed." Among the visitors were Red Cross captains Meade Detweiler, Bob Bates, and Gamble. In October Hemingway went back to the front, where he almost immediately came down with jaundice. Gamble accompanied him on the painful trip back to the hospital in Milan, and smoothed out all the bad part by making Ernest "perfectly comfortable." Soon after, he made the young ambulance driver a proposal that was very difficult to refuse: that he stay on in Italy for a year, all expenses paid, as his secretary and companion.

When Agnes got wind of the proposal, she advised strongly against it, since she was afraid such a life would turn Ernest into a bum, a sponger, and a floater. She had experienced similar feelings herself, she admitted: "When I was with Jessup [another of the nurses] I wanted to do all sorts of wild things—anything but go home—and when you [were] with Captain Gamble you felt the same way. But I think maybe we have both changed our minds—and the old États-Unis are going to look très, très bien to our world-weary eyes." He should go on ahead, and she would follow him to the States as soon as she could. Before he made up his mind to leave, however, Ernest went to visit Gamble at a villa he had rented in Taormina, Sicily—a visit he later took pains to deny to E. E. (Chink) Dorman-Smith, a young Anglo-Irish infantry officer whom he had met (and immediately admired for his wound stripes and combat experience) in the Officers' Club in Milan.

According to the yarn he told Dorman-Smith (later Dorman-O'Gowan), he had set out for Taormina in mid-December but never got there; he had "seen nothing of Sicily except from a bedroom window because his hostess in the first small hotel he stopped in had hidden his clothes and kept him to herself for a week." From the Gamble-Hemingway correspondence, however, it is clear that Ernest did stay with him at Taormina, and that they enjoyed a most pleasant time together. Indeed, these letters suggest that much of his bitterness at the "Dear Ernest" letter from Agnes, which reached him in Oak Park late in March 1919, may be traced to resentment over his having passed up the chance for a year in Taormina, Mallorca, and other resorts, in favor of a faithless woman. Viciously, Ernest replied to Agnes's letter of rejection by accusing her of trickery and bitchery, concluding with the wish that when she did return to the United States, she might "slip on the dock and knock out all of her teeth."

On March 3, before receiving her letter, Ernest had written Gamble an intimate note in an apparent attempt to keep his options open. Every minute of every day, Ernest said, he kicked himself for not being at Taormina with Jim, where they had strolled, pleasantly "illuminated," through the beautiful old place, watching the moon path on the sea below and Mount Etna fuming above, then returned to see the black shadows and the moonlight cutting down the stairway back of the villa. He was so sick to be back there that he raised a glass in transatlantic toast to Gamble, his "Chief."

Hemingway's letter crossed the ocean twice before catching up with Gamble at the Racquet Club in Philadelphia, whence he responded on April 16. Why he'd abandoned that magic place Taormina (so lovely, as Booth Tarkington once observed, that he could no more work there than he could in Hell) was beyond Gamble's comprehension. After Ernest had left, there was not a day in which Jim did not think of him and how the only thing lacking was a congenial spirit like himself to complete a nearly perfect situation. Two fellows had come down from Rome to recuperate from the flu and Gamble had taken them in for a few weeks, but they lacked imagination and a sense of humor. The standard set by Ernest, his first guest, was a bit too high. It was a shame that Ernest had missed the fragrance of the almond trees in bloom, but though Sicily was out, Gamble had another suggestion. He was going up to his "place in the mountains" at Eagles Mere, Pennsylvania, and asked Ernest to join him there. Together they could open one of the little cottages and enjoy the beauties of springtime in its budding glory with "practically nobody" around to disturb them. Gamble would paint while Ernest should bring his typewriter along, since Gamble had two or three stories to suggest. He would not, he concluded, take no for an answer. Ernest had to come. It would do him good.

Apparently Hemingway did not keep this rendezvous. But two years later, in the winter of 1921, Gamble once again proposed an Italian sojourn. From Rome he wired Ernest to come along, and this time Hadley Richardson played the Agnes role in advising him not to accept the invitation. Instead she asked him to visit her in St. Louis, he accepted, and six months later they were married. The two friends communicated by mail at least one more time. He had often wondered in the last two years, Ernest wrote Jim in December 1923, if Gamble were not somewhere nearby in Europe. In the future they must keep in touch so that they could "encounter" when fate pulled them toward each other. But that, apparently, was that: the Chief issued no more invitations to test Hemingway's ethical mettle.

Neither Agnes nor Hadley actually met Jim Gamble, but Bill Horne remembers him "as a very special swell guy" who, he thinks, offered to underwrite the European stay because he "recognized the greatness that was in Ernest." Gamble's name comes up only once in Hemingway's published writing, during a passage of nostalgic reminiscence in *A Moveable Feast* (1964). "Do you remember," Ernest asks Hadley, "when the horse chestnut trees were in bloom" and how he had tried to recall a story about a wistaria vine that Jim Gamble, he thought, had told him? It was a story that for the life of him he could not summon up.

Though he did not accept Gamble's largesse after the Sicilian adventure, Ernest Hemingway did rely on financial support, during much of his early career as a serious writer, from his first two wives. Before he and Hadley were married, he complained to her that if his mother hadn't insisted on having a cottage of her own up in Michigan, he'd be going to Princeton. But he didn't need a university, Hadley argued, and besides she was already supplying him with portions of her trust income (about $3000 a year) to invest in Italian currency against their trip to Europe in the fall. Soon after their marriage Ernest gave up his salaried job in Chicago as writer-editor of *Cooperative Commonwealth*, the monthly magazine of the Cooperative Society of America, but before they left for Paris in December 1921 he had firmed up a space-rate arrangement for his dispatches to the Toronto papers.

Though his newspaper correspondence helped support the newlyweds during the next few years, Hadley's trust fund provided the bulk of their expatriate income. Then, after a sojourn in Toronto in 1923 for the birth of their son Bumby (whose full name was John Hadley Nicanor Hemingway), the young writer took his family back to Paris in 1924 without any journalistic connection at all. With favorable exchange rates, the dollars from her trust financed Ernest's continuing and dedicated attempt to forge a new American prose style. But their quarters were functional at best, and the Hemingways were forced to do without the more expensive creature comforts.

Their situation worsened when, under the management of the husband of one of Hadley's friends in St. Louis, the income from the trust was drastically reduced. As Hadley recalls, Ernest virtually stopped writing in order to trace down this man, whom they both suspected of having absconded with the funds, and "finally we got about one-third of it back" through his epistolary persistence. "Of course, it helped him, you can say it was perfectly selfish on his part, but . . . we both needed it."

Indeed they did, and financial difficulties compromised his joy at hearing, in February 1925, that Horace Liveright would publish his first book of stories, *In Our Time*. The Hemingways were wintering in Schruns, Austria, largely because the exchange rates made it possible for them to profit by subletting their Paris flat for the winter and because Schruns was cheap. When the news of Liveright's decision reached him from New York, Ernest was in no mood to celebrate. The sublessees had skipped out on their agreement to keep the apartment for three months, Hadley's money manager in St. Louis had sent them a bum check, and so they were flat broke. Heaven knows he felt wonderful about the book, he wrote Harold Loeb, "even though simultaneously kicked in the balls."

Reading between the lines, it is possible to construe this letter as an indirect appeal for funds, especially when combined with the note he mailed the well-to-do Loeb the month before with the news that the humorist Donald Ogden Stewart had sent him an "enormous" check as a Christmas present to keep up the family morale. Back in New York, Don had already tried to interest two publishers (Doran and Knopf) in *In Our Time*, and had written Hemingway not to be a horse's ass and starve to death in a place with a name like Schruns, and, in short, Don was continuing to function as a hell of a good guy. He gave Hemingway the money, the affable Stewart later explained, not because he was backing any hunch as to Ernest's genius but simply because "I liked him—and Hadley—very much, and I had the money and he didn't."

Kathleen (Kitty) Cannell, who lived with Loeb for a time in Paris (and who is scathingly portrayed as Frances Clyne in *The Sun Also Rises*), maintains that Hemingway developed "a Tom Sawyerish way of getting money from people and then saying that they had embarrassed him by forcing it on him." One such touch occurred in the dead of winter, when Hem appeared in "a sweat shirt and a raggedy pair of pants," with a conspicuous hole in the backside. Some rich guy, he half-joked, ought to give him some pants so he wouldn't have "to freeze his ass in this weather." Loeb went right home, she recalls, and brought back his own new flannel slacks. Morrill Cody, another survivor of those days, recalls Hemingway as "a bad man to lend money to." He never paid for meals in restaurants, and Cody lent him cash that was never repaid: "Not a large sum of money but, you know, five dollars here and five dollars there." Trying to advance his career and make an occasional franc, Ernest did editorial chores both for Ford Madox Ford on the *Transatlantic Review*, and for Ernest Walsh and Ethel Moorhead on *This Quarter*; and both assignments led to quarrels over money. Ernest used to complain, for example, that Ford was always importuning him for loans, whereas (again according to Kitty Cannell) it was the other way around. And, after putting out an issue of *This Quarter* for Walsh, Hemingway complained that the editor seemed suspicious that he was trying to do him out of money. Many people might be trying to cheat Walsh, he added, but he was not one of them.

The composer Virgil Thomson, who hardly knew Hemingway, nonetheless offered a perceptive interpretation of the climax of his years in Paris. Hemingway never bought anybody a drink, according to Thomson; instead, "he paid them off in *The Sun Also Rises* (1926). He bought all his friends drinks in that book." What Thomson undoubtedly intended as a joke hits uncannily close to the mark, for Hemingway's first novel proposes an extremely high standard of financial responsibility and is organized around a strict morality of compensation which, on the evidence, its author had been unable to achieve during his period of apprenticeship in Paris.

The Morality of Compensation

While voyaging back to the United States in 1833, Ralph Waldo Emerson puzzled over a definition of morals. His thoughts, he admitted in his journal, were "dim and vague," but one might obtain "some idea of them . . . who develops the doctrine in his own experience that nothing can be given or taken without an equivalent." In Emerson's sublime optimism, he weighted the scales of equivalence in favor of the taker. Only the half-blind, as he observes in his essay on "The Tragic," had never beheld the House of Pain, which like the salt sea encroached in man on his felicity. But felicity was man's customary state, for he lived on the land, not at sea. If pain disturbed him, he could rest in the conviction that nature would proportion "her defence to the assault" and "that the intellect in its purity, and the moral sense in its purity, are not distinguished from each other, and both ravish us into a region whereinto these passionate clouds of sorrow cannot rise."

On this issue, Emerson's Concord voice sounds in off-key opposition to that of Emily Dickinson in western Massachusetts, who wrote of the primacy of pain in the equation:

> For each extatic instant
> We must an anguish pay
> In keen and quivering ratio
> To the ecstasy

> For each beloved hour
> Sharp pittances of years—
> Bitter contested farthings—
> And Coffers heaped with Tears!

For her, the transactions of life had been costly. Cosmic usurers demanded payments of anguish, at unconscionable interest, for each momentary joy. But the debt "must" be paid, however unfair the terms.

Ernest Hemingway throughout his fiction, but especially in *The Sun Also Rises*, sides with Dickinson in this hypothetical quarrel. The cost of joy, ecstasy, or happiness comes high—yet it must be met. Like the poet from Amherst, he expressed his view of compensation in the metaphor of finance—a metaphor which runs through the fabric of his first novel as a fine, essential thread. It is Jake Barnes who explicitly states the code of Hemingway's novel. Lying awake at Pamplona, Jake reflects that in having Lady Brett Ashley for a friend, he "had been getting something for nothing" and that sooner or later he would have to pay the bill, which always came:

> I thought I had paid for everything. Not like the woman pays and pays and pays. No idea of retributions or punishment. Just exchange of values. You gave up something and got something else. Or you worked for something. You paid some way for everything that was any good. I paid my way into enough things that I liked, so that I had a good time. Either you paid by learning about them, or by experience, or by taking chances, or by money. Enjoying living was learning to get your money's worth and knowing when you had it. You could get your money's worth. The world was a good place to buy in.

It is understandable that Jake, sexually crippled in the war, should think that he has already paid for everything; and it is an index of his maturity that he comes to realize that he may still have debts outstanding, to be paid, most often and most insistently, in francs and pesetas and pounds and dollars.

Jake's philosophical musing is illustrated time and again in the profuse monetary transactions of *The Sun Also Rises*. On the second page of the novel, one discovers that Robert Cohn has squandered most of the $50,000 that his father, from "one of the richest Jewish families in New York," has left him; on the last page of the book, that Jake has tipped the waiter (the amount is unspecified) who has called a taxi for him and Brett in Madrid. Between the beginning and the end, Hemingway specifically mentions sums of money, and what they have been able to purchase, a total of thirty times. The money dispensed runs up from a franc to a waiter to the 50 francs that Jake leaves for his *poule*, Georgette, at the *dancing*, to the 200 francs which Count Mippipopolous gives to Jake's concierge, to the $10,000 the count offers Brett for a weekend in her company. Mostly, though, the monetary amounts are small, and pay for the food, drink, travel, and entertainment that represent the good things in life available to Jake.

Hemingway reveals much more about his characters' financial condition and spending habits than about their appearance: the book would be far more useful to the loan officer of a bank, than, say, to the missing persons' bureau, which would have little more physical information to go on, with respect to height, weight, hair and eye color, than that Brett had short hair and "was built with curves like the hull of a racing yacht" and that Robert Cohn, with his flattened nose, looked as if "perhaps a horse had stepped on his face."

Hemingway had several good reasons to note with scrupulous detail the exact nature of financial transactions. Such a practice contributed to the verisimilitude of the novel, denoting the way it was; it fitted nicely with Jake's—and his creator's—obsession with the proper way of doing things; and mainly it illustrated in action the moral conviction that you must pay for what you get, that you must earn in order to be able to buy, and that only then will it be possible, if you are careful, to buy your money's worth in the world—essentially the same position taken by Hemingway's parents during his youth and young manhood.

In the early 1920s exchange rates in postwar Europe fluctuated wildly while the dollar remained stable, to the benefit of the expatriated artists, writers, dilettantes, and partygoers who settled in Paris. Malcolm Cowley and his wife lived there the year of 1921 in modest comfort on a grant of $1,000, 12,000 francs by that year's rate. By the summer of 1924, when Barnes and his companions left for the fiesta at Pamplona, the rate was still more favorable, almost 19 francs to the dollar. You could get breakfast coffee and a brioche for a franc or less at the cafés where Hemingway wrote when the weather turned cold. There were even better bargains elsewhere, as the Hemingways had found at Schruns in the Vorarlberg, where food and lodging for the young writer, his wife, and son came to but $28.50 a week. Europe was overflowing with (mostly temporary) American expatriates, living on the cheap. Any novel faithful to that time and that place was going to have to take cognizance of what it cost to live and eat and drink.

Hemingway regarded his fellow Americans on the Left Bank as "nearly all loafers expending the energy that an artist puts into his creative work in talking about what they are going to do and condemning the work of all artists who have gained any degree of recognition." The tone of moral indignation in this dispatch, one of the first that Hemingway had sent the Toronto *Star Weekly* from Paris in 1922, is emphasized by the anecdote he includes about "a big, light-haired woman sitting at a table with three young men." She pays the bill, and the young men laugh. "Three years ago she came to Paris with her husband from a little town in Connecticut, where they had lived and he had painted with increasing success for ten years. Last year he went back to America alone."

To the writer, single-minded in his dedication to his craft, the time-wasting of café habitués represented the greatest sin of all. It was the work that counted, and talking about art was hardly a satisfactory substitute. Observing the playboys and playgirls of Paris waste their lives on one long hazy binge, Hemingway as foreign correspondent felt much the same disgust that visits Jake after the revels at Pamplona, when he plunges deep into the waters off San Sebastian in an attempt to cleanse himself.

What distinguishes Jake Barnes from Mike Campbell and Brett, who at least make no pretenses toward artistic (or any other kind of) endeavor, and from Robert Cohn, a writer who is blocked throughout the novel, is that he works steadily at his regular job as a newspaperman. He is, presumably, receiving no money from home, and he spends his money, as he eats and drinks, with conspicuous control. Above all, he is thoughtful and conscientious in his spending. Sharing a taxi with two fellow American reporters who also work regularly and well at their jobs but one of whom is burdened, as he is not, by "a wife and kids," Jake insists on paying the 2-franc fare. He also does the right thing by Georgette, the streetwalker he picks up at the Café Napolitain. Not only does he buy her dinner as a preliminary to the sexual encounter she has bargained for, but, upon deserting her for Brett, he leaves 50 francs with the *patronne*—compensation for her wasted evening—to be delivered to Georgette if she goes home alone. The *patronne* is supposed to hold the money for Jake if Georgette secures another male customer, but this being France, he will, Brett assures him, lose his 50 francs. "Oh, yes," Jake responds, but he has at least behaved properly, and Jake, like his creator, was "always intensely interested in how to do a thing," from tying flies to fighting bulls to compensating a prostitute. Besides, he shares a double kinship with Georgette: she too is sick, a sexual cripple, and she pursues her trade openly and honestly.

The case is different with Lady Ashley, who acquires and casts off her lovers nearly as casually as Georgette, but does so without thought of the consequences to others. There is a certain irony in Brett's telling Jake that it was wrong of him to bring Georgette to the dance, "in restraint of trade." Surely this is a case of the pot and kettle, for she has arrived in the company of a covey of homosexuals. More to the point, it is women like Brett—and, to a lesser degree, Cohn's companion Frances Clyne—who provide unfair competition to the streetwalkers of Paris.

After an unsatisfactory time with Brett, Jake Barnes returns to his room, where he immediately goes over his bank statement: "It showed a balance of $2432.60. I got out my check-book and deducted four checks drawn since the first of the month, and discovered I had a balance of $1,832.60. I wrote this on the back of the statement." This is make-work, an attempt to delay thinking about the love for Brett that he cannot consummate. But it is also characteristic of Jake's meticulousness about money. The surprising thing, in fact, is that Jake should have spent as much as $600 in any given month, for he is a man who tries very hard always to get his money's worth. He knows to whom to write for good bullfight tickets, and he reserves the best rooms in the best hotels at the best price. In Bayonne, he helps Bill Gorton buy "a pretty good rod cheap, and two landing-nets," and checks with the tourist office to find out "what we ought to pay for a motor-car to Pamplona": 400 francs. At Burguete, he bargains to have the wine included in the 12-peseta-a-day hotel room he and Bill share, and they make certain at dinner that they do "not lose money on the wine." He is annoyed when Cohn sends a wire of only three words for the price of ten ("I come Thursday Cohn),") and takes revenge by answering with an even shorter telegram ("Arriving tonight"). After the fiesta, when a driver tries to overcharge Jake for a ride from Bayonne to San Sebastian, he first works the price down from 50 to 35 pesetas and then rejects that price, too, as "not worth it." Jake is careful to fulfill his obligations, but he will not be taken advantage of. Once, in church, regretting that he is such a rotten Catholic, he even prays that he will "make a lot of money," but here the verb is important, for he next begins thinking about how he might make the money. He does not pray or even hope to *have* a lot of money, or for it to descend upon him from the trees or the deaths of relatives. Robert Cohn and Mike Campbell remind him, often and painfully, of what inherited money, or the promise of it, can do to undermine a man.

Though physically impotent and mentally tortured, Jake Barnes remains morally sound, while Mike Campbell, Robert Cohn, and Brett Ashley, who are physically whole, have become morally decadent. As Carlos Baker observes, *The Sun Also Rises* has "a sturdy moral backbone," deriving much of its power from the contrast between Barnes-Gorton-Romero, who constitute the "moral norm" of the book, and the morally aberrant trio of Ashley-Campbell-Cohn. Money and its uses form the metaphor by which the moral responsibility of Jake, Bill, and Pedro Romero is measured against the carelessness of Brett, Mike, and Robert. Financial soundness mirrors moral strength.

Bill Gorton is the most likable of the crew at the fiesta. Gorton regales Jake with topical gags about Mencken, the Scopes trial, literary fashions, and middle-class mores. An enthusiast, he finds every place he visits equally "wonderful." The adjective is a private joke between Barnes and Gorton, for Bill knows as well as Jake that when things are really wonderful, it is neither necessary nor desirable to say so. Thus, hiking through the magnificent woods at Burguete, Bill remarks simply, "This is country." The five days they share at Burguete stand in idyllic contrast to the sickness and drunkenness which characterize both Paris and Pamplona. It is not that Bill and Jake do not drink together on the fishing trip; they drink prodigious quantities of wine. But it is drinking for the pleasure they have earned through hard work (in contrast to Cohn, Gorton is a producing writer) and through the rigors of the outdoor life they choose to pursue on vacation. Furthermore, Bill knows when not to drink. After dinner at Madame Lecomte's and a long walk through Paris, Jake proposes a drink. "No," says Bill. "I don't need it."

The first thing Jake says about Bill Gorton is that he is "very happy. He had made a lot of money on his last book, and was going to make a lot more." He has paid for his fiesta, and like all who have earned "the good things," he is careful of the rights of others. In Vienna, he tells Jake, he had gone to an "Enormous . . . prize-fight" in which a "Wonderful nigger" knocked a local boy cold and aroused the anger of the crowd. People threw chairs into the ring, and not only was the victorious fighter deprived of payment (he had agreed not to knock out the local fighter) but his watch was stolen. "Not so good, Jake. Injustice everywhere," Gorton remarks. Conscientious about money matters, he is disturbed by a world where fights are fixed and debts go unpaid. So, though tight and on holiday, Bill lends the black fighter clothes and money and tries to help him collect what's owed to him.

Bill's comic determination to purchase stuffed animals foreshadows Jake's serious reflections on compensation. Passing a Paris taxidermist's, Bill appeals to Jake to buy a stuffed dog: "Mean everything in the world to you after you bought it. Simple exchange of values. You give them money. They give you a stuffed dog." His fondness for spending money on the ridiculous emerges again at Pamplona, when he buys Mike eleven shoeshines in a row. "Bill's a yell of laughter," Mike says, but Jake, who unlike them has not had much to drink, "felt a little uncomfortable about all this shoe-shining." Still, Bill's expenditures buy amusement for himself and others (including, of course, the reader), and these otherwise merely amusing incidents serve to illustrate the principle of exchange of values: to obtain stuffed dogs, shoeshines, or drinks, you must deliver payment.

Robert Cohn, for whom Gorton conceives an immediate dislike, does not belong with the party at Pamplona. A romantic, he is understandably unable at first to conceive that his weekend with Brett at San Sebastian has meant nothing to her, but he forfeits any claim to sympathy by his subsequent stubborn and violent unwillingness to accept that obvious fact. Terribly insecure, he takes insult after insult from Frances and Mike without retaliation, though he is ready enough to fight with his "best friend" Jake over what he construes as insults to Brett and himself. A Jew in the company of gentiles, he is a bore who takes himself—and his illusions—far too seriously. Unlike Jake, he has not "learned about" things. He does not know how to eat or drink or love. It is no wonder that Harold Loeb, recognizing himself in Hemingway's portrait of Cohn, "felt as if he had developed an ulcer" and, decades later, attempted to vindicate himself in his autobiography.

Still, it would be possible to pity Cohn for his dominant malady (is romantic egotism a less lovely illness than nymphomania or dipsomania?) were it not for his callous and opportunistic use of the money he has not earned. His allowance (about $300 a month, from his mother) comfortably stakes him to his period of expatriation. He has written a novel which has been "accepted by a fairly good publisher," but it is not, clearly, a very good novel, and now the well has run dry. In his idleness, he hangs around Jake's office, disturbing his work, and even proposes to pay Jake's way as his companion on a trip to South America, a continent he invests with an aura of romance. How Hemingway felt about such proposals was later made clear in *A Moveable Feast*, when he reflected, in connection with the trip to Lyons with Fitzgerald, that he "had been a damned fool to accept an invitation for a trip that was to be paid for by someone else." But biographical evidence is hardly necessary to make the point that Cohn, whose money comes to him because of the accident of his birth, does not understand the proper way of spending it: the point is made implicitly by a number of incidents in *The Sun Also Rises*.

What comes too easily has a pernicious effect on him as a person. Having inherited a good deal of money, he wastes nearly all of it on a little magazine—and in purchasing the prestige that comes to him as its editor. But Cohn's most damning misuse of funds occurs when he attempts to buy his way out of obligations to women. Frances Clyne, one of the bitchiest women in Hemingway's fiction, reveals this practice of his in a devastating scene. Flat broke and not so attractive as she once was, Frances is being packed off to England, so that her paramour may see more of the world—and, he surely hopes, of Lady Ashley:

> "Robert's sending me. He's going to give me two hundred pounds [about a thousand dollars at the time] and then I'm going to visit friends. Won't it be lovely? The friends don't know about it, yet."
>   She turned to Cohn and smiled at him. He was not smiling now.
>   "You were only going to give me a hundred pounds, weren't you, Robert? But I made him give me two hundred. He's really very generous. Aren't you, Robert?"

"I do not know," Jake reflects, "how people could say such terrible things to Robert Cohn." But Frances can say them and get away with it because they are absolutely true. Cohn, in fact, has disposed of another girl, his "little secretary on the magazine," in just the same way, except cheaper. It is in his attempt to buy his way out of entanglements without expending anything of himself that Robert Cohn most viciously breaks the moral code of compensation.

Furthermore, there are suggestions in the book that Cohn is tight-fisted with his money. He has, apparently, tried to bargain with Frances. He directs Jake to buy him a double-tapered fishing line, but says he will pay later instead of now. After unleashing a stream of insults against Cohn ("Don't you know you're not wanted?"), Mike Campbell tells Bill Gorton, who is about to escort Cohn from the slaughter, to stay. "Don't go," Mike said. "Robert Cohn's about to buy a drink." The clear implication is that Robert Cohn rarely buys drinks.

Mike, on the other hand, is more than willing to buy drinks, whenever—which means rarely—he has any money. As is true of all the other major characters in the book, Hemingway reveals a good deal about Mike's financial condition and habits. Brett, Jake tells Robert, is going to marry Mike Campbell: "He's going to be rich as hell some day." Cohn refuses to believe that Brett will marry Mike—and the matter remains in doubt at the end of the novel—but there is no question about Mike's potential wealth. He is trying, Brett says, to get his mother to pay for her divorce so they can be married: "Michael's people have loads of money." But for the moment, he makes do on a rather skimpy allowance, and is not even allowed to write checks. When he needs funds, he must "send a wire to the keeper."

Mike Campbell is held under strict financial control for the best of reasons: he is totally irresponsible about money. With his anticipated wealth serving as a promissory note, he sponges off everyone in sight and simply does not pay his debts. And he drinks far too much. After suffering a business collapse, he has had to resort to bankruptcy, an ungentlemanly if legal way of evading creditors. These are, as Brett realizes when she introduces him, the two most important and typical things about the man she intends to marry: "This is Bill Gorton. This drunkard is Mike Campbell. Mr. Campbell is an undischarged bankrupt."

Mike is no more conscientious about settling his debts to friends than to his former business "connections." Yet he possesses a certain self-deprecatory wit, and Bill Gorton, especially, is drawn to him. Bill likes Mike so much, in fact, that it is very difficult for him to admit that Mike does not meet his obligations. Mike, Bill, and Bill's girl Edna are thrown out of a bar by the police one night in Pamplona. "I don't know what happened," Edna says, "but some one had the police called to keep Mike out of the back room. There were some people that had known Mike at Cannes. What's the matter with Mike?" "Probably he owes them money," Jake says. "That's what people usually get bitter about." The next morning, Bill remembers the incident more clearly: ". . . There was a fellow there that had helped pay Brett and Mike out of Cannes, once. He was damned nasty." The night before, Bill had emphatically defended his friend: "They can't say things like that about Mike." But in the light of dawn, he modifies the statement: ". . . Nobody ought to have a right to say things about Mike. . . . They oughtn't to have any right. I wish to hell they didn't have any right."

Bill's own loyalty to Mike finally crumbles when, after the fiesta, another incident makes it clear *why* they have the right. Jake, Bill, and Mike have hired a car together, and stop at "a very Ritz place" in Biarritz, where they roll dice to see who will pay for the drinks. Mike loses three times in a row, but cannot pay for the third round:

> "I'm sorry," Mike said. "I can't get it."
> "What's the matter?"
> "I've no money," Mike said. "I'm stony. I've just twenty francs. Here, take twenty francs."
> Bill's face sort of changed.

He had had just enough money for his hotel bill in Pamplona, Mike explains, though it turns out that Brett has given him all of her cash to pay his bill. Nor can Mike help pay for their car, and his promise to send Jake what he owes is hardly reassuring.

Mike continually banters about his bankruptcy, as if making light of the obligations might somehow cause them to disappear. "I'm a tremendous bankrupt," he remarks. "I owe money to everybody." He will not go down into the ring after the running of the bulls because "it wouldn't be fair to my creditors." As Mike observes, "One never gets anywhere by discussing finances," but he is unable to resist touching the wound by discussing his own. There is the story, for example, of the medals and Mike's tailor. Invited to a whopping big dinner in England at which medals are to be worn, Mike prevails upon his tailor to supply him with some medals that had been left by another customer for cleaning. Later he goes to a night club and passes the medals around. "Gave one to each girl. Form of souvenir. They thought I was hell's own shakes of a soldier. Gave away medals in a night club. Dashing fellow." The story delights his audience, but it had not seemed so funny to his tailor. Mike has fought in the war, and "must have some medals," but he does not know which ones and has never sent in for them. He is careless about them, quite as willing to don other people's ribbons as he is to spend other people's money.

Brett shares with Mike a carelessness of personal behavior which stems from a lifetime of having had things done for her. Her room in Madrid "was in that disorder produced only by those who have always had servants." She makes appointments and does not keep them. She accepts the generosity of others as if it were her due. The Paris homosexuals, one feels certain, were paying her way. Count Mippipopolous finances her champagne binge. "Come on," she says at Pamplona. "Are these poisonous things paid for?" In the bar of the Palace Hotel in Madrid, she asks Jake, "*Would* you buy a lady a drink?" She has been given, she admits, "hell's own amount of credit" on her title. Of course, she and Mike had jointly run up the bills they could not settle at Cannes. Moreover, she satisfies her demanding sexual appetites at the expense of others, effectively turning Robert into a steer, Mike into a swine, and Jake into a pimp. She is clearly not what Madame Duzinell, Jake's concierge, calls her after the bribe of 200 francs from the count, "très, très gentille."

Oddly, though, Brett observes a strict code in connection with her sexual activity. She will not accept money for her favors. Thus she rejects the count's offer of "ten thousand dollars to go to Biarritz [or Cannes, or Monte Carlo] with him." She pays Mike's way, not vice versa, out of the Hotel Montoya. Though the bullfighter Romero pays the hotel bill in Madrid, she will take nothing else from him. "He tried to give me a lot of money, you know. I told him I had scads of it. He knew that was a lie. I couldn't take his money, you know." In sending Romero away, against the urgings of the flesh, she has done the right thing at the cost of real personal anguish. She will be neither a whore nor "one of those bitches that ruins children."

Furthermore, Brett's apparent nymphomania can be at least partly excused by the unhappy circumstances of her past life. She has lost one husband in the war, and married another ("Ashley, chap she got the title from") who returned quite mad from serving as a sailor. "When he came home," Mike explains, "he wouldn't sleep in a bed. Always made Brett sleep on the floor. Finally, when he got really bad, he used to tell her he'd kill her. Always slept with a loaded service revolver. Brett used to take the shells out when he'd gone to sleep. She hasn't had an absolutely happy life." Like Jake, she still suffers from war wounds. Like him, too, she articulates her awareness of the law of compensation. If she has put chaps through hell, she's paying for it all now. "Don't we pay for all the things we do, though?"

The Sun Also Rises is, as has been amply demonstrated, a *roman à clef*, with roles clearly assigned to real people. Harold Loeb = Robert Cohn and Frances Clyne = Kitty Cannell; Pat Guthrie = Mike Campbell; Lady Duff Twysden = Lady Brett Ashley; Donald Ogden Stewart (with a trace of Bill Smith) = Bill Gorton; Niño de la Palma = Pedro Romero; Juanito Quintana = Montoya; and so on.

Stewart, especially, has been rendered unable to appreciate the book as a work of the imagination because its details, especially in regard to money, so nearly fit the actual circumstances of their visit to the Pamplona fiesta in the summer of 1925. The trip began as almost idyllic, Stewart recalled, with everyone having a glorious time, until the twin demons of sex and financial irresponsibility invaded the college-reunion atmosphere. "Everything was somehow changed," he remembered, "and, for me, spoiled. I wanted Hem and Hadley to be as they had been. I liked Duff and Pat Guthrie, but . . . when the devil of finance was added to my Garden of male Eden, I felt miserably conscious of how every one of us friends had suddenly turned into pumpkins." The tension heightened "when it was found that Guthrie didn't have any money though he had assured Ernie that he would pay his and Duff's share. In those days, especially for the Hemingways, the budgets were seriously close to the border line." As it happened, Don paid the Britishers' way out of embarrassment, but ever after "carried around the memory of that awful sickness which came . . . when we discovered that one of us had betrayed us about money."

Stewart's reminiscence underscores the novel's insistence on strict circumspection in money matters. The most circumspect of the major figures, of course, is Jake, and from the evidence of the first-draft manuscript of *The Sun Also Rises*, where the protagonist is never called Jake but instead Ernie and Hem, it is clear that Ernest Hemingway = Jake Barnes. But here, at least, the author took some liberties in his re-creation of the summer of 1925, for Hemingway, unlike Jake, was neither a working newspaperman with a steady job nor nearly so meticulous about finances as his idealized self in the book.

An Angel Named Gus

By the summer of 1926 the Hemingways' marriage was in disrepair, and Ernest, saddened and self-accusatory, turned for nourishment to those friends he had not "paid off" in *The Sun Also Rises*. He left the little apartment at 115 rue Notre-Dame des Champs and began to spend much of his time with Archibald and Ada MacLeish. The understanding was that Ernest could come to their flat for a bed or a meal whenever he wished. "He often wished." Gerald Murphy's studio served as a workplace where Ernest read proof on *The Sun Also Rises*, and Murphy also deposited a much-needed $400 in Hemingway's depleted bank account. Ernest was seeking his divorce in order to marry Pauline Pfeiffer, a petite, bright young woman, who, like Hadley, had gone to school in St. Louis, and who had come to Paris as a staffer for *Vogue*. Conscience-stricken about leaving Hadley, he promised to turn over to her all royalties from *The Sun Also Rises*. It was, he wrote, the least he could do in recompense for her love and "actual cash-support" over the years. The gesture was also one he could now comfortably afford, for Pauline, who was a few years younger than Hadley, was also considerably richer. Her father was a landowning squire in Piggott, Arkansas. Her uncle Gus, a childless bachelor who felt a proprietary affection for Pauline and her sister Jinny, held a controlling interest in Richard Hudnut perfumes.

Gus Pfeiffer could hardly have been more generous to the young man who married his niece. Prior to the marriage, he agreed to advance the money to pay the rent on their Paris apartment. News of the wedding in May 1927 produced a number of gifts of money from other relatives, including several $1000 checks, so that for the first time in his adult life, Ernest was virtually free of money worries. When the Hemingways decided in 1931 to buy their house in Key West, where Ernest could indulge his passion for game fishing, Gus supplied the $8000 purchase price as an outright gift. He also financed an elk-hunting trip to Montana, and anted up $25,000 to pay for their African safari of 1933. (Ernest was not entirely gracious in acknowledging this aid. In *Green Hills of Africa*, he complains about the disadvantage of hunting under a time limit. "The way to hunt is for as long as you live against as long as there is such and such an animal. . . . But here we were, now, caught by time, by the season, and by the running out of money. . . .") In late 1936 and early 1937 Gus set up separate trust funds, with Ernest as administrator, not only for Patrick and Gregory, Ernest and Pauline's two sons, but for Bumby as well. As John Dos Passos observed, "Ernest fascinated [Gus]. Hunting, fishing, writing. He wanted to help Ernest do all the things he'd been too busy making money to do." It pleased Gus to pay for things, but he need not have paid. For her own part, Pauline had quite enough money to support the Hemingways in style.

Though he and Pauline remained legally man-and-wife until 1940, theirs was essentially a ten-year marriage, for by 1937 Ernest had transferred his affections to the talented, ambitious, golden-haired Martha Gellhorn. In Ernest's fiction, there is ample evidence that his split with Pauline was motivated at least in part by a certain resentment of her wealth. In 1929 he wrote his first best seller in *A Farewell to Arms*, but the royalties earned from his writing, as he was well aware, could not pay for African safaris or even maintain the staff of five servants at their Key West house. Besides, though he produced two books of nonfiction (*Death in the Afternoon* and *Green Hills of Africa*) in the early 1930s, he also spent a tremendous amount of time hunting and fishing during his marriage to Pauline, and no Hemingway novels appeared between 1929 and the ill-received *To Have and Have Not* in 1937. In his private life, Hemingway reached a stage of almost constant truculence during the mid-1930s. In his fiction, he worked off this irritability in the remarkable African stories.

Both "The Short Happy Life of Francis Macomber" and, even more notably, "The Snows of Kilimanjaro" depict bad marriages held together by despicable financial binding. As Hemingway sarcastically summed up the Macombers' situation, "They had a sound basis of union. Margot was too beautiful for Macomber to divorce her and Macomber had too much money for Margot ever to leave him." Previously insulated against maturity by the possession of too much money, Macomber finally asserts himself in the rigors of the hunt, and is shot by his wife (whether accidentally or purposely remains a raging critical issue) as he bravely confronts a wounded, charging buffalo.

In "The Snows of Kilimanjaro," the writer Harry also dies at the end, though his demise is brought about by a physical gangrene that parallels his moral rot. He has married Helen, an extremely wealthy woman, and let his talent go to seed. Facing death, he cannot resist damning her for the idleness her money has purchased. She is a "rich bitch," and yet Harry knows that what has happened is no one's fault but his own. After all, he had let himself be bought: "It was strange, too, wasn't it, that when he fell in love with another woman, that woman should always have more money than the last one?" He had kidded himself that he would write about the very rich, that he was really a spy in their country, but in the end he had done no writing at all and, as the gangrene spreads, he lies thinking back over all the stories he had never written, and now would never write. It is a very powerful story, at least partly "a special and private . . . analysis of Hemingway's past failures as a writer of prose fiction, as of 1936." Characteristically Ernest denied that the story derived from so sensitive an origin. It had been suggested to him, he maintained, when a famous (but unnamed) lady of New York society connections offered to pay for his next safari, as long as she could accompany him and Pauline on the trip. But this yarn, like the one about the sex-starved innkeeper in Sicily, smacks of the apocryphal.

His divorce from Pauline, when he was forty, made Ernest Hemingway dependent upon his own financial resources for the first time. A month after he moved out of the house in Key West, on December 26, 1939, he urgently asked Max Perkins for a $1000 advance on his new novel, and in February of 1940, Pauline kept a promise she had made months before, and helped him to pay his taxes. According to the divorce settlement, the house which Uncle Gus had bought and which Pauline's money had improved remained hers to rent as long as she paid the taxes and insurance. If the house were sold, however, Ernest was to receive 40 per cent of the sale price, with Pauline getting the rest. (By the time the house was sold, for $80,000 in 1962, neither Pauline nor Ernest was alive to share in the proceeds.) Ernest also agreed to pay $500 a month child support for Patrick and Gregory.

Luckily Ernest had his biggest book in the works, the one which would climb off the top of the best-seller lists and command an unprecedented fee for motion-picture rights: *For Whom the Bell Tolls*. After that success, he could with some aplomb take on the role of provider that he had occasionally played toward the family in Oak Park since the suicide of his father on December 6, 1928. Significantly, Dr. Hemingway had been driven to the deed not only by ill health (he had contracted diabetes) but also by financial mismanagement. In 1925 he and Mrs. Hemingway had invested their entire savings in the Florida land boom, and had taken out a mortgage on their Oak Park home. But the boom turned to bust, and with his practice dwindling, Dr. Hemingway soon had trouble meeting the mortgage payments. His troubles came to a head, according to Ernest's brother, Leicester, when a relative (possibly Ernest's Uncle George) insisted on payment of a note that was coming due: relatives were relatives, but business was definitely business. Not to fulfill such an obligation was, to the doctor, unthinkable. As Leicester recounts the story, Dr. Hemingway finally asked Ernest for help and he promptly complied, but before his letter could reach Oak Park, his father had shot himself.

Word of the suicide reached Ernest when he and Bumby were en route by train from New York to Key West. He quickly sent the boy on ahead in care of the Pullman car porter, and with only enough money for the journey in his pocket, wired Scott Fitzgerald and his painter friend Mike Strater for emergency loans. Since Leicester, much younger, was still in high school, Dr. Hemingway's death placed Ernest in charge of seeing to the family's financial welfare. It was a position that simultaneously troubled and elated him.

To the older writer Owen Wister, he sent a disturbing letter telling of the suicide and his own deeply felt responsibilities. Wister responded with a $500 check that Hemingway returned, though he would have kept the check, he wrote, if things were that bad. Temporarily, at least, completion of the manuscript of *A Farewell to Arms* (which he worked on for six feverish weeks after the funeral) and the decision of *Scribner's Magazine* to pay $16,000 for the serial rights, had salvaged his finances. Perhaps he'd take Wister up on his offer later. To his mother, he wrote a letter full of good advice (he was glad she'd decided to rent out rooms in the Oak Park house and he advised her to sell the Florida lots) and ill temper (he'd take the hide off Uncle George if he didn't pay the mortgage, and his older sister Marcelline and her husband Sterling Sanford should certainly contribute to Grace's support, since they were "rich" and had not, like him, been ostracized).

As father-surrogate to the Hemingways, Ernest was entitled to his advice and ill temper, but not, perhaps, to the threat with which he ended the letter. He had never written about the family in his books, he said, because he did not want to hurt those he loved; now that his father was dead, perhaps he'd have to reconsider. To provide for his mother and to reinforce the message, he set up a $50,000 trust fund (Pauline chipped in $20,000) to support Grace Hemingway during her lifetime, with $30,000 to be split among the younger children in the event of her death and Pauline getting her share back. Where once he had been chastised as irresponsible and unconscientious, now he held the whip hand, and demanded of his mother the same kind of meticulous behavior she had earlier asked of him. Once he had revolted against the expectations of his mother and father; now he adopted them "as his own, applying them rigorously to himself and to everyone he met." His mother had accused him of being a sponger, and he clearly took a certain pleasure in knowing that the roles were reversed and she dependent upon him. He carried with him, then and always, the financial values that his parents had bequeathed to him.

The Artist as Businessman

So far as this code of values—a middle-western, upper-middle-class turn-of-the-century version of the Protestant ethic—applied to the world of business, it stipulated:

> 1) A man should make money in his profession, in order to prove that he has worked hard and well; the acquisition of financial rewards, by this yardstick, became a measure of manhood and maturity. (How one disposed of his earnings was another matter entirely.)
> 2) In the pursuit of this goal, a man should deal fairly, if astutely, with everyone.

In the case of Ernest Hemingway, as for many who were brought up according to this ethic, the first imperative sometimes came into conflict with the second, and, where they seemed incompatible, it was the first which proved dominant. Thus, in the end, Hemingway became the highest-paid writer of his time. He reached that goal as a consequence of hard work, of extraordinary talent, and sometimes as a consequence of rather sharp practices.

When he set off to cover the Greco-Turkish war in 1922, for example, Hemingway was under exclusive contract to the Toronto papers. Nonetheless, he made a secret agreement to cable spot news stories to the International News Service under the name of John Hadley. "That kind of action," Hadley recalls, "seared my Puritan soul." After the birth of their son Bumby in Toronto, he and Hadley decided to jump their six-month lease at the Cedarvale Mansions. To avoid having their personal possessions impounded, they asked friends to carry them off for safekeeping. When one of Ernest's fellow reporters was married in the Hemingway flat, nothing was left except the Murphy bed and the rented piano. Soon afterward the Hemingways were gone too, back to Europe.

Such indiscretions might have bothered Ernest more if he were not sure that everyone else was practicing them. The whole world was "crooked," he wrote Bill Smith early in 1925, and everything depended upon influence. If Bill came to Paris for a job, the second best thing was to look and act as though he really didn't need one, but the best thing was to have connections. Only a week before, Hemingway had seen this doctrine confirmed when the missionary work of Stewart and Loeb had resulted in his first American book contract with Liveright. The following year, he once more put his useful contacts to work in securing another, more attractive publisher.

From the start, relations with Liveright had been rather strained. Ernest was not entirely happy that his publisher had insisted on modification of a passage in "Mr. and Mrs. Elliot" and complete omission of "Up in Michigan," the seduction story Gertrude Stein had called *inaccrochable*. Nor did the size of the first printing of *In Our Time*, a mere thirteen hundred copies, please the author. Then Liveright had written in June 1925 asking Hemingway to line up other writers. Grabbing off writers, Ernest made clear in a sarcastic response, was beyond his capabilities as a simple country boy from Chicago. So far he'd only managed to grab off a publisher, and next he hoped to grab off some money. Then an advertisement could be arranged, Hemingway Before and After Being Grabbed Off By Horace Liveright, and with exhibits like that he could probably grab off other authors about as fast as he could get them drunk. Meanwhile, Fitzgerald was doing for Max Perkins just what Liveright had asked: trying to grab off Hemingway for Scribners. "He and I are very thick," Fitzgerald assured Perkins; though Ernest had signed a three-book contract with Boni and Liveright, there was a chance that the contract might be invalid.

The vehicle for breaking the contract was *The Torrents of Spring*, Hemingway's satire on Sherwood Anderson, which he wrote in a week late in 1925. Anderson was Liveright's most prominent author, and very much a Hemingway booster: he'd even composed a laudatory blurb for the jacket of *In Our Time*. But Hemingway had been disappointed with Anderson's recent work, and especially his novel *Dark Laughter*. So he composed his satire, partly to repudiate Anderson's influence, and partly, it appears, to sever his relations with Liveright, since if he refused to publish the book, Ernest would be free to negotiate elsewhere. Hemingway always maintained the innocence of his motives in this matter. He had "known all along," he wrote Fitzgerald, that Liveright "could not and would not be able to publish it as it makes a bum out of their present ace and best seller Anderson." But he did not, he insisted, "have that in mind in any way" when he wrote it. Hemingway's breaking the contract was not particularly unusual; a number of other writers were doing this kind of thing, as of 1925. What is surprising is that he always insisted he had not written *The Torrents of Spring* as a contract breaker.

In any case, he sent off the slim manuscript to Liveright on December 7, 1925, with a brash letter extolling its literary and commercial prospects. Fitzgerald, Dos Passos, and Louis Bromfield had all read and admired the book. Bromfield thought it the funniest book he had ever read. For his own part, Ernest suggested that it might stack up with Fielding's *Joseph Andrews*. With comic illustrations by the cartoonist Ralph Barton, Ernest thought it could sell twenty thousand copies and make them both a hell of a lot of money. (There was no mention in the letter about *The Sun Also Rises*, the novel whose first draft Hemingway had completed and whose commercial possibilities were appreciated not only by Liveright but by Perkins at Scribners and by the publisher Alfred Harcourt, whom Bromfield had interested in Hemingway's work.) This time, though, Liveright should merchandise the book properly, leaving off those jacket blurbs which had discouraged sales of *In Our Time*. In an exasperated reply, Liveright said he was eagerly awaiting the manuscript of *The Sun Also Rises*, but that he really couldn't publish *The Torrents of Spring*. The in-office readers unanimously disagreed with the assessments of Dos Passos, Fitzgerald, and Bromfield. Besides that, the book sketched a bitter caricature of Anderson and was entirely unmarketable. "Really, old top," Liveright inquired, even "admitting that *Torrents of Spring* is a good American satire, who on earth do you think would buy it?"

Well, both Scribners and Harcourt, Brace were eager to buy the book, if it would give them contractual access to the writer of *In Our Time* and the almost-completed *The Sun Also Rises*. In February 1926 Hemingway went the rounds in New York, first to Liveright's office for the formal separation, then, after a hard-drinking, restless night on the town, to Scribners and Harcourt, Brace next day. Perkins made the best offer, and that settled that; for the rest of his life (though in 1927 he flirted with the idea of letting Heinemann, the British publishers, bid on both British and American rights), Hemingway's New York publisher was Charles Scribner's Sons.

Though not precisely unethical, Hemingway's behavior in the Liveright-to-Scribners switch displayed a level of calculation that was characteristic of his dealings with publishers, editors, and agents. He conducted his business affairs with one eye cocked on the main chance, and the other alert for those who might try to cheat him. Popularity, he found soon after the success of *A Farewell to Arms*, spawned not only great opportunities but certain costly obligations as well. What was he supposed to do, he plaintively inquired of Sir Hugh Walpole, when he started getting letters? After *The Sun Also Rises*, the only mail had come in from maiden ladies who wanted to make a home for him, despite his presumed disability, or from drunks who claimed they had met him in one bar or another. But with *Farewell*, it was different; the letters kept pouring in, and so far he had answered them all. But that took twenty minutes and a franc and a half postage for each letter, and he had time for nothing else. What would happen if he didn't reply? Would "they" become angry, dig up his past sins, and get him indicted? Would "they" sullenly decide never to buy another book of his? Did Walpole answer such letters? This in late 1929, but by 1932 Ernest had come to suspect the motives of many correspondents. They were, he decided, out to receive, then sell his letters (as history has demonstrated, he was more right than he could have dreamed; a single Hemingway letter was quoted in 1974 at $1000). Thus he closed off a correspondence with a certain bookseller with the remark that he knew from "dirty experience" that the kind of man who brought out limited editions (as this man had done, of Faulkner's early ephemera) made it a practice to sell personal letters from writers. If the bookseller wanted to continue their correspondence, let him send the Hemingway originals back and just keep copies of them.

In the trough of the Depression, while the New Deal tinkered with the failing economy, Ernest Hemingway was becoming a hot literary property—and he knew it. So did Arnold Gingrich, who persuaded Ernest to contribute a monthly letter, usually on fishing or hunting, to his new *Esquire* magazine. Though Hemingway received but $300 a crack for these communiqués, he rather enjoyed writing them, and when he had a story in the works, his price shot up. Clearly Hemingway managed to bedazzle Gingrich, on the one hand writing him in 1933 that he was reluctant to reach a first-name basis (Max Perkins had asked him to stop calling him Mr. Perkins, he'd done so, and it had cost him at least $10,000), and on the other inviting him down in 1934 to an all-male fishing trip to the Dry Tortugas. Dos Passos, who was along on that voyage, watched in fascination while Ernest played the editor as he might have played a marlin. "The man never took his frustrated eyes off Old Hem. . . . Ernest was practicing up on skills he'd later apply to high literary finance. He got [Gingrich] so tame he even sold him a few pieces of mine for good measure."

The *Esquire* connection continued for most of the decade, and Hemingway revealed a strong sense of financial savvy throughout. From Gingrich he wangled a $3000 advance—promissory against a year's output—to help purchase the *Pilar*, his sleek black-hulled fishing boat. After Dave Smart, the publisher of *Esquire*, gave him a thousand shares of the company stock, he complained to Gingrich when the stock dropped in price. And at the very beginning of their relationship he laid down two rules which served him as guidelines in dealing with the magazines. First, unless the publication was noncommercial or put out on behalf of a charity, he would give nothing away. As he wrote the editor of an anthology some years later, whenever somebody stood to make some money and professional writers were involved, they should get their cut. Let others participate for the honor, if they wanted to be dopes. For his part, "if there is any dough involved let them pay. The hell with the honor." Second, and most important, his policy was to demand from all commercial magazines "the absolute top price" they had ever paid. Thus in selling "first serial rights only" for *Across the River and into the Trees* to *Cosmopolitan* he discovered that the highest they'd ever paid for a serialized novel was $75,000, and then asked for $10,000 more. Similarly, when a story he'd agreed to write for *True* stretched beyond the agreed-on two thousand-word limit, and the magazine's offer stayed stationary, Hemingway simply withdrew from the bargain. It was "too good and too long to sell for that sort of money," he tantalized editor Peter Barrett, but there were no hard feelings. He'd put the story away as "so much money in the bank." With this policy in operation, Ernest achieved the ultimate magazine price in 1960, when *Sports Illustrated* paid him $30,000 for a two thousand-word article on bullfighting: $15 a word.

As with magazines, so with stage and screen. Hemingway felt he'd been burned when *A Farewell to Arms* was sold to the movies for $80,000; after the agent took his 10 per cent, Hemingway split the remaining proceeds three ways ($24,000 each) with the producer and playwright who'd already adapted the novel for the stage. In the case of his play, *The Fifth Column*, he was going to allow no such mistake, and may have dickered with producers on his own despite having granted an option to Joseph Losey. So, at least, Losey suspected; Hemingway, he observed, was a hell of a guy to work with, and he did not mean it in a flattering sense. The triumph came with the "bloody wonderful" sale, in 1940, of the screen rights to *For Whom the Bell Tolls*. The price was $100,000 "plus ten cents a copy for each copy sold" including the Book of the Month Club printing of two hundred thousand copies, the highest price yet secured for the sale of a novel to Hollywood. When the downpayment check of $100,000 arrived, the euphoric Ernest conspicuously waved it under the bartender's nose at Lindy's in New York. Other sales at fantastic prices to the films, to radio and television followed. During the last twenty years of his life Ernest Hemingway proved time and again his extraordinary capacity to make money—more money than anyone else—from his writing.

iii

Money (CONTINUED)

Monumental Generosity

Among those who knew Ernest Hemingway well, a substantial difference of opinion exists as to whether he was generous or "careful" with his money. Though there are exceptions, as a general rule those who knew him during the first half of his sixty-odd years found him close-fisted; those who encountered him later characterized him as open-handed. Indeed, during the last three decades of his life, Ernest often displayed quite extraordinary generosity, a practice that suited oddly with his concurrent determination to sell his work at exorbitant prices. As Nelson Algren perceived, Hemingway befuddled his critics because "he never went for the money. He made the money, he liked the money, he spent the money. But he never went for the money." The observation applies in two ways. First, Hemingway did not cheapen his art by intentionally aiming for the widest possible audience. Second, once he began to make a great deal of money, he took clear satisfaction in getting rid of it like a sailor on liberty. For reasons that will bear exploration, Hemingway freely opened his purse, when it was full, to a number of the relatively impoverished, including other writers, fighters in the anti-fascist crusade, servants, casual acquaintances, and several young men in whom he saw intimations of his younger self.

One writer who benefited was his friend Guy Hickok, who had

been Brooklyn *Eagle* correspondent in Paris when Hemingway was covering Europe for the Toronto *Star*. He loaned Hickok $750 in 1931, despite Pauline's obvious disapproval. She went to visit the Hickoks in Paris privately, and when Guy mentioned her husband's offer of credit, piped right up like the proper watchful housewife that the money was all gone. "What do you mean," Guy wrote Ernest, "by offering me money that's all gone?" Ernest made the offer good, and seven years later, the debt had not been repaid. In 1933 Ernest sent John Dos Passos a check for $1000 when Dos came down with an attack of rheumatic fever, and issued other, smaller loans to him as well. In 1934, learning that aspiring writer Ned Calmer, his wife, and child were stranded in Paris without the funds for the trip home, Ernest "almost shyly slipped a cheque" for $350 across the table. Two years later, when Calmer wrote reaffirming his intention to repay the loan when possible, Hemingway told him to regard it as a present "to the kid" and offered to send him another $100 or $150, if he needed it. Calmer did his best to return the funds, but he was not entirely successful, for Hemingway didn't really want to be paid back. "After his death," Calmer observed, "the estate lawyer sent me one of my cheques made out to Ernest which he had never cashed." When he and Martha Gellhorn were off covering the war in the early 1940s, Ernest extended the use of his house in Cuba to the novelist Dawn Powell. And there were other literary beneficiaries as well, among them Ezra Pound.

An old friend from Paris days, where they played tennis, boxed, and Pound played literary tutor to Hemingway's apprentice, Ezra was one of the few writers who commanded Ernest's admiration from first to last, from an appreciative notice for the *Transatlantic Review* in the 1920s to the flattering portrait in *A Moveable Feast* written in the late 1950s. Financially, as well, Hemingway showed his loyalty, despite his own antifascism, contributing to the poet's defense in 1948, helping to support Dorothy Pound while she lived in Washington during her husband's confinement in St. Elizabeths Hospital, composing an eloquent letter urging Pound's freedom, and as a final gesture writing a check for $1500 upon his release. Pound never cashed Ernest's "monumental" check, instead having it "sunk in plexiglass as a token of yr magnanimous glory."

In January 1934 Hemingway turned down a proposal for a cooperative venture with six other writers, explaining that he was already supporting twelve direct dependents, loaning 35 per cent of his income to writers, painters, and fishermen that he thought worth supporting, and giving another 5 per cent away to worthless people he felt sorry for. Undoubtedly, there was some exaggeration in this account, but the advent of the Spanish Civil War furnished Ernest with a cause that he *did* support with near-incredible generosity.

One of the artists he had in mind, in the 1934 letter, was the Spaniard Luis Quintanilla, whose New York exhibition of etchings the previous fall Hemingway had organized, paying for the show, paying to have the prints pulled, paying the duty on the etchings, paying for the advertising, promising to buy fifteen if the show didn't produce enough other sales, writing an introduction himself, and getting Dos Passos to write another. Quintanilla was languishing in a Madrid jail at the time, charged with having been a leader of the October revolt. Two years later, when the real fighting in Spain started, Hemingway contributed personal notes for $40,000 to supply the Loyalists with ambulances, and donated cash as well as his services as writer-narrator to finance the propaganda film, *The Spanish Earth.*

Nor did his generosity cease after the hostilities. Anyone victimized by fascism or engaged in the antifascist crusade could count on his immediate and continuing help. According to Malcolm Cowley, "he supported . . . a great number of refugees from the Spanish war who would have starved if Hemingway hadn't helped them." (On a couple of occasions he tried to give Cowley money, too). No books were kept on these transactions, so only a few can be recounted here. To Margaret Anderson, an expatriate trapped in Paris without funds during the Nazi occupation, he sent a check for $400 to cover ocean passage. As long as any of us have money, he wrote her, we all have money: a remark of singular solidarity considering that she had depicted Hemingway as a lovesick oaf a decade before in *My Thirty Years' War.* But quarrels on other issues could not stem the flow of his generosity when Hemingway, and those he helped, shared a common hatred of fascism. Thus, he lent the communist Milton Wolff $425 to buy a chicken farm in the summer of 1942, a mere seven months after Wolff had accused Ernest, on the basis of reading *For Whom the Bell Tolls*, of having been no more than a "tourist" and a "rooter" in Spain.

Another way for Ernest to advance the cause of his beleaguered antifascist allies was to write prefaces to their books. He wrote one, for example, to introduce *The Great Crusade*, the autobiographical novel of the German novelist and soldier Gustav Regler. He also sent Regler a "substantial" gift of money and was instrumental in getting him released from an internment camp after the Spanish war. Similarly, he contributed a preface to Elio Vittorini's *In Sicily*, a novel of undercover liberalism written in fascist Italy, and promptly relayed his check for the job to Vittorini since he "had done the Introduction to help him and not to make money." For years after the war Ernest sent a monthly stipend to the Pamplona hotelkeeper Juanito Quintana, whom Franco had stripped of his hotel and livelihood. On Hemingway's trip to Spain in 1954 he looked up Quintana and took him along on an *aficionado's* tour of the bull rings; one day, after Quintana protested that he could not afford such travel, he found $500 stuffed in his coat pocket.

At times Hemingway impulsively pressed money on nearly total strangers. In 1938, at Brentano's bookstore in Paris, he ran into a young admirer named Tom Bennett, and hours later gave him enough money to buy clothes and to accompany the Hemingways on the ship back to the States. In this case, Ernest's generosity derived at least partly from the antifascist motive: Tom had been wounded while fighting with the Lincoln Battalion in Spain. But no such logic attended his decision to stuff $85 in bills in a half-empty wine bottle as a present to a farmer whose Montana land he hunted in 1940, or his contribution of a pile of pound notes to one-time Paris bartender Jimmy Charters in 1944, or his purchase of a pair of two-year-old bulls for a bellhop in Segovia who dreamed of becoming a bullfighter, or his financing a term at the Sorbonne for a worshipful youngster who wanted to learn French.

What, then, besides political conviction, accounted for Hemingway's streak of generosity? How can one explain his decision, though he was greatly annoyed by the book Philip Young had written about him, finally to allow publication and even to turn over to Young his own share of the permission costs? Perhaps, Young speculates, Hemingway needed to be generous. Perhaps he needed to be thought generous too. At times he was rather showy about his distribution of largesse, as when he pointed out "the International Whore" in Havana, and claimed that he had paid her daughter's way through college. He also told the rather sensational story, to several auditors, of his loans to escapees from the French prison on Devil's Island. As if to illustrate the tale, a young Frenchman shuffled down the path to Finca Vigia while Cowley was visiting there. His story was that he was a mason who had lost his tools while in the hospital. Ernest didn't believe him, but gave him $20 anyway. He was a sucker for hard-luck stories, he told Cowley; that was how he spent his money.

Hemingway may have enjoyed his bursts of generosity, his brother Leicester believes, because they took him back to his own "well-remembered days of low finances." Surely he did tend to glorify his years of comparative poverty. But another, more plausible part of the explanation is suggested by his deciding, on two separate occasions, to take young men—both of distinguished parentage—into his own home as surrogate sons.

One of these was the Venetian Gianfranco Ivancich, who came to live at the Finca in the early 1950s while he worked on a novel. Twenty years his junior, Gianfranco appealed to Ernest because of his beautiful sister, the nineteen-year-old Adriana Ivancich depicted as Renata in *Across the River and into the Trees*; because of his record in World War II, when he was wounded while fighting for Rommel in Africa, recovered, and later joined the American OSS; and because his own father had been brutally murdered. Hemingway put Gianfranco up at the guest house, provided meals, encouraged his writing, and tried to interest Scribners in his work. In addition, he gave Gianfranco the manuscript of *Across the River and into the Trees*, to dispose of as he wished and to the highest bidder. The visitor was treated, in fact, less like a member of the family than as an honored guest—so much so that when Hemingway's secretary complained that while the Hemingways were absent, Gianfranco and his friends had been holding noisy parties at the Finca and breaking glasses, Ernest responded that he had given Gianfranco the full run of the place, and she should not concern herself. For nearly three years the young Venetian stayed either at the Finca or nearby, one of his functions being to provide occasional male companionship to Mary Hemingway while her husband worked, shot pigeons, or fished the Gulf Stream.

More revealing of the motives behind Ernest's generosity was the case of the young Cuban aristocrat Mayito Menocal, Jr. The grandson of a one-time President of Cuba, Mayito dropped out of Cornell in 1942, and thinking himself ostracized by his own father, came to live at the Finca. Mayito, who was just Bumby's age, was immediately accepted into the family circle, and ever afterward regarded Ernest as a valuable, kind, and loyal mentor, a second father who taught him a great deal. One of the first messages Ernest conveyed was that Mayito should not despair, for he too had once been rejected as "a worthless character" by his parents.

Apparently, the memory of the condemnatory letters his mother and father had sent him in 1920 still rankled more than twenty years later. In any case, he had confounded their dire warnings that he would come to no good if he kept on with the "sponge game," and every time he gave money away, he re-emphasized, in a kind of long-range revenge, his capacity to make far more money than they had ever expected of him. Besides, as he like the other children of Oak Park had been taught, it did not do to worship, miserlike, at the altar of Mammon.

In letters, Hemingway justified his unusually generous gifts by invoking the axiom of limited emotional capacity. "You can have true affection," he told A. E. Hotchner, only a few times in your life. Getting rid of material things made sure he wouldn't be wasting affection on them that should be directed at human beings. Don't people, he inquired of another correspondent, always give other people things when they love them? Wasn't that the only way the things could have meaning to them? So he sent Pound his check "on the old Chinese principle . . . that no one possesses anything until they have given it to another." But the principle had still more recognizable roots in the Protestant-American doctrine that if the ability to make money measured a man's masculinity, his willingness to give it away measured his moral worth. It is this sense in which Hemingway best fitted Zelda Fitzgerald's perception of him as "sort of a materialistic mystic."

While Ernest played Lord Bountiful toward many outsiders, he was noticeably less openhanded with members of his immediate family. Thus, though he emerged from his three divorces in unusually good financial condition (Martha demanded nothing from him besides separation, and Hadley asked little beyond an occasional check for Bumby), Hemingway fiercely resented the terms of his divorce from Pauline. From 1940 until her death in 1951 he paid her with reasonable regularity $500 a month "blood money," muttering darkly the while that Pauline, a woman whose father (according to his calculations) owned seventy-six thousand acres of land and whose uncle was worth about $40 million, was out to break him. One thing you had to remember, he learned from that experience, was "that the economics of people having bust-ups" were almost fatal. The man not only lost the children but he went "straight into economic slavery" as well.

On at least a few occasions, Ernest and his fourth and last wife,

Mary Welsh Hemingway, apparently argued over money. In letters, Hemingway carefully pointed out how difficult it was to supply her with funds when the Internal Revenue Service commandeered seventy-five cents out of every dollar. This was not griping, only economics, and Mary could figure it out. On another occasion, Ernest enclosed a check with apologies for penny-pinching, and an insistence that he was not penurious, really, but was working on a long book against a bad tax setup. They'd have to make certain sacrifices together for the time being.

With the children, he took a sterner tone. In 1942, for example, he urged Hadley to take their son Bumby out of Dartmouth for a year. Six months a year he could fish, hunt, or box with his father; the other six months Bumby should spend working. College was a country club for him, and Ernest was sure that he had no idea where money came from or how hard it was to make. Ernest had in mind for his son very much the same program his parents had tried to impose on him in 1920. Sensing the analogy, Ernest told Hadley that one must be careful in disciplining kids of that age, because if the discipline was unjust in any detail they would turn against it as he had turned against the "hysterics, well-meant" of his parents. Nothing came of this proposal, for Hadley satisfied him by return mail that Bumby was being taught the value of a dollar, but a few months later, on the youth's visit to the Finca, Ernest reinforced the lesson. Bumby had come to Cuba after spending $60, too recklessly for his father's taste, in New York, and so when a man came to Ernest for that sum, desperately broke, a case of eat or die, he made sure that Bumby was on hand when he first turned the petitioner down, then gave him the money.

Financial quarrels, real or imaginary, frequently cropped up between Ernest and one or another of his friends. When he broke with Dos Passos in 1938, for example, the actual reason had to do with the two writers' varying interpretations of the way the Spanish Loyalist movement had treated a friend of Dos Passos's. But in a savage letter of dismissal, Hemingway first proposed that Dos might start paying back some of the money he owed him, then shifted to the Judas metaphor. Only an old friend, he wrote in choppy-sentenced wrath, would knife you in the back for a quarter. Anyone else would charge fifty cents. In 1938 Hemingway also quarreled violently with Archibald MacLeish over his contribution to *The Spanish Earth*. In all, Ernest put $3500 into the film, with $1000 of this sum added at the last minute in order to complete the picture. Ernest understood that this $1000, which he'd borrowed at interest in order to send to MacLeish, was to be returned out of the first revenues from the film. MacLeish understood nothing of the sort. Hence there issued from Key West a series of vituperative communications. MacLeish had given time and money to the Spanish cause, Hemingway acknowledged, but had not risked what could not be paid for, and hence would do well to keep his "Scotch" mouth closed while Ernest was around. He had been no saint in his life, Ernest admitted, but he had tried to be absolutely straight about two things: writing and money. Waking in the night, he had never felt pangs of conscience about either, which, by implication, could hardly be true of MacLeish. In the end, MacLeish wrote back in apology; of course the misunderstanding had been his fault, and he would clear it up. Five years later Hemingway attempted to repair the breach with MacLeish by inviting him to Cuba and promising not to be self-righteous, no-good, and bastardly as during his "great 37–38 epoch." But what has been committed to paper does not come so easily unsaid, and it does not seem possible that either Dos Passos or MacLeish was ever able to feel, after 1938, the same sort of affection for Ernest Hemingway that they once had felt.

Money Corrupts

Not only could financial quarrels drive a wedge between friends and family but throughout Hemingway's writing the lure of money is shown to have a morally disfiguring effect upon human behavior. Obviously, he took seriously Saint Paul's caveat that the love of money is the root of all evil. Follow that false god, he warns, and you may become a fomenter of wars, despoiler of women, ruiner of talent, and corrupter of sport.

On the issue of war profiteers, Hemingway took a position close to that of his one-time mentor Ezra Pound. "You seen a lot, and unpleasant," Pound wrote him in November 1936, "but WHY WAS IT? Because some sodomitical usurer wanted to SELL the goddamn blankets and airplanes." Though Hemingway lacked Pound's passionate obsession with usury, he had expressed similar sentiments earlier in that same year. International conflicts, he believed, were produced by power-mad leaders in league with the war lovers. And "the only people who ever loved war for long were profiteers, generals, staff officers and whores. They all had the best and finest times of their lives and most of them made the most money they had ever made." Especially in *Across the River and into the Trees*, he vented his scorn against the Milanese businessmen who had benefited from World War II without leaving their comfortable homes. Such profiteers were liable to produce shoddy merchandise for the troops, like the American manufacturer whose raincoats withstood the wind but were anything but waterproof. Who made the money on that one? Probably some jerk whose boy was "in Groton now . . . because our coats leaked."

Soldiers too faced extraordinary temptations during wartime, when the ordinary rules against stealing were suspended. "After Cherbourg," Colonel Cantwell explains to the rapt Renata, "we had everything," including the best brandy and negotiable German-printed French francs, but Cantwell stole nothing except an admiral's compass because he "thought it was bad luck to steal, unnecessarily, in a war." Most soldiers, of whatever army, did not share this superstition, so that during his trip to China in 1941, Hemingway found the Chinese custom of "squeeze" in full operation. Military truck drivers were selling their gasoline to private concerns, and he saw with his own eyes "tires being thrown off trucks loaded with them—evidently to be picked up by confederates later." Usually, Chiang Kai-shek's orders would be carried out immediately, but where money was involved, things slowed down drastically.

Given enough cash, one could even purchase immunity from the direst effects of war. Thus, Frederic Henry and Catherine Barkley in *A Farewell to Arms* can buy asylum in Switzerland, because they have passports and plenty of money. Their privileged status is contrasted with that of the two terrified virgins whom Frederic takes along during the retreat from Caporetto. When the trucks founder in mud, the best thing he can do for the young innocents is to give them a sum of money and aim them toward the main highway. "They did not understand but they held the money tightly and started down the road." So armed, perhaps they too will be able to avoid the worst consequences—to their minds, casual rape—of the corrupted standards practiced by men at war.

After delivering himself of his thoughts on the need to earn the good things through hard effort, Jake Barnes in *The Sun Also Rises* concludes rather cynically, "It seemed like a fine philosophy. In five years . . . it will seem just as silly as all the other fine philosophies I've had." Hemingway, however, did not abandon the code which Jake had enunciated, but continued to regard the lure of the easy dollar as a particular threat to the artist. Money, he wrote Dos Passos in 1929, had been the ruination of too many of their friends. Don Stewart had taken up with Jock Whitney, to say nothing of selling his soul to Hollywood for a $25,000 contract. John Peale Bishop's career had been spoiled by his wife's munificent income. The search for eternal youth had clearly sunk the Fitzgeralds. In *Green Hills of Africa*, he cited money as the first way in which American writers are destroyed. When they have made some money, they "increase their standard of living and they are caught. They have to write to keep up their establishments, their wives, and so on, and they write slop." How foolish to be so entrapped, when "a thousand years makes economics look silly and a work of art endures for ever."

The money culture acted perniciously in another province Hemingway held sacred, that of manly sport. Thus, in his first novel and in subsequent books and stories, he demonstrated how the cancer of commercialism had infected bullfighting. Pedro Romero, for instance, is forced to face a dangerously bad bull, whose deficient eyesight can barely detect the cape, because the promoters have paid for the bull and "don't want to lose their money." But the glory of Romero is that he remains immune to the disease of commercialism—and the caution unto cowardice it is likely to breed. He wants and expects to make money as a bullfighter. When Brett reads in his hand that there "are thousands of bulls" in his future, "Good," he says, and in an aside to Jake in Spanish, "At a thousand duros apiece." Yet he has not yet begun to compromise his bullfighting, as Juan Belmonte has, by insisting on manageable bulls with smallish horns. Appropriately, Hemingway invokes the metaphor of profit and loss when comparing Pedro's afternoon of triumph to the jeers that had greeted Belmonte: "Pedro Romero had the greatness. He loved bull-fighting, and I think he loved the bulls, and I think he loved Brett. Everything of which he could control the locality he did in front of her all that afternoon. . . . But he did not do it for her at any loss to himself. He gained by it all through the afternoon." His willingness to take chances, one of the ways, as Jake has reflected, in which you could pay "for everything that was any good," gives the bullfight, his relationship with Brett, and the fiesta itself a kind of dignity.

Hemingway further condemns Belmonte, in *Death in the Afternoon*, for his miserliness toward Maera, who served in his *cuadrilla*. Belmonte steadfastly refused to increase Maera's niggardly wages, until finally the youth struck out on his own to become one of the bravest of matadors. "A man's ranking" in Spain, Hemingway explains, "is made by the amount he receives for fighting," "the less he pays his subordinates the more man he is," and "the nearer he can bring his subordinates to slaves the more man he feels he is." In general, "there is no man meaner about money with his inferiors" than the Spanish matador. Maera himself was the exception to the rule. "He was generous, humorous, proud, bitter, foul-mouthed and a great drinker. He neither sucked after intellectuals nor married money." Best of all, he loved bullfighting enough not to be swayed by financial considerations. "There are bullfighters who do it just for the money," Hemingway once remarked, "—they are worthless." "The only one who matters is the bullfighter who feels it, so that if he did it for nothing, he would do it as well."

The hero of his story "The Undefeated" is such a man. Though badly in need of money and incapacitated by previous horn wounds, Manuel Garcia so loves his craft that he fights for a pittance and despite a valiant performance is seriously gored. But before he goes under the ether, Manuel sits up on the operating table to prevent the medics from cutting off his *coleta*, the pigtail that is his badge of status as a matador. He will die, but he will not die defeated.

A Moveable Disgust

In "The Snows of Kilimanjaro," Hemingway as narrator reflects on Scott Fitzgerald's romantic awe of the rich and his belief that they were a special glamorous race. Hemingway does not seem to have shared Fitzgerald's sense that the possession of great wealth could almost magically open up vistas forbidden to the sight of the less well-off. But the fact is that in his own fiction Ernest portrayed the rich as an entirely separate breed, more distasteful than the rest of mankind. Clearly, there was no doubt in his mind that an inverse relationship existed between money and morals. As he wrote to Owen Wister in 1932, people were much nicer since they were "all broke." Five years later he demonstrated the other side of the axiom in the vignettes excoriating the rich at the end of *To Have and Have Not*. These expensive people who lived on the yachts off Key West were immoral, sterile, and dull.

In the posthumously published "African Journal," an account of the African safari of 1954, Hemingway happily reflected on "how we had gone five months without breaking bread with a wealthy bore." It was this boring quality that he singled out, time and again, as the hallmark of the moneyed classes. The rich were "all good and wonderful and dull as hell." As fishing companions, they didn't know when to shut up or when to put up their money. In a 1934 *Esquire* letter, he suggested that deep-sea fishing ought perhaps to be subsidized, since as an expensive sport it was unfortunately restricted to those with lots of money. But all the people he knew who were wealthy enough to subsidize anything were "either busy studying how to get more wealth, or horses, or what is wrong with themselves, with psychoanalysis, or horses, or how not to lose what wealth they have, or horses, or the moving picture business, or horses or all of these things together, and, possibly, horses."

Only a few months before this satiric piece, however, Hemingway had written Gingrich suggesting that he might want to run horse-racing articles by young Alfred Vanderbilt, whom he had met hunting in Africa. Vanderbilt, he explained, knew all the workings of thoroughbred racing from the inside, and was a nice kid besides. Perhaps he could not write, but Gingrich could take a chance by paying $100 for a racing piece, and Hemingway would pay for it himself if it wasn't any good. Dull though they may have been as a class, in individual cases Hemingway was willing to cultivate and be cultivated by the rich. After World War II, especially, the Hemingways' circle of companions consisted more and more of members of the moneyed and titled classes. One of his closest friends during the last two decades of his life, for example, was the New York socialite Winston (Wolfie) Guest. Like Hemingway a virtual bear of a man, Guest served as fishing, hunting, and drinking companion to his friend the writer. During the early stages of the war Guest also assumed the role of first mate during the *Pilar*'s sub-hunting expeditions.

Nita Jensen Houk, who was Hemingway's secretary during the

1950s, vividly remembers a story her employer told about Guest. The two of them were driving home after a day of shooting and fishing, when Wolfie began to complain about his lack of ready cash:

HEMINGWAY: I can let you have a few bucks.
GUEST: No, thanks, I've still got a few left.
HEMINGWAY: A few dollars?
GUEST: No, a few million.

"Papa of course," Nita recalled, "loved to tell this story." Immediately after the war, Hemingway and Major General C. T. (Buck) Lanham, the Army officer whom Ernest befriended during World War II, went to a house party at the Guests' Gardiner Island estate. But Lanham simply felt out of place in such company, which seemed to him pretentious and dull. Nor was he entirely persuaded by Hemingway's insistence that though the very rich were not his people, he went into their country as he would go into any other foreign country.

It was a country that he inhabited more often as time wore on. "All of Ernest's friends that I ever knew," Mayito Menocal, Jr., remarked, "were either from the upper classes or—much less frequently —from the lower classes." Among these companions in Cuba were Mayito's father, Guest, Elicio Arguelles, Thorwald Sanchez, and Tommy Shevlin, all "rich members of the privileged elite of their respective countries." Except for the jai-alai players (all Basques), it was the same with the Spanish, and in Italy such companions as the Franchettis, Ivanciches, and Kechlers all belonged to the highest stratum of Venetian society. During the winter of 1954 Hemingway eagerly embraced Rupert Bellville's offer to put him up as a member of White's, the distinguished London club in St. James's, and casually invented a falsehood to advance his candidacy. He assured Bellville, a bullfight fan who had fought with Franco in the Spanish war, that no one should consider him anti-British, despite the slurring references to Field Marshal Bernard Montgomery and British soldiers in *Across the River and into the Trees*. At that moment (February 17, 1954, when he was still recovering from two airplane crashes the month before), he darkly intimated, he was placing his United States citizenship in jeopardy in order to serve the Queen on a mysterious, unspecified mission. Bellville duly put Ernest up for White's. Evidently he did not get in. "Ernest was not a snob," Menocal believes, nor did he ever assume "the special attitude toward life that the privileged seem to acquire at birth." Yet he did cultivate the companionship of "the aristocracy of whatever country he was in, and of the very rich."

What Menocal found striking about this proclivity was that it so obviously contradicted the attitude expressed in Hemingway's writing. As he put it, "In Ernest's books being rich was per se an indictment." The question, of course, is why. Why was he only at home among such people? Why did he consistently assume a position against them in his books? The book which suggests the most plausible answers is *A Moveable Feast*, a bittersweet memoir of his early days in Paris that is full of love and scorn. And the metaphor by which these emotions are articu-lated derives, once again, from the world of finance.

Brilliant in its style and for its portraits of the famous and near-famous, *A Moveable Feast* achieves its unity through evocation of the way it was for Ernest Hemingway, a young and unknown author, to practice his developing art in Paris during the 1920s. It is, then, a success story, and like most such stories, it emphasizes the accomplish-ment of its hero by exaggerating the depths from which he came. As he grew older (and *A Moveable Feast* was the last book he finished), Hemingway laid increasing stress on the poverty he suffered in Paris. Without question, Ernest and Hadley Hemingway lived on a relatively scant income during those years, but they were never so badly off as the writer, in retrospect, liked to believe.

In any case, poverty is vitually apotheosized in *A Moveable Feast*. As the title hints, a gnawing hunger for food and drink symbolizes Hemingway's indigence. According to the legend constructed in this book, Hemingway worked all day in his unheated garret, too poor to buy firewood or afford lunch. At least he does not tell here the unlikely yarn that appears in A. E. Hotchner's biography: the one about Heming-way catching pigeons in the Luxembourg Gardens in order to satisfy a rumbling stomach. But poverty, and its symbolic hunger, are nonetheless celebrated. "You got very hungry when you did not eat enough in Paris," Hemingway writes, because of the good things on display in the *pâtisseries* and at the outdoor restaurants. Mostly he and Hadley sur-vived on leeks (*poireaux*), but at least so frugal a diet enabled one to savor, truly, the joys of eating well when an unexpected windfall made it possible for them to dine out. Fasting offered another, more valuable compensation: a definite sharpening of the perceptions. Thus the Cézannes in the Luxembourg Museum "were sharpened and clearer and more beautiful if you were belly-empty, hollow-hungry."

Looking at these paintings in lieu of lunch provided "good discipline"; it was "healthy" to be hungry. Hemingway even wondered if Cézanne had not been hungry when he painted them. *A Moveable Feast* strongly supports the axiom, as Leo Hamalian has observed, that "the only good artist is a hungry artist," and it implicitly proposes the corollary that should you become fat and rich, you will be finished as an artist.

If the celebration of poverty comprises one side of the story Hemingway tells in *A Moveable Feast*, the other side consists of his diatribe against the rich. As the tale unfolds, it becomes clear that he holds this group responsible for destroying his idyllic first marriage, when he and Hadley and Bumby and F. Puss, the cat, lived together in joyous harmony in their barely adequate apartment. For the Hemingways, it was "poor everybody" else; they were the happy, the contented, the "rich feathercats with no money."

Years later Hemingway learned from Picasso how he "always promised the rich to come when they asked him because it made them so happy, and then something would happen and he would be unable to appear." But neither in the mid-1920s nor, very often, later did Hemingway know how to say no to such invitations. In his case, "the rich" followed him to Schruns for the winter skiing in the Vorarlberg, preceded by "the pilot fish who goes ahead of them, sometimes a little deaf, sometimes a little blind," always on the move, dabbling in politics and the theater, equipped with "the irreplaceable early training of the bastard, and a latent and long-denied love of money," moving "one dollar's width to the right with every dollar that he made." So Hemingway devastated, on the printed page, to be read by anyone who picked up a copy of *A Moveable Feast*, his erstwhile friend and fellow writer John Dos Passos. In a gallery of acid portraits, this one ranks as the most mean-spirited of all, with its gratuitous references to Dos's physical handicaps and his having been born out of wedlock, a circumstance then so little known that Hemingway must have learned of it from Dos Passos himself.

At least the book does not name Dos Passos outright, just as it does not explicitly identify "the rich"—"the good, the attractive, the charming, the soon-beloved, the generous, the understanding rich who have no bad qualities and who give each day the quality of a festival and who, when they have passed and taken the nourishment they needed, leave everything deader than the roots of any grass Attila's horses' hoofs have ever scoured." But the most elementary detective work reveals these sinister invaders to be Gerald and Sara Murphy, with whom Hemingway seems to have had no previous quarrel whatever. Still more obvious is the equation of Pauline Pfeiffer with the infiltrating rich girl who, "using the oldest trick there is," becomes the "temporary best friend of another young woman who is married, goes to live with the husband and wife and then unknowingly, innocently and unrelentingly sets out to marry the husband."

The burden of Hemingway's argument in *A Moveable Feast* is that he cannot be held accountable for leaving Hadley. The blame lay with Pauline, or rather with that vague group called "the rich" who sent her around and who taught him to value leisure more than work. In its attempt to acquit himself of charges brought by himself, the book testifies to the author's abiding sense of guilt for a mistake he had made more than thirty years before. As a consequence of that mistake, he married a rich woman and, having money, turned into a different kind of person, and writer, than he had imagined himself to be during the innocent 1920s. The guilt was too much for him to bear, and so he transfered it to Pauline and the Murphys. Reading the last few pages of *A Moveable Feast*, MacLeish felt as though he "had lost a quart of blood—the blood that once felt deeply about Ernest."

Throughout most of his adult life Ernest Hemingway was convinced, quite wrongly, that he teetered on the verge of bankruptcy. This conviction eventually turned into the delusion that people were out to rob him of his money, and that the Internal Revenue Service took particular and unflagging interest in his taxes. "At the end," as his son Jack (called Bumby as a boy) remembers, "he had a phobia about losing all of his money." When he first attempted suicide, in April of 1961, he had written a note which he stuffed in the pocket of his bathrobe and later disposed of. All she could detect about the note, Mary said, was that it seemed to be scribbled over with figures.

In his attitudes toward money (though not in his final delusions of persecution), Hemingway faced a dilemma characteristic of the American artist sprung from a middle-class upbringing. On the one hand, he learned from his environment that it was right and manly to make money, and in his career pursued that objective with remarkable success. As one who had proved his money-making capabilities, he took a certain pleasure in the company of others who understood how to enjoy the opportunities it gave them. In fact, when Ernest Hemingway was at play on the Gulf Stream or in Spain or in Italy, he encountered only the rich, for no one else could afford his strenuous kind of leisure living. On the other hand, Hemingway had also been indoctrinated to think that you had to earn your happiness and that easy money could ruin a man. Hence when he first married money, and then began to make it rather easily, he was assailed by guilt that he no longer lived the kind of life he once had as a young man in Paris, a city which "was always worth it" and where "you received return for whatever you brought to it." In *A Moveable Feast*, he purports to tell how it was "in the early days when we were very poor and very happy." Between the lines, the book tells another story about the self-disgust that visited Hemingway when his material circumstances had vastly improved.

iv

Sport

Hemingway as Walter Mitty

No major American writer devoted more time and energy to the world of sport than Ernest Hemingway. As a doctoral thesis on the subject has divined, sports are referred to in forty-three of his first forty-nine stories, and in a number of these ("Big Two-Hearted River," "Fifty Grand," "The Undefeated," and "My Old Man" come immediately to mind) the author conducts an extended examination of the techniques and mores practiced in a particular sporting subculture. Furthermore, Hemingway's journalism and correspondence frequently focused on bull-fighting, hunting, and fishing, as did three of his books—*Death in the Afternoon, Green Hills of Africa*, and *The Old Man and the Sea*.

Given the extent and duration of his interest in almost all sports, from six-day bicycle racing to boxing, from tennis to football, one might conclude that Hemingway was himself an accomplished athlete. This was an impression that he by no means discouraged; indeed, as Hemingway grew older, he tended to construct a myth about the athletic feats of his youth that hardly squares with the facts. Thus he wrote Harvey Breit, a writer and assistant editor of *The New York Times Book Review*, that he had been a football star at Oak Park high school, as well as an out-standing pitcher and hitter on the baseball team. Somewhere, he told Breit, there was a picture of his hitting the ball over the left-field fence, but he could not locate it. In point of fact, however, Hemingway never played high-school baseball, though he used to throw the ball around with Bill Smith in summer vacation pick-up games. As Smith recalls, Ernest would usually catch and Smith would pitch. "He wasn't so hot actually," Smith remembers, "but the picture he had of himself was pitching, not catching. He insisted on pitching in one game but I had to relieve him with three runs in and only one out in the first inning." As a ball player, his brother Leicester writes, Ernest was a pretty studious reader. His mother used to find him poring over a book, and propose that he go out to play some baseball. "Aw, Mother," Ernest would answer, "I pitch like a hen," and go on reading.

But it was football that, then as now, provided the test of courage and manliness for high-school boys. Hampered by mildly deficient eyesight, awkwardly stumbling over his outsized feet, Hemingway nonetheless gave that adolescent American rite an extended try, and even achieved some success. Two understanding English teachers, he later observed gratefully, were especially nice to him because he "had to try to be an athlete as well as try to learn to write English." The trial was complicated by Ernest's size; through junior year in high school he was only about five feet five inches tall, and played, without distinction, on the lightweight team. Then his growth spurt came, and by the fall of 1916, his senior year at Oak Park high school, Hemingway was nearly six feet tall and weighed more than a hundred and fifty pounds—a prime prospect, in terms of size, for the varsity. But his coordination had not kept up with his growth, and Ernest labored as a substitute right guard, which is not, in football terminology, one of the skilled positions. According to available records, he managed to get into only two games that year, including a victory over Waite High in Toledo, when Dr. Hemingway went along to watch his son perform. According to Philip M. White, one of the stars of the Oak Park eleven in 1916, Ernest "tried hard to be an athlete but did not make it." He won his varsity letter "just because of his weight." Another teammate, William C. Phelps, even less charitably recalled Hemingway's football career. Though larger than most of the others, Phelps said, Ernest "was a bluff and a blow hard" and used to pretend to be injured in order to attract sympathy.

From such unpromising beginnings began Hemingway's self-imposed legend of glory as an outstanding high-school tackle. In 1944, at the age of forty-five, he challenged Mike Burke, an authentic ex-football star, to informal tackling practice on the streets of Montmartre. While *bistro* patrons watched in fascination, Burke eluded Hemingway's tackle and stiff-armed him onto the cobblestones. As was usually the case when his bluff was called, Hemingway bounced up again full of laughter and high spirits.

Actually, his best high-school sport was swimming, in which he performed creditably in the plunge, an event that involved diving flat and coasting as far as possible before foundering. But even this limited skill received no mention in the Oak Park high-school *Trapeze* of March 21, 1919, which in reporting on Hemingway's dramatic return as a wounded veteran summarized his previous accomplishments thus: "While in Oak Park High he was prominent in the school's activities. He was on the *Trapeze* staff for two years and was one of the editors in his last year. Always interested in athletics, he won his monogram in football and was manager of the track team."

In sports as in other areas, then, the Hemingway image did not fit reality. Actually he had been a sensitive boy, something of a loner, given to shying away from head-on blocks and tackles on the football field. But while still in his early twenties, Hemingway set about altering the facts. Though he never really cottoned to team sports, he wanted, like Walt Whitman, to be regarded as "one of the roughs." So he spun apocryphal yarns about running away from home, about brawls in and out of the ring, about the tough neighborhoods he had frequented.

With delightful exaggeration, Ford Madox Ford satirized the unnamed Hemingway of the Paris years. "You are to remember," Ford wrote, "that in Paris I have lived for years buried under mountains of Middle-Westerners who there find it necessary to assume the aspects, voices, accents and behaviors of cow-boys crossed with liberal strains of prize-fighters and old-time Bowery toughs. They may have been born in Oak Park, that suburb of Chicago that is the mildest suburb in the world; but they are determined to make you and Paris think them devils of fellows who have only left Oklahoma of the movies ten months before." Similarly, when Archibald MacLeish first got to know Hemingway, Ernest gave him the impression, though he came from Oak Park and MacLeish from Glencoe, a similarly respectable Chicago suburb, that he had been "born on the wrong side of the railroad tracks and as a kid used to spend his time fighting up in Waukegan, which is a particularly miserable town just north of us, where he had suffered an injury to his left eye." This of course was all nonsense, for "he had exactly the same kind of bringing up I had." Hemingway was simply presenting himself "as the kind of boy he wanted to be" or wanted to be in relation to MacLeish. His six-foot frame filled out to manhood, Hemingway shadowboxed around the cafés and told his tales. Often these yarns were about contests in which the individual pitted himself against a powerful, and sometimes a brutal, opponent. Many of them had to do with boxing itself, one sport in which the participant has every opportunity to prove his strength, courage, and durability.

Boxing and Brawling

When Hemingway sailed off to war aboard the French Line's *Chicago* in the spring of 1918, he was accompanied by a hundred and twenty other Red Cross volunteers who were "too young, too decrepit, or too blind" to qualify as soldiers or sailors. His own deficiency was the bad eye he'd had since birth, but on board ship he rapidly converted the disability to an asset; he'd injured his eye, he told Bill Horne, "fighting in pork-and-beans fights around Oak Park." His boxing prowess, as his story went, had been earned through a course of brutal instructions at a downtown Chicago gym, and then he'd fought for dinner money in semi-pro bouts. Later, he would write back from Europe the inaccurate information that he was supplementing the family pocketbook by serving as a sparring partner to professional fighters. In fact, however, he never took boxing lessons in downtown Chicago, and never made any money as a sparring partner. He'd taken up the sport early in 1916, boxing with school companions in his mother's music room, and then, when she began to object, in his friend Tom Cusack's basement. These contests were informal and, according to his sister Marcelline, nobody ever really got hurt; in fact, she and her girl friends used to sail distracting cushions at the amateur gladiators.

But from that first exposure Ernest had learned that his developing size and strength gave him an advantage in boxing he did not have in sports which required greater dexterity and coordination. Upon arriving in Paris, he eagerly sought out opponents in that compulsion for competition that never left him. One of the first was the diminutive Lewis Galantière, who hospitably entertained the Hemingways at the behest of Sherwood Anderson, and had his glasses broken in an after-dinner set-to as a reward. Both Ezra Pound (who once, according to Robert Frost, managed to throw Frost over his head in a jiujitsu maneuver) and Harold Loeb were two-sport friends: tennis and boxing. Loeb, some fifty pounds lighter than the hundred and ninety-pound Hemingway, was not eager to take him on at first, but managed to survive the bouts through Ernest's forbearance and his habit of telegraphing punches by twitching his left eye.

Undoubtedly the most accomplished of his boxing partners in Paris, however, was the Canadian novelist Morley Callaghan. Before they began to box together in the late 1920s, Ernest put Callaghan through a demeaning ritual of initiation. Had Morley done any boxing, Hemingway asked? Yes, he had, quite a bit. Then Ernest rounded up some gloves, and proposed a trial: "Let's see." Somewhat miffed, Callaghan pulled on the gloves, and after a minute or two Ernest was satisfied. "I only wanted to see if you had done any boxing," he said apologetically, "I can see you have."

In the early months of 1929, these two writers fought together a number of times, with Hemingway on one occasion using his superior size and strength to isolate Callaghan in a corner, where he crouched low and "covered up like a turtle in its shell." Then Ernest stopped, smiled, and instructed his smaller opponent not to crouch so low, since he could not punch from that angle. Callaghan was, naturally, "dreadfully humiliated." On another occasion, after Callaghan's jabs cut his mouth, Ernest spat a mouthful of blood in his opponent's face. Their most notorious encounter, however, came one afternoon when Scott Fitzgerald, serving as timekeeper, became fascinated by the action and unwittingly let one round run to four minutes. Since they had agreed to abbreviated, one-minute rounds, and Hemingway had rushed out using up all his wind, the effect of this was to give Callaghan, with his greater quickness and jabbing ability, something of an edge. The extended round ended with Callaghan dumping Ernest on his back, hard. Fitzgerald, who virtually worshiped Hemingway, was distraught in his apologies, but Ernest tended to think he had made the mistake on purpose. Boxing, he lectured Fitzgerald, was not a sport of honor, and since he had been kayoed after the bell and thumbed in the eye during his apprenticeship, he had acquired the "complete habit" of suspicion where fights were concerned.

Though his friend Charles Thompson occasionally obliged Hemingway as a boxing partner in Key West, Ernest found it increasingly difficult, during the 1930s, to find worthy ring opponents among his friends. To keep himself in shape, however, he set up a ring in the back yard of the Key West house at 907 Whitehead Street, and invited the local prizefighters, for fifty cents a round, to spar with him. The better part of valor during those Depression years, for such boxers as the professional light heavyweight John "Iron Baby" Roberts, was to "take it easy on Mr. Ernest." At Bimini in 1935, his muscles hardened by fighting game fish, Hemingway issued a $250 challenge to any of the local Negroes who could stay with him for three three-minute rounds, using six-ounce gloves. Four Biminians tried their luck and all were defeated. As a climax to the summer, he boxed a few rounds with Tom Heeney, once a ranking heavyweight who had fought Gene Tunney. (In Cuba, in the early 1940s, Hemingway continued to propose a few rounds to nearly all visitors, including the mildly terrified Ambassador Spruille Braden, who was awed by Hemingway's chest, shoulder, and bicep development.)

What had begun with schoolboy pawings in the music room at Oak Park, then proceeded through friendly and not-so-friendly contests in Paris to more rugged encounters in Key West and Bimini. His competitive spirit in the ascendancy, Hemingway converted a sportsmanlike test of skill into a more brutal and bloody battle for supremacy. For most of his last three decades, in fact, he engaged more often in brawls than in bouts.

As early as 1926 Hemingway wrote Ernest Walsh not to worry about his slugging the expatriate writer Robert McAlmon, since he was really quite fond of him, and, besides, he had hit only two men, outside of boxing, in his life, and then only because they wanted to hit him. Twenty-five years later, in a letter to Carlos Baker, Hemingway stressed his obligation not to fight, since he was big, in good shape, and could hurt people, but insisted that some fights were unavoidable. Nobody ever gave him any credit for the fights he had avoided. Otto (Toby) and Betty Bruce, who knew Hemingway well in Key West and Piggott, Arkansas, during the 1930s, have testified to the frequency of altercations brought about more through Ernest's fame and force of personality than through any overt provocation. When he entered a bar, Betty Bruce recalled, there "was immediately something electric in the atmosphere—something like what happens when a cat comes into a roomful of ailurophobes, or perhaps more like what might happen if a huge jungle-cat suddenly entered a room." People turned and stared, and the rum-brave among them tended to fling insults, either at Hemingway or his companions.

A number of his fights commenced when he was pressed into action in defense of others. When working on the Kansas City *Star*, he slugged a bully who had been bothering fellow newspaperman Leo Fitzpatrick; and in Paris, Ernest once remarked, he would go out to drink with the myopic James Joyce, and when a fight would start, Joyce "couldn't even see the man so he'd say: 'Deal with him, Hemingway! Deal with him!' " Oftenest, though, these chivalric battles were waged in response to insults against his wives or other female companions. In the fall of 1949, for example, a drunken and foul-mouthed engineer on board the S.S. *Gargiello* made a slighting reference to whatever rich American bastards (the Hemingways) had brought their Buick on board. Mary took exception to his remarks, and Ernest challenged the engineer to a 5 a.m. duel. The engineer didn't show up. At other times, however, he took immediate corrective action. What were you supposed to do when someone called your wife a whore or a bitch? Ernest hit him, "automatically."

By no means were all of his brawls precipitated by such insults, however. In his letters he was given to issuing extremely provocative challenges to correspondents. Sometimes he even delivered such insults in published form. Thus the story, "Mr. and Mrs. Elliot," portrayed Chard Powers Smith and his wife in the most unflattering terms possible (in its initial form, the story was even called "Mr. and Mrs. Smith"). When Smith had the temerity to accuse Hemingway, by mail, of perpetrating "a cad's trick," Ernest responded by suggesting that Smith should fight him at the Deux Magots, where it would give him some pleasure to knock him down a few times, or only once, depending on his stomach for being knocked down. This altercation, like several others begun in letters or conversations, never reached the stage of actual fisticuffs. According to H. L. Mencken's brother, Hemingway once threatened to invade Mencken's office and beat him up, but when the Sage of Baltimore replied, "Come on in," he never appeared. In this case, Hemingway was apparently responding to Mencken's criticism of his work; and in fact, no segment of the population aroused his anger more easily than critics. Charles Fenton, while working on his book *The Apprenticeship of Ernest Hemingway*, conducted a short but lively correspondence with the author, who in a 1952 letter sent Fenton a check for $200 so that he might come down to Cuba and the two could settle their differences. He would like nothing better for his birthday, Ernest indicated, than to beat the hell out of Fenton in some enclosed place. The only critic Ernest actually did fight, however, was Max Eastman.

The bout with Eastman occurred in 1937, near the end of a period of irascibility in Hemingway's life. In 1934, for example, Ernest "totally humiliated" his wife Pauline by starting a fight during a respectable dance at a Key West night club. In 1935, at Bimini, he flattened a wealthy publisher named Joseph Knapp, who was unwise enough to pick a fight with the local champion; in celebration of the victory, a Bimini calypso group composed an impromptu number about the "big slob" Hemingway. Back at Key West, in 1936, the visiting poet Wallace Stevens apparently provoked a fight with Ernest, and was badly beaten. Meanwhile, Hemingway was also cutting his ties with a number of friends through ill-tempered letters and actions. In this period, too, he created the most notorious "tough guy" among his fictional heroes, Harry Morgan of *To Have and Have Not.*

Again in 1944–46 Ernest went through a streak of belligerent behavior. Waiting in Rambouillet for the liberation of Paris, he and his band of irregulars had virtually taken over the Hotel Grand Veneur, and when Bruce Grant, a six-footer from Chicago, complained about this state of affairs, the two briefly exchanged blows. A few months later he called William Saroyan "an Armenian son of a bitch" and started a brawl at the elegant George V in Paris. In New York, in 1946, he repeated the same act by directing a volley of insults at Charles Boyer, who was supping with Ingrid Bergman in the Stork Club. He referred to Boyer as "that small green-faced character," but on this occasion, perhaps because Mary Hemingway and Buck Lanham were along to cool the tensions, no brawl developed. General (then Colonel) Lanham had extensive experience as a fighting man, but as he later commented, "when Hem was nasty" he qualified as "The King of All Nasties."

Undoubtedly there are no simple explanations for these often childish displays of bad temper; but it does seem clear that Hemingway's fondness for boxing and tendency to settle differences with his fists stemmed in part from his twin drives toward competitiveness and toward professionalism. As a youth, Ernest had frequently converted the simplest activity—fishing, hiking, whatever—into a contest. Up in Michigan, at twenty-one, he insisted on walking over the shards of a broken milk bottle to prove his imperviousness to pain. Even in tennis, which was hardly his game, Hadley remembers his slamming his racket into the ground after a poor shot. "He didn't want to be bested in any line of life, at all. . . . He just could not bear not to be terribly good at anything." This motivation to excel led him, more or less naturally, into the cultivation of inside knowledge about a number of sports. In boxing, Callaghan reports, "he had all the lingo, he had hung around gyms, he had watched fighters at work. Something within him drove him to want to be expert at every occupation he touched . . . he had to feel he had a sense of professionalism about every field of human behavior that interested him."

His tennis game, for example, consisted of erratic groundstrokes, awkward volleying, and boundless enthusiasm. While married to Martha Gellhorn, he wrote Lillian Ross, they used to play a lot of singles, where he discovered that to make her happy he had to almost, but not quite, let her win. Martha had pretty, Bryn Mawr strokes, which he casually denigrated. As for himself, he wrote late in his life of the "pig ball" he had perfected playing against Ezra Pound in Paris. This particular shot was "a mysterious service" which "landed flat and dead but with speed, and did not bounce at all." He could only rarely hit this shot, he admitted, since it "was stroked heavily on top with a very violent but caressing motion which is extremely destructive to the ligaments of the right shoulder." But if he hit this bounceless serve only once, that would be once more than anyone else in the world has ever managed to do. Even in tennis, then, he demonstrated his compulsion to do something, somehow, with superprofessional skill.

As Charles Fenton observed, Hemingway was a man "with a high sense of craft," and nothing disturbed him more than watching supposed professionals debase that craft. Hired to cover the Joe Louis–Max Baer championship fight in 1935, he reported that ". . . Baer had no defense. He had never had any from his earliest days in the ring." The fight was disgusting, he wrote, because of Baer's naked fear before Louis's onslaught. As an analogy he told about the feisty behavior of the kingbird, a small but pugnacious bird with a sharp beak that could ward off "crows, hawks, and eagles which could all destroy him in an instant if he were afraid of them." Before Baer attempted "to fight publicly, for money, again, he should first be given a forcible feeding of kingbird eggs." There was nothing shameful in itself about being afraid. All human beings had fear, but fighters "should be trained not to be frightened while fighting." The fear would disappear if they knew their trade and thus had something else to think about. That was the cardinal omission in the make-up of the terrified fighter: "Max Baer had never bothered to learn his trade." For Ernest Hemingway, there could be no more damning sin.

Outdoorsman: Tyro to Tutor

Hemingway's most significant sporting accomplishments came in hunting and fishing, activities to which he had been introduced, very young, by a father who gave an unusual degree of guidance to his first son. Dr. (Ed) Hemingway, an enthusiastic outdoorsman, took Ernest fishing as a special present for his third birthday, and the boy "caught the biggest fish of the crowd." For a fourth-birthday treat, father and son spent all day on the water. Dr. Hemingway also gave his boy an early exposure to firearms: "Ernest was taught to shoot by Pa when 2-½ and when 4 could handle a pistol," Grace Hemingway wrote on the back of one boyhood picture. Later he graduated to air rifles, 22's, and marvelously, on his twelfth birthday, a shotgun of his own.

Blessed with "wonderful eyes," Ed Hemingway was a great fisherman and a crack shot, and he was an excellent teacher as well. Along with the weapons, he dispensed lessons in the proper care and cleaning of guns. He also taught Ernest, as Carlos Baker recounts, "how to build fires and cook in the open, how to use an axe to make a woodland shelter of hemlock boughs, how to tie wet and dry flies, how to make bullets in a mold . . . how to prepare birds and small animals for mounting, how to dress fish and fowl for the frying pan or the oven." By the time he reached junior high school, Ernest had absorbed, through the Agassiz Society lessons which Dr. Hemingway taught, a substantial body of nature lore, and could identify by name most of the birds, trees, flowers, fish, and animals that he encountered around Oak Park or in northern Michigan.

Ed Hemingway stressed the importance of kindness to dumb animals as well. "Instead of just seeing a tree," Marcelline recalls, "we learned from him to look between the branches of the trees and see the birds' nests cleverly hidden in the crotches. Often he would let us climb up very carefully and look into a bird's nest, but he never let us touch the nest or the eggs for fear the fluttering mother bird would not return." If he came across a wounded bird or animal, the doctor would prepare a splint and hope that it could be nursed back into healthy, independent life. Another part of his outdoor code demanded that nothing be caught or killed that would not be put to use. God, he believed, had provided wild life for the sustenance of mankind, and nothing was to be wasted. An incident that occurred at Walloon Lake when Ernest was thirteen illustrated both the doctor's tenderness and his utilitarian approach. A porcupine had stung an unwary dog with a mouthful of quills, and Dr. Hemingway, talking gently to the dog, managed to quiet him down and remove the painful quills. But Ernest and a friend, Harold Sampson, took revenge by shooting the porcupine, and as an object lesson Ed Hemingway made the boys cook and eat the animal. "We cooked the haunches for hours," Sampson recalls, "but they were still about as tender and tasty as a piece of shoe leather." The doctor, he thought, was a little unfair in making them eat the tough meat, but neither he nor Ernest ever killed another porcupine.

Curiously, though, Dr. Hemingway had little respect for man-made laws regulating fishing and hunting. On one occasion he illegally smuggled brook trout, packed inside ferns within bedroom slippers, across the Michigan state line to Illinois. And he was not above shooting "an occasional grouse or woodcock for the table, even though the game-law calendar and his appetite might not quite coincide." Marcelline remembers wondering, at one breakfast of what she thought was fried chicken, why he insisted on the children finishing their meal so rapidly. After every scrap was gone, he burned the feathers in the stove as well, in case a game warden might be happening by. How could he know, he innocently asked Mrs. Hemingway, that the bird he shot was going to be a grouse? Occasionally, too, his eagerness to demonstrate his shooting skill got the better of his hunting code. When the mood was upon him, the doctor could barely resist the temptation to shoot at any bird in flight. Once when Mrs. Wesley Dilworth objected that he couldn't shoot a robin, since it was against the law, he lowered his gun, stared at her, and shouted: "Never mind the law, madam. Shoot the birds!"

Such irregularities hardly troubled Ernest. By his example, Dr. Hemingway inculcated in his son a love of hunting, fishing, and the outdoor life that carried him from the rivers and streams of Michigan to the green hills of Africa. Ernest Hemingway spent a substantial portion of his life with rod and reel or gun in hand; in fact, he devoted so much of his time to the development of his skills as an outdoorsman that, in his writing, he was often moved to try to justify this near obsession.

The most persuasive justification, one which might have sufficed for a man less dedicated to the work ethic than Hemingway, was simply that hunting and fishing gave him an uncommon degree of pleasure. In a rhapsodic piece for *Esquire*, he invoked the thrills of the hunt:

> You can remember the first snipe you ever hit walking on the prairie with your father. How the jacksnipe rose with a jump and you hit him on the second swerve and had to wade out into a slough after him and brought him in wet, holding him by the bill, as proud as a bird dog. . . . You can remember the miracle it seemed when you hit your first pheasant when he roared up from under your feet to top a sweetbriar thicket and fell with his wings pounding and you had to wait till after dark to bring him into town because they were protected, and you can feel the bulk of him still inside your shirt with his long tail up under your armpit. . . .

"I think they were all made to shoot," he goes on, "because if they were not why did they give them that whirr of wings that moves you suddenly more than any love of country?" Why were they all so good to eat? "Why does the curlew have that voice, and who thought up the plover's call, which takes the place of noise of wings, to give us that catharsis wing shooting has given to men since they stopped flying hawks and took to fowling pieces? I think that they were made to shoot and some of us were made to shoot them and if that is not so well, never say we did not tell you that we liked it."

But the strident, no-need-to-apologize tone of this article about wing shooting was one that Hemingway rarely adopted in his outdoor writing. Nor could he always trace the emotion he felt to such specific criteria as the whirr of pheasant wings or the call of the curlew. Part of the thrill came from killing itself. He liked to shoot a rifle, he wrote Janet Flanner in the spring of 1933, he liked to kill, and Africa was the place to do that. Later that summer, tracking a buffalo bull on safari, he "felt the elation, the best elation of all, of certain action to come, action in which you had something to do, in which you can kill and come out of it." He could find no objective correlative for that sense of elation, or for the sense of quiet afterward. "Killing," he wrote in *Green Hills of Africa*, "is not a feeling that you share." But for him it was an essential part of existence. If he had not spent so much time shooting birds and animals and catching fish, he once observed, "he might have shot himself" instead.

Hemingway loved fishing still more than hunting. Fishing, he told Archibald MacLeish, was as exciting as war; it was, he told Waldo Peirce, another artist friend, certainly the best thing in the world. As a youth he had fished "the Black, the Sturgeon, the Pine Barrens, the Upper Minnie, all the little streams," and known the thrill of horsing a leaping trout out of the water. People "that have never horsed them out don't know what they can make you feel. What if it only lasts that long? It's the time when there's no give at all and then they start to come and what they do to you on the way up and into the air." Later, there was the deep-sea angling aboard the black-hulled "fishing machine," the *Pilar*, off Key West and Bimini, and finally off San Francisco de Paula in Cuba, where the deep blue river of the Gulf Stream he loved, "three-quarters of a mile to a mile deep and sixty to eighty miles across," lay but thirty minutes from the doorstep of Finca Vigia, and provided "the finest fishing" he had ever known. Cruising the Gulf Stream, Hemingway took "great pleasure in being on the sea, in the unknown wild suddenness of a great fish; in his life and death which he lives for you in an hour while your strength is harnessed to his; and there is satisfaction in conquering this thing which rules the sea it lives in."

Aside from the joy of the kill or capture, the life of the sportsman brought Hemingway into contact with the unspoiled world of nature he was constantly seeking. Whenever he attempted to set down, in capsule form, what it was that made his life worth living, Hemingway called up images of nature undefiled. What were the things he loved to do, he asked himself in 1934, and emerged with this list: "To stay in places and to leave, to trust, to distrust, to no longer believe and believe again, to care about fishes, the different winds, the changes of the seasons, to see what happens, to be out in boats, to sit in a saddle, to watch the snow come, to watch it go, to hear rain on a tent, to know where I can find what I want." El Sordo, facing death in *For Whom the Bell Tolls*, reflects that dying was really nothing, while "living was a field of grain blowing in the wind on the side of a hill. Living was a hawk in the sky. Living was an earthen jar of water in the dust of the threshing with the grain flailed out and the chaff blowing. Living was a horse between your legs and a carbine under one leg and a hill and a valley and a stream with trees along it and the far side of the valley and the hills beyond." Similarly, Thomas Hudson in the posthumously published *Islands in the Stream* (1970) recollects as the happiest days of his life those mornings when he was a boy and awoke knowing he would not have to go to school or to work:

> In the morning I was always hungry when I woke and I could smell the dew in the grass and hear the wind in the high branches of the hemlock trees, if there was a wind, and if there was no wind I could hear the quietness of the forest and the calmness of the lake and I would listen for the first noises of morning. Sometimes the first noise would be a kingfisher flying over the water that was so calm it mirrored his reflection and he made a clattering cry as he flew. Sometimes it was a squirrel chittering in one of the trees outside the house, his tail jerking each time he made a noise. Often it would be the plover calling on the hillside. But whenever I woke and heard the first morning noises and felt hungry and knew I would not have to go to school nor have to work, I was happier than I have ever been.

"Even than with women?" his companion, a Havana whore named Honest Lil inquires, thereby missing the point, which is the pleasure of waking into communion with nature, signaled by the first birds, and without any complications involving other human beings, such as would be encountered at school or work. In his preference for the company of birds and animals to that of people, and in his celebration of the morning, Hemingway echoes the sentiments of Henry David Thoreau, another sojourner in the world of nature whose books, Hemingway once remarked, he had not read and could not read.

What he was trying to say in *The Sun Also Rises*, Ernest wrote his editor Max Perkins, was embodied in the epigraph from Ecclesiastes (that "the earth abideth forever") and for his own part he "had a great deal of fondness and admiration for the earth, and not a hell of a lot" for his generation, lost or not. If it came down to a choice between nature and humankind, he was in no doubt where his affections lay. "I have loved country all my life," he wrote in *Green Hills of Africa*; "the country was always better than the people. I could only care about people a very few at a time." In *A Moveable Feast*, he struck a still more misanthropic note: "People were always the limiters of happiness except for the very few that were as good as spring itself." In one of the longest and best sentences he ever wrote, Hemingway compared the odious march of civilization to the eternal cleansing properties of nature:

> . . . when, on the sea, you are alone with it and know that this Gulf Stream you are living with, knowing, learning about, and loving, has moved, as it moves, since before man, and that it has gone by the shoreline of that long, beautiful, unhappy island since before Columbus sighted it and that the things you find out about it, and those that have always lived in it are permanent and of value because that stream will flow, as it has flowed, after the Indians, after the Spaniards, after the British, after the Americans and after all the Cubans and all the systems of governments, the richness, the poverty, the martrydom, the sacrifice and the venality and the cruelty are all gone as the high-piled scow of garbage, bright-colored, white-flecked, ill-smelling, now tilted on its side, spills off its load into the blue water, turning it a pale green to a depth of four or five fathoms as the load spreads across the surface, the sinkable part going down and the flotsam of palm fronds, corks, bottles, and used electric light globes, seasoned with an occasional condom or a deep floating corset, the torn leaves of a student's exercise book, a well-inflated dog, the occasional rat, the no-longer-distinguished cat; all this well-shepherded by the boats of the garbage pickers who pluck their prizes with long poles, as interested, as intelligent, and as accurate as historians; they have the viewpoint; the stream, with no visible flow, takes five loads of this a day when things are going well in La Habana and in ten miles along the coast it is as clear and blue and unimpressed as it was ever before the tug hauled out the scow; and the palm fronds of our victories, the worn light bulbs of our discoveries and the empty condoms of our great loves float with no significance against one single, lasting thing—the stream.

The novelist Wright Morris, acutely sensitive to this theme in Hemingway's work, concludes that there is one story "and one only he would tell us. Nature is good, man is a mess, but Nature will prevail." Barring a deluge, the earth would survive and the birds would sing, while "it makes no difference if the fountains play or not." Lurking behind "the armor of his prose, the shell of his exile," Morris writes, was "our old friend Huck Finn, American dreamer, the clean-cut boy who just wishes Aunt Sally would leave him alone, who wants nothing more, nor less, than a clearing of his own in the wilderness." In his

American way, Hemingway pushed ahead to frontiers, and lamented that they were so soon overrun. Cities, to him, represented sinks of iniquity. "Maggots of life," as an early poem put it, crawled in the hot loneliness of Chicago.

Through his writing runs a lament for the past, for the days when nature had been uncontaminated by exposure to swarms of people and machinery. When he'd grown up in Oak Park, there was nothing but the north prairie that ran all the way to the Des Plaines River. But by 1950 the prairie had become a subdivision, and there was no question, then, of going back home. "When you like to fish and shoot," he realized, "you have to move often and always further out." Even the woods of northern Michigan, he decided on a visit in the early 1950s, were "too civilized now," ruined by summer visitors and by the heedless destruction of the hemlock forests. Hired by the tannery at Boyne City, the Indians had felled the trees and stripped away the bark, so that eventually there was less and less forest and more of the "open, hot, shadeless, weed-grown slashing," with the unused logs rotting in the sun. Nick Adams, escaping from the game wardens in a posthumously published story, takes his younger sister along on his flight through the hot, ugly slashings to the spongy forest floor, free of underbrush. In this, "the last good country" where nobody would follow them, Nick and his sister feel the way they "ought to feel in church." The forest was like a cathedral, still and cool.

The mature Hemingway found his version of the last good country at Finca Vigía, well isolated from Havana and adjoining the sea, "the last free place there is." Cuba, he wrote in 1956, was all right until too many visitors came. Then he might take off to Spain or Africa or the Rockies, but all those places were being overrun "and nobody who knew them in the old days could live in them now." In a passage from *Green Hills of Africa*, he delivered a diatribe against his countrymen and their passion for progress:

> A continent ages quickly once we come. The natives live in harmony with it. But the foreigner destroys, cuts down the trees, drains the water, so that the water supply is altered, and in a short time the soil, once the sod is turned under, is cropped out, and next it starts to blow away as it has blown away in every old country and as I had seen it start to blow in Canada. The earth gets tired of being exploited. A country wears out quickly unless man puts back in it all

his residue and that of all his beasts. When he quits using beasts and uses machines the earth defeats him quickly. The machine can't reproduce, nor does it fertilize the soil, and it eats what he cannot raise. A country was made to be as we found it.

Finally, the only way he knew to recapture the pristine wilderness was through his imagination. The "mystical countries" of our childhood we "might remember and visit sometimes" when asleep and dreaming. In the dream they would be as lovely as they once had been. But if we ever went back to see them they were not there. Another way to recapture the past was through writing itself. In "Big Two-Hearted River," he had attempted "to do country so you don't remember the words after you read it but actually have the country."

At his best, Hemingway was so fresh in his perceptions, so attuned to "the country and how the weather was," that he could virtually bring the inanimate world to life. One can turn to any number of descriptive passages in his stories or novels and feel certain that no one else could have written them just that way or that well. To his landscapes, he brought not only a keen eye but the lessons he had learned from the paintings of Paul Cézanne. It was Cézanne, Hemingway acknowledged, who taught him "to make a landscape." The basic technique, as Emily Stipes Watts asserted in her book on Hemingway and the arts, was to reduce the complexity and haziness of nature "to a series of planes or geometrical forms," so that these forms emerged sharply even in the distance. Mountains, fields, and rivers acquired a solidity and clarity of definition which bespoke form rather than shapelessness, order rather than chaos. Both writer and artist took some liberties with photographic realism in order to accommodate this way of seeing, a way which involved a strong sense of identification with the world of nature.

With the creatures he hunted and fished, as with Nature writ large, Hemingway felt an almost mystical communion. Lying awake nights with the pain of a broken arm in 1930, he "thought suddenly how a bull elk must feel if you break a shoulder and he gets away and in that night I lay and felt it all, the whole thing as it would happen from the shock of the bullet to the end of the business and, being a little out of my head, thought perhaps what I was going through was a punishment for all hunters." If so, at least he could derive solace from the reflection that he had done "nothing that had not been done to me. I had been shot and I had been crippled and gotten away."

Occasionally Hemingway or one of his protagonists feels a transport of love for an animal he has killed. So with the beautiful kudu bull of *Green Hills of Africa*, "big, long-legged, a smooth gray with the white stripes and the great, curling, sweeping horns, brown as walnut meats, and ivory pointed," the "big ears and the great, lovely heavy-maned neck, the white chevron between his eyes and the white of his muzzle." Admiring the kudu, Ernest "stooped over and touched him to try to believe it" for "there was not a mark on him and he smelled sweet and lovely like the breath of cattle and the odor of thyme after rain." Or Miss Mary's lion in the posthumous "African Journal," beside whom Hemingway lay down "and talked to him very softly in Spanish and begged his pardon for having killed him" and while lying beside him felt for his wounds, all the time "stroking him and talking to him in Spanish" until the camel flies drove him away so he "drew a fish in front of him with my forefinger in the dirt and then rubbed it out with the palm" of his hand. As Karen Blixen (Isak Dinesen) once observed, in a remark Hemingway liked to repeat, "all real hunters are in love with the animals they hunt, but it is not reciprocated."

It was the same with game fish as with game animals. Santiago in *The Old Man and the Sea*, while battling his great marlin for three days and three nights, realizes that the fish is his true brother. In the end he kills him because it is his trade to do so, though not before he suffers twinges of conscience at having destroyed this creature he has come to love. "You loved him when he was alive and you loved him after. If you love him, it is not a sin to kill him. Or is it more?" In much the same way, young David Hudson, in *Islands in the Stream*, fights a giant swordfish for hours before losing him just as he is about to be boated. In such struggles both the fisherman and the fish suffer mightily, and, as David reflects, "in the worst parts, when I was the tiredest I couldn't tell which was him and which was me" and "then I began to love him more than anything on earth."

But the pleasure Hemingway took in the life of a sportsman, and the opportunity such an existence provided for communion with nature, did not supply reasons enough to satisfy those critics who could not or would not understand his passion for hunting and fishing. Hemingway himself saw no contradiction between loving animals and hunting them, but that point of view was emphatically unshared by, among others, Ezra Pound. He could not understand, Pound wrote in 1936, what motivated Hemingway to kill "pussy cats, however titanic, that ain't got no guns to shoot back with." What, he asked, "was the poor brute doin' to you?" In like vein, the Austrian "Kandisky," whom the Hemingways met on their 1933 safari, found it incomprehensible that Ernest, "an intelligent man, a poet" should want to hunt kudu. "Why should any man shoot a kudu?" To such challenges, Hemingway responded by stressing the elements of danger and endurance involved in the chase, and by insisting that only the initiate, practicing a strict code of ethics and skillful at his sport, could properly appreciate the pleasures of hunting and fishing.

Certainly the pursuit of dangerous game provided a test of courage. Only a brave hunter could face a wounded lion with steady nerves. And once he had done so, his appetite for such encounters naturally increased. As Hemingway wrote Marjorie Kinnan Rawlings in 1936, he was not interested in shooting bears. He still enjoyed shooting anything that flew well, but as for earth-bound creatures, he only liked to shoot animals that run "both ways."

Fishing, on the other hand, did not test courage so much as strength and endurance, though if you were on the ocean in a small boat there was always plenty of danger. "Fighting a really big fish, fast and unaided, never resting, nor letting the fish rest," was comparable to a ten-round fight "in its requirements for good physical condition." A two-hour fight was like a twenty-round bout. To kill a lion or boat a marlin under such conditions was to pass through a primitive rite of initiation. Thus David Hudson cut his feet, blistered his hands, and extended every ounce of strength he possessed in his struggle with the swordfish. The process was painful, even terrifying, but as his father remarks, "there is a time boys have to do things if they are ever going to be men."

One could not qualify as a proper sportsman, in Hemingway's judgment, until one had gone through the initiation and learned the rudiments of the sporting code. Basically, the code demanded three imperatives: (1) The good outdoorsman must not be wasteful, (2) He must kill cleanly and as humanely as possible, (3) He must not take advantage of fish or animal by letting mechanized or technological devices do his work for him.

To demonstrate the first axiom, Hemingway wrote of the time, in Wyoming, when he had fixed his sights on a moose at point-blank range, but refrained from firing. The moose "had a nice head but it was nothing to kill him for. He had plenty of meat and no one would eat moose meat when there is such a thing as elk. I put the rifle back in the saddle bucket. . . ." In Africa, too, he swung his sights away from a waterbuck upon reflecting that he "was the one animal we might get that I knew was worthless as meat and I had shot a better head than this one carried." In one of the posthumously published Nick Adams stories, Nick nets an old trout but then lets him escape "through the shallows, his back out of water, threading between rocks toward the deep current." He was, Nick decided, too big to eat. And one of the reasons why he had given up his fishing camp at Bimini, Ernest told Harvey Breit, was because too many big fish caught there were wasted. In Cuba, it was different. Nothing caught there was wasted.

The second imperative, killing cleanly, required a mastery of skills which, he felt, too few sportsmen had acquired. After all, Hemingway wrote Peter Barrett in 1950, "we have an obligation to kill cleanly and if we would wound an animal to follow it up all the way." For his part, he had lost but one wounded animal in his life. The real crime was to gun-shoot one's prey, and on the 1933 safari Hemingway was ashamed of gut-shooting a buffalo and a sable bull. "I felt like a son of a bitch to have hit him and not killed him," he wrote about the sable. "I did not mind killing anything, any animal, if I killed it cleanly, they all had to die and my interference with the nightly and the seasonal killing that went on all the time was very minute and I had no guilty feeling at all." Besides, "we ate the meat and kept the hides and horns." If he had not been overconfident and careless, he would never have gut-shot him.

Nick Adams, fishing for trout, customarily used grasshoppers for bait; he had tried a salamander once and crickets, but given them up "because of the way they acted about the hook." Nick liked to fish alone or with a few close companions, and not solely because such ventures brought him surcease from the sorrows of civilization, as in "Big Two-Hearted River" and Jake and Bill's fishing trip in *The Sun Also Rises.* "Years before when he had fished crowded streams," he remembers, "with fly fishermen ahead of him and behind him, Nick had again and again come on dead trout, furry with white fungus, drifted against a rock, or floating belly up in some pool." Other men had made the mistake of not wetting their hands before touching these trout. "If a trout was touched with a dry hand, a white fungus attacked the unprotected spot." It was one of the lessons that all trout fishermen should have learned. Since they had not, "Nick did not like to fish with other men on the river."

About the third axiom, taking no unfair advantage of one's game, Hemingway was still more adamant. "There are two ways to murder a lion," his June 1934 *Esquire* article begins. One was to shoot him from a car, and the other to blind him with flashlights at night. Such murderous perversions ranked, in his ethics, "with dynamiting trout or harpooning swordfish." Use of what white hunter Philip Percival called "those bloody cars" particularly enraged his sensibilities, since it was not only an illegal but also "a cowardly way to assassinate one of the finest of all game animals." One of the founders of the International Game Fish Association, Hemingway was also concerned that modern technology had eliminated those elements of strength and skill which made deep-sea fishing a challenge. "There is tackle made now," he wrote after World War II, "and there are fishing guides expert in ways of cheating at it, by which anybody who can walk up three flights of stairs, carrying a quart bottle of milk in each hand, can catch game fish over 500 pounds without even having to sweat much." Using the new winches and unbreakable gear, a beginning angler who "could not stay with a big fish ten minutes under regulation fishing conditions" might actually bring in a record-breaker. "The sport," he wrote in his introduction to Kip Farrington's *Atlantic Game Fishing*, was "about due for a good housecleaning. . . ."

Hemingway's sporting code is best dramatized in the magnificent "Short Happy Life of Francis Macomber." Rich and spoiled, Macomber panics upon his first encounter with a lion and then tries to evade responsibility for having gut-shot the beast. Macomber wanted, in the first place, to shoot the lion from a car, but his guide Robert Wilson, who knows and teaches the proper ethics, says simply, "You don't shoot them from cars." Then after the wounded lion takes cover, the frightened Macomber proposes to Wilson a series of unlovely alternatives to the only real one, that of following the beast into the bush and finishing him off.

> "Can't we set the grass on fire?" Macomber asked.
> "Too green."
> "Can't we send beaters?"
> Wilson looked at him appraisingly. "Of course we can," he said. "But it's just a touch murderous."

And finally, desperate to escape the second and more dangerous confrontation, Macomber asks, "Why not leave him there?" a question which makes Wilson feel "as though he had opened the wrong door in a hotel and seen something shameful." With patient tact, he explains that "it isn't done" and why—because the lion is certain to be suffering, and because someone else may run across him and be mauled. "In the ethics of shooting dangerous game," as Hemingway spelled it out, "the trouble you shoot yourself into you must be prepared to shoot yourself out of."

One snake in Hemingway's outdoor garden, a serpent lurking among fields and streams, was his competitive nature. Driven by the desire to master every activity he engaged in, Hemingway had the unhappy faculty of converting hunting and fishing into contests. Who would bring back the finest trophy? Who would catch the largest tuna? When he won such competitions, he was given to boasting; when he lost, to green envy.

The 1933 safari, for example, was virtually ruined for him by the comparative success, as bagger of the best hides and horns, of his companion Charles Thompson. His susceptibility to the competitive spirit, he realized, made little sense on safari, where luck figured equally with skill in shooting performance. Nonetheless, as Hemingway frankly confessed in *Green Hills of Africa*, he became intensely envious of Thompson's superior kills. Thompson gunned down the best buffalo, the best waterbuck, the best rhino, and then, as a final insult, the best kudu. After tracking for weeks, Ernest finally bagged two beautiful large kudu bulls and returned triumphantly to camp, only to discover Charles's trophy: "the biggest, widest, darkest, longest-curling, heaviest, most unbelievable pair of kudu horns" he'd ever seen. Weakly, he muttered congratulations, but inside he seethed with envy. "It's impossible not to be competitive," Percival consoled him. "Spoils everything, though." In succumbing to the spirit of rivalry—indeed, in the very act of shooting for trophies—Hemingway knew he was violating his own prohibition against wasteful destruction of wildlife. Yet when called upon to demonstrate his talents, he could not resist the urge to respond to the challenge. With deep-sea fishing, as well, Ernest was often tempted to go for records. In a hatchet-job of a magazine article, Arnold Gingrich referred to Hemingway as a "meat fisherman" who cared more about quantity than quality and who "was also—and this is what no true angler is—intensely competitive about his fishing, and a very poor sport." Gingrich, Hemingway's former editor at *Esquire*, had his differences with the novelist over the years, and his account betrays a touch of jaundice, but about the competitive strain he was surely accurate. Scornful of others who bent or ignored the rules to bring in fish of record weight, Ernest was not always so meticulous where he himself was concerned. While fishing off Key West he boated a huge sailfish which another member of his fishing party, a priest, had initially hooked but could not bring in. Technically, when two men fight a fish, neither can be said to have successfully brought him in, but the priest gave Hemingway full credit in a story for the Miami *Herald*, the Miami Rod and Reel Club displayed the mounted beauty in its lobby, and until the end of his life, Hemingway was technically listed as holder of the Atlantic sailfishing record. At first, Ernest was troubled by the subterfuge, but then subsided. "It's their lie, not mine," he told Charles Thompson.

There was never, however, any question about Hemingway's proficiency as a fine wing shot, a brave hunter of big game, and a strong and powerful fisherman. In the shark-infested waters off Bimini, for example, he caught the first two large unmutilated tuna (both weighed over five hundred pounds) ever taken there. He did it by fighting the fish absolutely without giving himself or the tuna any rest whatever, and thereby bringing them in while they were still fast enough to evade sharks on the lookout for slow-moving fish. It was Ernest's theory, as he expressed it to Kip Farrington, that for every minute the fisherman rested, the fish would acquire five minutes worth of additional energy. As a fishing technique, his method required extraordinary strength and determination, qualities which he possessed in abundance. Baron von Blixen-Finecke, fishing with him in 1935, saw Ernest fight a giant hammerhead shark for an hour and three-quarters, leaving the shark dead of heart failure and Hemingway half-dead as well. Admiringly, he referred to the author as "a gigantic fellow weighing . . . over fourteen stone, with shoulders like a wrestler and a chest like Hercules."

On other occasions, he was capable of shooting with the kind of truly remarkable skill his father possessed. Once, visiting Archibald MacLeish in Weston, Massachusetts, he pulled off a double on two grouse who wheeled above him in the clear fall sky. "He got both of them," MacLeish wrote. "Was he proud!" And one hungover dawn on a trip to the Dry Tortugas with John Dos Passos and Waldo Peirce, Ernest put on a remarkable shooting exhibition. He hit "a baked-bean can floating halfway to the shore" and "bits of paper spread out on wooden chips" from a distant skiff. "He shot several terns. He shot through a pole at the end of the pier. Anything we'd point at he would hit. He shot sitting. He shot standing. He shot lying on his belly. He shot backwards, with the rifle held between his legs." Yet this was the same marksman who in his awkwardness managed to shoot himself in the leg with his own rifle, and in his anger and jealousy demolished a toilet in a Paris hotel room with his pistol.

In his life as an outdoorsman, which was so extended and various as to constitute a second career rather than an avocation, Ernest Hemingway behaved very much like his father's son. He avidly mastered those lessons Dr. Hemingway first taught him on the prairie north of Oak Park and in the wilderness of upper Michigan. In his adult life he took every opportunity to practice what he had learned as a boy, in the process moving from tyro to accomplished sportsman. Finally, he assumed the role of instructor himself, tutoring his family and his readers in the proper way to hunt and fish.

He even inherited from Dr. Hemingway his scornful attitude toward game laws. The summer he turned sixteen, Ernest impulsively shot a rare blue heron up in Michigan, and was observed by the game warden's son. Frantically, he and his younger sister Sunny fled first to see Wesley Dilworth, who promised to intercede with the warden, and then to Uncle George Hemingway's. The upshot of this brush with the law was that the lad entered a guilty plea, and was let off with a warning and $15 fine, though in his imagination (and in "The Last Good Country," a posthumously published story) the event took on more dramatic colorations. But the episode taught him no lasting lesson. One of the reasons Key West appealed to him as a place to live, according to Dos Passos, was that "nobody seemed ever to have heard of Prohibition or game laws. The place suited Ernest to a T."

Hemingway, as sportsman-teacher, peppered his writing on the outdoors with *ex cathedra* advice. Earl Rovit draws a useful distinction between two kinds of heroes in his fiction: the tyro, who is easily hurt and often confused by the complexity of modern life, and the tutor, a simpler, happier man who has contrived to exist without "inner uncertainties." In his articles and books on sport, Hemingway moved along a chronological continuum from tyro to tutor, with intermediate stops to describe the experiences which qualified him as bona fide expert capable of delivering lectures or conducting tutorials.

With his own family, Ernest played the role of mentor from the time his three boys were youngsters, and subsequent events have made it clear that his teachings stuck. Jack Hemingway, his eldest son, went to live in Ketchum, Idaho, close to the good hunting and fishing country where his father spent many falls. "Papa got me started," he once said, "according to the W. C. Fields approach—'get the hell out of the way, you little bastard,' " and he was, naturally, intrigued. Once he had Jack interested at about six years of age, Ernest began to inculcate elements of his sporting code. He taught that "*nothing* was to be wasted, and no fish, bird or fowl was to be killed except expressly for the pot. . . . Not shooting sitting birds (ground sluicing), releasing fish carefully with as little physical damage to them as possible—all of these things we learned directly from him." For a time, Jack commented, his father had taken a certain pleasure in capturing game fish of record size, but "after the first triumphs with large marlin and the inevitable photographs that were taken afterwards, he never allowed the meat to be wasted there either." The sight of "marlin and other deep sea sport fishes left hanging out on the docks in the broiling Cuban sun, until the 'sports' deigned to come down to have their pictures taken with the rotting prey . . . filled my father with revulsion—and me too." What Hemingway caught, by way of contrast, "was generally distributed to the Cuban needy who flocked to the docks around Havana for a free handout in those days."

His second son, Patrick, who later taught wildlife conservation in the Tanzania which he, like his father, grew to love, was a still more apt pupil. His earliest recollection of his father was of watching him call and shoot the shore birds off Key West, where the family lived winters and springs. In the summers of those mid-1930s years the Hemingways traveled to the Bimini fishing camp, and the autumns were given over to hunting from the L-Bar-T Ranch in Wyoming. His father, Patrick believes, regarded fishing and hunting as "a reward for the routine of settling down and raising a family." Yet for Ernest "even sports could not be pure relaxation. They were always part of an education." One lesson Patrick did not forget was to fish in the old-fashioned way, using gut rather than nylon leaders and rods made by English craftsmen to provide the greatest test of the fisherman's skill. Jack, also, eschewed new-fangled glass rods in favor of bamboo. Later, he served on the Idaho game and fish commission.

Two of Ernest's wives, Pauline in 1933 and Mary in 1953, accompanied Hemingway on safari, where he saw to it, in the latter case assuming the role of white hunter himself, that they absorbed the proper ethics pertaining to shooting dangerous game, even when (as he put it) "the standard of ethics . . . was too rigid and slightly murderous." Both Pauline and Mary shot lions, following the code so that the killing was accomplished not the way such things were usually done but as they "should ideally be done." Mary, too, vividly recalled a rugged half-hour of tramping an Idaho field in search of a partridge she had shot and failed to mark. After that search, she vowed "never again to take my eyes off the spot a bird falls." She was simply following one of Ernest's rules: "never wound a bird and leave it to die, never kill a bird without retrieving it."

As they acquired greater maturity, Hemingway's protagonists seem to have worked off the competitive curse that spoiled the author's hunting and fishing in the 1930s. Colonel Cantwell, in *Across the River and into the Trees*, for example, observes that only one other duck hunter in the waters near Venice shot better or faster than he did, but that many "bad and fair shots" killed more ducks than he did, since he didn't "go by the numbers any more." Similarly, Thomas Hudson in *Islands in the Stream* tells his boys how necessary it is to stay calm and polite to each other while battling game fish. Fighting, he comments, never does any good, and Hudson will not be provoked into a fight. But it is Santiago, the champion Cuban fisherman in *The Old Man and the Sea*, who best exemplifies the role of accomplished master and excellent tutor. As the boy Manolin says to Santiago, exhausted after his struggle with the great marlin, "you must get well fast for there is much that I can learn and you can teach me everything." Whether Hemingway himself ever controlled his competitive drive enough to become a truly dispassionate and successful tutor, in these three characterizations— Cantwell, Hudson, Santiago—and in the outdoor lore he bequeathed to his sons he was obviously articulating an ideal for the true sportsman, himself included, to live up to.

When no other effort of justification for his divided life as artist and sportsman obtained, Hemingway resorted to the assertion that the two were complementary, and equally essential, parts of his existence. Hunting in Africa, he maintained, was every bit as necessary to him as looking at the Goyas and El Grecos in the Prado. Furthermore, both sport and art required lasting dedication and energy. "The way to hunt," he wrote in *Green Hills of Africa*, "is for as long as you live against as long as there is such and such an animal; just as the way to paint is as long as there is you and colors and canvas, and to write as long as you can live and there is pencil and paper or ink or any machine to do it with, or anything you care to write about. . . ." Practiced in maturity and with honesty, there was virtually no distinction worth making between the two activities. To become professional at either required an extraordinary measure of talent: "You can learn to play baseball, to box, or to sing, but unless you have a certain degree of genius you cannot make your living at baseball or boxing or singing in opera." But genius was never enough without a concurrent determination to nurture and train one's natural gifts.

Aficionado and Teacher

Nothing better illustrated Hemingway's conviction of the contiguity between sport and art than bullfighting, which he fell in love with while still a young man and followed with enthusiastic interest for the rest of his life. John Reardon has noted the similarity between two pronouncements in *Death in the Afternoon*, the remarkable book on Spanish bullfighting. One of the difficulties in writing, he reflected therein, was that real emotions were often obscured behind culturally approved ones. You had to know "truly what you really felt, rather than what you were supposed to feel, or had been taught to feel. . . ." Watching a bullfight properly, he observed in another passage, required for most Americans just such a suspension of previously implanted notions. Only when people resolved to "go open-mindedly and only feel those things they actually feel and not the things they think they should feel" could they discover whether they really liked what they saw or not. Matadors, like painters or opera singers, could only master their craft if they were "super-geniuses." When they practiced their genius, the journeyman artist observing them might even feel a trace of shame. "Tell him [the bullfighter Pedro Romero] I think writing is lousy," Bill Gorton remarks in *The Sun Also Rises*. "Tell him I'm ashamed of being a writer."

Death in the Afternoon repeatedly compares bullfighting with one or another of the more conventional arts. The chiseled brilliance of a well-performed bullfight, Hemingway asserted, surpassed any "modern sculpture, except Brancusi's," that he had ever seen. The difference was that bullfighting was "an impermanent art as singing and the dance are," so that an apter comparison might be made between the craft of the bullfighter and the musicianship of someone playing a pipe organ or steam calliope, in the sense that the bullfighter could only manipulate the force (the bull) he was presented with, just as the organ and calliope were instruments "in which the musician utilizes a force which is already there . . . rather than applying force in a varying degree himself to produce music."

But the artistic comparison Hemingway most insisted on was between bullfighting and classical tragedy. A bullfight was not merely *like* tragedy, in his view. It *was* a tragedy in three acts, which furnished certain death for the animal and danger for the man. As tragedy, the bullfight escaped being one of the major arts only because of its impermanence. But during those late afternoons when a skillful performance was going on in the arena, the sensitive and educated spectator might experience exactly the same kind of catharsis that comes from viewing a well-acted production of, say, *Oedipus Rex*. Watching the gypsy Cagancho on a good day, moving "the cape spread full as the pulling jib of a yacht before the bull's muzzle"; observing "a complete, consecutive series of passes with the *muleta* in which there will be valor, art, understanding, and, above all, beauty and great emotion"; transfixed by the moment of truth, "that flash when man and bull form one figure as the sword goes all the way in, the man leaning after it, death uniting the two figures"—these could take a man out of himself and make him feel immortal, possessed by an ecstasy "as profound as any religious ecstasy."

But not everyone had the capability to be so moved, and not everyone was prepared to put aside his scruples against bullfighting. Only the *aficionado*, who had a proper "sense of the tragedy and the ritual of the fight," could truly appreciate the bullfight as an artistic whole without being distracted by certain troublesome "minor aspects."

At the very beginning of *Death in the Afternoon*, Hemingway deals directly with the problem posed by these aspects. Having read the wrong books, he had gone to his first bullfight expecting "to be horrified . . . by what I had been told would happen to the horses." Most people who had written about bullfighting had condemned it "outright as a stupid brutal business, but even those that spoke well of it as an exhibition of skill and as a spectacle deplored the use of the horses and were apologetic about the whole thing." To such observers, it was bad enough that one dumb animal, the fighting bull, should inevitably be killed, but at least the bull was bred to fight, while the horses which were ridden into close quarters by the mounted picadors and almost invariably gored lacked both the ability to protect themselves and any relish for the contest. Hemingway described such a horse, his belly slit open so that his "entrails hung down in a blue bunch," still cantering jerkily as the picador spurred him to one more lance. Yet this sight did not, he insisted to Bill Smith in 1925, really bother him. He was no sadist and had never pulled the legs off grasshoppers, but he could no more care about the bone bags of horses, which were really comic characters in their awkwardness, than he did about impaling three hoppers on a fishhook.

What *happened* to the horses was not comic, for death was not funny; but since there were no homes for old horses, perhaps they had little to complain about. If wounded, they could be quickly dispatched with "an easy stroke by the puntilla . . . that solves all a horse's problems. . . ." Similarly, the bull could be sure of death within fifteen minutes, while the matador who fought him and suffered a goring might be kept "alive through times when death would seem the greatest gift one man could give another." Under the circumstances, "the horses and bulls will seem well taken care of and man to run the greatest risk." Besides, and always at the heart of Hemingway's apologia for the sport, he passionately loved bullfighting. "Gaw," he told Smith, what a wonderful show.

It was, of course, the dealing of certain death in the ring which distinguished the Spanish bullfight from more genteel contests practiced in other countries. Animals might be killed elsewhere, but not as part of a spectacle. Amateur sportsmen in England and America, in playing games, were not fascinated by death like Iberians. Instead, they were "fascinated by victory," and in the symbolism of their sports replaced the avoidance of death with the avoidance of defeat. It took "more *cojones*," Hemingway added, "to be a sportsman where death is a closer party to the game." The difference between English games and the Spanish bullfight was like that between playing cards with someone who, with nothing at stake, broke the rules and made a mockery of the game, and playing with another who had his fortune and his life at stake, followed the rules meticulously, and did "his best with utmost seriousness." It was Hemingway's eagerness to learn about death, one of the "simplest" and "most fundamental" things, that first took him in 1923 to the bull ring at Pamplona, the only place where "you could see life and death . . . now that the wars were over."

Another reason Hemingway was fascinated by bullfighting was that it required tremendous physical courage of the matador, especially after he had once been gored, recovered, and entered the ring again to face another fighting animal which desired nothing more than his adversary's death. Far more than big-game hunting, the bullfight provided the ultimate test of a man's courage; as a consequence, Jake Barnes observes, nobody "ever lived their life all the way up except bullfighters." Even the average bullfighter was by necessity "a very brave man"—that is, gifted with "the ability temporarily to ignore possible consequences." His courage stemmed as much as anything from the Spanish quality of *pundonor*, which "means honor, probity, courage, self-respect, and pride. . . ." With the Spanish, it was a matter of *pundonor* not to show cowardice, for once that was done by a bullfighter, his honor and his reputation were destroyed. "Courage comes such a short distance; from the heart to the head; but when it goes no one knows how far away it goes; in a hemorrhage, perhaps, or into a woman, and it is a bad thing to be in the bullfighting business when it is gone, no matter where it went."

In bullfighting, as with outdoor sports, Hemingway lamented the passing of what had presumably been a golden age, and inveighed against modern "decadence," his word, in *Death in the Afternoon*, for what had gone wrong with bullfighting by the early 1930s. Motivated by fear, the matadors had insisted on facing smaller bulls, or "bulls under the minimum age, stuffed on grain to make them seem big, giving the minimum of danger because of their lack of experience in using their horns." Motivated by greed, the breeders and promoters had gone along, so that the tragedy was virtually deprived of that element of danger which played so essential a part in the final catharsis. Instead of classical passes with the cape and *muleta*, the typical matador had taken to showy but safe tricks, picturesque touches like "putting his hand on the muzzle of the bull, stroking the horns, and all such useless and romantic things that the spectators like."

At the heart of the problem, though, lay the modern curse of specialization, as prominent and annoying in bullfighting as in medicine. In "the old days you went to a bullfight and the matadors were matadors; they had served a real apprenticeship, knew bullfighting, performed as skillfully as their ability and courage permitted with cape, muleta, banderillas, and they killed the bulls." But lately the "malady of specialization" had spread to bullfighting until now there were matadors who were only good with the cape "and useless at anything else." In a passage strongly reminiscent of Ralph Waldo Emerson's 1837 "American Scholar" address, in which he called for a rebirth of the whole, uncompartmentalized man, Hemingway proposed his remedy: "What is needed in bullfighting today is a complete bullfighter who is at the same time an artist to save it from the specialists. . . . What it needs is a god to drive the half-gods out." For a few years the superlative Maera had fulfilled the role, performing well in all areas of his art, "so brave that he shamed those stylists who were not," and so devoted to bullfighting "that, in his last year, his presence in the ring raised the whole thing from the least effort, get-rich-quick, wait-for-the-mechanical bull basis it had fallen to and, while he was in the ring, it again had dignity and passion." But by 1932 Maera was through, and Hemingway took it as his duty to "know what is good and what is bad, to appreciate the new, but let nothing confuse" his standards—and to write a book so that others might learn what those standards should be.

Why did Ernest Hemingway, with the success of *The Sun Also Rises* and *A Farewell to Arms* behind him, spend the better part of five years exhaustively researching, collecting photographs, and writing a book on so specialized an activity as bullfighting? Obviously, he was enthusiastic about the subject, not only in 1932 but as late in life as 1959, when he traveled round Spain with an entourage including A. E. Hotchner to observe and report, in a series of articles for *Life* magazine, on the "dangerous summer" of *mano a mano* confrontations between Luis Miguel Domingúin and Antonio Ordóñez. Just as clearly, in *Death in the Afternoon* he wanted to transmit his enthusiasm in language free of the kind of "bedside mysticism" found in such "one-visit" books as Waldo Frank's *Virgin Spain*. Furthermore, as he stated in the opening pages, "it might be good to have a book about bullfighting in English," a serious book which might even last. The result was Hemingway's most curious production, containing, along with its lessons on how to fight bulls and how to watch it being done, a series of brilliant vignettes that bring to life such figures in bullfight history as Joselito, Belmonte, Maera, and the most entertainingly sketched of all, El Gallo, the matador who once replied, when asked what he did for exercise, that he smoked cigars. At the end of most chapters, to break the rhythm, Hemingway inserted conversations between himself and an excessively curious

Old Lady, in which Hemingway relieved himself of opinions on writing and painting, love and sex, the crime of phoniness in art and life, the need for courage and genius, the importance that knowing about death holds for anyone who would fully savor life, and on the relationship between all these subjects and the art of bullfighting. Despite all its digressions, then, *Death in the Afternoon* achieves a sort of unity within diversity. But the highest encomium the book can be paid is that it remains interesting reading, and that it stands, more than forty years after it was written, as the best book in English on its subject.

Hemingway's strongest motivation for writing about bullfighting, however, was probably his compulsion to be the knower and conveyor of expert information. Very early, he was accepted into the small priesthood of true believers, those *aficionados* who could only be isolated by "a sort of oral spiritual examination" which, if one passed, would culminate with a touching, or laying on of hands. In his story "The Undefeated," Hemingway as implied narrator contrasts himself with the second-string bullfight critic for *El Heraldo*, a composer of empty clichés who smokes cigarettes and drinks warm champagne in his boredom while below, in the ring, Manuel Garcia fights a brave and doomed battle to recover his skill and his livelihood in the craft he loves.

Unlike the man from *El Heraldo*, Hemingway conceived of himself as truly knowledgeable about bullfighting. By the summer of 1959, in fact, he was ready to assume a position as the only expert alive. Nothing disturbed him more than pretensions by others to expertise. The "thing that makes Ernest really passionate," Eric Sevareid wrote after encountering him in Seville, "is a knowing remark from somebody about something he knows not"—like Kenneth Tynan, for example, being authoritative about a botched sword thrust. In the end, there was room for but one expert in the front row at the arena, or in Ordóñez's dressing room before a fight—and when he found Peter Buckley visiting Ordóñez on one such occasion, Hemingway warned him to get out of there within thirty seconds or he would "go in and kill him."

"A good writer," Hemingway remarked in *Death in the Afternoon*, "should know as near everything as possible. Naturally he will not," but truly great writers are capable of learning at such a rapid rate and with such amazing retention that they seem "to be born with knowledge." There were some things which could not be learned quickly—"the very simplest things and because it takes a man's life to know them the little new that each man gets from life is very costly and the only heritage he has to leave." His function as writer was to set down that "little new," to contribute "to the knowledge of the next writer" who came along. This is a statement of didactic purpose which Dr. Johnson could not have faulted. Hemingway saw himself as teacher as well as artist, and in no book is this view of his function more evident than in *Death in the Afternoon*.

v

Politics

"Some Sort of Y.M.C.A. Show."

As Europe smoldered during the 1930s, communists and fellow travelers courted the support of Ernest Hemingway, and for a time during the Spanish Civil War they thought they had won him over to their cause. Editorials and reviews in the *Daily Worker* and *New Masses* welcomed the intimations of social-political consciousness they detected in *To Have and Have Not, The Spanish Earth*, and *The Fifth Column*, the novel, film, and play Hemingway produced during 1937 and 1938. Eagerly, the Marxists awaited the appearance of the great book on the Spanish war which, as Cyril Connolly remarked, only Hemingway could write. When *For Whom the Bell Tolls* came out in 1940, the bubble burst and their hopes were frustrated. Yet there is nothing in *For Whom the Bell Tolls* that could not have been predicted from the political attitudes Hemingway expressed, before 1940, in books, stories, articles, and letters. In a classic case of selective perception, the communists miscalculated their man and misread his writing.

What were the basic planks in Hemingway's political platform? First of all, he paid little respect to politicians, whether domestic or foreign. As early as 1922 he labeled Mussolini "the biggest bluff in Europe." The Roosevelt-Hoover election of 1932 he characterized as a contest between "The Paralytic Demagogue" and "The Syphilitic Baby." Even the leaders of the Spanish Republic, he observed in 1934, made theirs a "lucrative profession" by pocketing a substantial share of the peasants' taxes. If it were up to him he would cheerfully machine-gun any political bastards who did not work for a living.

He disliked political systems at least as much as their practitioners. His hatred of fascism traced back to what had happened in Italy after World War I. Since he had "fought"—that is, served in the ambulance corps—there during the war, Hemingway felt a tug of the heart toward Italy and took the country's defection to fascism as a personal betrayal. The Italians were "the best people" in Europe, he wrote Ernest Walsh in the summer of 1925, but he could not live there because the political situation made him furious. The Hemingways would spend the fall and winter skiing in the Vorarlberg, but he doubted if they would leave the Austrian part of the Dolomites; he had promised himself never to go down into Italy again so long as the fascists were in power.

Two years later, having relaxed his rule to take a miserable trip through Italy with Guy Hickok, Hemingway outlined the ill effects of fascism in "Che Ti Dice La Patria?" In this bitter piece of reporting, originally published in the *New Republic* as "Italy, 1927," he uncovered the rottenness hiding beneath the façade of fascist efficiency and order. A whorehouse pretends to be a restaurant, a rude young Black Shirt arrogantly demands a ride in their car, a grasping policeman imposes a fine in order to fatten his own wallet. Since he and Hickok spent only ten days in Italy, Hemingway ironically concludes, "naturally . . . we had no opportunity to see how things were with the country or the people."

His antifascism, then, was no new phenomenon springing from the turmoil of the mid-1930s. He could not abide fascism early or late, because of its hypocrisy and especially because of its limitations on the freedom of the individual. "If we ever have a time when for a few days you may shoot anyone you wish," he wrote in *Death in the Afternoon*, he would certainly want to "bag various policemen, Italian statesmen, government functionaries, [and] Massachusetts judges" (possibly a reference to Judge Webster Thayer of the Sacco-Vanzetti case). In a letter to Owen Wister he added one more target for the days of "free shooting": Henry Ford. The assembly line, police brutality, fascist regulation, and bureaucratic red tape—all were anathema to the individualist strain in Hemingway.

Later, he conceived a distaste for communism, and for the same reasons. "I cannot be a communist now," he wrote the Russian critic Ivan Kashkeen in 1935, "because I believe in only one thing: liberty." He was willing to look after himself, his family, even the neighbors, but not the state. The same message went to John Dos Passos: Hemingway couldn't be a communist because he hated tyranny and even government itself. But if Dos Passos ever became a communist, he added in his generous way, it would be "swell with me."

Associated with this libertarian bias was a conviction that politics was inimical to art. In *Green Hills of Africa*, Hemingway elaborated on this theme: When you "serve time for society, democracy, and the other things quite young, and declining any further enlistment, make yourself responsible only to yourself, you exchange the pleasant, comforting stench of comrades for something you can never feel in any other way than by yourself." Though a writer could "make himself a nice career" by espousing a cause if his side won—"if his outfit gets in he can get to be an ambassador or have a million copies of his book printed by the government or any of the other rewards the boys dream about"—he set his own sights higher. Anybody who took politics "as a way out" of the hardest job in the world, which was to "write straight honest prose on human beings," was cheating. Going into politics was a sign that a writer was "afraid to go on" with his work, because it was too hard "and you have to do it alone."

Hemingway refused to be daunted by the necessity for solitude. "Everyone tries to frighten you now," he wrote Kashkeen, "by saying or writing that if one does not become a communist or have a Marxian viewpoint one will have no friends and will be alone. They seem to think that to be alone is something dreadful; or that to not have friends is to be feared. I would rather have one honest enemy than most of the friends I have known." (Kashkeen's reply bore the salutation, "Dear Enemy.") Being alone was a condition of his craft: "A writer is an outlyer like a Gypsy." All art was created by the individual.

But this acceptance of self-reliance, seemingly on the same grounds that Emerson had laid down in *Essays: First Series*, did not proceed as had the Transcendentalist's from a conviction of the near-perfectibility of the individual. Indeed, it was because he was anything but optimistic about the nature of man that Hemingway distrusted government. While a young foreign correspondent in the mid-1920s, he had learned about the "malady of power" from William Ryall (whose pen name was William Bolitho), the brilliant South African then reporting for *The Manchester Guardian*. According to Ryall, Lord Acton was right: power *did* corrupt. You could see what it had done to the leaders of the French Revolution, he said, "and it was because our forefathers in America knew how power affected men that they had limited the term of the executive."

Give men enough power, Ryall argued, and they would arrogantly lead their nations into futile and destructive wars. Working this vein, several of Hemingway's mid-1930s articles in *Esquire* focused on how to stay out of the European war he felt certain was coming. February 1934: "Europe has always had wars. But we can keep out of this next one. And the only way to keep out of it is not go in it; not for any reason. There will be plenty of good reasons. *But we must keep out of it*. If kids want to go to see what war is like, or for the love of any nation, let them go as individuals. Anyone has a right to go who wants to. But we, as a country, have no business in it and we must keep out." September 1935: "Not this August, nor this September; you have this year to do in what you like. Not next August, nor next September; that is still too soon. . . . So you can fish that summer and shoot that fall or do whatever you do, go home at nights, sleep with your wife, go to the ball game, make a bet, take a drink when you want to, or enjoy whatever liberties are left for anyone who has a dollar or a dime. But the year after or the year after that they fight." November 1935: "War is coming in Europe as surely as winter follows fall. If we want to stay out, now is the time to decide to stay out. Now, before the propaganda starts. Now is the time to make it impossible for any one man, or any hundred men, or any thousand men, to put us in a war in ten days—in a war which they will not have to fight."

Not only did he warn against blindly following powerful men down the road to war but he also adopted the stance of the conservative realist toward the possibility of reform. Asked what was going on in America, Hemingway as hunter-protagonist of *Green Hills of Africa* replied: "Damned if I know! Some sort of Y.M.C.A. show. Starry eyed bastards spending money that somebody will have to pay. Everybody in our town quit work to go on relief. Fishermen all turned carpenters. Reverse of the Bible." Like Huck Finn who leaves Tom Sawyer's make-believe pirate band because "it had all the marks of a Sunday school," Hemingway repudiated idealistic New Deal measures, especially welfare and the CCC. Certainly government was powerless to change human nature.

In unraveling his political thought in the years before the Spanish Civil War, one more thread emerges: his compulsion to play the expert, to secure inside knowledge. It was not knowledge arrived at through study in the conventional sense. Hemingway never read Marx, and the Roosevelt brain-truster Rexford Tugwell, meeting him in 1936, complained that though the writer seemed fascinated by the New Deal, he was "not willing to undertake an understanding of its issues." Instead, he preferred to acquire his inside information as it had been provided by Bill Ryall—and as he undoubtedly hoped it would be by Tugwell—accompanied by a drink and dispensed in the form of anecdotes.

Yet during the 1930s, when he was repeatedly attacked for his political neutrality, Hemingway often turned the tables on his challengers by claiming that he knew far more about communism than they did. In a 1931 letter to Scott Fitzgerald Ernest maintained that he had gotten communism out of his system long before it was taken up by Edmund Wilson. Ten years ago, he wrote Fitzgerald, when "we" were all paid-up party members, Bunny Wilson and the other members of the intelligentsia said it was all tripe, and they were right. Everybody, he supposed, had to go through a period of political or religious faith sooner or later, but he was glad he'd put his pink period and subsequent disillusionment behind him a decade earlier. (There is no evidence whatever to support this casual brag.) Similarly, when importuned by Paul Romaine to shift his views to the left, Hemingway began by insulting his correspondent for "the goddamned YMCA worker presumption . . . of [his] politico-literary well-wishing" and proceeded to assert that his own political beliefs were so much further to the left than Romaine's that he could be jailed for publishing them. Besides, why should he pay any attention to the opinions of Dreiser, Dos Passos, and Wilson, "these little punks who have never seen even street fighting let alone a revolution?"

Revolution, Hemingway argued in letters and magazine articles, was one thing he understood. Rather tentatively, he proposed to Owen Wister in 1932 the theory that no economic system had ever been overthrown without a great military defeat first. But in *Esquire* for December 1934 he converted the theory into a law of history: to achieve a communist revolution, you had first to suffer a complete military collapse. "You have to see what happens in a military debacle to understand this," he wrote, and personally he had witnessed such a debacle in Italy, a country which did not undergo a revolution after World War I solely "because her defeat was not complete; because after Caporetto she fought and won in June and July of 1918 on the Piave." That success encouraged "the merchants of Milan" to smash the socialist co-ops and socialist municipal governments and to install fascism instead.

"The Revolutionist," a story in *In Our Time*, provided a satirical showcase for the demonstration of the writer's wisdom on this subject. The title character is a young idealist who "believed altogether in the world revolution" and had come to Italy because it was "the one country that everyone is sure of." The narrator, who is a realist, does not say anything in response, but the story does supply one detail to symbolize the revolutionist's pipe dreams. He carries with him reproductions of paintings by Giotto, Masaccio, and Piero della Francesca, but "Mantegna he did not like": Mantegna, whose canvases, full of "nail holes," evoked the passion of Christ with painful realism. When last heard of, the optimistic young revolutionist has like the Saviour been imprisoned —but if he is executed, the tale suggests, his will be a futile, merely private martyrdom.

Since only the knowledgeable can afford to laugh, Hemingway also employed comedy as a device to underline his insider's stance. In 1933, for example, he outlined to Dos Passos his outrageous scheme to secede Key West from the Union. The first night they would massacre the Catholics and the Jews. The second night they would take care of the Protestants who had been lulled into a false sense of security by the events of the first evening. Next, they would butcher free-thinkers, atheists, communists, and members of the lighthouse service. Dos Passos could see how it would be: "one gay hilarious round" with everyone happily occupied.

Finally, in *Green Hills of Africa*, there is the following dialogue between Pop (based on Philip Percival, their hunting guide) and Hemingway:

> "Were you in Spain for the revolution?"
> "I got there late. Then we waited for two that didn't come. Then we missed another."

"Did you see the one in Cuba?"
"From the start."
"How was it?"
"Beautiful. Then lousy. You couldn't believe how lousy."

At this stage P.O.M. (Poor Old Mama, Pauline Hemingway) breaks in with the story of not spilling her drink during a street skirmish in Havana and of the children's asking to go out in the afternoon to see the shouting. Actually, Ernest Hemingway was fishing during most of the 1933 Cuban revolt against Machado, though Pauline and her sister Jinny reportedly were fired on in a Havana gunfight. On the basis of that experience Hemingway insisted that both he and Pauline were sick of revolutions. Nonetheless, he told Pop, he was contemplating a study of the subject and knew just how to go about collecting his material.

Courtship by the *Masses*

Despite Ernest Hemingway's aggressively apolitical remarks in *Green Hills of Africa*—the stench of comrades, the YMCA show, the disdainful dismissal of revolutions—the left-wingers' courtship of Ernest Hemingway continued apace. For one thing, he had offered them some encouragement in antiwar columns for *Esquire*, which demonstrated his awareness that the only ones who stood to gain from war were the profiteers and the politicians in power. For another, Hemingway was so big a catch as to demand untiring pursuit. "Let the boys yip," he had written, and yip at his heels they did, hoping to drive their famous stallion into the communist corral.

Did he succumb to their blandishments? In his life of Hemingway, Carlos Baker suggests that the arguments of Kashkeen and other correspondents may eventually have opened a fissure, "the thinnest of thin red lines," in his wall of resistance. But Baker also makes clear that, despite indications to the contrary, Hemingway never capitulated to Marxism. By and large, it was the tide of events rather than the arguments of "the persuaders" that accounted for his seeming drift to the left. He happened to be in Key West, for example, when a hurricane struck the Matecumbe Keys in September 1935 and wiped out nearly a thousand war veterans in the CCC camps. Chartering a boat to view the devastation at first hand, Hemingway returned to find a telegram from Joseph North of *New Masses*, asking for an article on the disaster. Though aware that the communist periodical was attempting to "use" him, he was angry enough about the stupidity and carelessness of the government to respond with a piece excoriating the "rich bastards" who had sent the veterans "to the Florida Keys and left them there in the hurricane months" when wealthy people, yachtsmen, and "fishermen like Herbert Hoover and Franklin Delano Roosevelt" knew enough to stay away.

A year later, after the outbreak of the war in Spain, Hemingway committed most of his energies to the Loyalists and the people of his "adopted country." His initial efforts were strictly humanitarian. First he raised money to supply the Loyalists with ambulances and medical equipment, and then in January 1937 he was named chairman of the Ambulance Committee, Medical Bureau, American Friends of Spanish Democracy. Soon after, he packed his bags and set out on the first of four trips to see the Spanish war for himself.

Hemingway's motives for going to Spain were not entirely altruistic. He carried with him credentials and a generous dollar-a-word contract from the North American Newspaper Alliance that would help to pay off the money he had borrowed for the ambulances. He escaped domestic troubles at home and planned to resume overseas his newly struck liaison with fellow correspondent Martha Gellhorn, whom he had met in Key West. He hoped to gain material for his fiction from close personal observation of the war. But insofar as his motivation was political, it derived from two consuming hatreds: of fascism and the horror of modern war.

In service of both feelings, he soon took on the role of propagandist. In April 1937, only one month after landing in Spain, Hemingway began work on the script of *The Spanish Earth*, a documentary film on the war produced and financed under procommunist auspices in the United States. Hemingway himself contributed about one-fourth of the $13,000 budget, and during filming traipsed around Spain with cameraman John Ferno and director Joris Ivens, a Marxist who attempted to indoctrinate his famous scriptwriter. By summer the movie was ready, and Hemingway and Ivens brought it back across the Atlantic. The completed film bore out Hemingway's conviction that politics and art did not mix well. In this case at least, so the *New York Times* review pointed out, the camera was mightier than the pen, for the commentary (which Ernest wrote and delivered himself), though occasionally powerful, nonetheless amounted to a "definitely propagandist effort" in its bitterness and vengefulness.

One theme of the narrative, repeated in Hemingway's 1939 elegy (in *New Masses* once more) for "The American Dead in Spain," harked back to the quotation from Ecclesiastes at the front of *The Sun Also Rises*. The "earth abideth forever," and the Spanish peasants who worked in that earth and were eventually to lie beneath it gave assurance that fascism, whatever its brutalities, could not hold "any people in slavery." Hemingway's script stressed the communion of the worker with the land, and the heretical violation of that holy compact by the tanks and airplanes of Franco's German and Italian allies. Mechanized doom might threaten and kill the good primitive people of Spain, but even in death they would live again in the Spanish earth, and "as long as the earth lives, no system of tyranny will ever prevail in Spain."

In July the film was shown at the White House, where Hemingway was repelled by Roosevelt's "Harvardian" manner, and in Hollywood, where his appeal for funds immediately drummed up enough money to put twenty ambulances in the field. As Scott Fitzgerald commented, Ernest swept in "like a whirlwind," relieved Miriam Hopkins of $1000 bills fresh from the gaming tables, and swept out again. There was "something religious about it."

Hemingway had exerted a charismatic effect on his listeners the previous month in New York, when he made the only public speech of his adult life to the League of American Writers. Chairing the meeting was former boon companion Donald Ogden Stewart. An irrepressibly funny man, Stewart got more laughs than anyone else present, though insisting that this was no time for good humor. Then the nervously perspiring Hemingway stepped to the microphones in Carnegie Hall to discuss the serious problems of a writer in wartime. The writer's problem was always the same: "to write truly and, having found what is true, to project it in such a way that it becomes a part of the experience of the person who reads it." The problem was very difficult, but really good writers could solve it under almost all conditions. "There [was] only one form of government that [could] not produce good writers, and that system [was] Fascism. For Fascism [was] a lie told by bullies. A writer who [would] not lie [could] not live or work under fascism." As in *The Spanish Earth*, he also inveighed against the intervention of the totalitarian fascist states in Spain's internal affairs—and against their slaughter of the innocent. "Every time they are beaten in the field," he said of the German and Italian forces, "they salvage that strange thing they call their honor, by murdering civilians." The audience responded with waves of applause as Hemingway, excited and wet, dashed offstage. He later tended to assume that his speech "was responsible for a lot of the guys coming over" to fight for the Loyalist cause.

He had originally left for Spain in February 1937, he told his wife's mother, as an "anti-war war correspondent." And this antiwar theme emerged clearly in the dispatches he sent back to be syndicated by the North American Newspaper Alliance. His cables zoomed in on grisly vignettes of the dead whose "remains took on the shape of curiously broken toys. One doll," he wrote, "had lost its feet and lay with no expression on its waxy, stubbled face. Another doll had lost half its head, while a third doll was simply broken as a bar of chocolate breaks in your pocket." The fascist shelling of Madrid "killed an old woman returning from market, dropping her in a huddled black heap of clothing, with one leg, suddenly detached, whirling against the wall of an adjoining house." Yet another dispatch, called "Old Man at the Bridge," survives in his collected short stories. The old man of the story, a saintly soul without politics who has been trying to take care of animals —goats, pigeons, and a cat—in the turmoil of battle, sits exhausted on a bridge on Easter Sunday. The fascists would surely bomb the bridge and strafe the roads soon, but on this day the ceiling was low: "That and the fact that cats knew how to look after themselves was all the good luck that old man would ever have." Such cables dramatized his conviction that modern warfare spread its violence indiscriminately, maiming innocent civilians as well as dedicated combatants.

The next year Hemingway wrote the strongest political statements of his life for a new left-leaning magazine called *Ken*, which was purportedly middle-of-the-road in outlook but actually left wing. In separate articles he denounced the American State Department for doing "their level, crooked, Roman, British-aping, disgusting efficient best" to deny "the Spanish government the right to buy arms to defend itself against the German and Italian aggression," and Neville Chamberlain and the French ministers for betraying their own countries and the Loyalist cause. His journalism of 1938, Baker observed, centered on a single theme: the absolute necessity of stopping fascist aggression in

Spain "before Hitler's Brown Shirts and Mussolini's Black Shirts overran the continent and precipitated a second world war." He was propagandizing against the spread of fascism and of war. If the United States, Britain, and France would see their duty and send arms to the Loyalists, he believed, World War II might be averted. But the politicians, acting out of shortsighted expediency and stupidly muttering about "peace in our time," sat on their hands and let the holocaust come.

The editors of *New Masses*, perhaps understandably, were unable or unwilling to perceive that Hemingway's bitter antifascism was accompanied by an abiding distrust of all politicians and political systems. If he was against fascism, he must be *for* the communists; and if he was on their side, it behooved them to reciprocate in kind. A chronological inspection of *New Masses* commentary on Hemingway's books reveals the ease with which the journal's editors adapted their artistic judgments to political purposes. In 1928, for example, Mike Gold dismissed the author of *The Sun Also Rises* by observing that "there is no humanity in Hemingway," that he was "heartless as a tabloid," "too bourgeois to accept the labor world," and (forgetting Dr. Johnson on this subject) that he affected aloofness as the "last refuge of the scoundrel." The still more vicious attack of Robert Forsythe, in 1934, prompted Hemingway to hope that he might one day have an opportunity to break the critic's jaw. Beginning with sarcastic emphasis on Hemingway's sensitivity to criticism, Forsythe ended by suggesting the writer's irrelevancy. Hemingway, he wrote, gives "the impression of a man who has been writing in a vacuum and is now ending in a vacuum." Hunting, Granville Hicks commented in his more conciliatory 1935 review of *Green Hills of Africa*, might be exciting to do but it wasn't exciting to read about. Hemingway should broaden his scope to write on different themes. Hicks would "like to have Hemingway write a novel about a strike, to use an obvious example, not because a strike is the only thing worth writing about, but because it would do something to Hemingway. If he would just let himself look squarely at the contemporary American scene, he would be bound to grow."

Once Hemingway started financing ambulances, making speeches, and writing documentaries, *New Masses* critics seemed to take total leave of their artistic senses. Hicks hailed *To Have and Have Not* as Hemingway's best novel so far, superior to *The Sun Also Rises* and *A Farewell to Arms* because of its author's new knowledge of the economic system. In making this judgment, Hicks must have swallowed hard, for in the novel Hemingway depicts a detestable camp-following novelist who is about to write a shoddy, phony, politically profitable novel—about a strike. (The popularity of *To Have and Have Not* with the left wing, incidentally, did not suffer when the Detroit Council of Catholic Organizations took steps to suppress the novel in the bookstores and libraries of that city. The real reason for this suppression, as three distinguished Americans—Van Wyck Brooks, Archibald MacLeish, and Thornton Wilder—insisted in a jointly signed letter, lay in "Hemingway's known sympathy for the Spanish government in the civil war in Spain and his activity in securing ambulances for the service of the Spanish army and the bombed population.") In a 1939 *New Masses* review, Edwin Berry Burgum praised Hemingway's play, *The Fifth Column*, and said of the "first forty-nine stories," which were published in the same volume, that they constituted "the record of the road that Hemingway has traveled through the confusions of modern life to a clearer insight into the relation between democracy and art."

As Hemingway's star rose among the communist critical fraternity, that of John Dos Passos, his erstwhile friend and once-dedicated left-winger, correspondingly sank. In a satirical piece which indicated that one journal on the left was amusedly watching another journal still further to the left, Herbert Solow in *Partisan Review* catalogued the change in the two writers' reputations as viewed by *New Masses*. The title of his article cleverly summed up its contents: "Substitution, at Left Tackle: Hemingway for Dos Passos."

The particular incident that prompted the Marxist disenchantment with Dos Passos also resulted in the end of the long, though often shaky, friendship between him and Hemingway. As an early and famous correspondent in Spain, Hemingway managed to open doors that remained closed to most of his colleagues. Thus General Hans Kahle, the anti-Nazi German who commanded the Eleventh International Brigade, took Ernest into his confidence and inspired his admiration. For a time, Hemingway considered writing a book about Kahle, but gave up the idea on the grounds that "we have too much together for me ever to risk losing any of it by trying to write about it." On Hemingway's first visit to the Twelfth International Brigade, to take another example, its Hungarian General Lukacz rounded up all the girls in the nearby village to put on a banquet in his honor.

Among Hemingway's friends in the Twelfth International was the then communist novelist Gustav Regler, who confided to the American "inside stories of operations and crises . . . feeling certain he knew what it was all about." At Gaylord's, the Madrid hotel occupied by the Soviets, Mikhail Koltsov, correspondent for *Pravda* and *Izvestia*, also filled Hemingway in on the way the war was actually being run. The ambience of Gaylord's—fixed bayonets at the entrance, uncommonly fine food and drink inside—suggested that it was a place where, once you had gained entree, you could pick up what Hemingway liked to call "the true gen," or intelligence. With friends and informants in high places, Hemingway felt very much the insider, and he adopted an attitude of rather smug superiority toward less favored correspondents.

It was this attitude that produced the final break with Dos Passos, who had come to Spain to work with Hemingway on the script for *The Spanish Earth*. They had their differences about the film, too, but the real quarrel between them involved Dos Passos's old friend, José Robles Pazos, a teacher of Spanish literature at Johns Hopkins University who returned to his homeland to fight for the Loyalists, encountered powerful political enemies, and was secretly executed after a drumhead trial. Unaware of this, Dos Passos spent much of his time in Spain trying to locate Robles and to clear his name. Hemingway understood how distressed Dos Passos was about his friend, yet when he finally got word that Robles had been killed, he callously broke the news to Dos Passos with the offhand assertion that—so his inside information revealed—it was all right, since Robles had been "worthless."

During the Spanish Civil War at least five parties on the left were competing for control of the government, and though Ernest never really understood the fine points of difference between them, he did come to feel that the rigorously Russian-organized Popular Front offered "the best discipline" for the successful conduct of the war. Hence he disapproved of the anarchist faction, which, he believed, Robles and Dos Passos represented. Hemingway broke with Dos Passos, Arnold Gingrich thought, "because he felt that Dos Passos was too sympathetic to the anarchist element in the Loyalists' ranks, and not 'regular' enough in his attitude toward the commissars." But to conclude, as Gingrich did, that "Ernest was going through a very brief period of being very red" was to mistake Hemingway's motivations. Normally, to be sure, his radical individualism would have led him to sympathize with the anarchists. But two other influences prohibited that reaction.

The first was his tendency to glory in his alleged inside information. The second, and more important, was his conviction that the anarchists hindered Loyalist chances of winning the war, and he was strongly committed to that goal.

Two Violent Heroes

Most critical reaction to *To Have and Have Not*, which was published in October 1937, found the novel aesthetically disappointing. The structure was uneven, the story episodic, the contrast between Harry Morgan and the novelist Richard Gordon heavy-handed, the vignettes excoriating the rich merely tacked on to the back of the book. Lionel Trilling, assessing both this novel and *The Fifth Column*, complained that "the man with a dull personal ax to grind" had supplanted the artist, and blamed the proletarian critics for insisting that Hemingway "give up his base individuality and rescue humanity and his own soul by becoming the mouthpiece of a party, a movement, or a philosophy."

For their part, the left wingers were glad to accept the onus. They appropriated Hemingway's name and *To Have and Have Not* in a promotion drive for *New Masses*, which asserted that "more leading writers were waking up to the historic necessity of joining the fight for a better life." The novel might be flawed, but "compare *To Have and Have Not* with *The Sun Also Rises*," Samuel Putnam suggested, "and you will have the measure of a great artist's growth in little more than a decade—a great artist and a brave one, brave enough to risk not writing a masterpiece once in a while, big enough to see the thing through." Philip Rahv, though he found "the contradiction between the old Hemingway manner and his new social direction" unconvincing and thought the writer still politically ignorant, nonetheless hoped that "Morgan's death [might] presage Hemingway's social birth."

The basis for these comments lay principally in Harry Morgan's dying words: "A man . . . One man alone ain't got. No man alone now . . . No matter how a man alone ain't got no bloody fucking chance" followed by the authorial comment that "It had taken him a long time to get it out and it had taken him all of his life to learn it." Surely, the critics concluded, Hemingway here was turning away from his earlier individualism. In his essay "Farewell the Separate Peace," Edgar Johnson spelled out the argument: since writing *A Farewell to Arms*, Hemingway had learned that it was impossible to make a separate peace, and in *To Have and Have Not* he had painfully "struggled through to affirmation"—the affirmation of human solidarity.

Though Harry's final speech is certainly important, it hardly represents a willing acceptance of human solidarity. In fact, the book illustrates time and again how badly men behave when they form in groups—especially political groups. Down and out in the Depression, desperately turning to crime to support his family, Harry can find no one to join forces with. The government offers no solution. When Morgan attempts to smuggle rum, "one bunch of Cuban government bastards" costs him an arm, and "another bunch of U.S. ones," represented by the pompous "alphabet man" Frederick Harrison, takes away his only means of livelihood, his boat. New Deal measures simply don't work, and even if he could, Harry wouldn't "dig sewers for the government for less money than [would] feed" his wife and kids.

Despite such comments, Harry is "no radical." He doesn't care "who is President" in Cuba or the United States; and the Cuban revolutionaries who charter his boat for Morgan's last job present an unlovely alternative to the status quo. One of them guns down the innocent Albert Tracy without reason, but is excused by his fellows as "a good revolutionary" since he kills in "a good cause . . . the best cause." Such rationalization does not persuade Morgan, who remains interested in his own problems:

> F____ his revolution. To help the working man he robs a bank and kills a fellow works with him and then kills that poor damned Albert that never did any harm. That's a working man he kills. He never thinks of that. With a family. It's the Cubans run Cuba. They all double cross each other. They sell each other out. They get what they deserve. The hell with their revolutions. All I got to do is to make a living for my family and I can't do that.

The American communist Nelson Jacks, who has not had much luck in organizing even the desperate, brutalized veterans in the camps, is more or less sympathetically portrayed, but Hemingway reposes little faith in the ideology which attracts men like John Hollis, a Hollywood director "whose brain is in the process of outlasting his liver so that he will end up calling himself a communist, to save his soul, his other organs being too corroded to attempt to save them. . . ."

Hemingway's deepest scorn, however, is reserved for the literary fellow traveler Richard Gordon. A hypocrite who mouths the slogan, "A writer . . . can't restrict his experience to conform to bourgeois standards," to justify a casual affair, Gordon is blind to political and emotional reality. His wife finally decides to leave him in favor of Professor MacWalsey, a lush who at least has the virtue of loving her. "If you were just a good writer," she tells her husband, "I could stand for all the rest of it maybe. But I've seen you bitter, jealous, changing your politics to suit the fashion, sucking up to people's faces and talking about them behind their backs. I've seen you until I'm sick of you." The communist Jacks has a similar reaction when he learns who Gordon is. Yes, he's read his books:

> "Didn't you like them?"
> "No," said the tall man.
> "Why?"
> "I don't like to say."
> "Go ahead."
> "I thought they were shit," the tall man said and turned away.

In the acid portrait of Gordon, Hemingway etched out his absolute refusal to join the company of party-lining writers.

But what of the rich yachtsmen, anchored off Key West, who are sketched as immoral, exploitative, homosexual, onanistic, alcoholic, suicidal, and untrustworthy? As Sinclair Lewis sarcastically commented, *To Have and Have Not* seems to demonstrate "that all excellently educated men and women are boresome and cowardly degenerates, while un-lettered men engaged in rum running and the importation of Chinese coolies are wise and good and attractive." Unconvincing it was. Besides, the one-sided diatribe against the rich hardly represented a new direction in Hemingway's thinking, since as early as *The Sun Also Rises* he had revealed his animus against the wasteful wealthy. His dislike of the rich rested on artistic and personal, not economic or political, grounds.

Whether Harry Morgan should be regarded as an admirable figure or as a modern antihero remains an issue of critical debate. One thing Hemingway clearly *did* admire about his protagonist was his strong self-reliance. Talking out the novel in advance, he saw as its theme "the decline of the individual" followed by (something that does not happen in the finished product) his eventual re-emergence. And when Charles Poore was putting together his Hemingway reader, Ernest specifically asked him to include, uncut, the first five chapters of "the most hated" of his books, chapters which showed "Harry Morgan pretty much in the round when he could still get by on *cojones* and improvising and his luck."

Repeatedly, Harry emphasizes that he would rather work by himself, and little good results when he carries helpers along on his buccaneering missions. Eddy the rummy stows on board for the Chinaman episode, and as Eddy lies asleep after the violence, Morgan wonders whether he should "do away with him," since he was liable to talk when he got drunk and since Morgan would have to pay a fine for bringing him in. Under the circumstances, Harry "didn't know how to consider him." Wesley, the Negro who accompanies him on the rum-running trip, complains so persistently after he is wounded that finally the more severely hurt Harry would have hit him if he'd been able to. On his final voyage, Harry reluctantly decides to take Albert along since he is "no rummy nor no nigger" and he might be useful. Still, Harry thinks, "It would be better alone, anything is better alone but I don't think I can handle it alone. It would be much better alone." As it develops, Albert is shot before he can be of any help, and the one-armed bandit Harry takes his last gamble—and loses—quite alone.

Twice in the course of the novel a minor character attempts to perform an act of brotherhood, but neither attempt is entirely successful. Captain Willie steers the insufferable bureaucrat Harrison away from Morgan's boat, and Harry calls, "thanks, brother," for a gesture which, while it probably kept Harry out of jail, could not prevent the government from impounding his boat. Later, Professor MacWalsey tries to take Richard Gordon, drunk and badly beaten, home in a taxi-cab, but Gordon will have none of it. "Is he your brother?" the taxi driver asks, echoing Harrison's query to Captain Willie, and the answer, "In a way," is also much the same. "I wish I could help that poor man whom I am wronging," MacWalsey thinks, but quite obviously he cannot.

Throughout the novel, then, Hemingway deplores the alternatives to individualism. Big government oppresses, revolution brutalizes, communism attracts the fashionable and insincere, politics ruins art, and there is precious little that any man can do for his fellows. To conclude with the left-wingers of the 1930s that Harry Morgan's last words signaled Hemingway's political change of heart would be to distort everything that the novel has to say. If one man alone doesn't have a chance, neither do two men on the *Queen Conch*, or forty communists at the veterans' camp, or any other larger association. Harry's hard-won stuttered words lament and do not celebrate the decline of the individual. In a better world, one man alone *would* have a chance.

The Fifth Column, written in Spain in the fall of 1937 and published the following year with Hemingway's collected stories, also heartened those critics on the left anxiously waiting for "more leading writers" to see the light, for the hero of this play openly embraces the cause of antifascism. The trouble is that he does so as much out of temperament as conviction, and evidently without sincerity.

Philip Rawlings, the protagonist, is a soldier of fortune employing his penchant for violence as a Loyalist counterspy in Madrid. The extent of his political commitment is supposedly conveyed by his deciding to give up his mistress, Dorothy Bridges, in order to devote himself to the cause. But giving up Dorothy does not constitute much of a sacrifice, for though attractive, long-legged, good in bed, and a Vassar graduate, Dorothy is also exceedingly dense. Throughout the first half of the play she is as unaware of what is going on as Richard Gordon in *To Have and Have Not*, and for the same reason: she is a political camp-follower, blinded by slogans. Thus she keeps nagging at Philip to stop being a playboy, to do "something *political* or something *military* and fine," "to study and write a book on dialectics," all the while remaining ignorant of the counterespionage he is carrying on under her nose. When he refuses to call her "Comrade," a word with special meaning, she exclaims rapturously, "Oh, Philip. *You're developing politically*." These and other stupidities pour from her mouth, while Rawlings indicates his continuing disenchantment with the breed of politicians she admires in a discussion of how badly they face death: "I have seen a politician on the floor . . . unable to stand up when it was time to go out. I have seen a politician walk across that floor on his knees and put his arms around my legs and kiss my feet. I watched him slobber on my boots when all he had to do was such a simple thing as die. I have seen many die, and I have never seen a politician die well."

Compared to Petra, the maid who has no politics but only works, or even to Anita, the honest Moorish tart who wants Philip for herself, Dorothy lacks dignity. She buys a silver fox coat with enough black market pesetas to pay a man in the brigades for four months. "I don't believe I know any one," Philip observes, "who's been out four months without being hit—or killed." Near the end of the play Philip daydreams about the trips he and Dorothy might take together—to St. Tropez, to Kitzbühel, to Paris, to Hungary, to Africa—as members of the pre-jet set. To her shallowness, all such prospects allure, but Philip and the reader understand that he has other work to do and so must give her up. "Granted she's lazy and spoiled, and rather stupid, and enormously on the make," he summarizes her qualities to Anita. "Still she's very beautiful, very friendly, and very charming and rather innocent—and quite brave." But it is the stupid and spoiled Dorothy, not the charming and brave one, that the play presents.

For a supposed parable of political awakening, *The Fifth Column* is remarkably flippant. "If the play has a moral," Hemingway commented by way of preface, "it is that people who work for certain organizations have very little time for home life." Occasionally, to be sure, Philip reveals some feelings about the cause. Thus upon hearing the comrades sing "Bandera Rosa," he confesses to Dorothy that "the best people I ever knew died for that song." And though he insists that he "is not supposed to be a damn monk," Philip finally decides to devote himself fully to the cause. "My time," he tells Comrade Max, "is the Party's time."

Why he makes such a decision, however, remains in doubt. The dedicated Max instructs him in the correct motivations: "You do it so *every one* will have a good breakfast. . . . You do it so *no one* will ever be hungry. You do it so men will not have to fear ill health or old age; so they can live and work in dignity and not as slaves," a speech which Philip laconically dismisses with, "Yes. Sure. I know." What Philip *does* know for certain is that "we're in for fifty years of undeclared wars and I've signed up for the duration." But he undercuts the apparent sincerity of that commitment by adding, "I don't exactly remember when it was, but I signed up all right," a speech which recalls the only other time Philip suffered from lapse of memory, the night he got so drunk he could not remember having moved in with Dorothy Bridges.

"Where I go now," he tells Dorothy in their farewell scene, "I go alone, or with others who go there for the same reason I go." That reason is never satisfactorily spelled out. It may even be, as Edmund Wilson speculated, that Philip Rawlings is driven by his lust for "the headiest of human sports . . . the bagging of human beings." On balance, Wilson decided, the play didn't do "very much either for Hemingway or for the revolution," a judgment Ernest himself later confirmed with his remark that *The Fifth Column* was "probably the most unsatisfactory thing he ever wrote." But if any political idea is affirmed in the wisecracking, tough-talking dialogue of this play, it is that of individualism. Where Philip goes, he goes alone, or with others who travel together in order to separate at the end of the journey, where each man will be free and independent.

The Bell Tolls

Whatever his reasons, Philip Rawlings did sign on for the duration, while Hemingway resigned from the antifascist struggle after witnessing a succession of Loyalist defeats during 1938. Convinced that the politicians had betrayed the Spanish people, certain that the cause was at least temporarily lost, Hemingway made his separate peace early in 1939, and set to work on his most ambitious novel.

His disillusionment had been festering for some time. In the beginning, he had invested the Loyalist cause, as symbolized by the Velazquez 63 (the palace which served as headquarters for the International Brigades), with a religious aura. The feeling, he wrote, was like the one "you expected to have and did not have when you made your first communion." But he could maintain that "purity of feeling" no longer than Robert Jordan: for about six months. By 1938 Hemingway was telling Joe North, "I like Communists when they're soldiers; when they're priests, I hate them," and trying to persuade Ring Lardner's son Jim not to join the Lincoln Brigade since it would be "sheer waste" to do so (Lardner enlisted anyway, and was killed anyway).

The extent of his disillusionment could be most clearly measured, however, in four stories about the war which he published in *Esquire* and *Cosmopolitan* during 1938 and 1939. In his articles for *Ken*, in his newspaper dispatches, in the film *The Spanish Earth*, and in *The Fifth Column* Hemingway had propagandized for the Loyalists. But in these stories—"The Denunciation," "The Butterfly and the Tank," "Night Before Battle," and "Under the Ridge"—he functioned as critical observer, introducing a number of themes which Marxist critics would later single out for condemnation when they read *For Whom the Bell Tolls*. Significantly, the stories are seen through the eyes of Edwin Henry, who shares initials and occupations with Hemingway. A war correspondent and therefore a noncombatant, he has risked his life yet remains essentially uninvolved.

In the first of these stories, "The Denunciation," the narrator encounters his old friend Luis Delgado in Chicote's (an actual Madrid bar that Hemingway and others found pleasant because "you did not talk politics there"). Delgado is an honorable, admirable man, but since he is now a fascist, Henry persuades a reluctant waiter to turn him in to the Seguridad. Afterward, the correspondent cynically reflects on his own motives: "impartiality, righteousness and Pontius Pilatry, and the always-dirty desire to see how people act under an emotional conflict, that makes writers such attractive friends." The war has set friend against friend, brother against brother.

"Under the Ridge," the most powerful in this group of generally undistinguished stories, demonstrates the cruelty of the communist battle police who follow orders from the Russians. Paco, a young Loyalist soldier, shoots himself in the hand to avoid combat, and though he tries to make amends, the police still execute him as an example. A middle-aged French soldier, apparently suffering from shock, attempts to walk away from his brigade and is summarily killed. These senseless brutalities, similar to those alleged against André Marty in *For Whom the Bell Tolls*, are associated with Russian intervention through the introduction of a dignified soldier from Extremadura who hates all foreigners and who proclaims proudly, "There are no Russians in Extremadura, and there are no Extremadurans in Russia."

"Night Before Battle" focuses on an American tank volunteer named Al, who spends his last night in Madrid before setting out on what he is certain will be a foolhardy and hopeless attack. Al, who is politically committed, knows what he is fighting for, but he'd "like things to be efficient and used as intelligently as possible," which is clearly not the case. "I don't mind dying a bit," Al says. "Dying is just a lot of crap. Only it's wasteful. The attack is wrong and it's wasteful." The next day, he will die uselessly and without advancing the cause.

"The Butterfly and the Tank" tells an anecdote about a drunk, reminiscent of the unfortunate Boggs whom Colonel Sherburn guns down in *Huckleberry Finn.* Hemingway's drunk harmlessly sprays Chicote's waiters with perfume from a flit gun. At first this seems amusing, but then the waiters object, and when the "flit king" will not stop, he is shot dead by some soldiers. The point of the story emerges when the narrator proposes to write about the incident and a "forceful girl" objects that he had better not, because "it would be prejudicial to the cause of the Spanish Republic." But the story, Henry objects, has nothing to do with politics; and if he sees a comic shooting in Chicote's during the war he will "write about it just as though it had been in New York, Chicago, Key West or Marseilles."

In so speaking, Edwin Henry echoed the conviction of Ernest Hemingway himself. He had worked for two years in the struggle against fascism, he wrote in refusing an invitation to address the League of American Writers in 1939. Now that the cause was temporarily lost, he was going to write his novel and stay with it until he finished it. He had reverted to his craft as a writer, and it was the job of a writer to tell the truth as he found it. The truths Hemingway decided to tell about the Spanish Civil War did not, however, necessarily coincide with the truths that other observers saw—or wanted to see—in that war. Consequently, when the brilliant *For Whom the Bell Tolls* came out in October 1940, it was greeted not only by tremendous popular acclaim but also by a cacophony of left-wing criticism. Those who had hoped that Ernest's experience in Spain would "inflame his heart and his talents" with revolutionary ardor were bitterly disappointed. Hemingway, they decided, had betrayed them, and as a traitor was fair game for vilification. He had pretended to be on their side, they wrote, and deserted when the going got tough, "leaving a trail of alibis, whines, and slanders." He had gone to Spain as a "tourist," for merely personal reasons. His work was limited, narrow; he was dumb, an unwitting spokesman for the bourgeoisie.

But the parts of *For Whom the Bell Tolls* that most enraged the crowd at the *Daily Worker* and *New Masses* basically reiterated three lines of thought which Hemingway had expressed, before and during the war, in letters, newspaper and magazine articles, and especially in his four Spanish Civil War stories. They were, first, the antiwar sentiment that refused to condone inhuman atrocities by either side and deplored the setting of brother against brother; second, the cynical insider's instinct to debunk the secular saints of any ideological cause and to discover criminal stupidity in high places; and third, the libertarian strain which only embraced communism as temporarily less likely than fascism to imperil the freedom of the individual.

The most powerful antiwar statement in *For Whom the Bell Tolls* comes early in the book, when Pilar relates in excruciating detail the brutalities with which the Republicans took over her home town. Pablo, an accomplished organizer, arranges that the leading fascists of the town walk, one by one, between two columns of Loyalists armed with flails. At the end of the column stands a cliff and oblivion. At first those in the movement are reluctant to strike a blow against the fascists, some of whom run the gauntlet with great dignity; but frustration and drunkenness eventually arouse the most savage instincts of the mob. That, she says, "was the worst day" of her life until three days later when the fascists recaptured the town, but Pilar does not provide the details of that day, nor is the execution of Maria's parents and her own rape rendered in the exquisite detail of the twenty-five pages it takes Pilar to describe the *Republican* atrocities. They are vivid pages, for Pilar tells her story well; she "had made him see it in that town," Robert Jordan reflects. Maria sees it as well. "Are there no pleasant things to speak of?" she asks Pilar. "Do we have to talk always of horrors?" But the horrors convey Hemingway's message, that war turns men—all men, whatever their politics—into murderers, and all Spaniards into savages. Within the guerrilla band, Agustín is even more bloodthirsty than Pablo had been. Watching fascist cavalry ride by, he feels "like a mare in the corral waiting for the stallion." "We do it coldly," Jordan thinks, "but they do not, nor ever have." Killing was their extra sacrament, blood lust an inheritance from the old Iberians.

In addition, the members of Pablo's guerrilla band fight more out of circumstance than conviction. If his father had not been a Republican, Andres reflects, he and his brother "would be soldiers now with the fascists. . . ." Andres and Eladio really have no choice. Like Sordo's soldiers atop the hill, like the fascist guardsmen in their comfortable sawmill who will be killed the next day, they are trapped in "Un callejon sin salida. A passageway with no exit." Keeping his lonely watch on those fascist sentries, Anselmo realizes that "they are the same men that we are." In peacetime, he could knock on their door and be welcome. "It is only orders," he thinks, "that come between us." Later, when he must shoot one of these men, Anselmo feels as if he has struck his own brother.

Similarly, when Jordan reads the letters of the dead fascist soldier from Tafalla in Navarra (a religious one from his sister, another from his fiancée, "quietly, formally, and completely hysterical with concern for his safety"), he cannot avoid thinking that very few of those he has killed "have been real fascists," and recalling that he likes "the people of Navarra better than those of any other part of Spain." Preparing to blow the bridge, Jordan gazes through his field glasses at a fascist sentry, unshaven, lighting a cigarette from a piece of charcoal, indisputably human, and drops the binoculars. "I won't look at him again," he tells himself.

The case of Lieutenant Paco Berrendo rounds off Hemingway's indictment of the war for setting brother against brother, just as his incipient death rounds off the novel. Berrendo comes from Navarra, he mourns the death of his friend Julian, and like Anselmo he suffers Christian remorse for killing ("What a bad thing war is"). He is, in short, a good man. At the end of the book, when Jordan focuses his sights on the mounted figure of Lieutenant Berrendo, he is about to commit the final, and unavoidable, act of horror to which the civil war has driven him.

"You're a bridge-blower now," Jordan thinks to himself upon arriving in Pablo's camp. "Not a thinker," He is holding his mind in suspension, he tells Karkov, for the remainder of the war, but that is hardly true. The dialogue within Jordan's mind continues throughout the novel, with the sensible, unquestioning half at variance with the part which wants to know, to understand, to moralize—one side assured, the other questioning. A college teacher before the war, Jordan cannot stifle the part of him that soaks up knowledge. "You learn in this war if you listen," he thinks after hearing Pilar's story. At the end he regrets that the learning process must end: "I wonder if you keep on learning or if there is only a certain amount that a man can understand . . . I wish there were more time."

His principal political teacher is the cynically wise Karkov. Talking with Karkov at Gaylord's, Jordan soon loses his original naïveté. But how else could it be? Who could keep "that first chastity of mind about their work that young doctors, young priests, and young soldiers usually started with?" Nor is Jordan, even at the beginning, really ignorant of politics, for he has read Emile Burns's *Handbook of Marxism*, "fifteen hundred pages and you could spend some time on each page." Still, Karkov opens his eyes to the comic-opera side of the movement, the initialed factions that might have been spelled M.U.M.P.S. or M.E.A.S.L.E.S., except the measles were more dangerous than, for example, the "infantile" P.O.U.M. The Russian instructs him in double-think: as a good communist he is opposed to political assassination, to "acts of terrorism by individuals," to "the duplicity and villainy of the murderous counter-revolutionary hyenas," but, on the other hand, "certainly we execute and destroy such veritable fiends and dregs of humanity and the treacherous dogs of generals and the revolting spectacle of admirals unfaithful to their trust. These are destroyed. They are not assassinated. You see the difference?" Karkov also reveals that the rapidly manufactured Spanish "peasant leaders" of the movement talk Russian they had never learned in Andalusia. These revelations do not shake Jordan's resolve to fight against the fascists. He "knew enough to accept the necessity for all the deception"; a real peasant leader might turn out to be a little too much like Pablo. Besides, he "liked to know how it really was; not how it was supposed to be."

As an insider Jordan/Hemingway specifically deflates the reputation of two actual communist heroes of the war, La Pasionaria and André Marty. Knowing how the communist propaganda machine worked and convinced that human beings were constitutionally incapable of perfection, Hemingway could not swallow the political sainthood of La Pasionaria (the Passion Flower), a Basque peasant woman named Dolores Ibarruri who, he privately told friends, "always made me vomit always," and whose propagandistic catchphrases, he publicly demonstrated in *For Whom the Bell Tolls*, collapsed under the stress of combat. Joaquin, a young member of Sordo's band, is a true believer in the legend of the Passion Flower. He refuses to accept that she has a son his age safely studying dialectics in Russia. "She alone can help us," he insists, and as he faces nearly certain death repeats her slogans, "Hold out and fortify, and you will win"; and "better to die on thy feet than live on thy knees" until, when the terrible roaring planes come to bomb them on the hilltop, he shifts suddenly to Hail Marys and acts of contrition. Though not even God can save him from the bombs, at least Joaquin does not die a heretic.

The other object of Hemingway's undiluted scorn was André Marty, once the hero of the French Navy's mutiny in the Black Sea but now a watery-eyed, double-chinned, pathologically suspicious Commissar of the International Brigades with "a mania for shooting" those he believes, on the flimsiest of evidence, to be spies. Marty is quite crazy, but in a position to render great harm to the cause; he delays Jordan's message from getting through to General Golz, for instance. Probably the delay did not matter, Hemingway points out, probably the ill-fated attack would have gone ahead of its own inertia anyway. But the incident illustrates things about the Spanish Civil War that Hemingway had shown about World War I in *A Farewell to Arms*: "the idiocy and murderous stupidity of the way it was conducted. . . ." Incompetence and dishonesty prevailed at the top; the Republic had been betrayed by its leaders who shared with Pablo the ethics of horse thieves. "Was there ever a people," Jordan thinks, "whose leaders were as truly their enemies as this one?"

Why, then, does Robert Jordan fight at all? Why does he proceed with the futile and deadly business of blowing the bridge? Why does he kill, knowing it to be wrong? "You were fighting," he reflects, "against exactly what you were doing and being forced into doing to have any chance of winning." Herman Melville's phrase sums up his dilemma: "the conflict of convictions spins against the way it drives."

To the extent that Jordan fights for a political cause, it is specifically not that of communism. He takes no interest in "the planned society and the rest of it." Marxist dialectics, he decides, "are for some but not for you" and afterward "you can discard what you do not believe in." In the original version of the novel, Jordan had actually joined the Communist Party while teaching in Montana. But Hemingway later deleted that passage to emphasize the point that Jordan's devotion is not to any political ideology. "Are you a communist?" he is asked. "No, I am an anti-fascist." Remember, he later thinks to steel himself for battle, "that as long as we hold them here we keep the fascists tied up."

To Jordan as to Hemingway, fascism represents the same repression of the individual which found its ultimate expression in killing him. He hates fascism and loves its opposite, freedom. What does he believe? He believes "in the people and their right to govern themselves as they wish." He believes that "all people should be left alone and you should interfere with no one." He believes in "Liberty, Equality, and Fraternity," in "Life, Liberty, and the Pursuit of Happiness." In service of these libertarian beliefs, Jordan accepted "Communist discipline for the duration . . . because . . . they were the only party whose program and whose discipline he could respect." When it was over, he could marry

Maria and write books and teach Spanish in Montana and live without the strain imposed by the conflict of convictions.

Secondly, Jordan fights out of a sense of duty, a solemn belief that commitments made must be kept. Doing one's duty, in wartime, becomes more important even than survival. "Neither you nor this old man is anything," Jordan thinks. "You are instruments to do your duty." He is not afraid of dying, he tells Pilar, only "of not doing my duty as I should." Anselmo, the most admirable character in the novel, shares with Jordan a devotion to duty. "Thou art an old man who always talks too much," Pablo tells him. "And would do whatever he said he would do," Anselmo replies. Thus he stays at his observation post obeying orders from Jordan, though he almost freezes from the snow and cold. By way of contrast, the gypsy Rafael abandons his guard duty to kill two hares for breakfast. The gypsy "is truly worthless" in Jordan's estimation, but Anselmo is a good man who will form the left flank—and die—in the battle.

In the third place, he continues the struggle as a means of serving the small band of guerrillas who have, in the space of seventy hours, become his surrogate family. Marxist critics like Alvah Bessie had rightly complained that the novel did not fulfill the promise of its title, taken from John Donne's famous sermon ("No man is an Island . . ."), by affirming the value of universal brotherhood. But *For Whom the Bell Tolls* does affirm the value of belonging to and sharing with a family (a word which Hemingway several times applies to Pablo's irregulars).

The point is emphasized through the metaphor of the gift. When Jordan first reaches the band, he jealously guards what is his. Upon meeting the newcomer, Pablo immediately assumes that the dynamite is a gift for his use. "How much have you brought me?" he asks. But Jordan replies, "I have brought you none." He answers Agustín's similar query, "Whose is the dynamite?" with the curt reply, "Mine." Jordan is also possessive about his absinthe. He tells Maria and Pablo that he cannot offer them any because he has so little left. When Rafael presses him for a taste, he grudgingly concurs: "Robert Jordan pushed the cup toward him. It was a milky yellow now with the water and he hoped the gypsy would not take more than a swallow."

After sharing danger and disappointment during his three days in the mountains, however, Jordan learns to put aside his selfishness and becomes "completely integrated" with the band. One of his teachers is the valiant El Sordo, whose generosity vividly contrasts with the American's possessiveness. He kindly procures a bottle of whisky for Jordan, and immediately offers him the use of his own dwindling supply of dynamite. Another is Pilar, who presents Jordan with the incomparable gift of Maria and love.

As his education progresses, Jordan willingly shares his absinthe with Anselmo and seals his faith in Pablo, who returns to engage in the climactic action of blowing the bridge, by offering him a drink of whisky from his flask. Pablo had deserted the band temporarily, largely because of his own covetousness about the horses, but he returns, overcome with loneliness, to become its leader once more. For the duration of the conflict, at least, Robert Jordan belongs to the guerrilla family. Thus he helps Pilar and Maria comfort Joaquin in his grief:

> "I am thy sister," Maria said. "And I love thee and thou hast a family. We are all thy family."
> "Including the *Inglés*," boomed Pilar. "Isn't it true, *Inglés*?"
> "Yes," Robert Jordan said to the boy. "We are all thy family, Joaquin."

He remains behind to cover the retreat of Maria and the others at the end, and so makes the ultimate gift of self. "Each one does what he can," he thinks as he lies crippled. "You can do nothing for yourself but perhaps you can do something for another."

Yet Jordan *does* do a good deal for himself in staying behind: he regains the dignity and self-respect which his own father had failed to bequeath to him. Visions of his brave grandfather and cowardly father course through his brain during his last hours, and it is only as one man alone that he can redeem the suicide of the father he cannot forgive. Like Anselmo, who, having been brought up in religion, misses God but realizes that "now a man must be responsible to himself," Jordan understands that the final test is within. Lying alone the day before the attack, he had longed for a squirrel in his pocket, "anything he could touch." But in his final agony, awaiting Lieutenant Berrendo and certain death, he sends his love away and cannot even find the flask for liquor's surcease against pain. "Where I go now," he tells Maria before embarking on his final voyage, "I go alone." As Harry Morgan and Philip Rawlings had. As all Hemingway heroes must.

In Dispraise of Government

For a brief period after the fall of Madrid, Ernest Hemingway's name cropped up on letterheads or lists of the famous who supported leftist causes. A few days in advance of the 1939 Hitler-Stalin pact, for instance, his name appeared with many others in newspaper advertisements advocating friendlier relations with Russia. Then, early in 1940, a letter went out over his signature requesting funds to fight "anti-alien" bills before Congress. It was natural that left-wingers should turn to him for such support, since he had openly committed so much of his time and money to the Spanish Republic's cause—so much that he was subsequently on a State Department "gray list" along with others who had been too enthusiastic about the Loyalists. After *For Whom the Bell Tolls*, however, and despite his service as correspondent and part-time soldier in World War II's struggle against fascism, Hemingway was no longer courted by the communists. And for his own part, in both public and private writings, he increasingly reasserted his cynical distaste for all politicians, re-emphasized his abiding lack of faith in governmental solutions to social problems, and reaffirmed his personal and artistic independence from all political parties and ideologies.

> "My Colonel, I have so little political development that I believe all honorable men are honorable."
> "Oh you'll get over that," the colonel assured him. "Don't worry boy. You've got a young party. Naturally you make errors."

This dialogue from *Across the River and into the Trees*—between the wise, experienced Colonel Cantwell and the naïve, young night porter at the Gritti Palace—reflects Hemingway's abiding distrust of "honorable" politicians. He had known several varieties of the breed, he wrote Harvey Breit in 1950, including the self-confessed patriot, the traitor, the regulator of other people's lives, and the regimentator, and they had all left him feeling as if he had been drinking out of a spittoon.

Colonel Cantwell develops a similar metaphor in explaining to Renata why he can't be President of the United States: he's never been an unsuccessful haberdasher, he doesn't have to sit on telephone books to have his picture taken, and he isn't "a no-fight general." The country, he continues, is "governed by what you find in the bottom of dead beer glasses that whores have dunked their cigarettes in." The only presidential candidate he'd ever voted for, Hemingway insisted in his letters of this period, was Eugene V. Debs. After Debs died, he'd retired from the giddy political whirl.

Hemingway was particularly outraged by the spectacle of congressmen setting themselves up as judges on the loyalty of their constituents. If he were called before the House Un-American Activities Committee (HUAC), he wrote Buck Lanham, he would tell them he wasn't and had never been a communist, declare his complete contempt for them, point out that he had known only four honest congressmen in thirty years, and deliver his judgment that a congressman, as a congressman, ranked slightly lower than snakeshit. The trouble was that you couldn't get decent people to run for office since it was hopeless working against the two rotten machines, Democratic and Republican.

As for Senator Joseph McCarthy, Hemingway amused himself after his 1954 plane crashes in Africa by wishing that the senator had accompanied him. "I have always had a certain curiosity, as one has about all public figures," he explained, "as to how Senator McCarthy would behave in what we call the clutch. Doubtless he would be admirable but I have always had this fleeting curiosity. I wondered if without his senatorial immunity he would be vulnerable to the various beasts with whom we had been keeping company." And in Hemingway's posthumously published account of the safari that preceded the crashes, the British white hunter Pop refuses to be informed about McCarthy, since "there are enough disgusting things in life without me having to read about the Senator whatever his name is."

Hemingway's feelings about the Cuban revolution of the late 1950s were mixed. On the one hand, he certainly disliked and disapproved of Batista, whose gang, he estimated, had looted the island of from $600 to $800 million, and whose soldiers on a predawn patrol of his Finca Vigia had brutally killed his dog Machakos. Under the circumstances, the rebels presented an attractive alternative. But by late 1958, he wrote his son Patrick, he "was fed" on living in a country where no one was right and both sides atrocious. He knew about the abuses of the Batista regime, but he also knew about the repression and murder that the insurgent government would bring. The future looked dark; confidentially, he was considering pulling out of Cuba. With Cuban politics as with American, Hemingway's attitude boiled down to: a plague on both your houses.

Many Cubans were desperately poor, but he could see no remedy, personal or political, for their condition. Thomas Hudson, the artist-protagonist of *Islands in the Stream*, used to take a drink along with him on the ride to Havana, for he needed the liquor to ward off the sight of "poverty, dirt, four-hundred-year-old dust, the nose-snot of children, cracked palm fronds, roofs made from hammered tin, the shuffle of untreated syphilis, sewage in the old beds of brooks, lice on the bare necks of infested poultry, scale on the backs of old men's necks, the smell of old women, and the full-blast radio. . . ." Once the girl he had been married to—Martha Gellhorn probably sat for this portrait—had tried to do something about it. She had stopped the car and given an old woman twenty dollars to "help her find a better place to live and to buy something to eat." Instead, the old woman stayed in her lean-to hovel and bought a dog who probably died, Hudson's chauffeur later guesses, of malnutrition, since "they have nothing to eat." "We must," Hudson sarcastically proposes, "get them another dog."

No one would call Hemingway a sophisticated political thinker, but Dos Passos was wrong to conclude that he "had no consistent political ideas." From adolescence to old age, his ideas were remarkably consistent. To give them a contemporary label, they were the ideas of conservative Republicanism, and probably were ingrained in Hemingway as a young man by his Republican parents and especially by the admired paternal grandfather who never in his life sat at a table knowingly with a Democrat.

These ideas stemmed from the main currents of American political thought—principally from the libertarian tradition of Jefferson and Emerson, salted by the philosophical pessimism of Hamilton and Henry Adams. With the Transcendentalists, Hemingway thought that government could provide no panaceas for social ills. What was needed was a whole man, uncompartmentalized, unspecialized, a modern Man Thinking—a god to drive the half-gods out of the political arena as a great bullfighter would drive the fake messiahs from the bull ring. But everywhere he looked, he encountered only fake messiahs: FDR the weakling, Truman the failed haberdasher, Eisenhower the "no-fight" general, and Richard Nixon, the prospect of whose ascendancy moved Hemingway devoutly to wish, in 1953, for Eisenhower's continued good health. Bad to begin with, these men invariably worsened once they gained power. "Power," Hemingway agreed with Adams, was "poison."

Like Jefferson, he could welcome the idea of integration into a small group or family or village while still expounding the virtues of as little government as possible. Ideally, the individual man, like the individual family, should be left alone to confront his destiny. The HUAC and McCarthy offended Hemingway by riding roughshod over the guarantees of individual freedom in the Bill of Rights. One of the worst things about Cuba in the late 1950s was that eventually there would be no freedom "coastwise" for the sailor and fisherman. Fascism represented the most repressive government, but all governments stifled and confined the individual. Thus the paranoid suspicions of Hemingway's last years, that the FBI and IRS were lurking in every shadow ready to clap him into jail, derived from a consistent pattern in his political thinking.

At the root of his support for individual liberty lay a longing for a golden, mythical past when each man (for Hemingway as for Jefferson, the self-sufficient man) lived free, unencumbered, and in harmony with nature. This ideal closely approximates the one which Hemingway's heroes seek, and do not find, in the complicated modern universe of his fiction. As the Marxist Christopher Caudwell accusingly put the case, Hemingway followed "the classic bourgeois party-line: 'Back to the Golden Age, back to the simple, natural, uncorrupted man, free from social restraints.'" Back his heroes went in quest of the territory behind, but restraints forever impinged, and could be escaped only at the moment of death, when the heart beat to the sway of the Gulf Stream or against the pine-needled floor of a Spanish forest.

vi

War

War Lover and Hater

Fresh off the ship in June 1918 Ernest Hemingway spent his first night in Paris chasing destruction. The Germans' Big Bertha was dropping shells on the city, and Ernest, with Ted Brumback, hired a taxicab to hurtle toward the sound of one explosion after another. Finally a shell landed near them, and they went to bed full of the adventure ahead. They had come to Europe to serve as Red Cross ambulance drivers, and to learn about war.

The ambulance service, as Malcolm Cowley pointed out in *Exile's Return*, offered an excellent position from which to develop a "spectatorial" attitude toward the war, for the drivers were officially noncombatants, traveling on the fringes of the battle, relatively immune from injury. So it was for young Hemingway, until he volunteered to supply Italian soldiers at the front with chocolate and cigarettes. Then, at Fossalta on the Piave, shortly after midnight on July 8, an Austrian Minenwerfer canister exploded in a forward trench and lodged 237 mortar fragments in his feet and legs. Somehow, despite these injuries, he carried another more seriously wounded man a hundred and fifty yards to the command post before collapsing; en route, a heavy machine-gun bullet ripped through his right knee.

Though later he wrote that he had "died then" and though as he

125

lay awaiting medical help among the dead and dying he contemplated suicide, Hemingway survived to revisit the scene of his wound, both in fiction and actuality. In *Across the River and into the Trees*, Colonel Cantwell returns to Fossalta, where he too had been wounded, and deposits his feces, and a ten thousand-lira note, as a memento of the occasion. Ernest's own private pilgrimage, in 1923, was less defiantly successful. Nothing was as he remembered it. The grass was green, the river blue, the wrecked houses rebuilt and occupied by those who'd spent the war as refugees in Sicily; there was almost no sign that men had fought and bled and died there. You could not, he wrote Bill Horne, go back to old things and expect to find them the same.

Nor was the setting the only thing that had changed. For many years after that night on the Piave, Hemingway was afraid of the death-dealing dark. Like Nick Adams in "Now I Lay Me" and "A Way You'll Never Be," two stories about his trauma, Ernest feared that if he ever shut his eyes in the dark and let himself go, his soul would fly out of his body like a handkerchief. Eventually his wounds healed, though he walked stiffly on his right leg, and eventually he was able to sleep without a night light; but that first terrifying wound had a lasting effect on Ernest Hemingway. His injury at Fossalta hardly provided the only key to unlock his writing and his personality (certainly he was not "destroyed" by his wound, a theory Hemingway labeled as so much "shit"). But he did abandon there his romantic concept of combat, to be replaced by a healthy disillusionment about war in general and World War I in particular.

A Farewell to Arms supplies Hemingway's most extended fictional statement of this disillusionment. Frederic Henry enlists in the Italian army for no better reason than that he is in Italy and understands the language. He does not join up in search of adventure; presumably, although he repudiates the abstract rhetoric in which the Allies clothe their cause, he thinks that the cause is just and that he will be useful as an officer in charge of ambulances. Very early on, however, he discovers his own insignificance. He goes on leave, and upon his return finds that "the whole thing seemed to run better" while he was away. Soon thereafter Frederic encounters an Italian soldier who has purposely slipped his truss to avoid returning to the front. Borrowing from Stephen Crane, Hemingway has Frederic suggest to the soldier that he "fall down by the road and get a bump" on the head, but though the soldier follows instructions and bloodies himself, his red badge does not work for him, and he is sent back to the front. "Jesus Christ," says the soldier, who has learned some demotic American in the States, "ain't this a goddam war?"

It is indeed, and Frederic takes a rather cynical view of it. All he knows is that he is stationed in a "very fine" house in a "very nice" town where the nightly routine is to bait the priest at dinner, get pleasantly drunk afterward, and adjourn to the government whorehouse for officers. The "Schio Country Club," Hemingway and his fellow volunteer ambulance drivers had christened their first Italian post, and it is much the same in Gorizia before the Austrians counterattack. The Italian is the "silly" front, the "picturesque" front, and to invest it with a spurious air of mystery Frederic sends off postcards to America with everything crossed out except, "I am well." He feels oddly uninvolved: "Well, I knew I would not be killed. Not in this war. It did not have anything to do with me. It seemed no more dangerous than war in the movies," he reflects, but at once adds that he "wished to God that it was over." If the war were over, he could travel to Austria, the Black Forest, the Hartz Mountains, Spain. The war has interrupted his Grand Tour.

Moreover, the conduct of the war seems idiotic, as in a B movie full of overacting. Frederic and his companions are supposed to wear steel helmets, even in Gorizia, "but they were uncomfortable and too bloody theatrical in a town where the civilian inhabitants had not been evacuated." At least these helmets fit, however, while the infantrymen doing battle with the Austrians are issued helmets so big that they come "down almost over the ears." Similarly the ambulance officers are "required to wear an automatic pistol" which jumps so sharply on firing "that there was no question of hitting anything." The pistol is window-dressing, and Frederic feels vaguely ashamed of carrying it when he meets English-speaking people. Italians, on the other hand, are fond of decorations, like the bad marble busts in Genoa which are so untrue to life, so "uniformly classical," that one "could not tell anything about them." It is appearances that count; the truth does not impede Rinaldi in his attempt to secure the Medaglia d'Argento for Frederic. Didn't Frederic do anything heroic? Didn't he carry anyone on his back? Didn't he refuse medical attention before the others? No, says Frederic, he was "blown up while we were eating cheese." But it hardly matters. He has been wounded, he is an American, the offensive has been successful, and Rinaldi thinks they can get him the silver. (Hemingway did get the silver—for somewhat better reasons.) It is all sham, as ridiculous as the "used swords" available at the Milanese pawnshop and as unfit for export as the extravagant Italian salute.

The symbols of war—pistol, medal, helmet, salute—take on a shabbiness that parallels the quality of combat generalship. In Frederic's company, no one knows what is going on, though they all speak "with great positiveness and strategical knowledge," and it is no different at the top. Napoleon would have whipped the Austrians, Frederic feels sure: "He never would have fought them in the mountains. He would have let them come down and whipped them around Verona." Still, he thinks, perhaps wars weren't won any more. "Maybe it was another Hundred Years' War." For three years, Catherine Barkley had "looked forward very childishly to the war ending at Christmas," but now she looks forward to the time when their son will be a lieutenant commander or a general or both. "If it's a hundred years' war he'll have time to try both of the services."

Under the circumstances, patriotism seems out of place, and indeed most of the patriots whom Frederic meets are at considerable distance from the combat zone. In Milan he encounters the barber who, mistaking him for an Austrian, warns the lieutenant that the razor is sharp and refuses payment: "I am not at the front. But I am an Italian." The X-ray doctor hates Austrians and asks Frederic how many he has killed. "I had not killed any but I was anxious to please—and I said I had killed plenty." The incompetent doctor who recommends a six months' delay before operating on Frederic's knee misunderstands his impatience with typical civilian wrongheadedness:

"You are in such a hurry to get back to the front?"
"Why not?"
"It is very beautiful," he said. "You are a noble young man."

The man who makes silhouettes takes pleasure in doing Lieutenant Henry wearing his cap ("it will be more military"), and like the barber will not accept payment. From across the ocean Frederic's grandfather sends money and patriotic encouragement.

The sole legitimate hero Frederic meets is Ettore Moretti, an Italian from San Francisco, who takes a vocal and persistent pride in his battlefield accomplishments and the honors—three wound stripes, four medals, an anticipated promotion to captain—that he has accumulated. "You're a great boy, Ettore," the man from the American consulate sums him up. "But I'm afraid you're a militarist." Ettore is not fighting for his country, but for personal reward, and would cheerfully shift to the American army where the pay is better. Stupidly, he assumes that Lieutenant Henry is a genuine hero like himself. He is a terribly conceited bore, "a dreadful, dreadful boy really," whose only talent is for killing.

As a hero Ettore practices skills which in peacetime would probably land him behind bars. During the war, however, normal prohibitions against lawbreaking collapse. Catherine gives Frederic a Saint Anthony medal for luck, but after he is wounded the charm has disappeared: "Some one probably got it at one of the dressing stations." He loses his revolver in the same way, and when purchasing a replacement realizes that it too had probably been stolen.

As an officer, Frederic attempts to maintain a certain moral order among his men. But they have no stomach for the war, and he himself has less and less, after his wound and after discovering that medical equipment and whores, as valuable items of government inventory, will be evacuated ahead of wounded men in the retreat. Once the retreat begins, however, he tries to serve as moral policeman for his unit. He and his men pick up two Italian sergeants as passengers. When these attempt to steal civilian goods, Frederic prevents them. When they attempt to desert rather than work for the group, he shoots one of them. But it does no good, for Bonello, one of his own men, deserts the next day. Finally all moral order descends into chaos at the Tagliamento, where the militant carabinieri are killing all officers who have been separated from their men. Faced with certain execution, Frederic dives into the river and makes his way, eventually, to safety in Switzerland and the arms of Catherine Barkley. He has made his separate peace from an unreasonable and immoral war.

In poems, as in this novel, Hemingway expressed his distaste for the first war. The men who had to fight the war did not die well:

> Soldiers pitch and cough and twitch—
>   All the world roars red and black;
> Soldiers smother in a ditch,
>   Choking through the whole attack.

And what did they die for? They were "sucked in" by empty words and phrases—

> King and country,
> Christ Almighty,
> And the rest.
> Patriotism,
> Democracy,
> Honor—

which spelled death. The bitterness of these outbursts derived from the distinction Hemingway drew between the men on the line and those who started the wars that others had to fight. He had written so much about war, Hemingway explained in an introduction to the 1948 edition of *A Farewell to Arms*, because it constituted the "constant, bullying, murderous, slovenly crime" of his time. But, he added, "it is the considered belief of the writer of this book that wars are fought by the finest people that there are, or just say people, although the closer you are to where they are fighting, the finer people you meet; but they are made, provoked, and initiated by straight economic rivalries and by swine that stand to profit from them." These swine included not only war profiteers, a class that earned his deepest contempt, but also demagogues and dictators who saw in international conflict a way to solidify their tyrannical regimes. Modern warfare was especially hateful because men killed indiscriminately, in cold blood, without so much as a glimpse of the enemy. "If a man has a conscience," Colonel Cantwell considers in *Across the River and into the Trees* "he might think about war power some time."

Judging in retrospect among the wars he had attended, Ernest concluded that only World War II made much sense. Certainly it was the war he most enjoyed, largely because he found such good companionship. After running his spy factory and U-boat hunting operation from Cuba, he went to Europe in 1944 and on July 28, in Normandy, attached himself as war correspondent to the 22nd Regiment, 4th Infantry Division, as it began its struggle to liberate France and invade Germany. In the course of this campaign Ernest made himself useful for his grasp of military terrain and his skill at interrogating prisoners. Though nominally a correspondent, he felt himself an integral part of a military group, and in that group he made several close friends, including particularly the feisty regimental commander, Colonel (later Major General) Buck Lanham. Never before, he later wrote, had he fought in his own language. Never before had he known such fine comrades in arms. Never before had he loved anything so much as he loved the 4th Infantry Division. His days with the regiment on the drive to the German frontier had, he decided, been the happiest of his life.

Despite such personal testimonials, Ernest did not encourage his own sons to participate in wars. He did not advise son Jack to enlist in naval aviation, he wrote Hadley in November 1942; he knew enough about war not to be a cheer leader, and would be glad to be shot himself if it meant that his children would not have to go. In the case of Patrick, he secured a medical statement and urged his son to present it at his preinduction physical for service in the Korean war. Reassuring Patrick that he thought him one of the bravest people he'd ever known, his father emphasized that it would be no disgrace for Patrick to sit out a war he was not in shape to fight. Furthermore, Ernest himself could muster little enthusiasm for the Korean conflict. With the prescience of a man widely read in military history, he was disturbed about the whole Southeast Asia theater. As he observed in July 1950, the British were contained in Malaya and Hong Kong, and the French were committed in Indochina; now, with the Americans going into Korea, each of the allies would end by fighting exactly where the enemy wanted them to fight and against native troops who knew the terrain and could be fed on locally grown rice. The United States would do well to stay out of such wars. In any case, he could promise that he wouldn't be the first man to jump into Northern Korea with the atomic bomb "up his ass."

Intellectually, then, Hemingway understood the idiocy of most wars. Yet, until the Korean war came along, he went to all the wars that were available to him. The question is why.

First of all, a foreign war offered Hemingway an opportunity, for a time, to escape domestic problems and enter an almost entirely masculine world. He knew it was supposed to be a terrible sin to have fun in war, but with good companions like Lanham, Ernest could not help enjoying himself. "I love combat," he used to say—and mean—in 1944. Furthermore, though there is no hard evidence that he ever killed any of the enemy—in World War I he drove ambulances, in subsequent wars he accompanied troops as a correspondent—Hemingway once "confessed" to having killed more than twenty and rationalized away the dealing of death as not only necessary but pleasurable. Killing cleanly, he remarked about hunting and fishing, had "always been one of the greatest enjoyments of a part of the human race" that included himself. Hunting man instead of beast, he believed, could produce still greater thrills.

In going off to war, Hemingway also purchased for himself a measure of superiority, both artistic and moral, over those who had not faced the rigors of combat. Thus he insisted to Scott Fitzgerald, in 1925, that war was the best subject of all to write about, and in *Green Hills of Africa* he elaborated on the point. The experience of war, he observed, offered "a great advantage . . . to a writer. It was one of the major subjects and certainly one of the hardest to write truly of, and those writers who had not seen it were always very jealous and tried to make it seem unimportant, or abnormal, or a disease as a subject, while, really, it was just something quite irreplaceable that they had missed."

When Archibald MacLeish mildly observed in 1940 that such novels as *A Farewell to Arms*, along with Remarque's *All Quiet on the Western Front* and Dos Passos's *Three Soldiers*, had instilled in the younger generation a distrust of all moral judgments and robbed the country of "the only weapon with which fascism [could] be fought— the moral conviction that democracy [was] worth fighting for," Hemingway replied with a bitter *ad hominem* attack to the effect that if MacLeish had fought as he had in Spain, "at Guadalajara, Jarama, Madrid, Teruel, first and second battles of the Ebro, he might feel better." Similarly, when Milton Wolff objected to Hemingway's portrayal of Loyalist atrocities in *For Whom the Bell Tolls*, Ernest responded with the inaccurate assertion that he "was in wars, commanded troops, was wounded, etc." before Wolff was "dry behind the ears."

So vain was Ernest of his supposed participation in combat that he bedeviled Lanham in letters with recurrent fears that twenty years after his death, or ten years after, or even before he died, "they" would deny that he'd ever seen action. For an official noncombatant, Ernest did see a great deal of action; indeed, he was one of the most decorated noncombatants in military history. For his work with the Red Cross in World War I (and his wound), the Italian government awarded him the Croce al Merito di Guerra and the Medaglia d'Argento al Valore Militare. For his "meritorious service" as a war correspondent in World War II, the United States gave him the Bronze Star. And had the

Loyalists won the war in Spain, surely they would not have left Hemingway unrewarded for his labors on their behalf. Among veteran campaigners medals were supposed to be regarded with a mixture of scorn and amusement—he'd thrown his in a drawer with the other scrap metal, Ernest used to say—but in fact as a young man he'd insisted on having wound stripes sewn on and medals attached to his Red Cross uniform before he would show himself in Milan, and in 1944 he complained to Lanham that he deserved not the dime-a-dozen Bronze Star but the much rarer Distinguished Service Cross for his World War II exploits. Mutely, a DSC would have testified to his courage and endurance in sweating out, among men he regarded with infinite love and compassion, some of the ruggedest days of combat that World War II had to offer.

Tests of Bravery

Most of all, going to war appealed to Ernest Hemingway because combat provided an ideal opportunity to test his private supply of courage. To sportswriter Jimmy Cannon, Hemingway seemed "like a man moving across dangerous terrain who knew that he was in the sights of a sniper and acted accordingly." He courted his danger, whether acquired vicariously while watching bullfights, or closer at hand while big-game hunting, when one might wait to sniff the lion's breath before squeezing off the trigger, but nowhere more persistently than under combat conditions. When he observed a similar propensity in others, Ernest recognized it as an indication of cowardice rather than bravery. Consider, he wrote, Mussolini's penchant for dueling: "Really brave men do not have to fight duels, and many cowards duel constantly to make themselves believe they are brave." But he did not see the parallel when he systematically exposed himself to mortal peril. That kind of danger, he thought, could purify a man.

This is not to say that Ernest practiced or condoned the foolhardy pursuit of thrills. (Indeed, during World War II he was outraged when a fellow correspondent recklessly paraded on the crest of a hill near Houffalize, Belgium, inviting fire from German batteries and endangering himself and his companions.) But over the years, Hemingway cultivated an impressive stoicism in the face of adversity. During the shelling of Madrid in 1937 he persuaded himself that fascist shells could not, mathematically, hit his room at the Hotel Florida, a doubtful position he calmly held to while the walls cracked and plaster fell from a series of close calls. Similarly he held his ground in September 1944 while dining with Lanham and other officers in the colonel's command post in Germany. As they prepared to eat, an 88 shell, traveling at the speed of sound and so giving no warning, ripped through one wall and out the other without exploding. All Lanham's men promptly "disappeared into a small potato cellar," but Ernest stolidly sat at table, cutting his meat and drinking his wine. When urged to take cover, Ernest reiterated his theory "that you were as safe in one place as another under artillery fire unless you were being shot at personally." Eventually the firing subsided, and the rest of the group came up from shelter to finish the meal. Some weeks later he once again maintained a monumental calm while, during the last of the fighting in Hürtgen Forest, a German plane strafed the ditch where he and correspondent Willie Walton had taken cover.

The behavior of men under stress was an endlessly fascinating topic of conversation for Hemingway, one he explored at length with professional soldiers, hunters, and bullfighters. He had learned from personal experience, he told Philip Percival on safari in 1933, "what it meant to be a coward and what it was to cease being a coward." Having conquered his fears, he took a hard line toward those who could not cast off their own. He'd always hated cowards, he wrote Lanham, and he did not feel any sympathy for victims of combat nerves or battle fatigue. The idea that each man had his psychological breaking point, Ernest regarded as so much hogwash: either he had guts or he didn't.

The first duty of a man, he believed, was to subdue fear, and he developed a full-scale theory of the best ways to accomplish that end. The essential requirement was a sense of personal pride and dignity. Given this quality, a man could prevent the onset of debilitating terror in several separate ways. First of all, he could learn not to think, not to conjure up dreadful images of what might happen. "Learning to suspend your imagination and live completely in the very second of the present minute with no before and no after is the greatest gift a soldier can have." Another secret of courage was to conceive a temporary hatred for the enemy. The recommended procedure involved taking a fairly deep breath, and saying, "Fuck you, you cocksuckers." Then nothing on earth could hurt you. A third technique was to concen. rigidly on the job at hand, since if you were thinking about what you were doing you couldn't be afraid. From Shakespeare came a literary rationale for casting off the fear of death, one Ernest heard first from Chink Dorman-Smith in 1918 and quoted approvingly both in "The Short Happy Life of Francis Macomber" and in his 1942 introduction to *Men at War*: "By my troth, I care not; a man can die but once: we owe God a death . . . and let it go which way it will, he that dies this year is quit for the next."

Nostrums like these, Hemingway maintained, helped him shake off the kind of fear that had, in World War I, made him sick to his stomach and so heavy in the legs that he had to force himself to move. "I was afraid as the next man in my time and maybe more so," he wrote. "But with the years fear had come to be regarded as a form of stupidity to be classed with overdrafts, acquiring a venereal disease or eating candies." Unnecessary fear, he concluded, was a child's vice; having overcome it, the only thing to be afraid of "was the presence of true and imminent danger in a form that you should be aware of and not be a fool if you were responsible for others." In the presence of such danger, a prickle came over the top of his head as a warning, and that "prickling was all that remained of the vast capacity for fear that some brave men start with."

If, as Harold Loeb once speculated, there are two kinds of courage—"the reflex courage of the man who knows no fear, and the acquired courage of the man who knows and overcomes"—Hemingway's was the second kind. When he was but three years old, Ernest began insisting he was *"fraid a nothing,"* but that was whistling in the dark. In his notebooks, Scott Fitzgerald characterized Ernest as a "reckless, adventurous" boy, but immediately added: "Yet it is undeniable that the dark was peopled for him." Indeed, the two protagonists in his fiction who are most clearly autobiographical in character and personality—Nick Adams of his first book and Thomas Hudson of his last—were both afraid of the dark in their boyhood, though only Hudson, in *Islands in the Stream*, admits to the weakness. In the case of Nick, Hemingway deleted the first few pages of "Indian Camp," the story which opens *In Our Time*, where the boy is depicted as terribly fearful of being left alone in the woods at night. Taken camping by his father and uncle, Nick stays in the tent while the two adults do some night fishing. Then in the awful silence he begins to think about dying, and fires the three rifle shots that, by prearrangement, will bring his father to his side. To justify his signal, Nick claims that a mysterious animal, "a cross between a fox and a wolf," has been fooling around the tent. Uncle George, an enthusiastic fisherman, is disgusted at the lie, but Dr. Adams is forgiving. "I know he's an awful coward," he says, "but we're all yellow at that age."

In other coming-of-age stories, Nick emerges as a rather apprehensive young man who sidesteps trouble whenever he can. Riding the rails in "The Battler," Nick is slugged by a brakeman and then comes across the punch-drunk prizefighter Ad Francis and his Negro companion Bugs. "You're a tough one, aren't you?" Francis asks him. "No," Nick answers. In "The Light of the World," Nick extricates himself and Tommy, his tough-talking companion, from one potential scrape after another. In a town in northern Michigan the youths meet a belligerent bartender who is loath to let them eat the free lunch of pickled pig's feet:

> "Put it back," said the bartender.
> "You know where," said Tom.
> The bartender reached a hand forward under the bar, watching us both. I put fifty cents on the wood and he straightened up.
> "What was yours?" he said.
> "Beer," I said, and before he drew the beer he uncovered both the [free-lunch] bowls.

But Nick's ameliorative gesture does not keep Tommy from picking another quarrel:

> "Your goddam pig's feet stink," Tom said, and spit what he had in his mouth on the floor. The bartender didn't say anything. The man who had drunk the rye paid and went out without looking back.
> "You stink yourself," the bartender said. "All you punks stink."
> "He says we're punks," Tommy said to me.
> "Listen," I said. "Let's get out."

In this fictional tandem, it is Tommy's role to invite trouble and make smart answers, Nick's to smooth things over. Thus at their next stop, the railroad station, where the boys encounter a homosexual cook and three whores, the cook asks how old they are and this dialogue follows:

> "I'm ninety-six and he's sixty-nine," Tommy said.
> "Ho! Ho! Ho!" the big whore shook with laughing. She had a really pretty voice. The other whores didn't smile.
> "Oh, can't you be decent?" the cook said. "I asked just to be friendly."
> "We're seventeen and nineteen," I said.
> "What's the matter with you?" Tommy turned to me.
> "That's all right."

In "Night Before Landing," the beginning section of Hemingway's early and abortive attempt to write a novel about World War I, Nick and a companion, en route to the war in Europe, climb out onto a lifeboat to talk and drink wine on the last night of the voyage. Though the climb is not difficult, Nick is frightened of falling, and he is sure he will be scared and no good in combat. In order to stave off such fears, Nick later reveals in "A Way You'll Never Be," he used to get drunk before every attack. Then, like his creator, he suffers his wound, makes his separate peace, and is visited by nightmares about being blown up in the dark. Despite such traumas, Nick apparently learns from his war-time experiences. Certainly, in "The Killers," he tries to be brave, taking it upon himself—however futilely—to warn Ole Andreson that the hired murderers have come to town. And his protagonists after Nick are customarily more courageous than Hemingway himself, whose personal fear of the dark, as well as his phobia about snakes, lasted for at least the first forty years of his life.

In his fiction, then, Hemingway set forth a standard of courage which anyone, including himself, would find it difficult to live up to. His acute sensitivity to reflections on his own bravery, furthermore, suggests his awareness of the discrepancy between fiction and fact. Thus Gertrude Stein, who understood where to place her barbs, outraged Ernest by referring to him, in *The Autobiography of Alice B. Toklas*, as "yellow." Rather more innocently, during a May 1947 talk at the University of Mississippi, William Faulkner roused Ernest's wrath by suggesting that he was less courageous, in the pursuit of his craft, than other writers. Asked to name the best contemporary novelists, Faulkner had listed Thomas Wolfe, Dos Passos, Erskine Caldwell, Hemingway, and himself. Among these he ranked Wolfe highest since he had been the most courageous, taken the most chances, in his fiction. By the same criterion, Faulkner ranked Hemingway last because he "stayed with what he knew. He did it fine, but he didn't try for the impossible." Incensed by what he took to be an accusation of cowardice, Hemingway immediately enlisted Buck Lanham as a champion to bear witness to his personal bravery. Importuned to write a registered letter to Faulkner, Lanham responded with four pages praising Ernest. Hemingway, Buck wrote, was "without exception the most courageous man" he had ever known, in war and peace, since he had both physical courage and "that far rarer commodity, moral courage."

Even as he was composing his letter, Buck was fully aware of the absurdity of the enterprise, for he could see, as Hemingway chose not to, that Faulkner's statement "had no reference whatever to Hemingway as a man: only to his craftmanship as a writer." The incident confirmed Lanham in his suspicion that Ernest lacked a full measure of self-confidence. Once before, in the summer of 1944, Lanham had observed Hemingway behave recklessly in response to a taunt he'd issued himself. During late August, the 4th Division hastily pressed the attack while Ernest enjoyed himself in liberated Paris. On September 1, Lanham's message—"Go hang yourself, brave Hemingstein. We have fought at Landrecies and you were not there" (a modernized version of Henry IV's jibe at the Duke of Crillon after a victory)—reached him, and he started early next morning on a foolhardy, dangerous journey to rejoin his comrades-at-arms. Only a man who did not quite trust himself, Buck decided, would react so violently on so little provocation.

When defending himself against imputations of cowardice, most of them directed from within, Ernest tended to lie like a trooper. Thus he wrote Carlos Baker that because he was not a fearful man, he fully expected that "they" would accuse him of cowardice. But that was nonsense, he went on in a casual lie, for any boy who'd been honorary president of the Unione Siciliano in Chicago at nineteen would not "spook" very easily. In a letter to Lillian Ross, Ernest admitted that he always overreacted when accused of lack of courage, and then, to il-lustrate his point, told a story about World War II fully as untrue as the one about the Unione Siciliano. On the road from Wassigny to Le Cateau, Hemingway wrote, giving his yarn the storyteller's verisimilitude of actual place setting, he'd been in charge of a crew of irregulars, and one of them, a Free French soldier, spotted a German antitank gun and asked Hemingway, "Aren't we going to attack?" When the reply was in the negative, the soldier spat, and Ernest, so challenged, decided to order the attack, which ended by killing six and wounding two of his eighteen men.

Miles Gloriosus

One critic, having finished *Across the River and into the Trees*, suggested that the book's hero should be regarded as a modern avatar of the *miles gloriosus*, or braggart warrior, made sport of in the Roman plays of Plautus. But Hemingway did not intend any such interpretation of Colonel Cantwell. Although his claims of universal knowledge and his calculated toughness of manner may occasionally seem comic, Cantwell is supposed to be taken seriously. Indeed, in his yarning about the wars, the colonel resembles no one more than Ernest Hemingway himself.

At the beginning, perhaps, in the tall tales about World War I which Ernest told for the benefit of the hometown folks, he was having some fun at the expense of gullible civilians. After an interview with the wounded returnee in February 1919, Roselle Dean of the *Oak Parker* reported soberly that "Lieutenant Hemingway submitted to having twenty-eight bullets extracted without taking an anaesthetic. His only voluntary comment on the war is that it was great sport, and he is ready to go on the job if it ever happens again." Two months later the Oak Park high school *Trapeze* printed an account of Ernest's speech to the school assembly, in which he suggested that he had served with the Italian Arditi, a group of devil-may-care soldiers made up (he said) of ex-convicts who had "committed some slight mistake such as—well— murder or arson." The Arditi, according to Hemingway, frequently fought stripped to the waist; one wounded captain, shot in the chest, "plugged the holes with cigarettes" and went on fighting. In time, such whoppers gradually hardened into a legend of the warrior that even Hemingway himself may have believed. The untruth about serving with the Arditi, for example, Ernest communicated to Chink Dorman-Smith; indeed, a book on Hemingway widely read in the United Kingdom today still circulates the fiction that Hemingway began in Italy as a volunteer ambulance driver but later became an infantry officer who "served on the Austrian front from October till the Armistice in November."

In the case of the Spanish Civil War, where Ernest functioned as war correspondent and propagandist on four separate visits, he once more undertook to convert his status to that of active participant. He strongly implied in letters to Lanham that he had actually fought with the Loyalists in 1937, where in the heat of battle the Maxim machine guns had become so overheated that he'd had to lubricate them with urine. So skillful was he in telling such tales that his second wife Pauline believed until her death that Ernest led troops during the Spanish conflict. The writer Vincent Sheean, who'd also worked as a correspondent in Spain, tried to disabuse her of this far-fetched notion. "Ernest was a correspondent for the North American Newspaper Alliance," Sheean said, "that's all." But the second Mrs. Hemingway held her ground, insisting that though Ernest pretended to be merely a correspondent, actually he'd held a high command post with the Loyalists. With R. Sturgis Ingersoll, Ernest claimed more modest rank. In his capacity as a "non-commissioned officer," he told Ingersoll, he had found it necessary to murder a truck driver in the course of shipping the art treasures of the Prado to safety in Switzerland. He also let Ingersoll know that he had fought in the Turkish army because he always hated Greeks. As Sheean concluded, Ernest's inventive capacities were deeply ingrained; he "created such stories as unthinkingly as others breathe" or appropriated others' war stories to his own purposes.

During World War II Hemingway's career as braggart warrior continued. He wrote his son Patrick that he'd landed at Omaha Beach on D-day, and that during the campaign that followed he would have been taken prisoner several times daily but for using his head and his balls. He told Milton Wolff, in exaggeration (but less, this time), that he'd entered Paris "ahead of anybody" and that he'd been present when the Siegfried Line was "busted." He told Charles Scribner, falsely, that he'd shot a German soldier who refused to respond to interrogating. He wrote Mary Welsh an embellished account of one hectic day when he and two companions came under fire from a German antitank gun. Ernest hurt his head and back diving into a ditch for cover, but in the retelling the antitank gun became a tank, and his injuries the consequence of the explosion of a tank shell, which supposedly left him with a bump on the head, a concussion, and double vision. Most, if not all, of this was exaggeration designed to impress Mary; when Ernest checked in to Lanham's command post immediately after the incident, he did not so much as mention any injury to his head.

The details of Ernest's conduct at Rambouillet, shortly before the liberation of Paris, remain somewhat indistinct. But it is certain that he got into trouble for his behavior there, and—in an ironic twist Plautus might have conceived—that in order to extricate himself from a court-martial he was forced to tell untruths which *belittled* rather than magnified his military accomplishments. The telling, naturally, came hard.

A week before the liberation of Paris Hemingway detached himself from the 4th Infantry Division. He did so because he wanted to get as close as possible to the French capital and to be among the first to enter the city. He accomplished both those goals, but in the process broke a number of rules set down at the Geneva Convention for war correspondents. On August 20, in the village of Rambouillet south of Paris, Ernest met and took charge of ten Free French irregulars looking for leadership. Under his direction these men patrolled to gather intelligence on the disposition of German troops and on roadblocks and ambushes they were preparing for the 2nd French Armored Division under General Leclerc, the division chosen for the honor of entering Paris first. In effect, Ernest commanded these irregulars; he worked in shirtsleeves, without displaying his correspondent's insignia; he carried weapons on his person, and his rooms at the Hotel du Grand Veneur housed a small arsenal. Knowing that he was violating the Geneva Convention, he secured a handwritten order from Colonel (later Ambassador) David Bruce of the OSS to justify taking command of the partisans. Bruce complied because Hemingway was useful to him: entirely brave, he possessed "a true scout's instinct" and a rare talent for interrogating prisoners and evaluating their information. In fact, the intelligence that Bruce, Hemingway, and others collected had a good deal to do with the relatively smooth passage of Leclerc's division over the final miles to Paris on August 25. During the preceding five days Ernest was more closely involved in actual warfare than he had ever been. But early in October he was summoned to defend himself before the Inspector General of the Third Army.

Among the accusations against Hemingway, brought by some of his fellow correspondents, were that he had removed his correspondent's badge in order to assume command of Free French forces in

Rambouillet, that he had persistently ordered and directed patrols, that he kept in his quarters "a stock of antipersonnel and antitank grenades, as well as mines, German bazookas, and sundry small arms," that he ran a "map room" in Rambouillet, that a full colonel had acted as his chief of staff, and that he had told another correspondent that he was no longer writing dispatches. Most of the charges were valid. Any of them, if proved, would have sent him back to the United States shorn of his correspondent's accreditation.

But none was proved, for under examination Ernest admitted very little of the truth. If he'd left off his tunic with insignia, it was because of the warm weather and for sanitary purposes. Resistance troops had asked him repeatedly to lead them, but he did not consent, instead merely offering advice to them. If they called him by a military title, it was an affectionate term, like the "Captain" assigned to New England dorymen. He'd stored weapons and ammunition as a convenience for the irregular troops he was advising. He had studied maps and gone on patrols, but only to gather material for his employer, *Collier's* magazine. If he'd issued orders to the irregulars, this was because his French was fluent and he was merely relaying the proper commands of an American colonel. In short, he lied to keep himself, and possibly David Bruce as well, out of trouble.

In explaining why he'd committed perjury, Hemingway told Dorman-O'Gowan (when he was Dorman-Smith) that the Inspector General's man had coached him on how to refute the accusations the night before he testified. But he also told Lanham that General George Patton himself asked him to lie under oath, and told Charles Poore that two of Patton's officers ordered him to deny everything. Probably Ernest needed no help at all in constructing his story, which lay well within the capabilities of his fertile imagination. But he did, without doubt, feel awful about it afterward.

If he'd simply told the truth, Ernest complained to Lanham a few days after his interrogation, he could have gone home a hero, and waited for the Key West Chamber of Commerce or the Havana Pigeon Shooters Club to strike off a medal honoring him. What was worse, he worried that the true story of what he'd done at Rambouillet would be forgotten, and in the early 1950s made a point of telling his version of the tale to Poore and to Carlos Baker, both of whom had expressed an interest in writing books about him. The trouble was that he'd "lied away everything [he] was ever proud of in October 1944," and now he didn't know how to straighten it out, since "false swearing" had a way of complicating the job of historians. Fifty years from now, he feared, some jerk would demonstrate, elaborately, that he'd never been at Rambouillet.

His lying under oath especially rankled because it went against the grain of his other war stories. When his official biographer Baker got around to writing about Ernest's World War II experiences, he relied for his first draft partly on letters that Ernest had written Mary. The result was so widely at variance with the truth that Lanham, reading it for accuracy, became physically ill. Buck could not understand, at the time, why it was that his friend wrote such "a lot of crap" to Mary, or "why of all people" he'd felt the need "to inflate himself," for the Hemingway he'd known during the summer of 1944, a brave man with a sound military mind, was beyond reproach. Some of the stories might have stemmed from the creative imagination at work, but Lanham could not avoid noticing, as Martha Gellhorn had some years before, that almost all of the lies ran in the direction of self-aggrandizement. Ernest had to have his image as "a very, very tough cookie" constantly reinforced. Buck knew better than to challenge him on tales designed to build up that image, but in the end the incessant boastful yarns compromised their friendship. Hemingway was one of those men, he concluded, who was "magnificent in war but insufferable in peace."

vii

Love

First Loves

Perhaps his elder sister Marcelline was right. Perhaps it was a consequence of being brought up in a predominantly female environment ("four sisters, his mother, a nurse-girl and the cook living in the house") that kept her younger brother Ernest from noticing girls. In any case, not until he was a junior in high school—"about time," Marcelline and Mama felt—did Ernest have his first date, and there weren't many dates after that.

Up in Michigan, he saw something of the Indian girl Prudy Boulton during the summers, but whether he knew her in the Biblical sense (as the one who "did first what no one has ever done better") or only so claimed in fictional reminiscence remains a matter of conjecture. What is clear is that Ernest Hemingway's interest in women blossomed rather late, and he was hardly prepared, as a wounded teen-ager, for the shock of falling in love with, and being rejected by, Agnes von Kurowsky. Aggie the Red Cross nurse, Ernie the wounded soldier in war-torn Italy—the ingredients were there for a romantic story, and Hemingway later used them in *A Farewell to Arms* and several short stories. But when Ernest came back to Oak Park in 1918, planning to marry Agnes and waiting impatiently for her to follow since he had only another fifty years or so to live and every minute away from her was wasted, he was

144

madly in love with "that kid" Ag, who was twenty-six years old to his nineteen. Then the months dragged on, the correspondence cooled, and in March 1919 the "Dear Ernest" letter arrived.

At first, the news so devastated young Hemingway as to send him, temporarily ill, to his bed. It may be that he never fully got over his first love. Years later in Paris he told Lincoln Steffens that if Ag came back, he'd have to leave Hadley and Bumby and follow her. But she didn't, and he didn't. He also did not, like the unnamed character in "A Very Short Story," take his juvenile vengeance by contracting "gonorrhea from a sales girl . . . while riding in a taxicab through Lincoln Park." Nor did he "cauterize" his wound, as he claimed to friends in 1919, through a steady diet of "booze and other women."

Ernest began to see other girls after his rejection, but hardly achieved Byronic wickedness while taking Kathryn Longwell canoeing on the Des Plaines River in the spring of 1919 or popping corn and telling tall tales to fourteen-year-old Grace Quinlan at Horton Bay that summer. With one waitress at the Dilworths' cabin, to be sure, he had the sexual encounter vividly described in "Up in Michigan." With another, Marjorie Bump from Petoskey, he formed a close liaison which, according to "The End of Something," almost developed into marriage. When he stayed up north in Michigan into the fall and winter months, however, he saw at least one other girl besides Marjorie. Attending a closed-cottage party, he met and immediately liked Irene Goldstein, who was home from college for the holidays. That evening they threw snowballs, constructed a snow fort, and made snow angels together. Later there were other dates and finally, the next fall, Ernest made a mild pass at her in Y. K. Smith's Chicago apartment.

Y. K. (or Kenley) Smith was the older brother of Bill Smith, Ernest's best friend during the summers in Michigan, and of Katy Smith, who later introduced Hemingway to each of his first two wives. She married his friend John Dos Passos in 1929, and if one takes literally a story called "Summer People," Ernest may have had an affair with her in the summer of 1920. Hemingway did not choose to publish the story during his and Kate's lifetime, for the best of reasons. At the end of "Summer People," which takes place at Horton Bay, a girl and boy make love twice in the forest. The girl is given no fictional disguise whatever, but is called Kate and "Butstein," Hemingway's and her brother Bill's special nickname for Katy Smith. The boy is Nick (Adams), but other characters in the story refer to him exclusively as

"Wemedge," which was Ernest's particular name in the Smith-Hemingway circle. Though the names represent real persons, it does not necessarily follow that the plot of the story mirrors reality. But the least that can be said is that imaginatively Ernest possessed Katy, that he later referred to her as one of the "first girls" he had, and that in the summer of 1921 he wrote Hadley Richardson, his bride-to-be, that one of the things he intended to keep to himself was his relationship with Katy Smith, a remark which inspired Hadley to suggest they should postpone their wedding for a few months.

Katy Smith and Hadley Richardson had both attended Mary Institute, a private school for girls in St. Louis, and when Hadley's mother died after a long illness in the fall of 1920, Katy asked her old school friend to visit her in Chicago. Red-haired Hadley stayed for three weeks, and left behind on her departure a budding romance with the "hurly burly," handsome Hemingway. The next summer, on the Saturday before Labor Day, they were married. Before the wedding Hadley had to overcome doubt which had bothered Agnes and would have troubled Katy, had the question of marriage come up. The three women had one thing very much in common: Agnes and Katy were seven years older than Ernest Hemingway, Hadley was eight.

For the first two or three years, Ernest and Hadley's marriage fairly bloomed. They were deeply in love, which was the only thing "worth a damn" to be; they lived in Paris, or went skiing in the Austrian Alps, or traveled to the bullfights in Spain; they were "poor" without really being deprived of anything that really mattered. Then came the discovery, in midsummer of 1923, that Hadley was pregnant. According to Gertrude Stein, this led Ernest to announce bitterly that he was "too young to be a father." According to his friend Guy Hickok, Ernest grumbled angrily in a conversation about birth control that there was "no sure preventative." In a July 1923 letter to Bill Horne, Ernest presented the dilemma more dispassionately. The baby was due in October, they were hoping for a boy, and he wanted Bill to act as godfather. Both he and Hadley were "crazy about" the idea of the baby, though it did mean they'd have to change their style of life. When it was only the two of them, it didn't much matter if they were broke, but Ernest figured he'd need a steady income during the "First Year of the Baby." Yet as soon as the baby got old enough, Ernest added, he'd have to take his or her chances with the rest of the family. The Hemingways' child, whom they called Bumby, turned out to be one of the most cheerful and healthy baby boys ever born. When he was but three months old, his parents decided, he was old enough to sail back to Europe, where, with the concierge's wife and F. Puss, the cat, looking after him, Ernest and Hadley were virtually as unrestricted in movement as they had ever been. Their marriage, in short, proved strong enough to survive a most agreeable child. But in 1925, with the appearance of the Other Woman, the bond that tied Ernest to Hadley began to weaken.

The Other Woman's name might have been—but probably wasn't—Lady Duff Twysden, the model for Brett Ashley in *The Sun Also Rises*. Ernest found Duff one of the most attractive women he'd ever met, fun, down-to-earth, good-looking, sexy, the best of drinking companions. Certainly the two achieved a degree of intimacy. Twice she applied to him, through notes left with bartenders, for personal loans. Fascinated as ever by the mechanics of how to go about things, Ernest copied down in his notebooks fragments culled from Duff's advice on the dangerous art of adultery. "You must make fantastic statements to cover things," she instructed. The thing to do was to have many admirers "so no one will know there is some one you love." Hemingway was jealous and upset when she went off for a weekend with Harold Loeb, and took his revenge on Loeb, as Robert Cohn, in *The Sun Also Rises*. But whether Duff and Ernest actually had an affair is doubtful, for as she also said for him to copy down, "We can't do it. You can't hurt people. It's what we believe in in place of God." Hadley herself, considering the question thirty-five years later, concluded that probably there was no affair, though as she pointed out she could hardly be sure: "That isn't the kind of a thing a husband talks to his wife about too much, don't you agree?"

About the relationship between Ernest and Pauline Pfeiffer, Hadley could not for long remain in doubt. "Everyone knew," as Hadley later recalled, that Pauline had come to Europe to find a husband. The one she found was Hadley's.

When they first met over drinks with Harold Loeb and Kitty Cannell in March 1925, Ernest was less taken with Pauline than with her sister Jinny, and Pauline thought Ernest rather lazy and unkempt. But in a few weeks' time, Pauline was playing adolescent ego-building games ("I was talking with so-and-so about you") for his benefit. In the fall when John Dos Passos and others expressed reservations about *The Torrents of Spring*, Hemingway's satirical attack on Sherwood Anderson, Pauline proclaimed it a masterpiece. For Christmas 1925 she journeyed to Schruns, where Ernest, wintering with his family, taught her to ski. In the summer of 1926 she ignored the quarantine on Bumby's whooping cough to stay with Ernest and Hadley at Juan-les-Pins on the Riviera. Such perseverance had its reward. In September 1926 Hadley agreed to a divorce, provided that Pauline and Ernest would first separate for one hundred days; in January 1927 the divorce became final, and in May Ernest and Pauline ("Pfife," as he called her) were married.

Not Getting Over Hadley

When Ernest broke faith with Hadley, he committed, in his own eyes, a sin which he was never able to expiate, though he tried to the end of his life. Ernest's first reaction was to excoriate himself. The divorce, he wrote Fitzgerald, was entirely his fault; he was a son of a bitch. Hadley, had been a perfect wife, lovely, loving, and understanding—a judgment which everyone who knew her seemed to share: if *he'd* had a son who married Hadley, Donald Ogden Stewart observed nearly half a century later, he'd have been "the happiest father in the world." In a letter to Pauline during their enforced period of separation, Ernest spoke of committing suicide in order to release her from the prospect of sinning against Hadley and to relieve Hadley of the pain of divorcing him. He was prepared to go to Hell, he wrote, in preference to the hell on earth he'd made of life for all three of them.

In his anguish, Ernest was anything but reassured by a letter from his friend Mike Strater, who told him that "all men of genius" were immoral and that therefore he might as well go on leading "an old-fashioned immoral life." That he could not do. Indeed, it may have been Hemingway's puritanical streak that made the divorce inevitable. If he hadn't been brought up in "that damned stuffy Oak Park environment," Hadley remarked to friends in 1929, perhaps he wouldn't have felt it incumbent on him to rush out and marry Pauline. Both his son Jack and his last wife Mary offered a similar explanation for Hemingway's four marriages and three divorces. As a healthy man, Mary said,

Ernest naturally had "more than one dame." But "in those days, people were more or less committed to marry the woman they wanted to shack up with." Hence, Ernest three times "faithfully got rid of one" wife in order to marry the woman he was having an affair with. It made for a complicated life. "Hemingway's mistake," William Faulkner remarked on hearing of Ernest's suicide, "was that he thought he had to marry all of them."

As a form of settlement with Hadley, who had supported him with her love and money during their years together, Ernest not only arranged for the royalties from *The Sun Also Rises*, both American and British, to be sent to her but also wrote a will which provided for all income from other books, past or future, to go to Bumby. Later these guarantees were amended to accommodate other times, other children, other wives; and even in 1927, when his books had not yet begun to sell and he was about to marry a rich woman, Ernest's conscience can hardly have been much assuaged by the financial sacrifice he proposed. Neither self-flagellation nor dollars could make things right. Time and again, in stories, novels, nonfiction, in letters, he returned to touch the still-festering wound.

The passage of time, in this case, only heightened the nostalgic glow surrounding his marriage to Hadley, so that the theme of paradise lost emerges most powerfully in the last books Ernest wrote. In *A Moveable Feast*, he attempts to transfer the blame for the breakup from himself to Pauline and the rich, but the tenderest and most convincing moments in the book evoke the joy of being young and in love in Paris with wife, child, and cat, and the agony of getting to love another, "new and strange," girl as well. Early in 1926, for example, Ernest returned to his family in the Vorarlberg after having dallied in Paris with Pauline: "When I saw my wife again standing by the tracks as the train came in by the piled logs at the station, I wished I had died before I ever loved anyone but her." As he wrote in *Death in the Afternoon*, he "would sooner have the pox than fall in love with another woman loving the one I have" (by then it was Pauline).

A similar strain of regret runs through Hemingway's posthumously published novel, *Islands in the Stream*. There, Thomas Hudson has much the same family situation as his creator. He has been divorced from each of his first two wives, who have between them borne him three sons. Now, living alone except for occasional visits from his sons, he is consumed with sorrow about the loss of "Tom's mother," his first wife and the only woman he ever really loved. The happiest times, like those in *A Moveable Feast*, were the days in Paris when they rode bicycles through the Bois and drank the double-size drinks served by the friendly waiter at the Closerie des Lilas. Hudson wishes he were still married to Tom's mother and worries his loss again and again. "But why did I ever leave Tom's mother in the first place? You'd better not think about that, he told himself. That is one thing you had better not think about." Even an unsympathetic reviewer of *Islands in the Stream* pointed out that there was "something moving in his [Hudson's] desperate attempt to survive, to cope with the rending loss of his first wife, of youth in Paris." That emotion came as truly from the heart as Ernest's reminiscence in "African Journal," another posthumously published work, of a magical trip to Switzerland with his first wife. His fourth wife, Mary, accompanies him on safari, but at night Hemingway's dreams take him back in nostalgia to Hadley and remorse and guilt:

> The wife I had loved first and best and who was the mother of my oldest son was with me and we were sleeping close together to keep warm and because that was the best way to sleep if both people love each other and it is a cold night. . . . I had bad dreams then as a residue, or inheritance, from a badly organized war, and sleep, or his brother death, were all that interested me at night. That was, of course, after we had slept together. . . . But tonight, in the dream, I slept happily with my true love in my arms and her head firmly under my chin and when I woke I wondered about how many true loves to which you were faithful, until you were unfaithful, a man could have and I thought about the strange strictures of morality in different countries and who it was that could make a sin a sin.

In his fiction written during and immediately after his marriage to Hadley, Ernest dealt subtly and indirectly with the cause for their breakup. In story after early love story, he depicted the male of the species—himself, at one remove—as unwilling to share, to give, to take responsibility. In "Cat in the Rain," for instance, a childless expatriate couple spend a rainy day in an Italian hotel. The obviously frustrated wife longs for affection, for someone—even a stray cat—to love, but her husband lies on the bed reading and will not respond to her appeals. In "Cross Country Snow," the male protagonist complains that the imminent arrival of a baby will send him back to "the States" and keep him off the Austrian ski slopes. In "Hills Like White Elephants," a brilliant story, the man keeps reassuring his girl/wife that the abortion he is determined she undergo really won't be dangerous, that he has known lots of people who've had abortions. So has the girl, and "afterward," she sarcastically comments, "they were all so happy." "A Canary for One" sounds in muted tones the desperate note of a marriage breaking up, as does the later, less successful "Homage to Switzerland." Some of these are more vignettes than stories, but where the characters are developed and a conflict emerges, Hemingway invariably invests his sympathy in the loving and responsible woman and implicitly condemns the man for selfishness and immaturity. This is also the pattern of *A Farewell to Arms*, the novel he wrote the year after the dissolution of his marriage to Hadley.

Frederic Henry, Selfish Lover

A Farewell to Arms has usually been interpreted as a tragic tale of two lovers, driven together by the war, who selflessly give themselves to each other in an affair that might have lasted in indefinite bliss had not fateful death unjustly intervened to snatch one away. The events of the novel, one critic remarks, take on a "fully idyllic" cast as Frederic Henry recalls them. Frederic and Catherine Barkley, according to another, represent counterparts "of Paolo and Francesca, of Lucy and Richard Feverel, of all great lovers," with only Hemingway's realistic presentation keeping them from "heroic scale." But to read *A Farewell to Arms* in this way drastically minimizes Hemingway's accomplishment. The construction of his 1929 book is far subtler and more complicated than that of the conventional sentimental novel, and the story it has to tell is anything but straightforward.

   Hemingway himself provided an important clue to his novel when he remarked to a group of University of Hawaii professors in 1941 that their students should not be reading *A Farewell to Arms*, since it was "an immoral book." Let them read *The Sun Also Rises* instead, he suggested; that was "very moral." In the earlier novel, Hemingway felt he had demonstrated the evils of wasting one's resources on dissipation and sex. The message of *The Sun Also Rises*, he assured dozens of correspondents, was that "promiscuity" didn't pay. In calling *A Farewell to Arms* immoral by comparison, Hemingway was applying the same ethical standards, and lamenting that he had not made clearer Frederic Henry's own complicity in the corruption that surrounds him.

Though Lieutenant Henry encounters in Europe a world he never made, he succumbs with suspicious ease to the temptations which the war's climate of moral ambiguity present to him. Like the sodden expatriates of Paris and Pamplona, he regularly drinks to excess, and when in his cups blasphemes and whores like a trooper. Having acquired Catherine as a replacement for the whores, he impregnates her and then returns to the front, where during the retreat he loses his ambulances, shoots one Italian soldier in cold blood, and leads another to his death before deserting to save his own life. Then he escapes to Switzerland with his girl, who later dies bearing his child, but to whom, until she lies dying in a Lausanne hospital, he gives very little of himself.

In short, the character Frederic Henry, whom Rinaldi calls "the remorse boy," has a great deal to be remorseful about. In dealing with his own sins, moreover, he tries to smooth them away, just as he had tried to brush the taste of harlotry away with toothpaste. The entire novel may reasonably be construed as his attempt to excuse himself from blame. But Hemingway does not let his storyteller off so easily. He makes it clear, between the lines, that we should take what Lieutenant Henry has to say with a grain of salt. The difficulty in grasping this point derives from the reader's tendency to identify with Frederic, who as first-person narrator serves as guide to what happens in the novel. He seems a trustworthy enough guide to the *action*. But as Hemingway warned, even when he wrote a novel in the first person, he could not be held responsible "for the *opinions* of the narrator."

People are always misspelling Frederic Henry's name, and no wonder: only once in the book does Hemingway supply it, in full, and those who know him best usually do not call him by any name at all. What is significant is what they do call him. Only during their last meeting, for example, does his great friend and roommate Rinaldi address him by name as "Federico" and "Fred." These nicknames (like the "Rinin" Frederic uses for Rinaldi) suggest how close these two "war brothers" are, but are not nearly as suggestive as the term of affection which Rinaldi consistently and repeatedly uses in talking to Frederic. That term is "baby."

In conversation together, Frederic naturally refers to the priest as "father," but the priest does not call him "son" in return. Instead, during an early encounter (a scene which does not actually take place in the book), the priest had called Frederic "a boy." This we discover when Catherine, who is mad "only a little sometimes," directs Frederic Henry through a charade designed to let her pretend that he is a reincarnation of the fiancé she lost in the "ghastly show" at the Somme. Do this, do that, touch me so, she tells him: Frederic follows directions, and she observes, in approval, that he is "a very good boy." That, he replies, is what the priest had said.

In the light of this curious scene, where Frederic is instructed to call her "Catherine" and to say "I've come back to Catherine in the night," it is the more remarkable that nowhere in the novel does Catherine Barkley refer to her lover by name. Her most frequent endearment for him is "darling," but on several occasions she too reverts to the use of "boy." Sending him off to the front, she cautions him, as one would a child, to "be a good boy" and "be careful." When he wants to make love again before his operation in Milan, she calls him "such a silly boy"; when he sleeps with his arm around the pillow, he reminds her of "a little boy." Nor are Catherine and the priest the only ones to see Frederic Henry as a boy. The first nurse at Milan calls him "a sick boy," and Frederic objects not to the noun but the adjective: "I'm not sick. I'm wounded." The house doctor cautions him to be "a good boy" until Dr. Valentini can come. Valentini arrives and cheerfully tells him he is "a fine boy." Rinaldi understands that Frederic must regard himself as "the fine good Anglo-Saxon boy." "Poor baby," he says when Frederic admits to being in love; "poor boy," Count Greffi remarks when Frederic admits to being in religious doubt.

Whether they use "baby" or "boy," then, the other characters in *A Farewell to Arms* clearly perceive Frederic Henry as young, inexperienced, and unaware. The officers in the mess conduct their priest-baiting ritual primarily for his dubious benefit as greenhorn, and in the same fraternity-initiation spirit his fellow officers involve him in drinking contests and propel him in the direction of the bawdy house. But the sense in which Frederic Henry most clearly qualifies for boyhood rather than manhood is illustrated at Stresa, after he and Catherine have been reunited. Appearing unexpectedly, Frederic breaks up the vacation trip of Catherine and her friend Ferguson, who is bitter about that and angry at Frederic for getting Catherine with child. "Be nice to her" anyway, Catherine tells him later, for "we have so much" and Ferguson has so little. "I don't think she wants what we have," Frederic says, which moves Cat to observe: "You don't know very much, darling, for such a wise boy."

Indeed he does not, and his inability to put himself in Ferguson's place is typical of a strain of selfishness characteristic of the young. A mere boy, Frederic Henry suffers at the beginning of the novel from a pervasive lack of awareness. He does not know why he has enlisted in the Italian army, nor what he is fighting for. He lacks any perceptible ambition or purpose in life beyond the securing of his own pleasure. During the course of his war experiences he does to some degree grow in understanding. Anyone exposed to such a series of shocks—the unreasonable wound, the bollixed-up retreat, the death of his lover— might be expected to acquire from them not only trauma but, as Hemingway himself put it, "a certain working knowledge." The question at issue involves the extent of his education, how far Frederic Henry moved along the continuum from ignorant, self-centered youth to knowing, caring adulthood.   .

The contrast between sacred and profane love is established in the very first scene of *A Farewell to Arms*. Frederic is drinking the afternoon away with a friend in the Villa Rossa, the officers' whorehouse, when the priest walks by. "My friend . . . pounded on the window to attract his attention. The priest looked up. He saw us and smiled. My friend motioned for him to come in. The priest shook his head and went on." Later the priest provides his definition of love, which has nothing to do with the passion and lust of the nights Frederic has told him about. "When you love," the priest—with Hemingway—insists, "you wish to do things for. You wish to sacrifice for. You wish to serve."

Henry learns from the priest that love is more than sex, that—as Count Greffi later assures him—being in love "is a religious feeling" as well, that true lovers wish to serve and to sacrifice. But actually living up to this gospel of sacred love is very difficult. Neither Catherine nor Frederic, in fact, manages to achieve the state of ideal, selfless love which the priest describes, though they fail for strikingly different reasons.

This difference is important, because it is one of the ways in which

Hemingway distances himself from his narrator. Their love, as Frederic re-creates it, was supposedly shared equally; yet Catherine is far more devoted to Frederic than he to her. Her devotion goes so far beyond proper bounds as to amount, in the end, to nothing less than heresy. When they first meet, Catherine is an emotional wreck because she had not given herself to the fiancé who had been blown up at the Somme, and she sets out to correct that error with Frederic. She throws herself —all of herself—into the affair. She arranges to be transferred to Frederic's hospital in Milan, and on arrival immediately climbs into his bed, a practice she continues repeatedly thereafter at some risk to her position as a nurse and with the eventual result of pregnancy. She willingly accompanies her lover up Lake Maggiore in a rowboat during a rainstorm on a dark night, never complains of the discomforts of being pregnant except to worry that Frederic may be bored, and even when dying thinks principally of him: "Poor darling" and "Don't worry, darling."

Her single goal is to serve and protect Frederic Henry. Sexually, Catherine wants to please him more than the whores he has known, and she can do so, for unlike them she has no ulterior motives: "I want what you want. . . . Just what you want." She comforts him after his desertion, and provides a world of physical sensation which keeps him, at least temporarily, from thinking about the war. She makes a tent of her hair for them to hide inside of, pulls his cape around to cover them both. "I can keep you safe," she says. "I know I can." Discovering that he might be arrested, she proposes that they leave Italy at once: "I'll get you some place where they can't arrest you," she tells him, "and then we'll have a lovely time."

Catherine's eagerness to serve and sacrifice for Frederic apparently stems from a powerful drive to obliterate herself. On several occasions, she insists that she has submerged her personality into Frederic's. "There isn't any me any more," she remarks after they make love. And again, "there isn't any me. I'm you. Don't make up a separate me." Then, on their last night together in Milan, she implies that a two-way merger has now been completed: "We really are the same one. . . ." During all these assertions, Frederic keeps his own counsel. Only once, near the end of the novel, does he repeat her theory about their unity, and then he does so, paradoxically, in order to keep her from trying to be more like him. Now large with child, Catherine proposes that he let his hair grow and that she cut hers and then "we'd be just alike only one of us blonde and one of us dark." But Frederic thinks his hair is long enough now, and adds, "I wouldn't let you cut yours." When she persists, he invokes the phrase which he hopes will reassure her:

> "Wouldn't you like it short?" [Catherine asks.]
> "I might. I like it the way it is."
> "It might be nice short. Then we'd both be alike. Oh, darling, I want you so much I want to be you too."
> "You are. We're the same one."
> "I know. At night we are."
> "The nights are grand."

Whatever Frederic may say, he is clearly not interested in losing himself in her or any unit they may form together. Nor are they "the same one," even at night, as Hemingway reveals in the scene immediately following. The lovers are both awake in the middle of the night, and Catherine starts a chat which Frederic abruptly terminates by suggesting that she should go to sleep. Catherine agrees, but adds: "Let's go to sleep at the same moment." "All right," Frederic replies, but she goes back to sleep promptly and he lies awake alone "for quite a long time." In her worshipful attitude toward Frederic, the best Catherine can hope for is that she might look like him, by cutting her hair, or act like him, by going to sleep at the same time. When the doctors sew her up after the Caesarean, the scene in the operating room looks "like a drawing of the Inquisition," and justly so, for she has committed the unpardonable sin of heresy. "You're my religion," she tells Frederic, and she means it.

If Catherine fails to meet the priest's ideal formulation by loving not wisely but too well, with the prudential Frederic the case is quite the opposite. As the book progresses, he becomes more loving and less selfish, but only as compared to an initial policy toward Catherine that can best be defined as exploitative. During their first meetings in Gorizia, Catherine poignantly reveals her vulnerability, but Frederic nonetheless treats her as he would any other potential conquest—as an opponent in the game of seduction he intends to win. He goes through the preliminary steps, saying "I love you" when he "did not love Catherine Barkley nor had any idea of loving her." In Milan he has his reward for playing the game well, except that when she turns up at the hospital, he finds himself suddenly "crazy in love with her" though "God knows . . . he had not wanted to fall in love with any one."

The love he feels is almost entirely sexual, however, and derives from the pleasure she gives him, pleasure far superior to that dispensed by the girls at the Villa Rossa who "climbed all over you and put your cap on backward as a sign of affection between their trips upstairs with brother officers." Since he is bedridden, she must come to him, a practice which symbolizes his role, then and later, as an accepter, not a giver, of services.

During the winter of 1918, according to Frederic's retrospective reminiscences, their love reaches its most idyllic stage. Waiting for Catherine's baby to come, they live in the mountains above Montreux, alone except for the landlord and his wife (who were "very happy together too"), and as Frederic remembers it, "We had a fine life. We lived through the months of January and February and the winter was very fine and we were very happy." The flatness of the prose and the ominous touch about having "lived through" two winter months tend to undercut the explicit statement, but even more contradictory is the novel's revelation of how they spent their time.

Happiness for Catherine consists of the opportunity to be alone, for the most extended period possible, with the man she worships. When they go to the racetrack in Milan with Mr. and Mrs. Meyers and others, she finds the company insupportable: "But, darling, I can't stand so many people." "We don't see many," he objects, but she leads him off anyway to watch the next race and have a drink alone. On this occasion she senses a certain reluctance in Frederic. Didn't he like it better when they were alone? Didn't being with the others make him feel lonely? He agrees but with monosyllabic curtness, and she capitulates, "Don't let me spoil your fun, darling. I'll go back whenever you want."

While recovering from his wounds in Milan, Frederic hardly lacks for fellowship—the doctors, the nurses, Simmons, Saunders, Ettore, the American vice-consul, the headwaiter at the Gran Italia—or for activity, once he is ambulatory and can go to the Ospedale Maggiore for his therapy treatments, to San Siro for the races, to the Anglo-American Club. In Switzerland, by way of contrast, he and Catherine know no one at all. For her, the Guttingens' cottage above Montreux represents the perfect location, since they can cut off all ties there. Earlier, when they'd considered where to spend his leave, she had expressed no preference: "Anywhere," as she put it, where "we don't know people." At Stresa, she had been resentful of the brief time Frederic spent in the billiard room with Count Greffi. But Frederic has no old friends or companions in Switzerland. "Isn't it grand how we never see any one?" she asks him. "You don't want to see people, do you, darling?" Frederic dutifully answers, "No," but there is evidence that he finds the exclusive pleasure of her company somewhat oppressive.

There is not much for the lovers to do in the mountains. They eat. They sleep. They read books and magazines bought in the town below. They buy a copy of "Hoyle" and play two-handed card games. They play chess. At the beginning Frederic had compared his sexual pursuit of Catherine to a chess game; now he prefers the game itself to making love:

> [Frederic]: "Now do you want to play chess?"
> [Catherine]: "I'd rather play with you."
> "No. Let's play chess."
> "And afterward we'll play?"
> "Yes."
> "All right."

In short, they kill time, since her job had ended with her pregnancy and his with his desertion.

In the way of "the winter sport," he and Catherine take walks together, but neither of them knows how to ski. The doctor says she can't risk it, but Frederic eagerly asserts to Mr. Guttingen's proposal that he learn how from their son. Sensitive to his moods, Catherine detects Frederic's restlessness and halfheartedly asks whether he'd like "to go on a trip somewhere by yourself . . . and be with men and ski." Because he knows she would be devastated if he did leave, he refuses the suggestion. As an alternative, she proposes that he grow a beard:

> "All right. I'll grow one. I'll start now this minute. It will give me something to do."
> "Are you worried because you haven't anything to do?"
> "No. I like it. I have a fine life. Don't you?"

But growing a beard does not really amount to "something to do," and two pages later, while he once more reassures her that he will stay with her, Frederic reverses himself about having "a fine life." "I won't ever go away," he promises. "I'm no good when you're not there. I haven't any life at all any more." The difference between them is clear-cut here. Catherine has no life without him, and desires none. Frederic has no life at all, and yearns for the occupation and companions he has left behind.

Short of idolizing her, Frederic could hardly have equaled the intensity of Catherine's love for him. But had he been more careful not to hurt her feelings, he would not have said that growing a beard would (at least) "give him something to do" or that he hadn't "any life at all any more." This latter gaffe repeats one he had made at Stresa, when he told her with exquisite lack of consideration that "My life used to be full of everything. Now if you aren't with me I haven't a thing in the world." But it is not her fault that, like "Othello with his occupation gone," he has left behind with Shakespeare's great warrior—the implied comparison belittles Frederic's relative lack of bravery and military accomplishment—the "pride, pomp and circumstance of glorious war!"

The most striking example of Frederic's insensitivity, however, comes in the scene where Catherine tells him she is pregnant. She brings up the subject reluctantly, afraid that the revelation will "worry" him or make him unhappy. She apologizes for her condition ("I took everything but it didn't make any difference"), offers him a drink to stop his worrying and make him more cheerful, promises that she will see to all the details of finding a place for the baby to be born, but Frederic merely lies in bed, does not reassure her or touch her. Finally she takes his hand, and this dialogue follows:

> "You aren't angry are you, darling?"
> "No."
> "And you don't feel trapped."
> "Maybe a little. But not by you."
> "I didn't mean by me. You mustn't be stupid. I meant trapped at all."
> "You always feel trapped biologically."
> She went away a long way without stirring or removing her hand.
> " 'Always' isn't a pretty word."

It certainly isn't, implying as it does that Frederic has had his share of affairs and gotten any number of girls pregnant, and they've always made him feel trapped when they got that way. "But you see," Catherine points out, "I've never had a baby and I've never even loved any one. And I've tried to be the way you wanted and then you talk about 'always.' "

He could, Frederic says, cut off his tongue, but he goes on to pick a quarrel with her as to whether or not she's "an authority" on the question of bravery and sends her away without the psychological comfort of love-making. She will visit him later in the night, but for the moment he prefers reading the old Boston papers with their stale news to making love.

Another instance of Frederic's callousness follows shortly thereafter, when on their last night together in Milan, having worked out the details in advance, he takes her to a hotel of assignation where no luggage is required, where the normal practice is to pay in advance, where the rooms are furnished in red plush with many mirrors, and where Catherine is made to feel, inevitably and unavoidably, like a whore.

Throughout their affair, Frederic rarely displays honest and thoughtful concern for Catherine's feelings. Where she invariably thinks of him first, he often does not think of her at all. Only when she lies dying of childbirth in the Lausanne hospital does he finally begin to want to serve and to sacrifice for her. As her pain intensifies, the doctor lets Frederic administer the anesthetic, and though he is afraid of the "numbers above two," he is also glad of the chance to be of help: "It was very good of the doctor to let me do something." Then her fatal hemorrhaging starts, and he asks, pleadingly, "Do you want me to do anything, Cat? Can I get you anything?" But there is nothing to be done, and in frustration he rails at the universe.

The creator of Frederic Henry believed in retribution, in rewards and punishments, in actions producing consequences. In correspondence, Hemingway scornfully condemned those who behaved badly and then "gaily" informed the world that it was not their fault at all. But this is precisely the procedure that Frederic follows near the end of *A Farewell to Arms*. In an attempt to justify himself, he fixes all blame on a deterministic world. "The world" stands against the lovers; a vague "they" are at fault: "Now Catherine would die. That was what you did. You died. You did not know what it was about. You never had time to learn. They threw you in and told you the rules and the first time they caught you off base they killed you." Adopting the rhetorician's device of the second person "you," Frederic tries to gain his audience's assent to this philosophy. But there is a logical inconsistency in the terrible game of life-and-death he posits: though he is at least an equal partner in any mistakes that have been made, he survives and Catherine dies.

This philosophy rings false, furthermore, in the light of two incidents which Hemingway includes in the final chapter. In each, Frederic has the opportunity to alter the course of events for the better; in each, he responds by doing nothing constructive, instead retreating into a passivity which enables him to see himself as a person things happen *to*, rather than one who makes them happen. The first incident involves a scavenging dog Frederic discovers nosing at a refuse can early on the morning of the day Catherine dies. "What do you want?" he asks the dog and looks in the can, but "there was nothing on top but coffee-grounds, dust and some dead flowers." Frederic says, "There isn't anything, dog," to underline the symbolic nihilism of the scene—but his efforts to help the dog find food have been halfhearted at best, since he has not looked beneath the surface layer.

The other incident takes the form of Frederic's reflection on a naturalistic death scene in his past:

> Once in camp I put a log on top of the fire and it was full of ants. As it commenced to burn, the ants swarmed out and went first toward the centre where the fire was; then turned back and ran toward the end. When there were enough on the end they fell off into the fire. Some got out, their bodies burnt and flattened, and went off not knowing where they were going. But most of them went toward the fire and then back toward the end and swarmed on the cool end and finally fell into the fire. I remember thinking at the time that it was the end of the world and a splendid chance to be a messiah and lift the log off the fire and throw it out where the ants could get off onto the ground. But I did not do anything but throw a tin cup of water on the log, so that I would have the cup empty to put whiskey in before I added water to it. I think the cup of water on the burning log only steamed the ants.

In this passage, the narrator crucially, if unconsciously, condemns himself while simultaneously making nonsense of the deterministic world picture he has been advocating. Here no omnipotent fate decrees the death of the ants. They die because a camper, who might have saved them, steams them instead while clearing his cup for a drink of whisky, since he knows that water should be added to whisky and not the other way around.

A number of readers have confessed to a certain uneasiness about Frederic Henry, among them Holden Caulfield, the young rationalizer of J. D. Salinger's *Catcher in the Rye*, who senses a certain "insincerity" in Hemingway's narrator. As E. M. Halliday observed, the philosophical reflections in the novel seem to be tacked on: "One is likely to feel not so much that Frederic Henry thought these thoughts at the time, as that Frederic Henry—or Ernest Hemingway—thought them retrospectively, and is delivering short lectures with his eyes on the audience rather than on the story itself." But it is not *either* Frederic Henry *or* Ernest Hemingway but only the created character who attempts under cover of the doctrine of determinism to evade responsibility years after the fact of his affair with Catherine Barkley. Worse yet, he does not love Catherine as she deserves. He takes without giving. He withholds. By showing us these shortcomings in Frederic Henry and by implicitly repudiating his philosophical justifications, Hemingway distances himself from his protagonist, who is one of those first-person narrators whose opinions are not to be trusted.

The Last Three Wives

To the extent that the author of *A Farewell to Arms* identifies with the narrator—and their *war* experiences (the wound, the girl in the Milan hospital) run along suggestively parallel lines—Ernest Hemingway is apparently chastising himself in the novel. By contrast Catherine Barkley emerges as a far more admirable character. A composite of the qualities of several women, her most obvious model is the American Red Cross nurse Agnes von Kurowsky, but Catherine's psychological disrepair and Britishness fit Duff Twysden better than Agnes, and her death in childbirth undoubtedly derives from Pauline's difficult Caesarean in the summer of 1928. Finally, in her loving and selfless nature, Catherine resembles no one more than Hadley Hemingway.

Hemingway rarely again portrayed a woman as believable and sympathetic as the heroine of *A Farewell to Arms*. The bitches who populate his fiction of the 1930s, like Margot Macomber in "The Short Happy Life of Francis Macomber" and Helene Bradley in *To Have and Have Not*, yield in later novels to such Latinized child-women as Maria in *For Whom the Bell Tolls* and Renata in *Across the River and into the Trees*. On the rare occasions when he created characters resembling his second and third wives, the fog of nostalgia that enveloped his first marriage evaporated and he saw these women with a critical, if not jaundiced, eye. The closet approximation to Pauline in his fiction, for example, is Helen in "The Snows of Kilimanjaro," who despite meaning well encourages her writer-husband Harry to indulge himself in luxurious idleness and so to destroy his talent. And Dorothy Bridges in *The Fifth Column*, who matches Martha Gellhorn, Hemingway's third wife, in background and long-legged blondness, is satirically depicted as lacking in perception and understanding because of her foolish, knee-jerk liberalism.

One reason Pauline and Martha fared so poorly in fictional renderings is that they could not measure up, in Ernest's estimation, to the standard set by his first wife. In letters written during marital crises, he made the comparison explicit. The more he saw of women, he wrote Hadley in 1939 while undergoing the unpleasantness of a divorce from Pauline, the more he admired Hadley. Perhaps they might be reunited in Heaven, unless they'd already had theirs in the Dolomites, the Black Forest, and the forest of the Irati. Then remarried to Paul Scott Mowrer, Hadley responded by asking Ernest to spend Christmas with them, an invitation he refused though he was "stinko, deadly lonely" all the time. When relations with Martha soured in 1942 and 1943, he sentimentally wrote Hadley once again with recollections of the first time at Pamplona when they were by themselves, and the Atlantic crossing on the *Leopoldina*, and the private songs and jokes they had shared. Paul would understand that he couldn't help loving her, his dearest "Miss Katherine Kat." (This nickname for Hadley supports the idea that Hemingway had her at least partly in mind when he created the character of Catherine Barkley, often called "Cat" by Frederic.) No future wife, obviously, could prosper by comparison with such a paragon.

His marriage to Pauline Pfeiffer lasted twelve years, and for much of that time was at least reasonably happy. Pauline gave him love and loyalty, and bore him two sons, Patrick and Gregory. Together they lived in Key West, from whose harbor Ernest ventured after the monsters of the deep aboard the *Pilar*. But Pauline was not always pleased when he left for extended periods on fishing expeditions, nor when he spent long hours among the town's disreputable residents at Sloppy Joe's bar. As if to distinguish himself from her monied world, Ernest frequently violated her notions of propriety by drinking and brawling. Yet it was not until Martha Gellhorn walked into Sloppy Joe's one day in 1937 that their marriage entered its terminal stage. During the Spanish Civil War, Ernest and Martha lived in Madrid's Hotel Florida, and during the next three years the two lovers continued their affair with only a modicum of discretion. The divorce and remarriage finally came in 1940.

His decision to leave Pauline bothered Hemingway almost not at all. In one sense, he felt, she had got no more than she deserved for her role in breaking up his first marriage. Those that live by the sword, he brutally commented, must expect to die by the sword. Pauline had also made a crucial mistake at the very beginning, Ernest revealed in a passage he eventually deleted from the published version of *A Moveable Feast:* "She undervalued the power of remorse." In addition, he felt he "had to" leave her for sexual reasons. As he explained matters in a letter to Carlos Baker, they had been forced to practice *coitus interruptus* after Pauline's two Caesareans, since for medical reasons she could not afford to become pregnant and for religious ones (Pauline was Catholic) she would not countenance the use of birth-control devices. Under the circumstances, Ernest said, he had no choice but to leave her. The divorce was not his fault at all.

After Ernest and Martha Hemingway's stormy marriage ended in 1945, both participants looked back on their union with distaste. Martha regarded her infatuation with Hemingway in much the same spirit as the high-school cheer leader, who grows up enough to know better, recalls her crush on the football hero. Aside from his work, she believed, Ernest possessed almost no redeeming qualities whatsoever; he was, in matters of the heart, about as trustworthy as a cobra. Ernest for his part referred to marrying Martha as the "biggest mistake" in a life full of mistakes.

One reason for the mismatch was that Martha, a published novelist when they met and later a practicing journalist and writer, insisted on pursuing her own ambitions wherever they might lead her. During

World War II they often led away from home to overseas theaters of war. As Hemingway wrote Dawn Powell at the end of January 1944, Martha had been away for five months and since he'd married her for a wife and not as an ideal to be worshiped from a distance nor even as "the Unknown Soldier," he was not happy.

Gifted with a sharp tongue and temper, Martha was not afraid of using either. Once, on receiving a manicure set from Mrs. Gustavo Durán, she turned to Ernest and sweetly exclaimed, "Oh, Pussy, now I won't have to go to Havana to have my toenails done." The Duráns, like other visitors, witnessed heated arguments at Finca Vigia, where the Hemingways settled in 1940. Martha was not awed by Ernest, nor loath to criticize his unpredictable hours, his noisy and often unwashed companions, his personal untidiness, and his drinking bouts at the Floridita. One summer afternoon in 1940 she stormed into the bar at four o'clock, obviously enraged that Ernest had kept her and her mother waiting for two hours. "You can stand me up," she yelled, "but you can't do that to my mother." Ernest mumbled an apology, and meekly left at her heels.

When World War II began she denigrated the importance of Ernest's Cuban spy network and U-boat-hunting team and went off on her own as a war correspondent. At a rendezvous in London, in 1944, Ernest cruelly and publicly stood her up to declare his independence. But it was *her* behavior, he insisted, which brought the marriage to an end. To his brother, Leicester, he maintained that Martha had openly cuckolded him and then published a story about it. To Archibald MacLeish, he wrote that she was a virulently ambitious girl after all.

As with his previous wives, Ernest did not finally break with Martha until he had another bride-to-be, this time Mary Welsh, waiting in the wings. Scott Fitzgerald theorized at the time of Ernest's divorce from Hadley that he would require a new woman for each "big book," a theory that applies rather well to his first three wives (Hadley: *The Sun Also Rises*; Pauline: *A Farewell to Arms*; Martha: *For Whom the Bell Tolls*), but breaks down in Mary's case, since neither the artistically flawed *Across the River and into the Trees*, the novella *The Old Man and the Sea*, nor the memoir *A Moveable Feast* qualifies as a "big" book. Furthermore, though he wrote about her in nonfiction pieces, Ernest did not create any characters who much resemble Mary Welsh. They met in 1944 in London, where she was working as a reporter for *Time*. Small, blonde, and whip-bright, with an excellent figure (Ernest called her his "pocket Rubens"), she came from Minnesota and was the only Hemingway wife who had not gone to school in St. Louis.

Mary was different in other ways, too—not the least of them being that she stuck with her famous husband, and kept him with her, through good times and bad. It was not always pleasant. It was not always easy.

At the beginning of their affair, Ernest treated her with both tenderness and passion. He would rather have the side of his foot touch hers, he said, than make love to any other woman. But Mary had reservations even then. Like Catherine in *A Farewell to Arms*, she had felt married the first time she and Ernest slept together, but she confided to her journal her doubts about the prospect of spending the rest of her life with the sometimes manic, occasionally belligerent writer. During the premarital period (late 1945–early 1946), while she was visiting at Finca Vigia for several months, the course of their love ran less than smooth. She complained to Ernest that she felt confined, that she was used to a normal life including parties and travel and the freedom of a reporter, that they needed better help around the place (a butler, as Ernest sarcastically commented, with the "probity" of Cardinal Newman and the "organizing capacity" of Henry Kaiser). Their wedding day itself, March 14, 1946, ended in such a bitter altercation that Mary would have left at once if she hadn't been so tired.

Despite an inauspicious start, and despite the tragic loss of a baby (through rupture of her left Fallopian tube) that summer, Mary Hemingway gradually accommodated herself to the multitude of roles—not merely wife but mistress, cook, bartender, and bouncer—required of her position. In an appreciation he wrote for *Look* in 1956, Ernest singled out his wife's most essential quality: "Miss Mary is durable. She is also brave, charming, witty, exciting to look at, a pleasure to be with and a good wife. She is also an excellent fisherwoman, a fair wing shot, a strong swimmer, a really good cook, a good judge of wine, an excellent gardener, an amateur astronomer, a student of art, political economy, Swahili, French and Italian and can run a boat or a household in Spanish." She could say in perfect Swahili, "Tupa ile chupa tupu," which means "take away the empty bottle," but when she was away, Ernest wrote, the Finca was "as empty as the emptiest bottle she ever ordered removed." She knew how to be lazy, but she also had great energy and could "stay the distance."

He also praised in print Mary's "wonderful memory for forgetting.

. . . She could forget in the loveliest and most complete way of anyone" he ever knew. "She could carry a fight overnight but at the end of a week she could forget it completely and truly. . . . She forgave herself in her memory and she forgave you, too." Forgetting was a talent which Ernest, in his periodic emulation of the Bad Boy, gave her plenty of opportunities to employ. During the two worst of these spells (which occurred approximately a decade apart, as he passed the milestones of his fiftieth and sixtieth birthdays), Ernest's behavior would have driven even an amnesiac to twinges of jealousy.

In November 1952 Mary Hemingway sent her husband a Thanksgiving note expressing her thanks that he had been so good for so long and that he did not feel it imperative to acquire ever younger and more beautiful wives. Ernest could hardly have missed what went unsaid: that Mary, herself nine years his junior, was grateful that he was getting over his passion for Adriana Ivancich, whom he had met and fallen in love with in Venice in December 1948, when she was but nineteen. As a daughter of Venetian society, Adriana was carefully chaperoned at all times, and there was no way that Ernest could see her alone in a gondola or a hotel room, though in his imagination he arranged such assignations for Colonel Cantwell and Renata in *Across the River and into the Trees*. In private correspondence, Ernest cultivated the romantic sorrow of his hopeless love for Adriana. His heart, a target of opportunity, was split in half, he wrote in one letter, since he faced once again his old dilemma of loving two women at the same time. After writing her into his novel as Renata, Ernest began a heated correspondence with Adriana, which she apparently cooled with a warning against being too explicit. He would always love her, Ernest responded in June 1950, but would not say so or write it in a letter if that was "better" for her.

Only when Louella Parsons reported that the Hemingways were splitting up because of his affair with an Italian countess (a false report which stemmed not from Adriana but from another young Venetian girl) did Mary erupt in anger. For the most part she regarded his relationship with Adriana, according to Ernest, as a *cosa sagrada*, a sacred thing as inevitable and irremediable as lightning at the crossroads. Wisely, she rode out the storm, but another one loomed ahead.

In May 1956 Ernest wrote a religiously inclined correspondent that a young woman had recently come through Cuba to see him, but he had made no play for her since he "was not born" to complicate the lives of children, no matter how attractive they were. But that resolution apparently dissolved in the summer of 1959, when he met an Irish girl named Valerie Danby-Smith. Valerie came to Spain that summer and attached herself to the Hemingway party—also including his friend Nathan (Bill) Davis, A. E. Hotchner, and two young American girls the men had "kidnapped"—which was touring from bullfight to bullfight. Her peaches-and-cream complexion sprinkled with freckles, the nineteen-year-old Valerie looked disarmingly innocent. But as they journeyed she constantly rode at Ernest's side, their bodies always touching. She also acted capably as his traveling secretary. Buck Lanham, who flew over to attend Ernest's sixtieth birthday party at "La Consula," the Davises' estate near Málaga, sized up the situation and proceeded to warn Valerie that Ernest, though old, was still vigorous and "a very dangerous man." Buck soon concluded that he might just as well have saved his breath.

The following year Ernest arranged for Valerie to come to the States, and sent Hotchner, as intermediary, a check for $1500 to help cover her tuition and living expenses while she studied at the American Academy of Dramatic Arts in New York. On October 25, 1960, the same day he sent Hotchner the check, he wrote a letter to Valerie herself, assuring her of his love and suggesting that she could correspond with him by enclosing a sealed letter in a typewritten envelope mailed to his Sun Valley doctor and with a return address to some name beginning with A. Such elaborate circumlocutions fit into the pattern of persecution that extended, in Ernest's final years, to the conviction that the immigration authorities were after him because of Valerie's immigrant status. He need not have gone through such round-about devices for the benefit of Mary, who, as in the case of Adriana, knew what was going on but kept her head. (Remarkably, Mary employed Valerie after Ernest's death to help straighten out his books and manuscripts. More remarkably, Valerie has since married Dr. Gregory Hemingway, Ernest's youngest son.)

The marriage of Ernest and Mary Hemingway lasted through some extremely hard times, for when enamored of his young ladies Ernest tended to treat Mary very badly. During the Adriana period, he showed his displeasure by taking plates of food that Mary had prepared for him and presenting them to the Finca's cats instead. And during the Spanish summer of 1959 with Valerie, he berated Mary for spending too much money on the elaborate birthday party she organized for him (she'd earned most of the money herself with a fishing piece in *Sports*

Illustrated), refused her any sympathy for the broken bone in her foot, and finally, at the party itself, cussed her out in public. But she would not panic and would not quit her loyal commitment to him, before or after his death. Marriage might be a gamble, as Hemingway wrote in a 1949 letter to Dos Passos, but the last time he "drew cards" he was lucky to come up with Miss Mary.

"Getting Connected Up."

D. H. Lawrence, after reading *In Our Time*, Hemingway's first book of stories, characterized the moral of the stories thus: "Avoid one thing only: getting connected up." Lawrence detected a persistent voice, running through the book, which warned against love and marriage as a trap. "Once a man's married he's absolutely bitched," Bill tells Nick Adams in "The End of Something." More than half of the fifty-odd stories Ernest Hemingway wrote dealt with love in one form or another; but not one of them depicted a satisfactory, lasting, mutually shared love between a man and a woman.

The fictional situation found its counterpart in Hemingway's private life. His penchant for older women when he was young, and for much younger girls when he was middle-aged and older, together with the taking of one wife after another serially, strongly suggest that he was unwilling or unable to make a total and binding commitment to one woman. Falling in love was, for Ernest Hemingway, a process fraught with dangers. The loving male, in his estimation, courted the pain of sorrow, took a chance on losing his manhood, and—most frightening of all—risked opening up his innermost self to invasion.

"If two people love each other," Hemingway wrote in *Death in the Afternoon*, "there can be no happy end to it," for one of them must die and the other remain bereft. In his fiction it was usually the man who was left, after the loss of a loved one, more or less desperately at liberty. In an ironic tale called "Now I Lay Me," an optimistic hospital orderly insists that the wounded Nick Adams must get married soon to cure his insomnia and nightmares. The naïve orderly "was going back to America and he was very certain about marriage and knew it would fix up everything." But "In Another Country," also a Nick Adams hospital story, demonstrates how wrong the orderly was. While under-going physical therapy for his wounded leg, Nick meets an Italian major who had been a champion fencer before the war but whose badly muti-lated hand will never recover its skill. Nonetheless, the major remains cheerful in his misfortune until word comes that his wife has died. This news he cannot resign himself to; bitterly he insists to Nick that "a man must not marry. . . . If he is to lose everything, he should not place himself in a position to lose that. . . . He should find things he cannot lose." In a passage Hemingway cut out of *A Farewell to Arms*, Frederic Henry similarly reflects on the injustice of his loss: "They say the only way you can keep a thing is to lose it and this may be true but I do not admire it. . . . And if it is the Lord that giveth and the Lord that taketh away I do not admire him for taking Catherine away. . . . All that we can be sure of is that we are born and that we will die and that every-thing we love will die too. The more things with life that we love the more things there are to die."

The quotation above is part of a long philosophical reflection, and it may be that Hemingway eliminated it in order to avoid weighing down his narrative with commentary. But he may also have decided to delete the passage because to let Frederic Henry have these thoughts would generate an unwanted climate of sympathy for him and also, since the sentiments expressed were so patently those of Ernest Hem-ingway, tend to link narrator and author too closely. That Hemingway himself *did* feel this way, he confirmed in the process of firing a baby-sitter Pauline hired in Key West to take care of their young sons Patrick and Gregory. The babysitter had to go, he explained, since he could see that the boys were starting to care for her too much. You could only love a person so much, but then you had to stop "or get hurt."

Another chance a man took in loving a woman was the loss of manhood. In correspondence and conversation, Ernest often expressed his lack of respect for men who let women run their lives. Scott Fitz-gerald had been ruined by Zelda. Evan Shipman had been dominated by his wife. Tommy Shevlin had always been under some woman's orders. And once a man gave up sovereignty to a woman, that was the end of him. There were really only two possible arrangements between a man and a woman: either you "must govern" or you must be gov-erned. As for Ernest, he did not intend to let women boss him around.

His own parents provided a sorry example, to his mind, of the emasculating marriage. In autobiographical fiction left unpublished at his death, Ernest as Nick Adams elaborated on his mother's techniques for controlling other members of the family, and he and his little sister fervently agreed that they had "seen enough fights in families." In one memorable assertion of her superiority, Mrs. Hemingway gathered up her husband's treasured collection of Indian arrowheads and tools and tossed them all into a back-yard bonfire, an event which Ernest transplanted to his story "Now I Lay Me" to illustrate the point that marriage was hardly likely to solve Nick Adams' problems.

Unlike his mother, other aggressive women in his fiction rarely succeed in taking over the role of dominance which, Ernest believed, rightfully belonged to the male. Lady Brett Ashley of *The Sun Also Rises* treats her lovers shabbily, to be sure, but she suffers for her sins when she meets Pedro Romero. Margot Macomber, the character in Hemingway's fiction who best fits Edmund Wilson's definition of the American bitch—"the impossible civilized woman who despises the civilized man for his failure in initiative and nerve and then jealously tries to break him down as soon as he begins to exhibit any"—shoots her husband, but only after she has come to see that in the future she would no longer be able to manipulate him to her will. Then the white hunter, who witnesses the killing, gains control over Margot. Like Brett, she must succumb to masculine domination.

In *Across the River and into the Trees*, Colonel Cantwell speaks for Hemingway when he insists on his superiority in the face of a fancied challenge from Renata. In one of their long conversations—as usual, Cantwell plays guru to Renata's rapt disciple—he thanks her for not asking him to tell any more war stories, and she lightly responds, "Oh, you are going to have to tell them to me later." The remark sets him off:

> *"Have to?"* the Colonel said and the cruelty and resolution showed in his strange eyes as clearly as when the hooded muzzle of the gun of a tank swings toward you.
> "Did you say *have to*, Daughter?"

She did, but she apologizes and he says he understands about the young's desire to command and she insists that she doesn't want to command but to serve and everything is smoothed over between them once more. Still, Cantwell's sudden reaction smacks of a raw sensitivity shared by his creator.

Very few women were outspoken and strong-minded enough to challenge Ernest's assumption of male dominance. Martha Gellhorn was one. Another was Buck Lanham's wife Pete, who told Ernest in 1945 that he might as well carry a bowler and umbrella, *à la* Chamberlain, considering his attitude of appeasement vis-à-vis the Russians. After that occasion, Ernest always specified in invitations to Buck that their reunions were to be strictly male, though Lanham noticed there were usually women around when he arrived. "I know wimmins," Ernest used to tell him, "and wimmins is difficult."

Men and women making love together could achieve a high level of happiness, he wrote in *Green Hills of Africa*: "I was happy as you are after you have been with a woman that you really love, when, empty, you feel it welling up again and there it is and you can never have it all and yet what there is, now, you can have, and you want more and more. . . ." When you have loved a woman like that, "happy and untragic," she will always love you no matter where she goes or whom she loves later on. But even such satisfactory heterosexual love did not, for Hemingway's Thomas Hudson, constitute the supreme happiness. He had been desperately, unbearably happy with women, so happy "that it was like being drunk or crazy." But he had been even happier, sober and sane, with his children and as a carefree boy.

How, Honest Lil asks Hudson, could he possibly be as happy by himself as with someone else? He submits no answer, but Hemingway implicitly suggested one in a 1950 note to his wife. Miss Mary must now understand him well enough to know, Ernest wrote, what he himself had learned in love and loneliness: that there were secret places in a man—or a woman—which no one had the right to enter or even the right to ask the way. To guard those secret places, to protect that inmost self, Ernest Hemingway constructed barriers against invasion. One such legal barrier, admirably designed to keep women from getting too close, was divorce.

Yet if there were hidden things about himself—pockets of weakness behind the façade of strength—that Ernest Hemingway did not "want out" (as Robert Frost said of certain of his most personal poems), he nonetheless made it a practice to leap from the frying pan of one woman, discarded, to the fire of another woman, betrothed, without more than the obligatory period of bachelorhood. He did so largely because he could not bear being alone, and it was the function of the female to kill a man's lonesomeness. Thus he praises Mary Welsh, coming gently to his hotel room in London during the war, not simply for bringing him love but for curing "all loneliness."

When he was left alone for a time, Hemingway usually succumbed to spells of depression. These spells were particularly acute during his separation and divorce from Hadley. "He was in the state," Archibald MacLeish recalls, "of being unable to endure being left alone. . . . Even at night, somebody had to be within reach, he had to be able to call out to somebody." There was nothing faked about this need: "it was very real . . . and very touching." Thus Hadley's proviso that he and Pauline stay apart for a hundred days caused him terrible anguish. To carry out the agreement, Pauline came to the States, while Ernest remained in Paris. What he missed worst of all, he wrote her, was not having any intimacy with her, no feeling of the two of them against the others. Even after he and Pauline were married, Ernest indicated how bereft he felt when, in filling out his 1928 *Who's Who* questionnaire, he crossed out "Home: 1 rue des Italiens, Paris, France" and scribbled underneath "No Home." A decade later, when he left Pauline for Martha Gellhorn, and Martha subsequently abandoned him, in 1939, to cover the Russian invasion of Finland, Ernest suffered another attack of loneliness and applied to Pauline for permission to spend the Christmas holidays with her and their boys in Key West. She refused.

Characteristically, Hemingway's fictional protagonists finish alone, a pattern which becomes increasingly dominant in his later writing. The fear of loneliness implicit in these final fictions reflects what Erich Fromm calls the "deepest need of man . . . the need to overcome his separateness, to leave the prison of his aloneness." Hemingway as an individualist refused to subdue that separateness by blending into the herd or by following a numbing, nine-to-five work routine. He also found bumpy and dangerous the alternative route to integration, that "fusion with another person, in *love*," which Fromm calls the "full answer" to the terror of aloneness.

In defining his terms, Fromm distinguishes between *symbiotic* love and *mature* love. In symbiotic love, one partner normally assumes a passive, masochistic, inferior role to the other's active, sadistic superiority. Most of Hemingway's love stories, which usually assume a dominant-submissive relationship, focus on this kind of love. Mature lovers, on the other hand, share equally: they give and gain by giving.

In a process which Fromm defines as "union under the condition of preserving one's integrity," the paradox occurs "that two beings become one and yet remain two." In this paradox resided Hemingway's dilemma. Like all men he dreaded aloneness; he dreaded it more than most. But he also feared that love would deprive him of his own individuality, of his own inmost self.

Among his fictional counterparts, Robert Jordan in *For Whom the Bell Tolls* comes closest to achieving the Frommian state of mature love. Like Frederic Henry with Catherine, he resists Maria's desire to become exactly like him, to passively submerge herself in him. "I would be thee because I love thee so," she says, but he counters, "It is better to be one and each one to be the one he is." Unlike Frederic, though, during his three days among the Spanish guerrillas, Jordan comes to understand the beauty of giving and the importance of selflessness to those in love. "He knew he himself was nothing, and he knew death was nothing. . . . In the last few days he had learned that he himself, with another person, could be everything."

At least once in his fiction, then, Ernest Hemingway created a hero who loved maturely and selflessly without giving up his own integrity. The evidence of his life and of the bulk of his writing, however, suggests that he himself kept barriers standing against such total commitment. In *Islands in the Stream*, Thomas Hudson's first wife returns for a short visit, and after they make love together, they quarrel over what it was that broke up their marriage. "Couldn't you be more needing and make me necessary and not be so damned give it and take it and take it away I'm not hungry?" she asks. But the answer to the question, which refers not so much to sexual need as to his deeper reluctance to betray any need at all, is no; for to confess such dependence would, Hudson is afraid, make him "a baby like the men" she has since loved and cared for. Hudson loves her desperately, but cannot unbend to her or unburden himself to her. The final words in the book render a judgment on Thomas Hudson which his creator may have intended for himself as well: "Oh shit," his mate Willie says to the dying artist. "You never understand anybody that loves you."

viii

Sex

Great Lover . . .

According to Hemingway, he learned practically everything there was to know about sex while still a teen-ager. He insisted, for example, that he'd suffered the unpleasant consequences of casual couplings while still in high school: that he'd "had the clap" twice before his older friend Bill Smith ever got laid. This assertion, totally unsupported by biographical evidence, formed part and parcel of the tough-guy aura with which he invested his youth. He'd missed reform school so close it wasn't funny, he said, and missed the penitentiary so close it *was* funny. Also contributing to that aura were his claims of youthful experience with prostitutes, claims the more dubious in that the whores in his fiction—Alice in "The Light of the World," Georgette in *The Sun Also Rises*, Honest Lil in *Islands in the Stream*—emerge as stereotypes of the scarlet woman with heart of gold.

The fictional Alice, he maintained, was based on a real 258-pound whore he'd met while a young boy up in northern Michigan; what's more, Alice had been so satisfied with his performance that she would not accept her customary $2 fee, and even loaned him money. Lest one accept that story as gospel, however, Hemingway in the next breath recalled with spurious nostalgia the good old days when he used to break his hand every Saturday night during the weekly fistfight at the whorehouse in Billings, Montana. By way of contrast, Howell Jenkins, a fellow ambulance driver in World War I, remembers Ernest blushing furiously when accosted by a prostitute at the officers' brothel in Italy.

Ernest's double impulse—on the one hand to pose as a man of the world who could not be shocked, on the other as a naughty boy who was determined to shock everyone else—may have accounted for his consenting to write an introduction to *Kiki of Montparnasse*, a book which, having been composed "by a woman who was never a lady at any time," might, as he said, provide a welcome alternative to books "written by present-day ladywriters of all sexes." The same paradoxical impulse probably also inspired his later tales, mostly confided to the gullible, of having consorted with Havana prostitutes nicknamed Xenophobia or Leopoldina or the International Whore. Ernest did, apparently, bring Xenophobia along for an embarrassingly public lunch with Miss Mary one spring day in 1950, but a more elaborate yarn of his about this particularly "young and crisp and really beautiful" whore seems constructed of whole cloth. While Mary was away, the story goes, Xenophobia visited the Finca on a number of occasions for Ernest's entertainment. All might have gone well, Hemingway explained while reveling in his naughty-boy role, had not one of the servants, enamored of his new camera, taken three snapshots of Xenophobia, wearing *a different dress* in each one, and proudly showed them to Miss Mary on her return. Though there were those who swallowed such stories from Ernest, this one sounds too clever and coincidental to be credible. Mayito Menocal, Sr., who knew Ernest from 1939 until his death, observed that he never knew him to have sex with a prostitute. Ernest may have said that he slept with the outsized Alice or Xenophobia or Leopoldina, but that didn't mean that Menocal—or anyone else—had to believe it.

It was not merely prostitutes but women in general who, according to Hemingway, were forever yielding their persons up to him. He had never, he told Ella Winter, asked a woman who'd refused him. He had had every woman he ever wanted, he told others, and some he didn't. He converted sexual performance, like everything else, into a competition. Thus he was, by his own repeated accounts, incredibly virile. His sex drive was so strong, he wrote Thornton Wilder, that in the early days in Paris he could not be satisfied by making love only at night and in the morning; if he could not also have sex in the afternoon, he had to relieve himself privately. On a shipboard crossing in the 1920s, he ostentatiously consumed saltpeter to quiet his raging libido. He also chewed some sort of sex-sedating nuts while in Spain during the civil war. To Buck Lanham, especially, he insisted on his extraordinary prowess, as in a 1948 letter comparing intercourse to six-day bicycle racing (the more you did it, the better you got at it) and calculating the family screwing ratio at a hundred times per month, which made a "bum" out of Dr. Kinsey. The older Ernest got, Lanham noticed, the more he insisted on his bedroom accomplishments.

Though Lanham hardly credited such tales, he did become convinced, over a period of time, that Ernest was "totally amoral sexually," and that he had achieved liaisons late in life with at least a few of the young girls who came to hover about him in admiration. Menocal, Sr., told Hemingway in 1953 that a man of their age (past fifty) could awaken in young women only two emotions: if the young women were kind and good-hearted, the emotion of pity; if they were tough and calculating, the emotion of greed. But Ernest apparently disagreed. According to his own account and that of others, he conducted several affairs during his fourteen-year marriage to Mary, besides resisting the attempts of a Greek princess and a "middle-aged contessa" to seduce Ernest—occurrences fictionally reflected in *Islands in the Stream*, where Thomas Hudson speaks of the "only princess . . . he had ever made love to outside of Italian princesses, who did not count. . . ." But the evidence remains skimpy. Perhaps a negative inference can be drawn from the fact that no woman has yet come forward with a memoir of her love affair with the famous author. Ernest may have made love to any number of women when a mutual attraction existed: or he may not have and implied that he had, even—or especially—to Mary. But he did relate a number of cock-and-bull stories, often in considerable detail, about sexual conquests which he patently did not make.

The most flagrantly apocryphal of these was Ernest's claim that he had coupled with Mata Hari. Chronology tripped him up here: the famous spy died a year prior to the supposed date of their affair. Another alleged sexual encounter, duly recorded in A. E. Hotchner's *Papa Hemingway*, nearly rivals that one for lack of credibility. According to this yarn, Ernest met an exquisite Italian girl at "21" in New York (the year is not specified) and enjoyed the charms of her "pure Renaissance beauty, black hair straight, eyes round at the bottoms, Botticelli skin, breasts of Venus Rising" before discovering, the next day, that she was the girl friend of mobster Legs Diamond.

He also asserted that he maintained a black harem while on safari with Pauline in 1933 ("bloody optimist," Philip Percival chortled) and that he made love to Debba, another native African girl, while on safari with Miss Mary in 1953. Then there are tales about an unspecified older woman's offer to finance a safari on a *quid pro quo* basis, his fictional counterpart Thomas Hudson's "wonderful" evening in bed with three Chinese girls, and his seductions by passionate innkeepers in Paris and Sicily. Finally, in a letter to Charles Poore, Ernest presented his version of the day during World War II when a famous French writer came to his Paris hotel room, so that she might have the "literary experience" of love-making with Hemingway. As Ernest spins the yarn, he was at the time rendered virtually impotent by the stress of battle, but nonetheless managed to satisfy the lady before he started to cough and bled all over her, a postcoital reaction which, he thought, impressed her.

In Hemingway's fiction the man usually reacts less violently after sex; instead he grows cold, and has little time for his woman. After his brutal fornication with Liz in "Up in Michigan," the whisky-besotted Jim simply falls asleep. Nick Adams, in "Fathers and Sons," brags about the manly havoc he will wreak on his Indian girl Trudy's half-brother if the boy should dare to come close to Nick's sister. In "Summer People," Nick calls Kate "slut" after they have made love, and leaves her to spend the night alone in the woods. Though the earth may move for Robert Jordan as for Maria in *For Whom the Bell Tolls*, once their passion is spent he thinks principally of his duties as warrior and bridge-blower; thoughts of love must wait until one's job is done. In Hemingway's estimation, then, sex tended to turn a woman soft and a man hard. After intercourse, he told an aspiring writer in 1931, a man's head clears "and is cold." In that coldness the male of the species achieves a measure of superiority over his sexual partner/opponent. Some measure of satisfaction might even accrue through organizing other men's sexual pleasure, as Hemingway did for Milton Wolff in Madrid during the Spanish Civil War, and did so often for companions from the 22nd Infantry Regiment in Paris during World War II as to compromise his standing, as he cheerfully put it, as "an amateur pimp." He even tried, unsuccessfully, to arrange an afternoon of dalliance for Marlene Dietrich and Buck Lanham.

All this suggests that Hemingway took the metaphor of sexual conquest literally. By sleeping with a woman, a man might prevail, at least temporarily, in the everlasting struggle between the sexes. But there are good reasons, besides the laws of probability, to challenge the veracity of his sexual boasting: Hemingway's background and his cultural heritage militated against his developing into a sexual libertarian.

. . . or Sexual Puritan

Paris in the 1920s offered a virtual paradise of profligate possibilities to those young Americans who, in nominal revolt against the "Victorianism" or "repression" of their native culture, had come to the artistic capital of the world to pursue their genius without conventional restraints. But Hemingway could not comfortably shrug off those restraints. He struck Donald Ogden Stewart, for example, as "a bit priggish" during those expatriate days. Another companion, Harold Loeb, thought Ernest "a Puritan." Loeb never saw him "out" with a woman other than his wife. When he did go out, as for a night on the town in Montmartre, Hemingway was liable to attacks of morning-after remorse. He couldn't help wanting to make love to some of the girls in those dance halls, he told Max Eastman after one such night, but he always came home disgusted with himself for having such feelings. The only reason a man went to a night club or cabaret, he was convinced, was to locate an unattached and willing female companion. All the rest amounted to a wasting of time in bad air.

In behavior and sentiments both, Hemingway revealed the strength of his Oak Park conditioning. When it fell to Dr. Hemingway's lot to instruct his son in the mysteries of sex, he issued enough *caveats* to frighten any adolescent lad. In the autobiographical story, "Fathers and Sons," Nick Adams reads that Enrico Caruso has been arrested for "mashing," and asks his father what that means. Dr. Adams' vague reply that it was "one of the most heinous of crimes" evades the issue and encourages in Nick fanciful pictures of "the great tenor doing something strange, bizarre, and heinous with a potato masher to a beautiful lady who looked like the pictures of Anna Held on the inside of cigar boxes." Nick privately resolves, "with considerable horror," that he will try mashing at least once when he grows up, but Dr. Adams goes on to deliver a broadside against all sexual activity: "His father had summed up the whole matter by stating that masturbation produced blindness, insanity, and death, while a man who went with prostitutes would contract hideous venereal diseases and that the thing to do was to keep your hands off of people."

Lacking the rudiments of sex education, Ernest later cooked up or acquired at secondhand some eccentric theories on the subject; among them that each man at birth was allotted a certain number of orgasms (which therefore must be carefully spaced out) and that if you had enough sexual intercourse, you could eat all the strawberries you wanted without contracting hives. Foolish though they were, these ideas were not much more ridiculous than those reticently advanced by Dr. Adams/Hemingway in "Fathers and Sons." But one lesson the young boy in Oak Park did absorb and take to heart was that only those in love were entitled to make love. Later in life, perhaps, he was able occasionally to ignore that lesson, though not without suffering subsequent pangs of guilt.

Nowhere in Hemingway's fiction does he celebrate sexual activity for its own sake. After casual sex, in his stories, men (and boys) turn into unfeeling monsters, or they contract gonorrhea. The evidence of his writing supports the view that Hemingway strongly disapproved of sexual promiscuity (the whole *point*, he maintained, of *The Sun Also Rises*). With the exception of Thomas Hudson, his fictional protagonists, even when like Frederic Henry they fail to love completely, *always* maintain trust with one woman. They do not, however, have to love that woman forever, since the crack of doom (in the form of death or disease) intervenes to keep their love from dissipating during a longstanding commitment.

In a long passage in *Death in the Afternoon*, Hemingway lectures about syphilis, which had been brought to Europe by the Crusaders and which was "a disease of all people who lead lives in which a disregard of consequences dominates." He scornfully writes of college men who, in their sheltered existence, had not been exposed to the joys of sex until coming out into the world after college, and who, "delivering themselves to these joys, seemed to believe that they had discovered, if not indeed invented, sexual intercourse." On finding that they had contracted a disease, these same "citizens" would be apt to limit "their activities to a much narrower social circle" thereafter and to take a high moral tone in discussing matters of sex.

Favorably contrasted to these overeducated "believers in Yale in

China" were boxers, bullfighters, and soldiers—men who had learned in the course of their education-by-experience to take risks. Though all fornicators "who continued their careers far enough" could expect to be infected eventually, Hemingway's obvious preference lay with those who "from their habits of mind would rather take chances than use prophylactics." This distaste for the mechanical paraphernalia of "safe" sex is vividly conveyed by Helen Gordon, the most sympathetic female character in *To Have and Have Not*, as she tells off her husband Richard. He speaks to her of love, but she has learned from him the ugliness of that word: "Love is ergoapiol pills to make me come around because you were afraid to have a baby. Love is quinine and quinine and quinine until I'm deaf with it. Love is that dirty aborting horror that you took me to. Love is my insides all messed up. It's half catheters and half whirling douches. I know about love. Love always hangs up behind the bathroom door. It smells like lysol." Like social diseases, babies were the natural products of love-making, and Hemingway found abhorrent any sexual arrangement which slipped off the proper path into unnatural byways. Even Honest Lil, the prostitute in *Islands in the Stream*, feels a repugnance for the "piglike things" that some men like: "If I could be rich doing perverted things and be poor doing normal things, I would be poor."

Above all, Honest Lil absolutely draws the line at "doing anything with girls," for like Hemingway she regards lesbianism as a particularly unsavory form of abnormality. In one story, "Mr. and Mrs. Elliot," Ernest adopts a tone of superior amusement in depicting a lesbian relationship; in another, "The Sea Change," the tone shifts to bitter irony as a lovely girl explains to her male companion that she must go away with another woman. According to *A Moveable Feast*, the reason why Ernest broke off with Gertrude Stein was that he could not feel the same about her after overhearing a lesbian conversation in her pavilion at 27 rue de Fleurus—sounds such as he "had never heard one person speak to another; never, anywhere, ever." Undoubtedly there were other reasons for the Stein-Hemingway split, but one stemmed from her lesbianism and her subsequent conviction, as Ernest believed, that all homosexuals were talented, and that only homosexuals were talented.

The Mincing Gentry

Talented or not, Hemingway could not stand male homosexuals, especially when they congregated in groups. In letters and throughout his published works, he went out of his way to articulate his virulent scorn for homosexuals—so far out of his way, in fact, as eventually to lay himself open to counterattack by psychologically-oriented critics.

Obviously, his Oak Park upbringing had not prepared him for sexual arrangements overtly practiced in other parts of the world. From Europe in the early 1920s, he gossiped relentlessly on the topic. Readers of the Toronto *Star Weekly*, for example, read about "utterly charming young men, with rolling white sweaters and smoothly brushed hair," who wintered in the best hotels in Switzerland on the proceeds from their bridge games "with women who are old enough to be their mothers and who deal the cards with a flashing of platinum rings on plump fingers." The select audience of *The Little Review* learned more about the Lausanne Peace Conference than they bargained for:

> Lord Curzon likes young boys.
> So does Chicherin.
> So does Mustapha Kemal.

Nor did Hemingway's fascinated disgust for homosexuals leave him in later years, though the subject is nowhere more insisted upon than in *Death in the Afternoon*. In the frequent digressions which characterize that book, Ernest came back time and again to express his contempt for homosexual writers—Jean Cocteau, Raymond Radiguet, Oscar Wilde, Walt Whitman, and André Gide among them. In more substantial detail, he relates the anecdote of the two fine, clean-cut Americans, one rather richer and older than the other, who meet on the boat to Europe and who quarrel terribly when they check into a Paris hotel room. The younger man desperately knocks on the door of the newspaperman in the next room to escape the advances of his friend, but finally returns after the friend reassures him that there will be no more trouble. Later that same night the newspaperman is awakened "by what sounded like fighting in the next room and someone saying, 'I didn't know it was that. Oh, I didn't know it was that! I won't! I won't!' followed by . . . a despairing scream." When he hammers on the wall and yells an offer of help, the screams subside to sobs and the older, richer friend advises him through the wall to mind his own business. As it turns out, the newspaperman sees the two rather often after that, having breakfast outside the Café de la Paix, riding in an open taxi, sitting on the terrace of the Café des Deux Magots, where, the last time he saw them, the poorer and younger of the two, "the one who had said he would kill himself rather than go back in that room, had had his hair hennaed." Oddly, *Death in the Afternoon* also contains Hemingway's sole expression of admiration for a man he took (from the way he depicted male genitals) to be a *maricón*—El Greco. By any standard, El Greco was a great painter, and if he was a homosexual, Hemingway wrote, "he should redeem, for the tribe, the prissy exhibitionistic, aunt-like, withered old maid moral arrogance of a Gide; the lazy, conceited debauchery of a Wilde who betrayed a generation; the nasty, sentimental pawing of humanity of a Whitman and all the mincing gentry. Viva El Greco, el Rey de los Maricones."

Hemingway's stories and novels abound with evidence of his antipathy to homosexuals; several, in fact, have no real point other than to illustrate the author's scorn for the "the mincing gentry." In "The Mother of a Queen," for example, Hemingway chronicles with disgust the unwillingness of a highly paid homosexual bullfighter to spend $20 for his mother's proper burial. Besides his miserliness, the bullfighter has yet another quality which the narrator of the story finds detestable —he refuses to be insulted: "I told him what I thought of him right there on the Gran Via, in front of three friends, but he speaks to me now when I meet him as though we were friends. What kind of blood is it that makes a man like that?"

Another story, "A Simple Enquiry," sketches the unsuccessful attempt of an Italian major to seduce his young orderly. Is the lad "quite sure that he loves a girl?" The theme of the unsuccessful homosexual seduction comes up again in *Islands in the Stream*, where Thomas Hudson's eldest son, while still a schoolboy, learns backgammon from an older man. Inadvertently the boy arouses the man's interest by confessing to having read Gide's *Si le grain ne meurt*, but he quickly repels the subsequent overtures with polite firmness: "Mr. Edwards, I take only an academic interest in homosexuality. I thank you very much for teaching me backgammon and I must bid you good day."

Implicit in these incidents is the superiority of the heterosexual to the homosexual. "I think fairies are all awfully sad," as another character in *Islands in the Stream* remarks. "Poor fairies." In Hemingway's estimation, they tended to be dishonest both in art and in life, like the "little bit pédéraste" painter of Renata's portrait in *Across the River and into the Trees*. The portrait is "very romantic" and inaccurate, showing Renata's hair twice as long as it has ever been and still dry, though she is just rising from the sea. For his part, the painter "goes with very many women to hide what he is. . . ." They affect false accents and poses, like the young novelist Robert Prentiss, in *The Sun Also Rises*, who is from New York by way of Chicago with "some sort of English accent" and whose pretended indifference to the charms of Paris makes Jake Barnes almost ill.

It is Jake, himself unmanned through a war injury, who most powerfully articulates the unrestrained anger which he and his creator felt toward homosexuals. Early in the novel, Jake takes Georgette to the "dancings" and then two taxis come up and "A crowd of young men, some in jerseys and some in their shirt-sleeves, got out. I could see their hands and newly washed, wavy hair in the light from the door. The policeman standing by the door looked at me and smiled. They came in. As they went in, under the light I saw white hands, wavy hair, white faces, grimacing, gesturing, talking. With them was Brett. She looked very lovely and she was very much with them." Just as Hemingway was annoyed by Duff Twysden's homosexual friends in Paris (perhaps, he suggested to Harold Loeb in planning the 1925 trip to Pamplona, they should arrange to have a band of local fairies meet Duff's train in Spain so as to make her feel at home), Brett Ashley's companions disturb Jake: "I was very angry. Somehow they always made me angry. I know they are supposed to be amusing, and you should be tolerant, but I wanted to swing on one, any one, anything to shatter that superior, simpering composure." To control this impulse, Jake walks down the street for a beer, but when he returns the fairies are still there, one of them has asked his *poule* Georgette to dance, and he knows then that they will "all dance with her. They are like that."

Legends abound as to Hemingway's belligerent behavior toward homosexuals. One given currency in a recent book maintains that a Key West lawyer used to bedevil Hemingway by telling homosexuals who wandered into Sloppy Joe's bar that Hemingway was really queer and would welcome a pass. Then, when one of these victims made his approach, Ernest would knock him out cold. Another, circulated by the Brooklyn-born bullfighter Sidney Franklin, held that Ernest so over-reacted to homosexuals that he once crossed the street in Spain for the sole purpose of knocking one to the ground. Neither this yarn nor the one about Sloppy Joe's squares with the incontrovertible fact of Hemingway's pleasantness toward Tennessee Williams in 1959. Williams attended their luncheon meeting in Havana with dire misgivings, having heard in advance that "Hemingway usually kicks people like me in the crotch." But the two writers talked affably together, and Ernest did not even wince when Williams said he had met Antonio Ordóñez in Spain a few months earlier and found the matador "a lovely boy, very friendly, very accessible." Perhaps, to be sure, Hemingway's fighting days were over by the time of that encounter, in his sixtieth year, but even in his youth, his voiced dislike of homosexuals expressed itself more in scornful talk than in fisticuffs.

Discussing homosexuality in *A Moveable Feast*, Hemingway wrote that as a boy he carried a knife as a safeguard against attack: "When you were a boy and moved in the company of men, you had to be prepared to kill a man, know how to do it and really know that you would do it not to be interfered with." This, presumably, was during those nonexistent days when, he liked to believe, he had run away from home and was riding the rails with tramps and hoboes. Later, during the 1920s, Ernest did issue real threats to Robert McAlmon, who had published Hemingway's first slim book of *Three Stories and Ten Poems*, but who later turned to slandering Ernest as a wife-beater and closet homosexual and Pauline as a lesbian. This last piece of defamation, which McAlmon circulated around New York in 1929, got back to Ernest by way of Fitzgerald, and prompted the comment that he'd have to beat up McAlmon, pitiful though he was. Despite such threats, however, nowhere in Carlos Baker's meticulously documented life is there an account of Hemingway actually hitting a homosexual. Still, Mc-Almon certainly touched a nerve when in his gossiping he challenged Ernest's masculinity. Though he did not slug homosexuals simply be-cause they were the way they were, he stood ready to defend himself against any imputation that his own masculinity was suspect. Just such an accusation, by another writer, led to the most celebrated brawl of Hemingway's life.

The writer was Max Eastman, who in a June 1933 *New Republic* review of *Death in the Afternoon* (entitled "Bull in the Afternoon") speculated about Ernest's psychological make-up. He had no doubt, Eastman wrote, that Hemingway was "a full-sized man," but it seemed from the aggressively masculine positions taken in the book that Hemingway himself lacked "serene confidence" in his own manhood. "Most of us too delicately organized babies who grow up to be artists," Eastman went on, "suffer at times from that small inward doubt." In Hemingway's case, it had led to an unfortunate "literary style . . . of wearing false hair on the chest."

Two outraged responses to this review soon arrived in the *New Republic*'s offices. The more effective (because more disinterested) came from Archibald MacLeish, who pointed out that Eastman's "scurrility" merely gave circulation to a commonplace bit of gossip "among the young sensitives, the old humanitarians and all the rest of the literary impotent to whom Mr. Hemingway's vitality [was] an implicit reproach." These gossipers whispered that Ernest's artistic accomplishment proceeded, "by some psychological hocus-pocus, from the fact that Mr. Hemingway himself believes himself unvirile." Why, the rumor ran, would he go so conspicuously out of his way to excoriate homosexuals had he not detected in himself an abhorrent tendency in that direction? McAlmon said as much, and Gertrude Stein implied it in *The Autobiography of Alice B. Toklas*, also published in 1933, but earlier than Eastman's famous review. MacLeish hoped his letter would stop the rumor mills from grinding, but they have stayed in operation ever since. Thus Otto Friedrich proposed in 1957 that Hemingway like Rudyard Kipling should be classified with women writers since their male characters were "always nervous of being mistaken for women" and were forever trumpeting their manhood. And Lewis Galantière wondered in 1964 whether Hemingway might have been "better satisfied to be a woman? Was his carefully cultivated hardy masculinity a means of concealing from others, and perhaps even from himself, the inward wish to be . . . a woman?" Where there was smoke, wasn't there fire?

Hemingway's behavior in the Eastman case only added fuel to such speculations. MacLeish had responded by testifying to Ernest's undoubted personal courage and by referring Eastman for evidence that his friend was indeed "a full-sized man" to the birth records of his sons in Paris and Kansas City. In more sardonic mood, Ernest put several nasty questions to the editors of the *New Republic*: "Would it not be possible for you to have Mr. Max Eastman elaborate his nostalgic speculations on my sexual incapacity?" speculations which would make amusing reading in Havana. And, on a more *ad hominem* tack: "Mr. Alexander Woollcott and the middle-aged Mr. Eastman having both published hopeful doubts as to my potency is it too much to expect that we might hear soon from Mr. Stark Young?"

At the *New Republic*, editor Bruce Bliven attempted to paper things over with assurances that neither he nor anyone else he knew (except MacLeish and Hemingway) had read the review as an attack on Hemingway's virility. In a letter to Hemingway, Eastman allowed that for his part he was doing his best to spike such rumors. But in a letter to the editor, Eastman also reiterated his "conviction that Hemingway [was] gentle and sensitive, and rather puritanical, and that there [was] a lot of unreal bluster in his roaring about whore-houses and bull's blood." This, emphatically, was not the sort of recantation to satisfy Ernest, and he was still seething when, four years later, he ran into Eastman in Max Perkins' office at Scribner's.

During the ensuing contretemps, Ernest (1) ripped open his shirt to reveal a hirsute chest, (2) unbuttoned Eastman's shirt to reveal an expanse of bare skin, (3) angrily accused Eastman of accusing him of impotence, (4) refused to reread the offending passage, and smacked Eastman in the face with the book which contained a reprinting of the review, and (5) wrestled himself and Eastman to the floor where, the physically smaller and older Eastman having landed on top of Hemingway, tempers abated and Ernest grinned up at the aghast Perkins as though the melée was the sort of thing that happened every day at Scribner's. That, presumably, would have put an end to the matter, except that the newspapers got wind of the fight and printed Eastman's version that he had bested Hemingway in a wrestling match. In retaliation Hemingway told the reporter from *The New York Times* that Eastman had "clawed at him like a woman" and challenged the critic to a real fight: "If Mr. Eastman takes his prowess seriously, let him waive all . . . legal claims to damages, and I'll put up $1000 for any charity he favors or for himself. Then we'll go into a room and he can read his book to me. . . . The best man unlocks the door." Which having said, in the serenest confidence imaginable, Ernest sailed off to resume covering the war in Spain.

As this incident demonstrates, Hemingway was extraordinarily sensitive to any imagined slights about his manliness. But there is no evidence that this sensitivity, or his fictional habit of celebrating excessively masculine characters and denigrating effeminate ones, served as a smokescreen to hide any propensities of his own. Privately he admitted to having been approached by a homosexual only once in his life, after he was wounded in World War I. While he lay in the Milan hospital recovering from his wounds, Ernest wrote thirty years after the fact, he was forced to rebuff the attentions of an older, aristocratic Englishman:

> This Englishman used to bring me Marsala. That was fine, but then he got wet about wanting to see my wounds dressed. At that time I didn't know well-brought-up people were like that. I thought it was only tramps. I explained to him that I was not that way and that he couldn't come to the hospital any more and that I couldn't take his Marsala.
>
> He felt very badly and said he must have something to remember me by. By now it was getting comic and awfully like Proust when you know Albertine is the chauffeur. So I said I would keep the Marsala and I gave him a handful of beautiful pieces of cutoff sections of metal rods that had once been a part, if not an integral part, of me and he left in tears.

The flippancy of this tale suggests that it qualifies as one of Hemingway's frequent inventions. If there were actual encounters in other rooms, he did not write of them. In all likelihood, he followed the road taken by Nick Adams and his friend Tom in "The Light of the World." When the homosexual cook, at the end of that story, asks the boys which way they're going, Tom replies, "The other way from you."

Macho and Midwesterner

What constituted ideal male behavior, for Ernest Hemingway, jibes almost exactly with the images of the *macho* as Octavio Paz describes it in *The Labyrinth of Solitude*. The *macho* is a stoical creature, capable of magnificent feats of bravery or endurance in the face of adversity, feats like those of such Hemingway heroes as Pedro Romero of *The Sun*

Also Rises and Manuel Garcia of "The Undefeated," Cayetano Ruiz of "The Gambler, the Nun, and the Radio," El Sordo of *For Whom the Bell Tolls,* and Santiago of *The Old Man and the Sea*—all admirable men, all of Spanish heritage. In combat, under actual fire, Hemingway demonstrated a high level of courage himself, but he resembled the *macho* still more in withdrawing from intimacy with others. The *macho,* Paz writes, "is a hermetic being, closed up in himself"; he never "opens up," for to do so would be to demonstrate weakness and invite rebuff. He constructs walls to keep himself "remote from the world and from other people." So Yousuf Karsh, finding Hemingway "the shyest man" he had ever photographed, sensed that he had thrown up around himself, for self-protection, "a wall of silence and myth."

In his fiction Ernest also adopted the European model of the good subservient woman, who nurtures and sustains her man through the gift of herself, sexually and in all other ways. Thus his heroines, so often criticized as "too good to be true," are characteristically foreign, from the English Catherine Barkley to the Spanish Maria and the Italian Renata. And his own "loveliest dreams," he confessed in 1938, were, like those of Robert Jordan, inhabited by "Miss Dietrich, Miss Garbo and others . . . they always being awfully nice (in dreams)." The perfect woman, then, usually comes from Europe; the hateful one (Margot Macomber, Nick Adams' mother, Mrs. Krebs in "Soldier's Home," the mother in "A Canary for One," Helene Bradley in *To Have and Have Not*), who frustrates and dominates men, comes from the United States.

Hemingway's admiring portraits of the stoical, distant male and his submissive, serving female closely match the ideals of the *macho* and his good woman. He was driven to embrace these models because the alternatives provided by his own culture proved so abhorrent. In his middle-class, Midwestern world, Mom, from her pedestal, nagged man and boy off to the woods and wars, in a flight from the female famously represented in classical American literature from the days of Deerslayer and Huck Finn to those of Nick Adams. In Ernest's own family, the traditional pattern was only magnified by an extremely powerful and domineering mother, who for several years dressed her first son as a girl, at least on special occasions. Marcelline was born first, and when Ernest came along a year later, Mrs. Hemingway, who had always wanted twins, "was determined" (as Marcelline has written) "to have us be as much like twins as possible. When we were little, Ernest and I were dressed alike in various outfits, in Oak Park in gingham dresses and in little fluffy lace tucked dresses with picture hats, and in overalls at the summer cottage on Walloon Lake." Mrs. Hemingway continued this practice into the school years, holding Marcelline back so that she and Ernest might enter first grade together. Even at that postkindergarten period, their play knew no sexual distinctions. As Marcelline recalled, "we played with small china tea sets just alike; we had dolls alike; and when Ernest was given a little air rifle, I had one too—Mother was doing her best to make us feel like twins by having everything alike." But not quite everything, and her son grew up proclaiming his virility, angrily lashing out at effeminate men, and cursing his mother.

ix

Friendship

A Gift for Friendship

In "The Doctor and the Doctor's Wife," one of his earliest stories, Hemingway first expressed himself on the preferability of male to female companionship. Nick Adams' father backs down from a fight in the story and then suffers worse humiliation from his wife, who assumes that her husband must be to blame in the dispute. Sent to fetch Nick home, Dr. Adams instead takes him hunting for black squirrels in the cool woods. Together, the two of them escape the inhibiting presence of Mrs. Adams, who lies resting her eyes in a darkened room, a copy of *Science and Health* at her side. Elsewhere in *In Our Time*, Hemingway's most autobiographical book of stories, Nick realizes that the outdoor life is much better shared with an experienced fisherman, like Bill in "The Three-Day Blow," than with a girl, like Marjorie in "The End of Something," who has to be taught how to skin a perch for bait. Valuing Bill's friendship more than Marjorie's love, he cuts her adrift.

Another semifictional fragment, which went unpublished until after Hemingway's death (the passage was originally written as a possible conclusion to the story, "Big Two-Hearted River"), reinforces the autobiographical relevancy of these Nick Adams stories. In this fragment, Nick/Ernest reflects on what his marriage to Helen/Hadley (these names are disguised, but no others are) has cost him: "When he

191

married he lost Bill Smith, Odgar, the Ghee, all the old gang . . . lost them because he admitted by marrying that something was more important than the fishing." Bill had been closest of all his friends, and like a woman forgiving him his previous lovers, Bill "forgave him the fishing he had done before they met. He forgave him all the rivers." They were all, Hemingway writes, "married to fishing. Ezra [Pound] thought fishing was a joke. So did most everybody. He'd been married to it before he married Helen. Really married to it. It wasn't any joke."

Not a joke, but a source of happiness: the sunniest scenes in *The Sun Also Rises* occur when Jake Barnes and Bill Gorton and the Englishman Wilson-Harris fish the Irati and drink together in male fellowship. At Burguete all's right with the world, while the demon of sexual jealousy converts the Pamplona fiesta into hell. "Women were very important in Hem's code," as Donald Ogden Stewart observed, "but it was a subdivision kind of thing that must not impinge on the solidarity of [male] companionship." Giving expression to that masculine solidarity, however, was a touchy business. On the strength of several bottles of wine, Wilson-Harris can bid his new friends good-by with "I say, Barnes. You don't know what this all means to me." But the less said the better, as Jake knows. "You're a hell of a good guy," he says to Bill on their fishing trip, "and I'm fonder of you than anybody on earth. I couldn't tell you that in New York. It'd mean I was a faggot." At one and the same time, American society promoted the development of male friendship and discouraged its expression in any terms more endearing than "Old Bill" and "You bum!"

Hemingway himself possessed an extraordinary capacity for inspiring the affection and admiration of other men. A shortcoming of Carlos Baker's biography, Malcolm Cowley feels, is that the book "gives hardly any notion of the immense charm" Hemingway exerted—a charm deriving from his "tall, handsome, broad-shouldered" presence, from his seemingly boundless vitality, and from his "habit of paying undivided attention" to people, one at a time, of really listening to what they had to say. In the Paris years, Hadley recalls, Ernest could "get right into the center of another person's heart and just make them feel perfectly grand." He was the kind of man "to whom men, women, children, and dogs were attracted. It was something."

Many people "were not only content," as Baker *does* comment, "but even eager to tan themselves like sunbathers in the rays he generated." The relationship between Hemingway and Don Stewart provides an example of this charismatic quality. When he came to Paris in the fall of 1923 Stewart followed two suggestions from John Peale Bishop—first, that he should read a new poem by T. S. Eliot called "The Waste Land"; second, that he should look up "an interesting young writer" named Hemingway. Eliot's poem struck a chord with Stewart, but he was even more grateful to Bishop for the tip about Hemingway, whom he liked immediately. "I didn't know anything about him as a writer," Don recalled, "but he seemed to be my kind of guy, which meant, among other things, that there wasn't any phoniness about him and he liked good food and liked to drink and he understood my kind of humor." On his first night in Paris they met at a restaurant and got on so well that Ernest insisted that Don stay at his apartment. There Stewart woke up the next morning, very happy, with a note from Hemingway telling him where he could get eggs and milk.

Not only was Ernest friendly and generous, Stewart wrote, but "he was so full of life and so full of beans" that Don ended by sharing his enthusiasms, especially for bullfighting. Thus, Stewart went along to the Pamplona fiesta, in 1924 and 1925, and "was so damn anxious to please Ernest" that he "wouldn't have dared to criticize bullfighting." In 1924 he even climbed into the ring with the rest of the amateur *toreros*: "I wouldn't have gone into the goddamn ring, but there was Ernest in there going around chasing bulls, and . . . I was sort of hanging around the outside of the crowd not wanting to—because I'm scared to death of animals. Especially bulls. Even though they're young bulls with their horns wrapped and everything. I was just trying to show Ernie that I was there—'old Don'—I didn't really want to face it." But he went on in, and someone gave him a cape, and since he didn't understand how to execute a *veronica*, Stewart was tossed twice and broke a couple of ribs and got his picture in the papers. He never would have done it, Stewart realized, but that he wanted Ernest to like him. "I wanted to live up to his ideal of manhood, you see. It was as simple as that, and all I got were two broken ribs and a lot of hangovers." They were great friends from 1923 to 1926, when Hemingway read a scurrilous poem about Dorothy Parker at a party, Stewart told him off, and that was the end of that.

Another Hemingway sporting interest, during those years, was bicycle racing. Stewart went along to watch this too, though as he observed in 1972, he'd "run 8000 miles rather than go to see one of those damn things." Allen Tate was also a convert to the six-day races at the Vélodrome d'Hiver. "I never thought I'd like a bicycle race," Tate remarked, "but [Ernest] had the gift of imparting enthusiasm for anything he was enthusiastic about."

Especially as a young man, Hemingway made people want to please him, to do things for him. The poet and horse player Evan Shipman, for example, gave up Joan Miró's painting *The Farm* in order to win Ernest's approval. Shipman bought the painting on time from a Paris gallery on the rue Bonaparte. But when he told Hemingway about it, Hemingway's mouth fell and he said, "Ezra Pound took me to see that picture a year ago, and ever since I have wanted it more than any other single thing I can think of." Ernest was too broke to make an offer, but Shipman, taking pity, offered to flip a coin. "I want the picture myself," Evan told his friend, "but I'm willing to toss you for it. After all, you saw it first." Shipman won the toss, but he "sold" the painting to Hemingway anyway, at cost and on easy installments, when "his face showed me that he felt worse than I would have felt if I had happened to lose." At last report, Miró's great painting was still on display in Mary Hemingway's apartment. Whatever Ernest wanted, Ernest got.

"The Career, the Career"

What he wanted most of all, those early years in Paris, was literary success, and in this quest Hemingway's abundant charm undoubtedly served him well. The novelist Nathan Asch, a fellow expatriate, noted how Ernest "managed to have it important for visitors to Paris to meet him." He "*was* a conscious careerist," Asch concluded, but "finally he did have the stuff, and he delivered." Ernest had originally come to Paris with the auspicious endorsement of Sherwood Anderson. There he managed to cultivate most of those in a position to give him a leg up. The most famous of these were Gertrude Stein and, later, the British novelist Ford Madox Ford, but there were others as well. All, for a time, befriended Hemingway as a prepossessing young man and promising young artist; nearly all, in due time, were dismissed from his roster of friends as unworthy. Ezra Pound proved to be the exception, but Ezra was more than merely a literary companion: he boxed and played tennis with Ernest as well. Yet when Pound and Hemingway were first introduced, in Sylvia Beach's bookstore, Ernest announced, with at least some degree of calculation, "I have traveled four thousand miles to see *you*." Even Scott Fitzgerald, who virtually worshiped Hemingway, sensed an opportunistic strain in his friend. "Ernest," he wrote, "would always give a helping hand to a man on a ledge a little higher up."

Anderson occupied a place very near the top of the mountain when Hemingway, as would-be writer, first met him in Chicago in 1921. Anderson launched the Hemingways in Paris by giving Ernest letters of introduction to Stein, Pound, Beach, and the witty Lewis Galantière. The letters described the couple as "delightful people to know" and spoke of Ernest's "extraordinary talent," which would take him far beyond journalism. (Except for high-school juvenilia, Hemingway had yet to publish a short story anywhere.) As a gesture of reciprocation, Hemingway brought the older writer a knapsack full of provisions the night before he and Hadley left Chicago for Europe, a "magnificent broad-shouldered man" shouting up the stairs with "a hundred pounds of perfectly good rations." What a nice idea, Anderson thought, "bringing thus to a fellow scribbler the food he had to abandon." But it was Anderson's gift of entrée that was the more valuable. Four years later his advocacy of Hemingway helped persuade Boni and Liveright to bring out *In Our Time*.

Ernest's relationship with older, more established writers tended to follow a pattern. First acquaintance would quickly ripen into friendship, then the better-established artist would give Hemingway's career a boost, and finally Ernest would repudiate his benefactor. In Anderson's case, the repudiation took a public form because Hemingway was trying very hard, in *The Torrents of Spring*, to do away with the critical assumption that his work derived from Anderson, that he was in effect Anderson's protégé. In fact, Ernest Hemingway's prose did reflect Anderson's influence. As Archibald MacLeish put it, "Anderson was the bone on which [Ernest] cut his teeth. He got to be a big dog on Anderson." In style, Hemingway adopted the direct simplicity of language that Anderson had pioneered; in subject matter, both writers focused on apparently unsophisticated people, often from the world of sport. What Hemingway took from Anderson, or from Gertrude Stein, his genius shaped into something singularly his own. Yet during his apprenticeship, he wrote some stories ("My Old Man," for example, seems to borrow its racetrack milieu and theme of disillusioned innocence from Anderson's "I Want to Know Why") which strike the critical eye as derivative.

Such borrowings Hemingway proceeded to write off in *The Torrents of Spring*, which ridicules Anderson's naïvely romantic obsession (especially in his financially successful 1925 novel *Dark Laughter*) with primitive and inarticulate people. As Morley Callaghan remarked, people were saying, "Ah yes, you can see where this came from, this came from Sherwood Anderson." And Hemingway, "being rather violent," knew that "you must kill your father."

In breaking the news to Anderson about *The Torrents of Spring*, Ernest justified himself on artistic grounds. He maintained in a May 1926 letter that Anderson, who was capable of writing very great things, needed to be told when his fiction went rotten, so that he could stop writing "slop." Ernest meant nothing personal by his satire. He "had done it," so Anderson interpreted his patronizing letter, "in the interest of literature. Literature, I was to understand, was bigger than either of us." Decades later Ernest stuck to the same reasoning in an unpublished 1959 essay on "The Art of the Short Story." While admitting that his satire had been cruel and he had been a son of a bitch to "throw at" Anderson, his motivation had been of the best: to show Sherwood the error of his ways and try to straighten him out. But if that were true, a letter might have served as well as the book (though it wouldn't have broken his contract with Boni and Liveright). Wright Morris has called the book "a sustained, carefully planned, and extremely clever effort of annihilation." *The Torrents of Spring*, Morris believed, was "not the act, to put it charitably, of a self-reliant man." Instead it was the "skillfully tactical ploy" of a man who was frightened both of creditors and of competitors.

Where Anderson's influence on Hemingway came by way of example, the Buddha-like Gertrude Stein served more directly as copy editor, examining and criticizing Ernest's first efforts at fiction. "There is a great deal of description in this," she said of Ernest's 1922 novel, which Hadley later lost in the Gare de Lyon, "and not particularly good description. Begin over again and concentrate." Ernest's dark eyes showed her that he was "passionately interested" in what she had to say. For the moment, he sat at her feet, a rapt devotee. But that too passed, and in time they quarreled, Stein to accuse Hemingway not only of cowardice but of careerism ("What a story that of the real Hem, and one he should tell himself but alas he never will. After all, as he himself once murmured, there is the career, the career"); Hemingway to accuse Stein—in *Green Hills of Africa*—of letting her talent turn "to malice, and nonsense and self-praise" and—in correspondence and again in *A Moveable Feast*—of being "patriotic" about her lesbianism.

On the issue of influence, Stein wrote, in exaggeration, that "Hemingway had been formed by the two of them" (Sherwood Anderson and herself), and that they enjoyed teaching him because "it is so flattering to have a pupil who does it without understanding it, in other words he takes training and anybody who takes training is a favorite pupil." Ernest, in retaliation, simply turned the tables. "You know a funny thing," he remarked in *Green Hills of Africa*, "she never could write dialogue. It was terrible. She learned how to do it from my stuff. . . . She never could forgive learning that and she was afraid people would notice it, where she'd learned it. . . . But I swear she was nice before she got ambitious." Pauline rounded out the denunciation of Stein. "She's just jealous and malicious," she told Ernest. "You never should have helped her. Some people never forgive that." By 1948, in a letter to W. C. Rogers, Hemingway was ready to admit that both he and Gertrude had profited from their friendship. But, once again, his explanation of what happened between them revealed more about Ernest's own motives than about Stein's: "She had . . . a sort of necessity to break off friendships. . . . She had to attack me because she learned to write dialogue from me just as I learned the wonderful rhythms in prose from her."

Another benefactor-turned-victim was Ford Madox Ford. On the strength of Pound's recommendation (Hemingway ranked, Ezra told Ford, as "the finest prose stylist in the world"), Ford gave Ernest an unpaid post as assistant editor of *Transatlantic Review* in 1924. At their first meeting, Ford was somewhat taken aback by the young American, who danced around on his toes shadowboxing, acting and talking rather like "a bayonet instructor." Yet he soon proclaimed himself an admirer of Hemingway's abilities. "The best writer in America at this moment (though for the moment he happens to be in Paris)," Ford wrote in 1925, "the most conscientious, the most master of his craft, the most consummate, is my young friend Ernest Hemingway."

To such generosity, Ernest replied with ridicule. One reason was that he could hardly look at the author of *The Good Soldier*—fat, asthmatic, washed-out eyes beneath colorless lashes and brows—without acute discomfort. Then Ford earned Ernest's further displeasure by yarning about his improbable encounters with English royalty, and—according to the belittling sketch in *A Moveable Feast*—by ignoring whatever anyone else said. In the sketch, Ford announces to Hemingway that he has discovered an amusing *bal musette* on the rue du Cardinal Lemoine, and, not listening to Ernest's response that he had lived on that very street for two years, insists on providing him with directions. The two men fell out about the magazine as well. On one occasion Ford criticized his subeditor in print for including too much American material in an issue Hemingway had put out alone; on another he gently chastised him, also in print, for gratuitously including an attack on T. S. Eliot in a Joseph Conrad memorial number (if he could bring Conrad back to life "by grinding Mr. Eliot into a fine dry powder and sprinkling that powder over Conrad's grave," Hemingway had written, he would "leave for London early tomorrow morning with a sausage grinder"). Finally, Hemingway and Ford fell out entirely. "Pay for your own drinks," Ernest yelled to Hadley across a crowded room late in 1924. "Don't let [Ford] buy you anything."

Among Ernest's other supporters during his early years as a writer were Edward O'Brien and Owen Wister. O'Brien, editor after World War I of anthologies containing the year's best short stories, met a dejected Hemingway in Rapallo in 1923. Ernest's spirits rose when O'Brien read "My Old Man" in manuscript and immediately took it for *The Best Short Stories of 1923*, though normally he only reprinted stories which had first appeared in magazine form. Further, the editor was enough impressed with Ernest, on this brief acquaintance, to dedicate the volume to him. When this news reached Hemingway, he gratefully replied that he couldn't have been more pleased by a combined gift of a million dollars, the Victoria Cross, a permanent pass for the royal suite on the *Mauretania*, and a seat replacing Anatole France in the French Academy. In other letters to O'Brien, he discussed more practical problems, complaining about the shortsightedness of most editors and seeking advice on the best magazine markets for his work. With one such letter, Ernest enclosed several stories, asking O'Brien to ship them along to an agent. Then he inquired: Should he enter the *Harper's* story contest? How many stories would he need for a book? By August 1927, however, three of Ernest's books had been published, his work was in demand, and his manner became less submissive. When they'd talked in Paris earlier in the summer, Hemingway had promised O'Brien that he could have "Fifty Grand" for his forthcoming anthology. Now it turned out that Scribners wanted to include the boxing story in Ernest's next collection, and, besides, the publishers had sent him an advance of $750 and he needed the money. O'Brien had done more for him than anyone, Ernest concluded, but he hoped that he'd ask for something other than "Fifty Grand." O'Brien did, and without, one suspects, ever regretting the change in plans. The story he took as replacement was "The Killers."

Hemingway and Owen Wister met in Paris during the winter of 1927–28. Then sixty-eight years old and still vigorous, Wister had achieved success in a number of fields, including music and law, but he was best known as the author of *The Virginian* and several other best sellers. He was also a personal friend of Theodore Roosevelt, whose biography he later wrote, and his reformist opinions on political and social issues carried a good deal of weight. This illustrious man was at once impressed by young Hemingway, forty years his junior, though as he commented in the lively correspondence that ensued, he was rather fussy about bestowing his friendship and guidance. Such others as Upton Sinclair, John Steinbeck, Frank Norris, and Hamlin Garland had courted his favor, Wister wrote, but none of them appealed to him so much as Hemingway. He detected in Ernest something the others lacked —a streak of independence.

In the same long letter, which was mailed in February 1929 (six weeks after the suicide of Ernest's father), Wister praised the younger man's writing, asked after his health, and enclosed his personal check for $500. Hemingway replied that he didn't really need the money now, but perhaps in the future he might want to call on Wister, and confusedly assured the older man in one sentence that he was just fine and wondered in the next if he would live long enough to finish another book. That summer, when the two men foregathered in Paris, Ernest made a botch of the meeting, at which he had planned to find out more about Wister's friend Rudyard Kipling, by talking too much of himself. Ernest felt especially guilty, he wrote in an apologetic note, because he had just been instructing his son Bumby that he should dispense with "I, I" the "detestable" perpendicular pronoun, for a week.

But Wister and Hemingway did not really fall out until the fall of 1929. Max Perkins sent Wister galley proofs of *A Farewell to Arms*, asking for an endorsement. But the endorsement was not forthcoming, and Wister wrote Ernest that though he admired the novel's vitality, he found the ending painful and the profanity gratuitous. Up to this time

Hemingway had gratefully accepted criticism from the older writer. But now he rebelled, curtly responding that he hoped Wister meant the good things he said about the book; as for the criticism, he had worked so hard on the novel that he could not judge it dispassionately. Hemingway's next letter, in January 1930, respectfully insisted that every man had to write for himself. And that December Ernest took over the role of editorial adviser himself, telling Wister that his biography of Roosevelt (which had appeared serially in the *Saturday Evening Post*), had not succeeded because Wister was too close to his subject. A year later Hemingway sent a letter and telegram apologizing for his ill temper, and several decades later he told Charles Fenton that Wister was one of the writers he'd known whom he considered a friend. But by refusing Wister's fatherly offer of financial help and by rejecting his literary advice, Ernest had asserted his independence—the very quality the older writer most admired in him—and so broken the bonds of friendship.

Hemingway and O'Brien drifted apart quietly as Ernest became more prominent, and the break with Wister was communicated privately. Closer contemporaries, notably Harold Loeb, were not so fortunate. According to Loeb's own account, it was he who rescued *In Our Time* from the rejection pile at Boni and Liveright, and so helped set Hemingway's publishing career in motion. According to all accounts, it was Loeb who met Lady Duff Twysden for a week of dalliance just prior to the 1925 fiesta at Pamplona. Ernest thus had two reasons to dislike Loeb: fierce independence which would not acknowledge indebtedness and sexual jealousy. At Pamplona these emotions flared into open insult, and the morning after one such clash Ernest sent Loeb a note saying that he was thoroughly ashamed of the way he'd acted and of the "stinking" things he'd said the night before. The next year, with the publication of *The Sun Also Rises*, Hemingway revealed the insincerity of these remarks by modeling his "miserable character" Robert Cohn very obviously after Loeb. In his portrait of Loeb/Cohn, Ernest worked off whatever jealousy remained and disposed of one more man who had given his career an upward shove.

At the beginning of the career, Hemingway angled for and obtained the friendly assistance of a number of influential people in the literary world. Then, in his paradoxical determination to prove that he needed no one's help in achieving success, he found ways to announce to the world—or to himself—his independence of such benefactors. If you did him a favor, as Robert M. Coates put it, you were dead. In Don

Stewart's phrase, Ernest was "a dangerous friend" to have—dangerous to those who helped him, doubly dangerous to helpers who might be regarded as potential literary rivals. Both conditions were operative in the sad story of the relationship between Ernest and Scott Fitzgerald.

Scott versus Ernest

Even before they met, Scott Fitzgerald was blowing Ernest Hemingway's horn. As self-appointed talent scout for Scribners, Fitzgerald alerted his editor Maxwell Perkins, in the fall of 1924, to the existence of "a young man named Ernest Hemingway, who lives in Paris (an American), writes for the *Transatlantic Review* and has a brilliant future." Fitzgerald had seen the remarkable sketches of *in our time*, and could guarantee that Hemingway was "the real thing."

Six months later, on a spring afternoon in 1925 at the Dingo Bar on the rue Delambre, Fitzgerald and Hemingway met. The two men became friends immediately, though aside from being Midwesterners and writers they had not much in common. Fitzgerald had followed a conventional path through prep school and Princeton, succeeded by a stateside career as a second lieutenant in World War I. He had then achieved unusual early literary success—*The Great Gatsby* was published in April 1925, less than a month before he met Hemingway, and that great novel was Fitzgerald's fifth published book. By contrast, Ernest's writing had not yet appeared between book covers in America. (*In Our Time* would not come out until November of that year.) He was also three years younger than Scott, but he had accumulated enough experience to seem—and act—years older.

Fitzgerald admired the younger man's obvious dedication to his craft, and what he had seen of his work. But he was still more admiring of Hemingway the man—seemingly simple but actually complex, at once adventurous and sensitive, courageous and shy. And then, of course, there was Ernest's famous charm. For these reasons, and undoubtedly because Scott took a certain pleasure in playing the role of patron, Fitzgerald began a full-scale campaign to promote Hemingway's career.

In service of that goal, Scott sought aid in some unlikely quarters, including even Glenway Wescott, between whom and Hemingway no love was lost (Hemingway was to pillory Wescott as the shallow novelist Robert Prentiss in *The Sun Also Rises*). It was all very well that their books—Fitzgerald's *The Great Gatsby* and Wescott's *The Apple of the Eye*—were succeeding in America, Scott argued, but surely Glenway would agree that Hemingway as an artist was superior to both of them and deserved their help. What could Wescott do to launch him? Why didn't he write a laudatory essay? (Scott did himself, for *The Bookman.*) Wescott was impressed, at the time, by what seemed a strange naïveté and lack of calculation on Fitzgerald's part, and he wondered too if such apparent abasement of the self at Ernest's shrine was good for Scott.

But Fitzgerald plunged ahead, his major effort directed to wooing Ernest to his side as a fellow Scribners author; in a series of letters to Perkins, he plotted and schemed to that end. Max's first offer to sign up Hemingway reached him five days after he had committed himself to Horace Liveright. But Hemingway, "a fine, charming fellow," had appreciated Perkins' initial letter enormously, Scott told Max, and if "Liveright doesn't please him he'll come to you." That, eventually, was what happened, though not before Fitzgerald had advised Perkins to send a wire eagerly soliciting Ernest's work, filled him in on the competition from Liveright and Harcourt, Brace, warned him to soft-pedal his own role in the negotiations, and—privately to Hemingway— stressed that one of the advantages of dealing with Scribners was that they also published their own excellent magazine, in those days under the editorship of Robert Bridges. So when Hemingway came to New York in the winter of 1926, Perkins was prepared to meet him with a generous offer for both *The Torrents of Spring*, his satire on Sherwood Anderson that did double duty as contract-breaker with Liveright, and the promising novel *The Sun Also Rises*, and to assure him that Bridges would publish "The Killers" in *Scribner's Magazine*. To such blandishments, Ernest capitulated, and with his friend firmly in the fold, Scott's function altered slightly from promoter to protector. "Do ask him for the absolute minimum of necessary changes" on *The Sun Also Rises*, Fitzgerald advised Perkins in June 1926, adding that Hemingway "was discouraged about the previous reception of his work by publishers and magazine editors" and so far had earned almost no money at all from his writing. Besides, Fitzgerald was acting as editor at the source. On his recommendation, Ernest had cut a thousand words out of "The Killers" and several thousand out of *The Sun Also Rises*.

Fitzgerald read a carbon copy of the manuscript of *The Sun Also Rises* in June 1926, while type was being set in New York, and urged Hemingway to chuck his entire first chapter, some thirty-five hundred words of "careless and ineffectual" writing which originally began with chatty casualness. "This is a novel about a lady. Her name is Lady Ashley and when the story begins she is living in Paris and it is spring." Elsewhere in his critique, Fitzgerald accused the younger writer of verbosity, easy irony, and "maladroit" writing, but ended with a tactful reminder that he thought Ernest's "stuff" was great.

Ernest lopped off that abortive beginning, just as Scott told him to, but he never admitted it. In *A Moveable Feast*, he strongly implied that Fitzgerald had nothing to do with any alterations. "That fall of 1925," Ernest wrote, Scott "was upset because I would not show him the manuscript of the first draft of *The Sun Also Rises*. . . . Scott did not see it until after the completed rewritten and cut manuscript had been sent to Scribners at the end of April." This account, while technically true, tells a good deal less than the whole truth, which was that when Scott *did* see the manuscript on the Riviera that summer and recommended the changes, Ernest wisely followed his advice.

Asked for his recommendations on *A Farewell to Arms* in 1929, Fitzgerald in nine pages of handwritten commentary once again proposed that the book could profit from careful pruning. There were places, he felt, where Ernest had become "a little hypnotized" with himself, sections which "ought to be *thoroughly* cut—even rewritten." He was especially bothered by the characterization of Catherine, who seemed to him "too glib." Ernest was seeing Frederic Henry "in a sophisticated way as now you see yourself then—but you're still seeing her as you did in 1917 through 19 year old eyes. In consequence unless you make her a bit fatuous occasionally the contrast jars—either the writer is a simple fellow or she's Eleanora Duse disguised as a Red Cross nurse." Scott also asked whether it was in character for Frederic Henry to shoot the fleeing sergeant, and proposed "a burst of eloquence" for the ending. Once more, as with *The Sun Also Rises*, the criticism was harsh; as Scott remarked parenthetically, perhaps their friendship wouldn't survive but "better me than some nobody on the Literary Review that doesn't care about you and your future." And he ended with praise: "A beautiful book it is!" which elicited a written obscenity in the margin from Ernest.

This time, Ernest did not make the suggested changes, and then proceeded, when the Fitzgerald revival got under way in the 1950s, to tell others what a lousy critic Scott had been. To Charles Poore, he derided Fitzgerald's insistence that Lieutenant Henry should not be allowed to shoot the sergeant (still a touchy point among interpreters of the novel) and with rather more reason hee-hawed at Scott's proposal that after Catherine dies Frederic should go to the café and read about the Marines holding firm at Château Thierry. Scott had made some fifty criticisms, Ernest wrote, and not one "made any sense or was useful." Furthermore, he lied, "I had learned not to show [my fiction] to him a long time before."

Ernest need hardly have repudiated this editorial debt to Fitzgerald so vigorously. Indeed, he could have done away with the evidence by destroying the notes Scott sent him on his first two novels. But he did not destroy them; perhaps with an eye cocked on immortality, he destroyed practically nothing. For his part, Scott cautiously minimized his role as editor, writing John O'Hara in 1936, for example, that though he and Ernest talked "back and forth at each other . . . the only effect he'd ever had on him [Ernest] was to get him in a receptive mood and say let's cut out everything that goes before this. Then the pieces got mislaid and he could never find the part that I said to cut out. And so he published it without that and later we agreed that it was a very wise cut." Then, perhaps disturbed at having twisted the facts, Fitzgerald modestly added: "This is not literally true and I don't want it established as part of the Hemingway legend, but it's about as far as one writer can go in helping another." The letter concluded with Scott's recognition that he had been wrong about the ending of *A Farewell to Arms*. Hemingway, he said, had been in doubt about the ending and "marketed around to half a dozen people for their advice. I worked like hell on the idea and only succeeded in evolving a philosophy in his mind utterly contrary to everything he thought an ending should be, and [it] later convinced me that he was right and made me end *Tender Is the Night* on a fade-away instead of a staccato."

After 1929 Hemingway no longer tolerated any criticism from Fitzgerald. Actually, the roles were reversed, and so Scott wrote Ernest in May 1934 pleading for his reaction to *Tender Is the Night*: "For

God's sake drop me a line and tell me one way or another" (he was to find out, soon enough).

Initially the two writers felt a genuine tenderness for each other. "I can't tell you how I miss you," Scott wrote Ernest in 1927. If you don't mind, you are the "best damn" friend I have, Ernest wrote Scott the same year. And remnants of the feeling remained even after they went their separate ways in the 1930s. His friendship with Ernest had been one of the high points of his life, Scott wrote Perkins; he had "loved" Scott, Ernest wrote Arthur Mizener.

During the years when their friendship flourished (from 1925 to 1929), Fitzgerald and Hemingway also demonstrated their affection through a singularly good-natured and carefree literary spoofing contest —an exchange in which they made fun of each other, of each other's work, and even of themselves. To his notebooks, for example, Scott confided the observation: "*This Side of Paradise*: A Romance and a Reading List. *The Sun Also Rises*: A Romance and a Guide Book."

In September 1926 he sent Ernest a scatological satire based on five of the eighteen short interchapters to *In Our Time*:

> We were in the back-house at Juan-les-Pins. Bill had lost control of his sphinctre muscles. . . . When the King of Bulgaria came in, Bill was just firing a burst that struck the old lime-shit twenty feet down with a *splat-tap*. All the rest came just like that. The King of Bulgaria began to whirl round and round.
> "The great thing in these affairs—" he said.
> Soon he was whirling faster and faster. Then he was dead.

In December 1927 Scott poked gentle fun at his friend's growing notoriety by asking Ernest if it was true that "you were seen running through Portugal in used B.V.D.'s, chewing ground glass and collecting material for a story on *boule* players; that you were publicity man for Lindbergh; that you have finished a novel a hundred thousand words long consisting entirely of the word 'balls' used in new groupings, that you have been naturalized a Spaniard, dress always in a wine-skin with 'zipper' vent and are engaged in bootlegging Spanish Fly between San Sebastian and Biarritz, where your agents sprinkle it on the floor of the Casino."

Hemingway also joked with Fitzgerald in correspondence, but with a certain edge to the humor deriving from his position as the aftercomer to literary prominence. In a long "set-piece," Ernest both suggested his debt to Fitzgerald and made sport of the novel of matricide (which eventually, after many transformations, turned out to be *Tender Is the Night*) that Scott then had in mind. Purportedly, Ernest was outlining the plot of *The Sun Also Rises*:

> The hero, like Gatsby, is a Lake Superior Salmon Fisherman. (There are no salmon in Lake Superior.) The action all takes place in Newport, R.I., and the heroine is a girl named Sophie Irene Loeb who kills her mother. The scene in which Sophie gives birth to twins in the death house at Sing Sing where she is waiting to be electrocuted for the murder of the father and sister of her, as then, unborn children I got from Dreiser but practically everything else in the book is either my own or yours. I know you'll be glad to see it. *The Sun Also Rises* comes from Sophie's statement as she is strapped into the chair as the current mounts.

In yet another note Ernest jested about the high prices Scott commanded for his magazine work, some of it mediocre. His son Bumby, the letter ran, had taken up writing, and the Hearst papers had offered him "182,000 bits" for a serial about lesbians wounded in the war who found it so difficult to have children that they started drinking and cavorting all over Europe and Asia. Scott's version of Heaven, Hemingway speculated in a July 1925 letter, would be populated by powerful and wealthy monogamists, all belonging to the best families, steadily drinking themselves to death. By contrast, his own version of Heaven consisted of holding two *barrera* seats at a bull ring with an exclusive trout stream outside and two houses nearby—one for his wife and children, the other for his nine gorgeous mistresses. In these communications, Ernest as sportsman was insisting on his difference from the essentially indoor Fitzgerald.

From the very beginning, though, Ernest was distressed by what he considered Scott's unfortunate weaknesses. According to the abrasive reminiscence in *A Moveable Feast*, Fitzgerald's very appearance augured ill: "Scott was a man then [in 1925] who looked like a boy with a face between handsome and pretty. He had very fair wavy hair, a high forehead, excited and friendly eyes and a delicate long-lipped Irish mouth that, on a girl, would have been the mouth of a beauty. His chin was well built and he had good ears and a handsome, almost beautiful, unmarked nose. This should not have added up to a pretty face, but that came from the coloring, the very fair hair and the mouth. The mouth worried you until you knew him and then it worried you more." One of the things he came to worry about was Fitzgerald's habit of twisting his good fiction into the formula that guaranteed acceptance by the *Saturday Evening Post* (for up to $4000 a throw). Ernest warned him that this was whoring and that he did not believe "anyone could write any way except the very best he could without destroying his talent."

Another shortcoming had to do with liquor. The first time they met, Scott passed out. Later he often seemed stupefied with drink. In November 1925 he came to call on the Hemingways one afternoon, and (so the tale is recounted in *The Torrents of Spring*) "after remaining for quite a while suddenly sat down in the fireplace and would not (or was it could not, reader?) get up and let the fire burn something else so as to keep the room warm." In humorous expiation, Fitzgerald explained by letter that "the man who entered your apartment . . . was not me but a man named Johnston who has often been mistaken for me." But such comedy wore thin, and Ernest rather scornfully concluded that his friend was simply a drunkard, though it was hard to accept him as such "since he was affected by such small quantities of alcohol."

But Scott's worst failing, in Ernest's eyes, was that he let Zelda control his life and, finally, "destroy" him. Hemingway maintained that he recognized at once the madness of Zelda, with her "hawk's eyes and a thin mouth and deep-south manners and accent." He was also sure that she was jealous of Scott's work and enjoyed exploiting his weakness for liquor. One day the Fitzgeralds invited the Hemingways to lunch, and "Scott was being the good cheerful host, and Zelda looked at him and she smiled happily with her eyes, and her mouth too, as he drank the wine. I learned to know that smile very well. It meant she knew Scott would not be able to write." Not only did she encourage her alcoholic husband to drink, but she "really ruined" him, Ernest felt, by complaining that he was no good in bed. According to *A Moveable Feast*, she told Scott that he had never satisfied her sexually because his penis was too small. Scott believed her, and brought this problem to Ernest. Hemingway did his best to reassure Fitzgerald through comparative examinations in the water closet and among the statues at the Louvre, but Scott remained doubtful and unsure of himself. Before she was certified as officially "net-able" and placed under institutional care, she had, Ernest felt, successfully emasculated her husband.

The antipathy was mutual. On first reaction, Zelda found Ernest Hemingway "bogus," a "poseur," and she did not change her mind. She belittled his writing. She tried to keep Scott from lending him money and from exerting his influence at Scribners in his behalf. Finally she accused Scott of a homosexual liaison with Ernest. As Fitzgerald understated the case to Perkins in 1932, "there has always been a subtle struggle between Ernest and Zelda," based on jealousy. Therefore, he advised Max, when he saw Hemingway, not to mention that Scribners was bringing out Zelda's novel, *Save Me the Waltz*: *"do not praise it, or even talk about it to him!"* Ernest would be upset, since his *Death in the Afternoon* was also scheduled for publication, and he would expect Max's "entire allegiance" to his work. Once, Ernest had told Scott that he would "never publish a book in the same season" with him because it might lead to ill feeling. Since there already existed plenty of ill feeling between Ernest and Zelda, it was best not to let a literary rivalry stir up the troubled waters.

Meanwhile, Scott and Ernest could hardly avoid conducting between themselves a competition that strained the ties of friendship, a rivalry only intensified by the explicit comparisons others were constantly making. Christian Gauss, the great Princeton educator who looked up Fitzgerald in Paris in 1925, was moved on the strength of a brief meeting with Hemingway to this exercise in contrast: "You two take your places at the opposite ends of the modern spectrum. Without disrespect to him I put Hemingway down at the infrared side and you on the ultra-violet. His rhythm is like the beating of an African tom-tom—primitive, simple, but it gets you in the end.

"You are at the other end. You have a feeling for musical intervals and the tone-color of words which makes your prose the finest instrument for rendering all the varied shades of our complex emotional states." Such a contrast did not trouble Fitzgerald, who must have sensed Gauss's preference for his kind of light. But he *was* disturbed when Gertrude Stein essayed a metaphorical comparison, remarking in the presence of the two young authors that their "flames" were not at all the same.

After brooding over that remark, Fitzgerald became convinced that Stein meant his "flame" was inferior to Hemingway's and wrote Ernest a letter complaining about it. Hemingway replied by saying, first, that Stein had meant just the opposite (that she preferred Fitzgerald's flame) and, second, it really didn't matter, since such comparisons were all nonsense. Why didn't Fitzgerald forget about who was superior? Among serious writers, there could be no such thing as competition anyway. They were all in the same boat, and to compete within the boat was as silly as playing deck sports. But this high-minded and very reasonable letter came from a man whose fierce desire for pre-eminence could not be subdued by mere common sense.

Furthermore, Scott was constantly confronted, as his own literary fortunes declined, by the rapidly growing reputation of his erstwhile friend and protégé. His letters illustrate, time and again, his awareness that "I was silent for too long after Gatsby, and then Ernest's vogue succeeded mine."

What most galled Scott was the conviction that Scribners, to whom he had in effect delivered Hemingway, later came to treat Ernest, and not himself, as most favored author. In September 1933 Scott wrote Perkins asking if *The Great Gatsby* could not be brought out in the Modern Library edition, and then drew the lines of his complaint: ". . . a novel of Ernest's in the Modern Library and no novel of mine, a good short story of Ernest's in their collection and a purely commercial story of mine." Again in 1938, Scott linked his own fading reputation to Ernest's increasing success: "Since the going out of print of [*This Side of*] *Paradise*" he wrote Perkins, "and the success (or is it one?) of *The Fifth Column* [*and the First Forty-Nine Stories*] I have come to feel somewhat neglected. Isn't my reputation being allowed to let slip away? I mean what's left of it."

Clearly Scott felt diminished by Hemingway's success. Fitzgerald's own life and career had, in Ernest's phrase, "a very steep trajectory," and it seemed to Scott, finally, as if Ernest's eminence hovered above him, announcing "I told you so," as he plunged toward obscurity.

During his final Hollywood years Scott proposed to Thornton Wilder that Hemingway was the reason why he wasn't writing any fiction: "Ernest," he said, "has made all my writing unnecessary." And when Hemingway as Byronic foreign correspondent and propagandist for Loyalist Spain swept through the film capital in 1937 to raise money for ambulances, Scott was literally terrified at the prospect of seeing him. In his notebooks, he spelled out the reason: "I talk with the authority of failure—Ernest with the authority of success. We could never sit across the same table again."

Suffering through those final years when his reputation was in such precipitous decline, Fitzgerald found some consolation in hoping for a more favorable judgment from posterity. "After all, Max," he wrote Perkins, "I am a plodder. One time I had a talk with Ernest Hemingway, and I told him, against all the logic that was then current, that I was the tortoise and he was the hare, and that's the truth of the matter. . . ." In the fullness of tortoise-time, Fitzgerald's reputation has been fully restored. But while he lived, it was at the very least frustrating for him to plod in futile pursuit of so rapid and visible a hare as Hemingway. Armed with a touch of genius, Hemingway provided a standard against which Fitzgerald was forever measuring himself to his own disadvantage.

One escape from such invidious comparisons was to make Ernest into a creature of superhuman proportions, above compare with mere mortals, and from the start there was a strong element of hero worship in Fitzgerald's attitude toward him. Ernest functioned both as Scott's "artistic conscience" and as a model to be admired for his physical prowess as boxer, outdoorsman, pseudosoldier—all roles which Fitzgerald himself did not or could not fill. There seemed a toughness about Ernest, Scott thought, the "quality of a stick hardened in the fire," that lay beyond emulation. Ernest was fully aware of Scott's propensity to adulation. It was embarrassing, he wrote Mizener, to be somebody's hero and have all sorts of qualities attributed to you.

This hero worship found its literary embodiment in the incomplete and badly written novel of the Middle Ages which Scott began in the mid-1930s. Tentatively entitled "Philippe, Count of Darkness," it recounted the adventures of an eleventh-century French nobleman. In all, Fitzgerald completed four installments of the novel, which appeared in *Redbook* for October 1934, June 1935, August 1935, and (posthumously) November 1941. In the first installment, Philippe, who was consciously modeled upon Ernest, returns to France after a childhood spent in captivity in Moorish Spain to take over the territory bequeathed him by his father, Bertram of Villefranche, but finds his land overrun by Normans. The next two installments show Philippe battling these Normans, surviving a dangerous encounter with the cowardly King Louis the Stammerer, brutally killing a number of men, and treating women with masterful roughness and superiority—every inch the medieval warrior-hero. But in the final installment, the formerly invicible Philippe falls victim to the wiles of the Lady Griselda, his lover and secretly chief priestess of the Witches of Touraine, and of Ja[c]ques, who like her worships at this pagan shrine. Earlier Philippe had been all-brave, all-wise, totally self-sufficient; now he has fallen under the spell of Griselda and Ja[c]ques, and they lead him around by the nose.

In this fourth and final installment, written late in 1934, Fitzgerald may have been seeking covert revenge against his more successful rival. Certainly Ernest had already given him, and would continue to give him, plenty to be upset about. "Ernest—until we began to walk over each other with cleats," goes an entry in Scott's notebooks, but while Scott would "half bait, half truckle" to Ernest, it was Hemingway who wore the cleats.

The punishment began with Ernest's May 1934 letter castigating Fitzgerald for succumbing to self-pity in the portrait of Dick Diver in *Tender Is the Night*. "Forget your personal tragedy," Hemingway directed him. "We are all bitched from the start. . . . But when you get the damned hurt use it—don't cheat with it. . . . You see, Bo, you're not a tragic character. Neither am I. All we are is writers and what we should do is write." What Fitzgerald next chose to write from the depths of his depression, however, only earned Ernest's further scorn. The "Crack-Up" articles of 1935 in *Esquire*, he thought, amounted to a miserable whining in public. Fitzgerald had leaped straight from youth to senility without achieving manhood. He had "confused growing up with growing old."

Nor did Ernest warm to Scott's judgment that *Green Hills of Africa* was his weakest book. With mock jocularity, Ernest responded that he could see from Scott's letter that he still didn't know when a book was good or what made it bad. Meanwhile, he had a suggestion: Why didn't Scott come down to Key West and they could travel to Cuba together for the next revolution? There ought to be a good story in it, and besides, "if you really feel blue get yourself heavily insured and I'll see you can get killed. . . . I'll write a fine obituary that Malcolm Cowley will cut the best parts out of for the new republic and we can take your liver out and give it to the Princeton Museum, your heart to the Plaza Hotel, one lung to Max Perkins and the other to George Horace Lorimer. . . . We will get MacLeish to write a Mystic Poem to be read at that Catholic School (Newman?) you went to." The good-natured joshing of the past had depended upon a closeness and a recognition of near equality in their trade that no longer existed. The pupil had graduated to master, and would brook no insubordination. His wit turned macabre.

But the cruelest and most telling blow came not in correspondence but with the publication, in the August 1936 *Esquire*, of "The Snows of Kilimanjaro." There, in black and white for the perusal of all, Hemingway dismissed Fitzgerald as a serious writer. In a reflective passage, Hemingway's narrator comments that the rich as a class were dull and played too much backgammon. Then, gratuitously, there follows: "He remembered poor Scott Fitzgerald and his romantic awe of them and how he had started a story once that began, 'The very rich are different from you and me.' And how someone [presumably Hemingway] had said to Scott, yes, they have more money. But that was not humorous to Scott. He thought they were a special glamorous race and when he found they weren't it wrecked him just as much as any other thing that wrecked him."

As a form of attempted literary assassination (for Scott, though near the end of his rope, was still very much alive), this comment was indefensible. Yet when Fitzgerald wrote in measured tones to request that his name be deleted in any future reprintings, before reluctantly agreeing (when the story was collected in book form in 1938, the name "Julian" was substituted for "Scott Fitzgerald") Ernest insisted that inasmuch as Scott had chosen to expose his private life so "shamelessly" in "The Crack-Up" articles, he'd assumed that it was open season on him. Nor did Hemingway later recant his cruelty. Hadn't Fitzgerald realized, he rhetorically asked in 1951, that the narrator of "The Snows of Kilimanjaro" would naturally have spoken of him by name just as he spoke of other actual things, cars, or places? But Scott was not a thing or a location. Unlike such inanimate objects, he could be both deeply hurt and remarkably forgiving. "Somehow I love that man," he wrote Perkins, even though Hemingway's referring to him in print as a "wrecked" man "was a damned rotten thing to do."

Considering its origin, Ernest's making Scott the butt of the anecdote seems still more contemptible. According to Perkins, the joke was originally on Ernest himself. Three of them—Max, Ernest, and the writer Molly Colum—were lunching together when Hemingway remarked that he was "getting to know the rich" and Molly said, "The only difference between the rich and other people is that the rich have money."

In the face of such insults as the one in *Esquire*, Fitzgerald eventually traded his picture of Hemingway as Byronic hero for one of Hemingway as psychiatric case. "He is quite as broken down as I am," Fitzgerald wrote in September 1936, "but it manifests itself in different ways. His inclination is toward megalomania and mine toward melancholy." However erratic Ernest's behavior, though, Scott remained a steadfastly loyal friend. Until the end, in his letters Scott was constantly asking Perkins about Ernest, a man whom, as Edmund Wilson commented, he "began by adoring and by whom he remained more or less obsessed." Then, in the last months of Fitzgerald's life, Hemingway scored his greatest popular success with the publication of *For Whom the Bell Tolls*. With a trace of bitterness, Scott wrote Zelda that the novel had been selected as a Book of the Month. "Do you remember," he added, "how superior he used to be about mere sales?" But he also sent Ernest his judgment that *For Whom the Bell Tolls* was "a fine novel, better than anybody else could do" and his congratulations on the book's success, which would buy him time (Scott himself had but six weeks left) to do what he wanted. He signed off "With Old Affection," and meant it. Did you know, Arthur Mizener inquired of Hemingway in July 1949, "that, till the day he died [Scott] would come up fighting—as boldly and ineffectually as always—for you at the drop of an adjective?"

Mizener corresponded with Hemingway while doing research for *The Far Side of Paradise*, his 1951 biography which spearheaded the Fitzgerald revival. Perhaps resentful of the attention being lavished on his former friend, Ernest sent Mizener a series of comments on Fitzgerald's failings. "Poor Scott," he observed, "how he would have loved all this big thing about him now." One time in New York, Hemingway recalled, "we were walking down Fifth Avenue and he said, 'If only I could play football again with everything I know about it now.' I suggested that we walk across Fifth through the traffic since he wanted to be a back-field man. . . . But he said I was crazy." Then Scott had this "great fantasy about going to war and asked me how he would have been. I told him that for his actions in civil life as a criterion he would probably have been re-classified or shot for cowardice." The trouble with Fitzgerald was that he lacked discipline and "was fragile Irish instead of tough Irish." Furthermore, he was uneducated "and refused to educate himself in any way. He would make great studies about football say and war but it was all bull-shit." Scott had let Zelda destroy his confidence in himself and when that happened he was through. His work wasn't much, either, and *The Last Tycoon*, "after the part that is written, and was as far as he could write, is really only a scheme to borrow money on." The only thing Hemingway had respected about him was "his lovely, golden, wasted talent." Compared with dedicated writers he had known, "Scott seemed like a child trying to play in the big leagues."

For more direct public consumption, Ernest dramatized these shortcomings in *A Moveable Feast*. The book focuses on a trip the two men took to Lyons to pick up an automobile which the Fitzgeralds had left there for repairs. Ironically, Scott included that June 1925 journey, "Auto Ernest and I North," in a list of "Most Pleasant Trips," and wrote Gertrude Stein about their "slick drive through Burgundy." But in the course of that trip, as Hemingway later presented it in a maliciously funny reminiscence, Scott revealed himself as a literary prostitute, a financial fool, an ignorant hypochondriac, a hopeless drunk, and an emasculated weakling. As if driven by some compulsion, Ernest in *A Moveable Feast* delivered a series of what Fitzgerald's daughter has aptly called "Mr. Hemingway's piercing jabs at that prone body."

The virulence of that attack may be laid to three causes. First, Hemingway insisted on his friends' observing a strict code of conduct. He turned away in disgust from Fitzgerald's drinking and his misuse of his talent and his willingness to be dominated by women, perhaps fearing that some trace of these weaknesses might rub off on him. Second, Fitzgerald had been his benefactor in the early years, and Hemingway could not abide being beholden to any man. During the late 1920s, while Ernest suffered through his divorce from Hadley and his father's suicide and the fiasco of a fight with Morley Callaghan, Scott was forever proferring what aid and comfort he could. "I'm sorry for you and for Hadley and for Bumby and I hope some way you'll all be content and things will not seem so hard and bad," Scott wrote sympathetically about the impending divorce. In the meantime, if there was anything he could do, "anything about your work, or money, or human help under any head—remember," Scott reminded Ernest, that he could always call on his devoted friend. But Hemingway did not like anyone feeling sorry for him, and rejected the role of the poor petitioner. Third, and perhaps most important, the two men had been very close friends indeed, and Ernest did not want anyone quite *that* close. He had many friends, but very few of them lasted—and it was invariably Hemingway who broke off the relationship. "Madame," as he himself put it in *Death in the Afternoon*, "it is always a mistake to know an author."

A Small Club for the Faithful

One thing about Hemingway and friendship: he rarely left people in doubt as to where they stood. If anything, he grew steadily more brutal in breaking off old ties as the years wore on. Even in his youth, however, he demonstrated his considerable capacity for righteous ingratitude in cutting off from Y. K. Smith, who had provided him during his post-World War I days in Chicago with room, occasional board, and companionship. Grace Hemingway, unaware that her son and Y. K. were feuding, invited the Smiths to a party she was giving in honor of Ernest and Hadley's wedding in 1921. This gave Ernest the opportunity to disinvite them, and to add insultingly that he would soon drop in to pick up his belongings and his "probably well-thumbed correspondence." When Y. K's younger brother Bill, once Ernest's closest friend, sided with his family in the dispute, Hemingway sent him a brutal poem in reply:

> "Blood is thicker than water,"
> The young man said
> As he knifed his friend
> For a drooling old bitch
> And a house full of lies.

The bitch he referred to was Bill's aunt in northern Michigan who, Ernest felt sure, had been poisoning Bill against him for years. He expounded this theory in a letter appealing to Howell Jenkins for his support. Hadn't they had a great time bumming around? Was Ernest such a leper now? What was wrong with Smith anyway? In 1925 he got an answer when Bill turned up in Paris subject to fits of depression and very much down and out. He'd tried to show Bill a good time, Ernest wrote Jenkins, and to find him a job, but it was no use. It would have been better if Bill had killed himself when he first began to suffer his periods of depression.

Similarly when he and John Dos Passos quarreled over the politics of the Spanish Civil War, Ernest let his old friend know in person, by letter, in a magazine article, and through the portrait of Richard Gordon, the fellow-traveling novelist in *To Have and Have Not*, just how naïve and contemptible he thought Dos had been. Yet when Dos Passos depicted Hemingway as a character in his 1951 novel, *Chosen Country*, Ernest raged that he'd trained a fierce crew of cats and dogs at the Finca to attack one-eyed Portuguese bastards on sight. "He was a wonderful, irreplaceable, but an impossible friend," as Archibald MacLeish observed, "a man you couldn't get along with, a man you couldn't get along without." MacLeish had reason to know. When he traveled across the country to visit Ernest, hospitalized after his 1930 automobile crash, Ernest accused him of making the trip only to see him die. Later he initiated unpleasant disputes about politics and money in order to signal the end of the friendship. He was through liking every dull bastard who liked him, he explained.

Sensitive to the powers of language, Hemingway knew what he was doing when he wrote off these former friends. He also meant what he said when he wrote a noted life-winger who dared to object to his depiction of André Marty in *For Whom the Bell Tolls* that he really couldn't be concerned with the opinions of "shits." And he intended the hurt when he referred in print to ex-friend and *Esquire* editor Arnold Gingrich as "a con man." "You wouldn't call Poppa mean or nasty," said Leicester Hemingway in summing up his brother's capacity for putting people down. "You'd call him malevolent." Once Ernest got down on a person, he added, he treated him as a nurse might treat a fly who accidentally entered a hospital room. Furthermore, despite subsequent attempts at reconciliation, no one he'd banished ever quite returned to favor. "If he took exception to anyone," Hadley remembers, "that was it; there was no reasoning with him about it." And eventually he "turned on almost everyone" they knew, "all his old friends." Friends and family as well, including Leicester: if his younger brother were a magazine, Ernest once commented, he doubted if he would renew his subscription.

This bleak record of broken friendships suggests what was patently the case: that Hemingway demanded a great deal of those few who were admitted to his private club of companions and never subsequently blackballed. Among other qualifications, members of the club were expected to demonstrate unstinting loyalty, eternal cheerfulness, and extraordinary achievement in a challenging career other than writing.

Hemingway valued loyalty primarily because he knew it was such a rare commodity. The only way to prove people worthy of your trust was to extend it to them, he understood; yet he also advised Buck Lanham that the best policy was to trust nobody and never "show it." Very few people, he believed, merited trust; most were basically insincere, and it was best to break with them before they disappointed you. Let someone praise him to the skies, for example, and Ernest's guard immediately went up. "Praise to the face," an old Oak Park saying ran, "is open disgrace." But if too fulsome praise bothered him, so did criticism, implied or explicit. Thus Dos Passos felt that their relationship started to crumble when he irreverently started sailing his Panama hat at the bust of Ernest that Pauline had ensconced in their Key West home.

The kind of loyalty Ernest sought was like that of Mike Ward, the bank teller in Paris who introduced him to bicycle racing. He was so devoted a friend, Pauline asserted, that if Ernest killed his own mother, Mike would simply say, "Well, it was *his* mother, wasn't it?" On the other hand, no persistent swearing of oaths could persuade Hemingway of a man's loyalty once he had failed him in any way, whether intentionally or not. Any liar, as he put it during the McCarthy era, could take an oath. A close companion of Ernest's during the last decade of his life, A. E. Hotchner, had in effect sworn an oath many times over: according to Mary Hemingway, if Ernest had known that Hotchner would one day write a book exposing the paranoid behavior of his last years, he "would have killed him"—perhaps not have killed him personally, but seen to it that he was disposed of in an automobile accident, say, or out on the Gulf Stream.

Another quality essential to friends of Hemingway was personal cheerfulness. The world might be in terrible shape and the sky falling, but the people Hemingway liked would not succumb to sadness. Robert Cohn, a victim of self-pity, is described as "sad." So is Jackson, Colonel Cantwell's driver in *Across the River and into the Trees*. The "sads" bored him; they were expendable. Jake Barnes and Bill Gorton, by way of contrast, enjoy life, and one reason the colonel has earned the love of his young Venetian countess is that "he had never been sad one waking morning of his life." (This was a claim Hemingway liked to make about himself as well, right up to the last morning.) As a soldier in combat, Cantwell had been exposed to plenty of anguish and sorrow, and in the course of the novel he has but a few days to live, but he lives them with zest and happiness. All the best men, as Robert Jordan reflects in *For Whom the Bell Tolls*, "were gay. It was much better to be gay and it was a sign of something too. It was like having immortality while you were still alive. . . . There were not many of them left though," not many happy comrades for the trials of life.

Such trials were important in Hemingway's scheme of things. Indeed, only those who had exposed themselves to adversity could earn status as permanent members of his club. To an unusual degree, his abiding friendships were based upon his appreciation of those who had exhibited skill under duress, men who had courageously faced imminent death in combat. He felt, as the citation for his Nobel prize expressed it, "a natural admiration of every individual who fights the good fight in a world of reality overshadowed by violence and death." Most notable among these were Chink Dorman-Smith, Irish captain of His Majesty's Fifth Fuseliers, whom Ernest met while recovering from his 1918 wounds in Milan, and Major General (Ret.) C. T. (Buck) Lanham, alongside whom Ernest endured some of the heaviest fighting in World War II. With Chink, he had hiked around several countries and drunk beer and talked about the war and about writing in the early 1920s. But then their "ways had gone a long way apart." Similarly the intensity of Ernest's devotion to Lanham and his troops necessarily dwindled after the war (it was, he told Buck, too strong a feeling for him to write about), but they remained close friends until Hemingway's death, after which Lanham said of Hemingway that he was "one of the most compassionate, sensitive, gentle people" he had ever known.

There were other military men Hemingway admired as well, including soldiers-of-fortune Colonel Charles Sweeny and General Morris Abraham Cohen, and a number of soldiers-by-conviction who fought bravely in the Spanish Civil War. Ernest's attachment to such men was strengthened if they had shared his experience of being wounded in battle. Like Colonel Cantwell, Hemingway was "a sucker for crips . . . any son of a bitch who has been hit solidly, as every man will be if he stays, then I love him."

Let personal disagreement enter the picture, however, and even these men would be stricken from the rolls. That is what happened to Gustavo Durán, a hero of the Spanish Civil War. After Franco's vicrory, Durán escaped to the United States, where Hemingway wined and dined him and told his wife that he considered Gustavo a great man. Ernest first tried unsuccessfully to land Durán a job in Hollywood and then arranged through diplomatic channels to have him naturalized as an American citizen in 1942 and sent to Cuba to act as a "real pro" in the spy-hunting Crook Factory which he had established. But Durán displeased Ernest by bringing his wife to Cuba (the Crook Factory was supposed to be an all-male operation), and by finding most of the espionage activities useless. Durán felt much more at home at the American embassy, where his Old World manners and command of languages made him particularly useful. In time he turned down a Crook Factory job that Ernest assigned him as not worth the time or trouble. For that defection, Hemingway punished his former friend by attributing to him the worst possible motives. At an embassy cocktail party in the spring of 1945, Ernest turned an apparently polite conversation into overt insult.

HEMINGWAY: "And how is your child?"
DURÁN: "Fine, thank you, but you know we have a baby now too."
HEMINGWAY: "Oh yes, you managed quite well to keep out of the war, didn't you?"

How can one account for the savageness with which Hemingway dismissed so many erstwhile friends? In some cases, his powerful sense of self-sufficiency—and the need to *appear* fully self-sufficient—led him to repudiate former benefactors. In other instances his competitive instinct drove him to break with men whom he considered inferior, since doing so would symbolize his superiority. But another, less obvious motive was also at work.

From the days of his youth, those closest to Hemingway noted his capacity for keeping his distance. Ernest used to be annoyed by Fitzgerald's ingenuous way of asking the most personal questions imaginable. Do you enjoy sleeping with your wife? Scott would ask, and halfexpect an answer. Hemingway did not ask such questions, but he was a remarkably acute listener: witness the nuances of different voices in

The Sun Also Rises, for example, or in the brilliant short story, "Hills like White Elephants." This gift of mimicry extended, according to Edmund Wilson, to the sketches in *A Moveable Feast,* where he reproduced "for one who has known them the hoarse British gasps of Ford Madox Ford, the exasperating nonsense of Scott Fitzgerald so faithfully that one can hear them speaking." But he did not, Wilson maintained, penetrate below the surface. With real people, as with many in his fiction, Hemingway remained something of a stranger.

Working in Toronto in 1923, Ernest rather cold-bloodedly set down his impressions of fellow newspapermen Greg Clark, ex-major of infantry, friend, and (Ernest thought) the best writer on the *Star.* He did not yet know all about Greg, he wrote, for he had not yet seen him cry ("Sooner or later you will see every man cry. It is like chemistry. When he cries is when he is separated into his component parts") or seen him drunk ("I like to see every man drunk. A man does not exist until he is drunk"). As these reportorial notes indicate, Ernest sought knowledge rather than friendship, and he was no respecter of persons or of the conventional pieties. On another occasion, asked why he had not attended the funeral of a well-known acquaintance, he shot back, "a son of a bitch alive is a son of a bitch dead." When it came to human relationships, as MacLeish remarked, Ernest was "cross-grained, all narrowed and knotty."

Yet he was also, in his twenties, "perhaps the nicest man" Morley Callaghan had ever met, reticent, "often strangely ingrown and hidden, with something sweet and gentle about him." His undoubted capacity to inspire warmth in others suggests that his coldness and cruelty were learned reactions, and not the result of an innately deformed personality. The picture Hemingway projected, Earl Rovit noted, was that of a man very much on his guard, "hypersensitively ready to strike out against a potential foe before he himself is struck." Though he liked to make each close companion feel that he was his best, practically his only, friend (as Fitzgerald believed for a time), Ernest did not want anyone to act as a good friend would, to presume to intimacy. Not willingly would he let any man penetrate his armor. As MacLeish put it: "There seemed to be implicit in his nature, in his relationships not only with other men but with women, a sort of what they call in spy stories, self-destructive device. His relationships always self-destructed. He never was able, I think, in his relations with anybody, to give himself. He had an iron reserve, a steel reserve, a crystalline reserve."

And this reserve, Leicester implied, he had acquired at home. His adamant unwillingness to readmit banished friends to favor was, his brother wrote, "a psychological device Ernest learned from having had it used on him," presumably by his mother.

On safari in Africa in 1933, Ernest and his gunbearer M'Cola came close to achieving what was, to Hemingway, an ideal if necessarily unequal relationship. M'Cola does a sloppy job of cleaning a weapon, but Ernest forgives him because the native worships him: he runs after the car taking Hemingway away at the end of the safari, screaming, "B'wana! I want to go with B'wana!" Together with M'Cola, Hemingway meets the handsome Masai tribesmen, and together they are admitted to instant brotherhood with the disinterested friendliness characteristic of the Masai as well as "the best of the British, the best of the Hungarians and the very best Spaniards." This makes Ernest feel marvelous, but it is "an ignorant attitude," he adds, because it puts too much faith in others, and "the people who have it do not survive."

As Mayito Menocal, Sr., writes, Hemingway loved to have "some person who would take care of 'the details.' " In Key West, this was Toby Bruce; later, in Cuba, it was Roberto (Monstruo) Herrera. These men, devoted to Ernest, took care of the nuisance chores, and so, to a lesser degree, did Hotchner in the last years of Ernest's life. A professional writer, Hotchner made a lot of money recasting Ernest's stories for radio and television, and made still more from *Papa Hemingway*. But the Hemingways expected him to run errands, to act as agent for articles Mary had written, to shop at Abercrombie and Fitch for Ernest, to amuse with funny stories. "Yes, Papa," was the response of most of those around Hemingway during his last fifteen years.

Severing his ties to all who might be in a position to hurt him or to disagree with him left Ernest, as he wrote in 1959, with "very little depth on the bench in friends." Those who remained, if not servants or stooges, were often sporting companions. This was not true of Bill Horne or Gianfranco Ivancich, both of whom came to his funeral. But the category of sportsmen embraced yet another mourner, Charles Thompson of Key West, who had accompanied the Hemingways on the 1933 safari. Among the seven pallbearers were five hunting companions and his doctor—all from in or around Ketchum and Sun Valley, Idaho and George Brown, his New York boxing coach who, at Mary's request, had driven the Hemingways out west from the Mayo Clinic. There were no men of letters.

x

Religion

Oak Park Piety

When Ernest Hemingway was a boy, his family offered a blessing before every meal, and that was standard practice in the churchly community of Oak Park. "Everyone we knew," his sister Marcelline recalled, said grace, but the Hemingways outdid most of their neighbors in piety by conducting a prayer service after breakfast as well. Parents, children, and even the cook and the maid gathered in the parlor for this service, at which Grandfather Ernest Hall presided. He read, usually, from a thick, gold-trimmed volume called *Daily Strength for Daily Needs*. After receiving the lesson for the day, his listeners all knelt on the carpet in silent prayer before going off to school or work.

Grandfather Anson Tyler Hemingway was even more religious than Grandfather Hall. A friend and associate of Dwight L. Moody, the famous evangelist, A. T. Hemingway was for ten years employed as general secretary of the Chicago YMCA. After moving to Oak Park he became a pillar of the First Congregational Church, acting as Sunday school superintendent, deacon, and finally deacon emeritus. He helped raise funds for the church and was active in the temperance movement. He brought his six children up in the stern religious discipline of the day and sent them all to Oberlin College. According to the brief biography printed for his funeral service in 1926, each of his four sons "made enviable places in the world." One became a leading businessman, one an educator, one a missionary physician in China, and one—Ernest's father—"a highly esteemed doctor."

Where religion was concerned, Dr. C. E. Hemingway was very much his father's son. He forbade his four daughters and two sons to participate in any games or entertainments on Sunday. His letters to Ernest were full of pious sentiments. And when his elder son left home for the first time (if the scene in *For Whom the Bell Tolls* accurately reflects what happened), Dr. Hemingway saw him off at the train with a kiss and an emotional prayer, "May the Lord watch between me and thee while we are absent the one from the other," that in its earnestness and "damp religious sound" made Ernest, looking back on the incident twenty years later, feel sorry for him.

As a youth, though, Ernest usually behaved with the circumspection one would have expected from his background. He later took delight in painting himself as a young rapscallion, a "Huck Hemingstein," but in fact he was rather more a Tom Sawyer than a Huck Finn. At fourteen he starred in a Sunday school play given by the Third Congregational Church of Oak Park, appearing on stage in a flowing kimono that made him look "almost saintly." The following year the family changed its affiliation from the Third to the First Congregational. There, together with Marcelline, Ernest joined in the activities of the young people's Plymouth League, serving as program chairman, treasurer, and speaker for the group's Sunday-afternoon meetings. After he had graduated from high school, Lloyd Harter, of the church's Boys' Department, prevailed upon him and four other graduating seniors to tell the younger boys "some of the deeper things about your high-school experience and especially what the Church . . . has meant to you. . . . Put your soul into it," Harter advised, "and bring them a message that they will never forget. . . . Give the chaps the best you've got right from the shoulder."

No record of Ernest's talk survives. Considering the satiric bent of his writings in the high-school newspaper, however, it seems likely that the best he had was rather more free of cant than the run of Sunday school presentations. In this connection, it is worth observing that Dr. William E. Barton, the minister of First Congregational, was the father of Bruce Barton, the advertising man and author whose book, *The Man*

Nobody Knows, depicted Jesus as the forerunner of the modern businessman, as "the most popular dinner guest in Jerusalem," and as the writer of parables which were "the most powerful advertisements of all time." Barton's book, which became one of the best sellers of the twentieth century, appeared in 1925, the same year that Ernest published his grand but relatively ungodly collection of stories, *In Our Time*. By then he had rebelled against his religious heritage. The citizens of Oak Park, he proposed, could be divided into two groups: the "Christer element" and a lot of fine people.

The pious pronouncements of his home town, Ernest found, little suited him for confronting the world beyond its borders. He objected, for example, to the repressive climate generated by conventional religious norms. As an early poem has it:

> The age demanded that we sing
> And cut away our tongue.
>
> The age demanded that we flow
> And hammered in the bung.
>
> The age demanded that we dance
> And jammed us into iron pants.
>
> And in the end the age was handed
> The sort of shit that it demanded.

His upbringing had provided him with a rosy picture of existence that did not square with the brutality of modern life he found everywhere about him. World War I, especially, served as a catalyst in crystallizing Ernest's disillusionment with Oak Park religion. "The war itself," as Frederick Hoffman remarked, "had been so violent a departure from custom, from the 'rules,' that it was impossible to return to them." So Harold Krebs, of "Soldier's Home," back from the war, cannot readjust to his middle-class environment. Before the war, he had attended a Methodist school, belonged to a fraternity, and worn "exactly the same height and style collar" as his companions. But now he has no desire to conform to the community's patterns. He'd like to have a girl, but lacks the energy to go through the courtship rituals. He'd like to talk about the war, but no one wants to hear how it really was. Above all, he'd like to lead a life without complications or consequences, but his parents, and especially his mother, keep urging a complicated existence upon him. They insist, for example, that he find a job. "God has some work for everyone to do," his mother says. "There can be no idle hands in His Kingdom." But Krebs replies, "I'm not in His Kingdom." Such talk shocks Mrs. Krebs, and she eventually forces her son to lie that he loves her, but he is quite unable to join her in prayer. And so Krebs plans to get away from home and parents, as Ernest himself did after the war, realizing that "the world they were in was not the world he was in." His world was full of unreasonable pain and unconscionable suffering and inexplicable violence, a world in which, as Frederic Henry remarks, there "isn't always an explanation for everything"—though both he and Catherine Barkley had been brought up to think that there was.

Convert to Catholicism?

In Ernest's own case, the wound he suffered at Fossalta in July 1918 led him to abandon Congregationalism for Catholicism—or so he later claimed. The morning after his injury he lay in an Italian dressing station while Don Giuseppe Bianchi, a priest from the Abruzzi, passed among the wounded, anointing each in turn. Thus, he told some correspondents, he was baptized in the faith. Thus, he told others, he received extreme unction. In any case, he wrote Guy Hickok, his "conversion' was somewhat fortuitous. He got religion, he explained, because he was scared as hell, on the verge of death, and a priest happened to be handy. If the chaplain had been a Mormon elder or a muezzin, he would cheerfully have become a Mormon or a Muslin. But he happened to be a priest, and so Hemingway became a Catholic. At the time, apparently, the experience made little impression on him. Agnes von Kurowsky could not remember his talking about religion at all. What's more, she added, her Catholic friends on the nursing staff in Milan would surely have said something if Ernie "had been converted to Catholicism."

Nor did his behavior in the years immediately following the war indicate such a conversion. He was married to Hadley Richardson in a Methodist country church at Horton Bay, Michigan, and their son was christened in St. Luke's Episcopal Chapel in Paris. Whatever may have happened in Italy in 1918, circumstantial evidence suggests that Ernest did not really embrace Catholicism until after he met and determined to marry the ardent Catholic Pauline Pfeiffer.

"Dear Saint Joseph," Pauline said by way of nightly prayer, "send me a good, kind, attractive Catholic husband," and Ernest did his best to meet those qualifications. "If I am anything," he wrote Ernest Walsh and Ethel Moorhead in January 1926, after his affair with Pauline had begun, "I am a Catholic. . . . Am not what is called a 'good' Catholic. Think there is a lot of nonsense about the Church, Holy Years, etc. What rot. But cannot imagine taking any other religion seriously." A year later, in the depths of despair over the prospect of divorcing Hadley, Ernest traveled through Italy with Hickok and, in Rapallo, held a reunion with the priest who had anointed him nine years earlier. After that meeting, he several times insisted on stopping to pray and then returned, tear-stained, to the car.

When he and Pauline were married, Ernest concurred in the fiction that he and Hadley were never really man and wife, since they had been married outside the faith. A few months later, in a letter to a Dominican father, he drastically misrepresented his religious history. Though he had drifted away from the Church during 1919–27, he wrote, he had been a Catholic for many years. Now, however, he was going to Mass regularly, and had set his house in order. One who did not entirely accept the sincerity of Ernest's religious transformation was Scott Fitzgerald, himself a fallen-away Catholic. "Well, old Mackerel Snapper," he wrote Hemingway in July 1928, "wolf a Wafer and a Beaker of blood for me."

But for a time, at least, Hemingway faithfully performed his religious duties. When his father killed himself late in 1928 Ernest arranged that a Mass be said for him, and he advised his brother Leicester to join him in praying hard for the release of Dr. Hemingway's soul from purgatory. He and Pauline faithfully attended Mass, both at Saint-Sulpice, their parish church in Paris, and at various other ports of call. In wide-open Wyoming, during 1932, he undertook a round-trip drive of nearly four hundred miles so that Pauline could attend the First-Friday Mass for August. At least once, he also made a small financial contribution to the faith, sending a check for $25 to the Jesuit Seminary Missionary Fund of New Orleans in February 1935. (Thereafter the grateful members of the order saw to it that the Hemingways received copies of *The Southern Jesuit*.) Such observances hardly repaid his debt to the Church, however. "Hell," he told Chub Weaver in 1931, "any man could become a Catholic for a million seeds."

Whatever his obligations, Ernest disapproved of the Church's positions on sex and politics. Both of Pauline's sons were delivered by Caesarean, and the second birth, especially, endangered her life. Angrily Ernest proposed that if the Church continued to insist on production of more and more Catholics, it ought to at least provide some relief for those who had to risk death to conform to papal encyclicals. Then, after Patrick and Gregory were safely delivered, the Hemingways ran afoul of the Catholic taboo against the use of contraceptive devices.

Politically, the Church earned his wrath by siding with the fascists during the Spanish Civil War. In *Ken*, Hemingway warned American Catholics against being influenced by the Spanish Catholic Church. The fascists were war criminals, and so, he believed, were the priests who supported their cause. As evidence, he cited a photograph which showed several luminaries of the Church giving the fascist salute, and wondered if there were not a connection between their political support and the fascist bombing of women and children in Barcelona. He advised his readers to discount Cardinal Hayes's assertion that Franco would not bomb children. If that were true, and since it was clear that the Loyalists had not bombed the city they held, the only possible explanation was that the children had bombed themselves. The depth of Hemingway's bitterness emerged in that article, as in the offhand comment in *For Whom the Bell Tolls*, that the old man Anselmo was "a Christian. Something very rare in Catholic countries." As an institution he cordially detested the Spanish Church. But he could admire and respect the occasional individual priest who, like the Basque Don Andrés he later befriended in Cuba, had maintained his Republican convictions and was exiled from Spain.

During World War II he delighted in disproving the old saw about there being no atheists in foxholes. Did William S. Boice, the division chaplain, still believe that? "No, sir, Mr. Hemingway, not since I met you and Colonel Lanham." But how, the chaplain asked, could Ernest and the colonel face their God each day with sins weighing on their souls? Chaplain, Ernest answered, we take these sins into an attack as you might carry K rations. And all we have to do is make an act of contrition if we have time. What if there were no time? Then, Ernest replied, he'd have to rely on the parish priest and the chaplain to pray for him. In December 1944 he found a curious way of demonstrating his independence of the Church. The regiment set up headquarters in a house said to have belonged to a priest who collaborated with the Germans. Ernest located some bottles of sacramental wine in the cellar, drank the contents, and then urinated them full again, calling the noisome product "Schloss Hemingstein, 1944."

Two letters Ernest wrote Mary Welsh in September 1945 suggest his ambivalent feelings about Catholicism. In the first, he declared that he and Mary need not believe in Mary Baker Eddy or God and his beard or anyone at all except each other. But, in the second, he complained about the intractable anti-Catholic talk of Buck Lanham's wife, Pete, who was convinced all priests were immoral and would give no credit even to the lonely priest trying to do his job and trying not to be a rummy. He was on record as opposed to the Church and in favor of Republican Spain, but he could not accept such wholesale indictments.

In his last decade, particularly after the near-fatal airplane crashes of 1954, Ernest once again began to tilt toward religious conviction. In the spring of that year he stopped to pray in the Cathedral at Burgos, and told A. E. Hotchner afterward, "Sometimes I wish I were a better Catholic." The following year, in Cuba, he expressed similar sentiments when Fraser Drew, who had come to pay his respects to the author, happened to mention that he was a Catholic. "I like to think that I am," too, Ernest responded, "insofar as I can be." He could still go to Mass, for example, despite his divorces and remarriages. Don Andrés prayed for him every day, he added, "as I do for him. I can't pray for myself any more. Perhaps it is because in some way I have become hardened."

His inability to pray for himself, however, may be better interpreted as growing religious maturity, for throughout Hemingway's fiction the characters pray, childlike, for the granting of favors, even—in some cases—offering to strike a bargain with God if He will only give them what they desire. Hemingway himself took a long time to get beyond this stage. In September 1920, for example, he reported going to a Catholic Church, praying for all the things he wanted and wouldn't ever get, and being rewarded for his efforts with a sexual adventure. His pleas were also answered in 1927, he told Hotchner, when "a short prayer" at Saint-Sulpice enabled him to overcome a spell of sexual impotence.

Similarly Hemingway's fictional protagonists often pray for relief in time of trouble. Thus the frightened Nick Adams, flattened out in a trench under bombardment, seeks to purchase his safety through prayer: "Dear jesus please get me out. Christ please please please christ. If you'll only keep me from getting killed I'll do anything you say. I believe in you and I'll tell every one in the world that you are the only one that matters." Nick survives the bombardment, but the "next night back at Mestre he did not tell the girl he went upstairs with at the Villa Rossa about Jesus." His prayer is only temporarily efficacious, anyway, for Nick like his creator is eventually wounded and thereafter suffers terrors which prayers do not help to exorcise.

Generally, in fact, such self-serving prayers do Hemingway's characters little good. Even when one asks God to intervene on behalf of someone else, the appeal goes unanswered. Frederic Henry, for example, bargains unsuccessfully for Catherine's life: "Oh, God, please don't let her die. I'll do anything for you if you won't let her die." Maria promises the "Sweet Blessed Virgin" that she will do anything at all if only She will take care of Robert Jordan during the blowing of the bridge. Honest Lil reposes "absolutely blind faith" in the ability of the Virgen de Cobre to look after young Tom Hudson, who is, ironically, already dead.

One particular kind of prayer, offered by a weak and fearful man under stress, Hemingway obviously disapproved of. It was all right, in his judgment, to ask, with Anselmo, for the courage to perform one's military duty well and without fear, but it was wrong to expect heavenly aid in escaping or minimizing a dangerous task. Thus Ernest scornfully depicts the unmanliness of a "cowardly bullfighter," who prays, sweating in his suit of lights, to the Blessed Virgin for a bull that will charge frankly and follow the cloth well, for a day without wind, "promising something of value or a pilgrimage, praying for luck, frightened sick." He stopped praying for himself, Ernest wrote, during the shelling of Madrid, when the sight of so many others being destroyed by fascist shells made it seem egotistical and wicked to ask God for divine intercessions. He missed a certain ghostly comfort as a consequence, Ernest admitted, but understood that no amount of praying could produce courage, a quality a man had to acquire on his own, or guarantee survival, which was a matter of luck.

Superstitions and Rituals

Though he was by no means always cordial to inquiries from scholars interested in his work, Hemingway engaged during the 1950s in friendly correspondence with those who, like Robert M. Brown and John C. Pratt, inquired about his religious beliefs. Clearly he did not wish to be depicted, in whatever form these men chose to express themselves, as a heathen. In 1958 he reassured his hunting companion, the actor Gary Cooper, that Cooper's recent conversion to Catholicism would probably turn out all right. He himself, Ernest added, certainly "believed in belief." And he took no official steps to sever himself from the Catholic Church, an omission which made it possible for the Reverend Robert J. Waldman, pastor of Our Lady of the Snows Catholic Church in Sun Valley, to conduct his funeral and to supervise at his burial rites in a Catholic cemetery, though Hemingway's son Jack told an inquisitive reporter that, no, his father had not actually been a Catholic at the time of his death.

Ernest's decision not to reject Catholicism officially may have been partly based on expediency, in just such a spirit as that in which he asked Chaplain Boice, on a mid-1950s Christmas card, to remember "us sinners" to God if he ever managed to make contact. Such attempts to play it safe in the remote possibility of warding off disaster smack rather more of superstition than of conventional religious faith. Indeed, Betty Bruce felt that Ernest's respect for the Catholic Church was founded on grounds of superstition, and Mary Hemingway's testimony suggests the same thing. Her husband's religious views, she said in 1972, were far from orthodox. When he visited a cathedral or a basilica, he might "light a few votive candles because that was the normal thing to do," but not out of deep belief. "It was probably like horoscopes are today."

In his biography, Carlos Baker concludes that Ernest was "as superstitious as a medieval peasant." Like all superstitious men, he inhabited an unpleasant world in which bad luck seemed to predominate. It did not make sense to court evil consequences. He thought it "very bad luck," for example, to work on a Sunday. He believed that you would be moonstruck and fall ill if you slept with moonlight on your face. Above all, he was convinced that language had the power to jinx a man. Thus he erupted in anger when Scribners sent him the proofs of *Death in the Afternoon*, with each galley slugged "Hemingway's Death." His fiction yields several examples of this superstition. In *To Have and Have Not*, Harry Morgan is appalled when Bee-Lips, the crooked lawyer, puts "his mouth on his own self." In recruiting Harry to pilot the Cuban revolutionaries (and bank robbers) away from Key West, Bee-Lips tries to reassure him about the danger:

> "Nothing's going to happen to anybody."
> "With those guys?"
> "I thought you had cojones."
> "I got cojones. Don't you worry about my cojones. But I'm figuring on keeping on living here."
> "I'm not," Bee-Lips said.
> Jesus, thought Harry. He's said it himself.

Hemingway illustrates the principle of the spoken jinx once more in *Islands in the Stream*, where Andrew Hudson talks too volubly about how to boat the gigantic fish his brother David is battling. *"Oh keep your mouth off of him, please,"* David demands, and—of course—he later loses the fish.

Since so many omens augured ill, Hemingway armed himself during most of his adult life with one kind or another of compensating good-luck piece designed to ward off catastrophe. These were invariably secular talismans. During his years in Paris, for example, he kept a rabbit's foot, its fur worn away from long use, in his right-hand trouser pocket, where, feeling its claws, he could be reassured that his "luck was still there." His next lucky piece was a red stone that Bumby had found. When it disappeared, early in July 1944, he quickly located another charm—a champagne cork from a bottle of Mumm's—to see him through a stint as observer on a low-level flying mission over occupied France. "Damned good thing I had it," he told Hotchner. "Every plane on that flight got chewed up except ours." Ernest was doubly distressed when he lost the lucky cork in 1950, on the very morning when he'd planned to make a killing at the Auteuil racetrack. This time, however, he settled for a horse chestnut as a lucky piece, and when his horse did win, he held on to the chestnut for eleven years before giving it to Hotchner, in 1961, in exchange for a carved wooden figure from the latter's key ring. As another remedy for bad luck, Ernest was forever knocking on wood, or rather, in his private version of the ritual, touching wood three times with his finger tips.

Hemingway also believed in premonitions and forewarnings. Though his protagonist in *For Whom the Bell Tolls*, the college instructor and presumable rationalist Robert Jordan, consistently denies the validity of such premonitions, Pilar sees Jordan's imminent death in his hand, and she turns out to be right. Pilar had also been right about Kashkin, Jordan's predecessor, who, she says, had "smelt of death." Jordan jeers at the idea, but Hemingway himself obviously did not share his skepticism. Twice during World War II, in fact, he claimed to have smelled impending doom. During the Normandy campaign he suddenly abandoned the command post at Château Lingeard because, he said, "the place stank of death." The next day, several officers were killed and others wounded there. Later, in the Hürtgen Forest, he told Lanham that one of his officers would not long survive, for he too gave off the stink of death. Minutes later, word came that the officer had been killed. Such warnings came to him, Ernest felt, as much because of his experience as because of any mystical power. So he was disinclined to accept others' claims of foreknowledge—the fictional Pilar, who had gypsy blood, being an exception—or adopt their substitutes for formal religion. Marlene Dietrich tried to interest Hemingway in astrology, but he had his own rituals against the forces of darkness that surrounded him, and in any case he did not, he told her, want his life "run by the stars."

"I think we are born into a time of great difficulty," Robert Jordan observes in *For Whom the Bell Tolls*. "I think any other time was probably easier." His times, and those of his creator, were made especially difficult by the collapse of pre-World War I values, which left a generation foundering, if not lost, in a sea of chaos. There is but one "single, simple truth" that Hemingway's work has to tell us, according to Alan Lebowitz: that "life is harsh and dull, that God—if He exists— is not on our side, and that man, under sentence of annihilation, is while he lives only a human punching bag . . . with an innate resilience and courage to make do." If God was not dead, he was certainly no friend to man, and in "A Natural History of the Dead," Hemingway said his satiric farewell to the concept of a benevolent Deity. In that macabre sketch, he repeats the question the explorer Mungo Park had posed when, lost in the desert, he was inspired by finding a small plant: "Can that Being who planted, watered and brought to perfection, in this obscure part of the world, a thing which appears of so small importance, look with unconcern upon the situation and suffering of creatures formed after his own image?" Park had asked, and his answer was "Surely not." But Hemingway dramatically undercuts this conclusion by examining in detail how modern warfare has mutilated and killed men, women, and children, all "formed after his own image." "Most men," he concluded, "died like animals, not men." If there was benevolence or order at work in the universe, Hemingway could not find it.

What he did find, in "A Clean, Well-Lighted Place," was a universe stripped of meaning. In that most philosophical of Hemingway's stories, an old man, bereft, comes nightly to a clean, well-lit Spanish café to sit and consume enough brandy to get drunk. Two waiters at the café talk about the old man. One, a young waiter, wants to go home and impatiently wishes the old man, the last customer, would leave. The other, an older waiter, is more understanding, for he senses a kinship between himself and the old man. Much of the story is told in dialogue between the two waiters, beginning with this exchange:

> "Last week he tried to commit suicide," one waiter said.
> "Why?"
> "He was in despair."
> "What about?"
> "Nothing."
> "How do you know it was nothing?"
> "He has plenty of money."

But it is more than lack of money that troubles the old man. It is more than the loneliness of the eighty-year-old who once had a wife and now is "taken care of" by a niece. It is more than the inability to sleep at night—"probably only insomnia"—which, the older waiter rationalizes, must afflict many.

His suicidal despair is shared by the older waiter, who also cannot confront a meaningless universe without the comforts of good lighting and orderly surroundings. In a famous passage, the older waiter articulates in blasphemous terms what it is that they dread:

It was a nothing that he knew too well. It was all a nothing and man was nothing too. It was only that and light was all it needed and a certain cleanness and order. Some lived in it and never felt it but he knew it all was nada y pues nada y nada y pues nada. Our nada who art in nada, nada be thy name thy kingdom nada thy will be nada in nada as it is in nada. Give us this nada our daily nada and nada us our nada as we nada our nadas and nada us not into nada but deliver us from nada; pues nada. Hail nothing full of nothing, nothing is with thee.

Building on the foundation of this story, critics have attempted to make a case for Hemingway as existentialist. His depiction of a meaningless universe matches the *Weltanschauung* of the European existentialists, they point out; his *nada* parallels Sartre's *néant*, Heidegger's *Nichts*. Furthermore, Hemingway agrees with existentialist doctrine in affirming that only the individual who maintains his separate identity can possibly face down the powers of Nothingness and achieve final dignity. The crucial distinction, however, is that Hemingway was not a philosopher; in his fiction he merely reported on life as he found it. "To Sartre," as John Clellon Holmes commented, "the meaninglessness is basically an idea; to Camus, the absurd is a concept." To Hemingway, on the other hand, they form part of his experience. And what primarily interested him was the individual's attempt to overcome despair in the face of such chaos.

Driven to seek a substitute for the outmoded faith of their fathers, Hemingway's characters often turn to primitive rituals for comfort. They invest physical love-making with mystical import; they ritualize the mundane business of eating and drinking; they follow elaborate procedures derived from games. Such rituals, as they have always done, help to satisfy his characters' yearning for order and meaning in their lives. Sometimes they serve a therapeutic purpose as well. In this sense, Cowley points out, Nick Adams' fishing trip in "Big Two-Hearted River" may be regarded "as an incantation, a spell to banish evil spirits." In this sense, too, Hemingway qualifies as a religious writer.

A Religious Writer

Brett Ashley finds it difficult to take Jake Barnes's professions of faith seriously. "Oh, rot," she tells him. "You don't look very religious, Jake." As with Jake, so with Ernest Hemingway's fiction: the tendency has been to see his work as non-Christian because it doesn't "look" religious. His characters constantly commit sinful acts, to the point where one exasperated critic remarked in the mid-1930s that he'd gladly "settle for just one story in which the Ten Commandments did not get kicked all over the place." Back home in Oak Park, Ernest's parents had much the same reaction. Why, they asked in dismay, couldn't he emphasize the good things in life? Such attitudes undoubtedly stemmed from an inability to separate what happens in Hemingway's fiction from what ought to happen. Thus, when *The Sun Also Rises* came out in 1926, many readers assumed that Hemingway approved of the drunkenness and fornication of the expatriate crowd, a mistaken reading that half a century of close critical explication has not entirely put to rest.

Actually Hemingway's first novel is rather carefully organized around a contrast between paganism and Christianity. The initial scenes in Paris establish that cosmopolitan city as the home of paganism. Sexual aberrations proliferate there. Notre-Dame squats "against the night sky," but the characters frequent the Dingo Bar instead. Statues honor secular heroes: Marshal Ney, the men who invented pharmacy, and the developer of the semaphore system. But as soon as Jake enters Spain, a far more devout Christian country, the references to churches multiply, and Jake goes to pray in them as he had not done in Paris. These two strains commingle during the fiesta of San Fermin ("also a religious festival") at Pamplona, where Brett is elevated to the status of a pagan idol by the drunken crowd. The *riau-riau* dancers form a circle around her and will not let her join the dance, since they want her "as an image to dance around." She is forbidden entrance to one church because she has no head covering, and finds herself unable to pray for her lover Romero in another, because the experience makes her "nervy." She even asks to hear Jake's confession, but that, he tells her, is not allowed "and, besides, it would be in a language she did not know."

Jake, on the other hand, is "pretty religious." Even during the fiesta, when the formalized piety of the Spaniards gives way to free spending and heavy drinking, Jake walks to Mass in the mornings. As he keeps insisting, Jake is hardly an ideal Catholic. He becomes angry when the Catholic "pilgrims" on the train take over the dining car and prevent all others from getting a meal. When he, Bill Gorton, and Wilson-Harris go to see the cathedral at Roncesvalles, the site of the last great struggle between Charlemagne and the Saracens, he is happy to adjourn with the others to a nearby pub when the obligatory visit is over. And the Church, as an institution, has not helped him much in his efforts to cope with his emasculating war wound. The Catholic Church simply advised him not to think about the wound. "Oh, it was swell advice. Try and take it sometime. Try and take it." Still, Jake regrets that he is such "a rotten Catholic" and remains, in the end, one of those who "have God . . . quite a lot."

Neither in *The Sun Also Rises* nor anywhere else in Hemingway's writing is an individual Catholic, as a Catholic, presented unfavorably. The priest in *A Farewell to Arms* is a sympathetic figure who, despite his youth, provides the novel with its moral touchstone. In "The Gambler, the Nun, and the Radio," Hemingway created the delightful Sister Cecilia, a character modeled upon a Sister Florence who cared for Ernest when, in 1930, he was painfully recuperating from a broken arm in the Billings, Montana, hospital. A sports fan and firm believer in divine intervention, Sister Cecilia prays for the Athletics ("Oh, Lord, direct their batting eyes!") to win the World Series and for Notre Dame ("They're playing for Our Lady") to be victorious on the football field. Radiating a childlike innocence, she wants desperately and openly to become a saint: "All I want is to be a saint. That is all I've ever wanted. And this morning I feel as though I might be one. Oh, I hope I will get to be one." Taken aback at first, Mr. Frazer, the spokesman for Hemingway in the story, then offers reassurance. "You're three to one to be a saint," he tells her. Saint or no, she is certainly one of the most likable characters in all of Hemingway's fiction.

Ernest was sometimes given to blasphemies like those of a preacher's kid out to shock his elders. As young men up in Michigan he and Bill Smith used to sing the Lord's Prayer "in recitative very loudly" when drunk on hard cider. In 1927 he published his short "Neo-Thomist Poem"—

The Lord is my shepherd, I shall not
want him for long

—intended, as he later explained, to "kid" Jean Cocteau for switching his allegiance from opium to Neo-Thomism. When John Dos Passos wrote him that it looked as though *U.S.A.* would turn out to be a trilogy, Hemingway irreverently replied, "Trilogies are undoubtedly the thing— look at the Father Son and Holy Ghost—Nothing's gone much bigger than that." On his 1953 safari to Africa Ernest invented an elaborate myth for the benefit of the natives. According to his religion, he told them, it was necessary that the Memsahib (Mary Hemingway) kill a particular marauding lion before the birthday of the Baby Jesus.

In title and contents, Hemingway's published fiction reveals a similar sacrilegious strain. One early example is "A Divine Gesture," a brief fable published in "The Double Dealer" in 1922. Using mock-Biblical language—"And then when all was come and gone, the Great Lord God strode out of the house and into the garden"—the story trivializes Christian doctrine by reducing God to a Mussolini-like dictator who insists on using bad grammar, and the angel Gabriel to his bootlicking yes-man. The better known "Today Is Friday," Hemingway's playlet about the Crucifixion, contrasts the comments of two verteran Roman soldiers as they drink wine on the evening after the event. The first soldier frankly admires Christ's bravery. Surreptitiously, he had slipped his spear into Christ's body to relieve His suffering: "It was the least I could do for him. I'll tell you he looked pretty good to me in there today." The second soldier remains skeptical about the incident. To him Jesus Christ is a "false alarm" who really wanted to come down off the cross. What's more, he says with a wink, he'd known Jesus' girl "before he did." His cynical view is reminiscent of Hemingway's own assertion, in a letter to Dos Passos, that Christ "yellowed out" on the Cross. Two other stories which, like "Today Is Friday." appeared in *Winner Take Nothing* (1933), apparently reflect an anti-religious bias. Both have ironic titles. In "The Light of the World," two whores confuse the Messiah with the prizefighter Stanley Ketchel, whom they both call "Steve" and whom they both claim to have laid. "God Rest You Merry, Gentlemen," despite the suggestions from the Christmas carol, contains plenty to dismay the reader. In that tale, a devout Catholic lad, who takes his Church's preachments too literally, cuts off his penis to avoid the lustful thoughts he regards as a sin against purity.

Yet for all their surface irreverence, such stories emerge as positive Christian statements. In his open admiration of Christ and his willingness to take a personal risk to stop His agony, the first soldier is far more sympathetic than his disbelieving companion. Nick correctly perceives that the massive whore Alice, despite her profession, is capable of love, the true "light of the world." The hero of "God Rest You Merry, Gentlemen" turns out to be the Jewish emergency-room doctor, who demonstrates a competence and understanding beyond the capabilities of his nominally Christian colleague. What annoyed Hemingway was the assumption of virtue by those who observed the formalities and practiced the hypocrisies the Church required of them. So in each of these stories he introduced at least one good character, one person not formally associated with Christianity in any way, who nonetheless possesses the cardinal Christian virtues.

The apparent blasphemy of the stories conceals an underlying reverence for the goodness potential in man. In this sense, as Ernest himself put it, no one but a Christian could blaspheme properly. Besides, he remembered what James Joyce had told him: that blasphemy was not a sin—the sin was heresy, and a heretic he was not.

Affirmations

Hemingway used Christian symbolism in his fiction as it suited his artistic purposes, not so much out of calculation as instinctively. Thus, two very dissimilar protagonists, Colonel Richard Cantwell of *Across the River and into the Trees* and Santiago of *The Old Man and the Sea,* are both symbolically associated with Jesus Christ. Cantwell is very much a man of this world, experienced in food and drink, love and death. Before he succumbs to the heart attack which he knows will come, he enjoys one last fling with his nineteen-year-old Venetian mistress, the Countess Renata. These are most unlikely materials from which to construct a modern version of the Saviour, but Hemingway nonetheless invests Cantwell with Christ-like qualities. What they have most in common is suffering, and it is his wounded places, especially his misshapen right hand, that Renata most loves. Cantwell acquired his wounded hand "Very honorably. On a rocky, bare-assed hill," like Calvary, which was surrounded by Christmas trees. At night Renata dreams that the colonel's hand "was the hand of Our Lord," and though Cantwell reproves her ("That's bad. You oughtn't to do that"), he too is guilty of sacrilege when he asks her whether she'd "like to run for Queen of Heaven."

In addition, the only miracles he believes in have secular origins. One is sex, which is mixed up in his reflections with religion: "he was assisting, or had made an act of presence, at the only mystery that he believed in except the occasional bravery of man." Though he must die, he will not, the colonel decides, "run as a Christian" in the end. That would be hypocritical, since he resembles the Messiah closely only in the courage and endurance with which he faces suffering and death. Suffering was the natural condition of man and death his inevitable end, but each man could face these tyrants as he chose. Hemingway finds his heroes among those who, like Cantwell and Santiago, confront their fate with courage, endurance, and dignity.

Santiago is virtually inundated with religious imagery. His very name, which Hemingway said was no accident, means Saint James, the fisherman, martyr, and apostle of the Lord. Furthermore, the real story from which the book comes—a tale of a Cuban fisherman Ernest told in the April 1936 *Esquire*—is significantly altered to suggest parallels between Santiago and Christ. The old man of the *Esquire* story fights his giant marlin for two days and nights, and when he comes to shore, the predatory sharks having stripped his prize, he is crying in the boat. This bare sketch is retouched, in *The Old Man and the Sea*, with religious coloration. Instead of two days on the water, Santiago spends three days. As Christ fell beneath the cross, Santiago falls beneath the mast as he struggles, exhausted and beaten, up the hill to his shack. As the heart of Christ broke, so Santiago feels something break inside him. Santiago's hands like Christ's are mutilated, though by fishing line instead of nails. Hemingway underlines the similarity when the old fisherman, seeing the sharks for the first time, calls out "Ay," a word for which there is no translation but "perhaps . . . just such a noise as a man might make, involuntarily, feeling the nail go through his hand and into the wood."' Despite all the religious imagery, however, *The Old Man and the Sea* is not a Christian fable. Hemingway nowhere suggests that we are all fallen with the persecutors of Christ or saved by His example. What he *is* celebrating is the capacity of one man to endure terrible suffering and pain with dignity. The most telling alteration, from fish story in *Esquire* to minor masterpiece, comes at the very end. The real fisherman, "half crazy with his loss," had to be helped from his boat. The fictional one does not succumb; he brings in the boat and struggles home quite alone. Santiago is one of those who look "pretty good in there," one of those rare ones who are "not made for defeat." As he himself puts it, "a man can be destroyed but not defeated."

In exalting the value of the struggle itself, and in celebrating the endurance and bravery a man might summon in the face of suffering, Hemingway affirmed the grandeur of which the individual human being was capable. And there was one other article in Hemingway's private creed: a worship of the natural world around him. Santiago, for example, feels a powerful affinity for the sea which supports him. Bereft of family and friends, and deprived of Manolin's company, he still loves his fellow creatures—the sea birds, the flying fish, the great marlin, even the sharks—and is "glad we do not have to kill the stars." Should there be nothing else to love, man can still love the earth and the sky and the sea, which, though they be indifferent to our fate, are nonetheless beautiful and abide forever and may even give comfort to man, as Nick Adams finds while fishing "in the good place" on the banks of the Big Two-Hearted.

This kind of piety, which Nathan Scott calls "a sense of the radical holiness" of the world, is pervasive in Hemingway's writing, especially in the Nick Adams stories and in *The Old Man and the Sea*. Infused with this spirit, man looks beyond everyday existence to a realization of "the beauty and stability and permanence of Creation." This reverence for the natural world, then, constitutes a kind of glory for Hemingway, but it is balanced—often overbalanced—by his concurrent sense of the blank, dark meaninglessness of our existence. In his feeling for nature, Hemingway stems from Emerson and Thoreau; in his consciousness of the blackness "ten times black," he derives from Hawthorne and Melville. His unsolved problem—a basic problem of modern faith—was to reconcile the two, the "glory and the blackness" both.

xi

Art

Forging a Style

Ernest Hemingway was not much interested in philosophical puzzlements about the nature of the universe. The focus in his life, as in his writing, was on conduct. "I did not care what it was all about," as Jake Barnes articulated the position in *The Sun Also Rises*. "All I wanted to know was how to live in it." As an afterthought Jake added, "Maybe if you found out how to live in it you learned from that what it was all about," but the emphasis lay on *how* a man should live his life. A fictional character posed this problem, and the answers also emerge from Hemingway's books. A man should maintain his individuality; he should seek the truth and not kid himself or others; he should stick to his commitments; he should behave with dignity and courage under stress; above all, he should work, and work hard. Furthermore, these maxims applied with equal force both to a man's life and to his craft. "Artist, art, artistic!" the young Hemingway had railed at the Chicago avant-garde assembled in Y. K. Smith's apartment. "Can't we ever hear the last of that stuff?" Yet he was from the first a highly conscious, careful craftsman who in time developed and set down the principles of his own private aesthetic.

Foremost among the principles was that each writer must forge his own style. "I could have written the old prose as it should be

241

written," Ernest told Charles Poore. "But it had been done so well and I thought we needed a new prose to handle our time or that part of it I've seen." His new prose did not so much abandon the past as build on it, and especially on the groundwork of such immediate predecessors as Sherwood Anderson and Gertrude Stein, but such borrowings were inevitable. "Every novel which is truly written contributes to the total of knowledge which is here at the disposal of the next writer who comes," he observed in *Death in the Afternoon*. Most writers could only absorb that knowledge properly if they had enough experience to know what to assimilate and what to discard. The great writer, however, seemed to possess such experience instinctively; he could go "beyond what has been done or known" to make something of his own.

Above all, it was vital to avoid the pitfall of outright imitation. Hemingway's own style, for example, was so distinctive and well known that it inevitably spawned a school of imitators. Some of the copies were brilliant, others shoddy, but none came close to reproducing the original. In a 1953 letter to a beginning writer, Ernest admitted that the young man wrote better than he himself had done at nineteen. The trouble was that the lad wrote like Hemingway. That was no sin, but it wouldn't get him anywhere. The best advice he could give was to read a lot of other writers, including Kipling, de Maupassant, Stephen Crane, Ambrose Bierce, and Flaubert, to see and hear with his own eyes and ears, and to write it his own way.

Actually, it is inaccurate to speak of the Hemingway style, for he practiced at least two styles, moving from an early economy of language and objectivity of presentation to a much longer, more discursive, and, for almost all observers, less successful later style. It was the first style that became famous and imitated: the wiry short sentences based "on cablese and the King James Bible" (as John Dos Passos thought) that Hemingway struggled to perfect during his young manhood in Paris. This was the style whose words, Ford Madox Ford remarked, "strike you, each one, as if they were pebbles fetched fresh from a brook." In its economy and discipline, the style bespoke the man. Nothing was to be wasted, nothing given away.

Very little happens in "Cat in the Rain," one of the stories of *In Our Time*. An American couple stop at an Italian seaside town, out of season, and the wife does her unsuccessful best to rescue a cat that has been left out in the rain. That's all, or almost all, and yet the story conveys meanings which one would almost be ready, on the first reading, to swear did not exist. Here is the opening paragraph of the story, which exemplifies Hemingway's early and famous style:

> There were only two Americans stopping at the hotel. They did not know any of the people on the stairs on their way to and from their room. Their room was on the second floor facing the sea. It also faced the public garden and the war monument. There were big palms and green benches in the public garden. In the good weather there was always an artist with his easel. Artists liked the way the palms grew and the bright colors of the hotels facing the gardens and the sea. Italians came from a long way off to look up at the war monument. It was made of bronze and glistened in the rain. It was raining. The rain dripped from the palm trees. Water stood in pools on the gravel paths. The sea broke in a long line in the rain and slipped back down the beach to come up and break again in a long line in the rain. The motor cars were gone from the square by the war monument. Across the square in the doorway of the café a waiter stood looking out at the empty square.

The most unusual thing about this passage is its radical simplicity of presentation. It proceeds as if in response to a series of consecutive questions from an inquisitive child. Were there any other Americans at your hotel? Did you know anyone there? Where was your room? Did you have a nice view? What did the place look like? Did you have good weather? The American couple follow a direct sequence of time as they go up the stairs, into their room, and look out from the balcony whose doors are thrown open for them, no doubt, by the help. The sentences are simple or compound, not complex. The diction, too, is simple, made up of concrete nouns like hotel, room, stairs, monument, garden, and sea; of few and inexact adjectives (the colors of the hotels are "bright," the palms "big"), and a limited number of verbs which function principally to link subject and predicate, with special reliance on the wooden verb "to be," which college students in Freshman Writing have been advised, immemorially, to shun like the plague. Whatever emotional charge the story may carry is concealed behind the formidable impersonality of what is very nearly Basic English: concrete nouns, common adjectives, inactive verbs.

Despite these limitations, the passage manages to suggest what later will prove to be true: that all is not well with the marriage of the "two Americans" who stop at the hotel. The strongest clue falls with the repetitive rain outside. Gertrude Stein had taught Ernest the value of repetition, and he uses the word "rain" here five times, once with unmistakable emphasis: the war monument "glistened in the rain. It was raining." Furthermore, in the longest and most rhythmic sentence of the paragraph he associates the rain, a temporary phemomenon, with the endless movements of the sea: "The sea broke in a long line in the rain. . . ." It is a persistent rain and a disheartening one, for it keeps the tourists away and everyone else inside. What the rain suggests is confirmed by the last line of the passage, for this contains the only connotative word in the entire paragraph. The word is "empty" where it might have been the more neutral "unoccupied" or "vacant." It will turn out, subsequently, that the life of the American couple is similarly empty and that there is no child, inquisitive or not, to put the questions which the scene-setting introduction, in all-seeming innocence, sets out to answer. To read the passage this way is to take it out of context; without knowing the rest of the story, no one would be likely to glean so much from its beginning. But when one has finished "Cat in the Rain" and is wondering why he feels as desolate as he does and reads it over again, it eventually becomes clear that Hemingway has strewn the driftwood of desolation everywhere. Prose like this, or like the far more famous opening of *A Farewell to Arms*, must be read like poetry, as encoded language whose implicit message will only yield itself to a painstaking cryptographer.

Icebergs and Swords

Such code-breaking was made the more difficult by Hemingway's determination to dispense with the customary services to the reader offered by practitioners of the nineteenth-century novel. For example, he tried to write without "pointing" or intruding as authorial voice to deliver emotional or moral lessons. In his early work he was largely successful, as Thornton Wilder realized at once. What wonderful control, Wilder wrote Hemingway after reading *The Sun Also Rises*. The novel was full of dozens of incidental successes, but the greatest success of all was that "of keeping your hands off."

Not only did Hemingway avoid the more blatant forms of authorial intrusion—"As you will remember, gentle reader" (except to poke fun at them in *The Torrents of Spring*)—but he also took pains to avoid even the appearance of directing the reader. One best kept hands off, he thought, by stripping down to the bone. Thus, Chapter II of *In Our Time*, a sketch of the retreat from Constantinople which begins "Minarets stuck up in the rain out of Adrianople across the mud flats," is a drastically reduced and more powerful version of an account Hemingway, as foreign correspondent, cabled to the Toronto *Star* in October 1922. The newspaper version ran to 241 words and contained 30 adjectives, along with a number of other phrases designed to point toward the proper emotional reaction: "in horror," for example, and "ghastly." But when journalism was transformed to literature, the signposts fell away along with much of the verbiage. The 241 words of the original, already telescoped into brevity by the demands of cablese, were reduced to 132, with but 10 adjectives in place of the original 30.

Hemingway used a memorable figure of speech to describe his most striking technique as storyteller: that of leaving out critical details. "I always try to write," he put it, "on the principle of the iceberg. There is seven eighths of it under water for every part that shows. Anything you know you can eliminate and it only strengthens your iceberg." If you left things out because you lacked knowledge, there would be "a hole in the story," but omitting from knowledge only made the story stronger, like the submerged portion of the iceberg. At its best, as in "Big Two-Hearted River," this device worked brilliantly. Did you know, Ernest asked a correspondent in 1951, that the story is about a boy who had come home badly wounded from the war and yet the war is never mentioned? Perhaps not, but one can see how such a trauma might account for Nick's slow, careful, ritualistic way of working and fishing and eating in the story.

As time wore on, the iceberg theory became less and less applicable to Hemingway's fiction. For one thing, he could seldom resist the opportunity to point his moral through irony. It is in terms of his use of irony that he may most accurately be called (what many have called him) a sentimentalist. His writing was not sentimental, of course, in the usual sense of calling for overblown emotional responses to trivial matters. In fact, if sentimentality is that error which exacts of the reader more emotion than the event calls for, Hemingway might be regarded as a sentimentalist in reverse, since in its understatement his writing apparently asks for less emotional expenditure than is warranted. Sometimes, though, he intrudes with irony to help make up for the unseen portions of his iceberg.

Hemingway's irony usually functions to separate the mechanical, unfeeling, unperceptive, and therefore immoral character from the one who feels deeply and sees well below the surface. Such distinctions abound in his fiction, and occasionally—as at the end of *A Farewell to Arms* and *Across the River and into the Trees*—the irony seems to be tacked on gratuitously. In the first novel, two nurses come hurrying along the hallway, laughing at the prospect of witnessing the Caesarean that will take Catherine's life. In the second, Hemingway takes a last parting shot at the dull Sergeant Jackson who had spent his leave in Venice reading comic books. Colonel Cantwell has suffered his fatal heart attack, and his driver Jackson, opening the letter in which the colonel had asked for the painting of Renata and his two shotguns to be left for her at the Gritti Palace, determines to let red tape handle the job for him. "They'll return them all right," he thinks, "through channels."

Though too strong a moralist to resist underlining with irony, Hemingway was almost never guilty of adorning his tale. "Goddam," he told a fellow reporter on the Toronto *Star*, "I hate refinement"; and even in the later stages of his career, where the once lean prose took on superfluous weight, he rarely descended to "fine writing." With Ezra Pound, he went in fear of abstractions and abhorred empty rhetoric. The most famous expression of this repugnance came in *A Farewell to Arms*, where, reflecting with Frederic Henry, Ernest bade his own farewell to such words as "sacred, glorious, and sacrifice and the expression in vain" as hollow abstractions repeatedly invoked to justify the slaughter of young men.

This powerful abhorrence of the abstract discolored Hemingway's own critical judgments, especially of American writers. In *Green Hills of Africa*, he excoriated those of his predecessors "who wrote like exiled English colonials from an England of which they were never a part to a newer England that they were making." Who were these men, he is asked, and in his reply he lists "Emerson, Hawthorne, Whittier, and Company" all of whom he accuses of being too genteel, too respectable, too euphemistic. None of them used "the words that people always have used in speech, the words that survive in language." Such an answer betrays ignorance and misjudgment of his own literary heritage, for it was the unmentioned Longfellow, with his celebration of the ideal world of poetry over the real world of fact, who might most have earned his displeasure, and certainly not Emerson, who like Hemingway passionately advocated using the language of the street.

Hemingway wanted to write an antiliterary literature, after the model of Mark Twain, and his admiration for Twain is on record. What Ernest meant when he said that "All modern American literature comes from one book by Mark Twain called *Huckleberry Finn*" was that Twain had there reclaimed the common language and reoriented American writing from the rhetorical to the colloquial. Alongside Twain, he found Henry James pallid and unsatisfactory. Pauline had been reading to him from James's *The Awkward Age*, he wrote Waldo Peirce in December 1927, and he could hardly stand it. James kept reverting to the drawing room rather than face what his characters might do elsewhere, all his men talked like homosexuals and, in short, he seemed to Ernest "an enormous fake." Was that right, he asked Peirce? Was James a fake?

Though later he amended his view of James and even recommended that young writers read such tales as "Madame de Mauves" and "The Turn of the Screw," Ernest never did like T. S. Eliot's work. Eliot, he felt, never would have been heard from but for the tutelage of Pound. Actually Pound taught both Eliot and Hemingway how to recreate emotions, not through a general ooze of feeling, but through specific concrete images. Eliot gave this process a title, the "objective correlative," and supplied a theoretical rationale which argued that the only way of evoking emotion in art was through communicating "the external facts" which amounted to the "formula of that *particular* emotion." In *Death in the Afternoon*, Hemingway in precisely similar vein articulated his quest for "the real thing, the sequence of motion and fact which made the emotion and which would be as valid in a year or ten years, or with luck and if you stated it purely enough, always. . . ."

To get at the real thing, a writer required two rare qualities: an extraordinary gift of perception and a priestlike devotion to the truth. If you wanted to communicate the feeling given when a great fish jumped clear of the water, Hemingway instructed a young writer in an October 1935 *Esquire* article, you must "remember back until you see exactly what the action was that gave you the emotion. Whether it was the rising of the line from the water and the way it tightened like a fiddle string until drops started from it, or the way he smashed and threw water when he jumped. Remember what the noises were and what was said. Find what gave you the emotion: what the action was that gave you the excitement. Then write it down making it clear so the reader will see it too and have the same feeling that you had. That's a five finger exercise." It was also a "five finger" exercise which must go on continuously, however difficult that might be. "Even if your father is dying and you are there at his side and heartbroken," Ernest told Morley Callaghan, "you have to be noting every little thing that's going on, no matter how much it hurts." A novelist himself, Callaghan was struck by the ruthlessness of Ernest's dedication to his craft.

"A writer's job," according to Hemingway, was "to tell the truth," and his permanent value could be measured by his ability to stick to that obligation with "as great probity and honesty as a priest of god." When he had accomplished his job well, he got from it "the same pleasure and satisfaction . . . that a blacksmith or anybody who works with tools gets out of his day's work." Others might object to the result of his labors, but if they did, he could only explain, as in a January 1927 letter to Isidor Schneider, that though Schneider might not like or approve of the people in *The Sun Also Rises*, there was nothing to be done about it, because *"that is the way they are."*

Hemingway reserved his deepest scorn for those who faked a knowledge of what they were writing about, especially if the subject was war. Some good but dull books about war had been written, Colonel Cantwell lectures Renata, by boys who "were sensitive and cracked" after only a few days of combat. Other authors who dealt with war included those who wrote "to profit quickly from the war they never fought in," those who ran back to tell the news ("The news is hardly exact. But they ran quickly with it"), and professional writers "who had jobs that prevented them from fighting," but nonetheless "wrote of combat that they could not understand, as though they had been there." In this last and most sinful category, he placed Willa Cather, whose battle scenes in the Pulitzer-prize winning *One of Ours* (1922) were, he thought, cribbed from the footage of *Birth of a Nation*. Such novels were phony, and began to stink after a while. What was important was the ability to detect the scent. "The most essential gift for a good writer," he proclaimed, "is a built-in, shock-proof, shit detector. This is the writer's radar and all great writers have had it."

In "The Three-Day Blow," Nick Adams and his friend Bill get pleasantly tight and talk about books they've enjoyed. They both admire G. K. Chesterton and Hugh Walpole. They agree that Maurice

Hewlett's *Forest Lovers*, "the one where they go to bed every night with the naked sword between them," is a "swell book," but Nick has reservations:

". . . What I couldn't ever understand was what good the sword would do. It would have to stay edge up all the time because if it went over flat you could roll right over it and it wouldn't make any trouble."
"It's a symbol," Bill said.
"Sure," said Nick, "but it isn't practical."

Like the literal-minded Nick, Hemingway was wary of symbols artificially applied. As he said of *The Old Man and the Sea*, "I tried to make a real old man, a real boy, a real sea and a real fish and real sharks. But if I made them good and true enough they would mean many things." He was after what was real, and took a pragmatic approach to the problem of transforming the real into the fictional. Art could not reproduce life, but it was important to observe the probabilities. Thus he regarded Shirley Jackson's famous short story, "The Lottery," as a failure because its ending—the ritual stoning of one member of the community—was too incredibly harsh. You had to write, he thought, so people could believe it. Similarly, he lectured Fitzgerald that in using real people in fiction, he should stick to what had happened, or what logically would happen, in their lives.

For all his pragmatic devotion to the actual and probable, though, he still insisted on the value of invention. "The only writing that was any good," he said, "was what you made up, what you imagined." The difficulty was that you could only create out of what you knew. "You invent fiction, but what you invent it out of is what counts. True fiction must come from everything you've ever known, ever felt, ever learned." What you had learned one place could be used in another, just as Tolstoy could write *War and Peace* after having been at the battle of Sevastapol, though not, like his Prince Andrei, at Borodino. But if you had been at some Sevastapol of your own and if you were, like all good novelists, a "superliar," the fiction you invented out of your experience and talent would become truer than what actually happened. What Hemingway sought, finally, was more than the facts, more even than the empirical truth itself: "From things that have happened and from things as they exist and from all things that you know and all those you cannot

know you make something through your invention that is not a repres-
entation but a whole new thing truer than anything true and alive, and
you make it alive, and if you make it well enough, you give it immortality."

Critics and Competitors

From first to last, Hemingway went out of his way to berate critics as
camp-following "eunuchs" of literature who were paid to have attitudes
toward things. There were already eleven critics to every authentic
writer, he observed in January 1924; now that Van Wyck Brooks had
won the *Dial* prize, he expected the ratio to increase to fifty-five to one
or worse. Later, when his own work began to draw widespread commentary, Hemingway redoubled his attack upon the critical fraternity,
which found his fiction saturated in drink and sex or overpopulated by
tough guys or obsessed by violence or lacking in social awareness or
fixated upon the self. Sarcastically, he composed a piece of doggerel in
response:

> Sing a song of critics
> Pockets full of lye
> Four and twenty critics
> Hope that you will die
> Hope that you will peter out
> Hope that you will fail
> So they can be the first one
> Be the first to hail
> Any happy weakening or sign of quick decay.

The critics' most grievous fault, in his view, was that they refused
to measure him against the august company he wanted to be compared
with. An intensely competitive man, Hemingway constantly assessed
himself against the great writers of the past: "the only people for a
serious writer to compete with are the dead writers that he knows are
good." It was like "a miler running against the clock rather than simply

trying to beat whoever [was] in the race with him." Unless he tested his skill against time, he would never find out how fast he was capable of running. In his Nobel Prize acceptance speech in 1954 Hemingway put the same idea in slightly different words: "It is because we have had such great writers in the past that a writer is driven far out past where he can go, out to where no one can help him." All he wanted, he wrote Lillian Ross in May 1950, was to be champion of the world.

He did not like being compared with living writers, since most of them, he was sure, were false "geniuses" the critics had created for the season. Ernest was often generous with younger or beginning writers. Certainly there was no sign of rivalry involved when he arranged for novelist Nathan Asch and his critically ill wife to take a trip to the Pyrenees in the mid-1920s, or when he read and extensively commented upon and recommended to Arnold Gingrich at *Esquire* during the middle 1930s the stories of a beginning writer named Joseph M. Hopkins who'd asked for his help, or when he took time during the 1944 military campaign in Europe to provide a morose young enlisted man named J. D. Salinger with what Salinger called the only encouraging moments of his service overseas. Yet he also subjected actual or potential rivals to scorn and cruelty. Besides breaking off friendships with Fitzgerald and Dos Passos, he dismissed John O'Hara in 1956 as one of the "writing Irish" who could not stand either failure or success, and he feuded, more or less viciously, with Sinclair Lewis.

No other writer, though, brought out his competitive instincts so powerfully as William Faulkner. Both men must have been aware that they were engaged in a contest for literary pre-eminence, in their own country and their own time, and that awareness created an inevitable tension between them. At the beginning of his literary career, Faulkner was inclined to think Hemingway the best writer among his contemporaries, who included Dos Passos, Erskine Caldwell, and Thomas Wolfe. After World War II, however, he remarked for publication that Hemingway did not take enough chances as a writer, and lacked the courage to experiment, an observation that spurred Hemingway to a furious denial that he was anything but courageous under fire. Ernest's frantic reaction apparently surprised the writer from Mississippi. "Hemingway tries too hard," he observed. "He should be a farmer like me and just write on the side." Yet Faulkner did support Hemingway, in *Time* magazine, against the more vicious attacks on *Across the River and into the Trees*, and he later praised *The Old Man and the Sea*, the novel which quieted some of the critical grumbling about Hemingway, as no less than "his best." Still, the eternal comparisons must have rankled, and on Faulkner's trip to Japan, he was delighted to go unrecognized. "Here's somebody," he said of an old Japanese woman, "who doesn't know what I am, care what I am, and doesn't give a damn what I think of Ernest Hemingway."

If such comparisons bothered Faulkner, they drove Hemingway almost to distraction. As early as 1932, in one of the digressive conversations which function to end chapters of *Death in the Afternoon*, Ernest isolated Faulkner as a potential rival worth poking fun at. Because of the groundwork laid by Faulkner, Hemingway tells the Old Lady who serves as interlocutor, "publishers now will publish anything rather than to try to get you to delete the better portions of your works." Ernest was clearly referring to *Sanctuary*, a novel he regarded as blown-up and no good. Still, he planned to follow Faulkner's lead, he said, by writing extensively about the time he'd spent in whorehouses. In a backhanded compliment, Hemingway encouraged the Old Lady to go ahead and buy Faulkner's works. "Madame, you can't go wrong on Faulkner. He's prolific too. By the time you get them ordered there'll be new ones out." He could hardly understand, he'd told Mike Strater in 1930, how writers like Faulkner and Robert McAlmon could express themselves so freely. "It just comes out of them," Ernest said, "as though they were evacuating their bowels."

Hemingway's attitude toward his rival worsened with the announcement that Faulkner had been awarded the 1950 Nobel Prize for literature. After that, his comments on Faulkner became progressively more strident and personal. "No son of a bitch that ever won the Nobel Prize," he proclaimed, "ever wrote anything worth reading afterwards." The trouble with Faulkner's novels, he told Harvey Breit, was that he didn't know how to finish them. He'd get started pretty well, but then he'd get tired, or suffer from heat prostration, or hit the sauce too hard, and the book would fall apart. Besides, Faulkner had one incurable defect: you couldn't reread his fiction because when you tried to you were always conscious of how he had fooled you the first time around.

In the early days, when Faulkner wasn't very well known in Europe, Ernest maintained he'd built him up as the best of the American writers. Now he heard that Faulkner was telling students what was wrong with his work. Ernest was getting tired of this, and he was pretty well fed up with "Anomatopoeio County," since anything that needed a genealogical table to explain it reminded him of James Branch Cabell, and besides he'd feel cramped in that county, or any county. It was all right for "Old Corndrinking Mellifluous" to go after catfish there if he wanted to, but Ernest preferred fighting marlin in the Gulf Stream. "Some of the Southern stuff" was good, and "The Bear" was worth reading, he told a correspondent in July 1956, but Faulkner's last book, *A Fable*, was so full of phony, pretentious religiosity that it amounted to "impure diluted shit" and there wasn't a single "shit tester at Ichang where they ship the night soil from Chungking to but would fault it." Maliciously, he suggested to Breit that Faulkner should write an introduction to Breit's collection of interviews, *The Writer Observed*. Hemingway would pay Faulkner $350 for the job, "while he, for no financial consideration at all, would write a rival introduction based on an interview with the Deity, which he was almost certain he could obtain, once he explained the circumstances and the high honor being afforded Him of appearing there with Dr. Faulkner."

The Work Ethic

It is a cliché of Hemingway scholarship that as a member of the lost generation he repudiated the received values and rejected the old guides to conduct. His own correspondence seems to support this view. He had found it necessary, he wrote Mary Welsh in September 1945, to get rid of various unsound Puritan conceptions from the past and to make his own rules. He refused to accept any principles, he insisted, which had been handed down from on high in an abstract language he did not trust. His private standards were ones he'd tested in the crucible of experience.

But these standards turned out to be not very different from those he was presumably rebelling against. His fiction almost always asks for moral judgments, based on conventional ethical norms, against characters who fail in courage, dodge commitment, or cause suffering through their own lack of awareness. In this sense, his books fall within the classical American literary tradition, for, as D. H. Lawrence observed, "it is especially true of American art, that it is essentially moral!. Hawthorne, Poe, Longfellow, Emerson, Melville: it is the moral issue which engages them." Like these canonical nineteenth-century writers, Hemingway privately attacked "the old morality" while continuing to pay allegiance to it in his writing.

Many readers of Hemingway have argued that he was an immoralist, or at least an amoralist. James T. Farrell, for example, leaped from the observation that most of the characters in *The Sun Also Rises* act like "people who have not fully grown up" (a remark with which Hemingway would certainly have agreed) to the conclusion that the author's "moral outlook . . . amounts to the attitude that an action is good if it makes one feel good." Jake Barnes reflects along these lines, to be sure, and in *Death in the Afternoon* Ernest restates the idea: "So far, about morals, I know only that what is moral is what you feel good after and what is immoral is what you feel bad after." But the key word here is "after," for only the essentially good act could make Hemingway feel good afterward, whereas he was overcome by "awful puritanical" remorse the moment he began cultivating his vices. His code was not hedonistic at all, but rather its reverse, for the thing that made him feel best of all, as he reiterated time and again, was hard work. "What I had to do was work," he wrote in *Green Hills of Africa*. "To work was the only thing, it was the one thing that always made you feel good. . . ." He had always been happy when he was working, he told Breit in a 1952 interview; if he could not work, he usually did something bad and suffered remorse and his conscience would make him work once more. Work was the best therapy, he concluded in *A Moveable Feast*: it "could cure almost anything, I believed then [as a young writer in Paris], and I believe now."

Like many adolescents, he had instinctively resisted the preachments about the sanctity of work dispensed at home and at Oak Park high school, where, during the winter and spring of 1916, he reported on the meetings of the school's Hanna Club in the school newspaper. This club, organized for the benefit of the high-school boys, featured a series of inspirational speakers all bearing approximately the same message, which was "if at first you don't succeed, try, try again," or "the race is not to the swift," or, to quote the actual words of one Mr. Quayle who addressed the February meeting, "Genius and success are ninety-eight per cent perspiration and two per cent inspiration." In writing about the speech of the Reverend A. B. Gray, another visitor who was introduced as "one of the 'big guns' of Chicago," Ernest allowed a trace of cynicism to dampen his enthusiasm. Mr. Gray predictably told his audience "that initiative, not genius, is what is important in life, and that persistence is what makes men great." He then backed up his statements with "many convincing proofs," so that his talk was enjoyed "by every fellow in the room. In fact, it was so great a speech that there was no discussion afterwards."

The irreverent high-school junior apparently suspected that genius was not necessarily so great an affliction as it was represented to be in the oratory of Mr. Quayle and Mr. Gray, and took their rhetoric with a grain of salt. Nor did he embrace the work ethic after returning from World War I, when Grace Hemingway found it necessary to squelch his scheme of shipping out to the Orient with three buddies by refusing him the money for a passport and the fare to San Francisco. Both his parents were relieved when their son married Hadley Richardson, for now "they felt sure," as his sister Marcelline observed, "that Ernest would stick to a job."

They were righter than they knew, except that it was not a "regular" job (or even Hadley herself) that Ernest decided to stick to, but, instead, his consuming drive to write surpassingly good fiction. To that task, in the Paris of the mid-1920s, he brought both a talent bordering on genius and a willingness to perspire that would have brought an approving grin to the iron visage of Andrew Carnegie. As Lincoln Steffens remembered him in those days, Hemingway "was gay, he was sentimental, but he was always at work."

Ernest undoubtedly absorbed more from those Hanna Club meetings than he was willing to admit. More importantly, the parental accusation of idleness, like the related one of financial irresponsibility, left its barb in him. Not only did he work, he was determined to work harder than anyone else. Thus he was outraged when Max Perkins told him in 1928 that Fitzgerald worked at his writing eight hours a day. What's your secret, he later inquired of Scott in mock admiration, before coming to the point, which was that Fitzgerald was a dirty liar to claim that he wrote eight hours a day. Even Ernest couldn't do that, and he prided himself on his endurance and capacity for hard work.

Work he did, as his wives agree. According to Martha Gellhorn, working was Ernest's one "absolutely respectable aspect." For her part, Mary Hemingway found it remarkable that her husband could continue writing in the Cuban tropics during "the midst of our perpetual weekend." He only managed it, she explained, by getting up very early in the morning before the rest of the household was awake. Rising with the sun formed part of Hemingway's regular writing routine. As a way of getting started at dawn, he customarily reread what he had already written on the book at hand and proceeded from there, without following any outline or hard-and-fast structural plan. Then he quit for the day, usually about noon, while he still had some "juice" left, and pursued other activities, doing his best to shut the writing out of his mind until the next morning, when he would return, refreshed, to his work.

He did not normally take notes, but relied instead on an unusually retentive memory. After he and Max Eastman visited the eminent British humorist Max Beerbohm in 1922, Ernest noticed Eastman scribbling in his notebook, smiled, and tapping his forehead, said, "I have every word of it in here." Usually he wrote in longhand, since the typewriter made writing seem too easy and the product looked so solidified in type that he hesitated to make any changes by way of improvement (late in life, he sometimes wrote stories on the typewriter, although the first drafts of *Islands in the Stream* were still in longhand). He refused to dictate fiction, for it led to rhetorical excesses that did not untangle well on the page.

Usually Hemingway wrote slowly, keeping daily word counts of his progress in a conscious attempt to avoid the merely facile. In writing dialogue, though, his speed increased dramatically. "When the people are talking," he said in 1950, "I can hardly write it fast enough." He did not place much stock in psychic geography, and could work well almost anywhere. Madrid, he observed in the 1938 preface to his collected stories, "was always a good place for working," but so were Paris, Key West in the cool months, the ranch near Cooke City, Montana; Kansas City; Chicago; Toronto; Havana—a roster that included almost everywhere he had ever lived. Once, in the midst of an argument about the best place to write—"in or out of cities, north or south, facing the sea or the mountains, in America or Europe, and at what sort of desk, in what sort of room or office or study"—Hemingway put the question to rest. "Shit," he said, "the best place for a writer to work is in his head." It was important, though, that the writer work alone and that he keep what he was doing to himself. Writing represented a kind of catharsis for Ernest as for the character Nick Adams, who knew that if he wrote about his father's suicide he could "get rid of it. He had gotten rid of many things by writing them. But it was still too early for that." A corollary was that you could lose the emotion and the tension that stimulated the work by talking it away.

The one thing Hemingway did frequently talk about was the laboriousness of his chosen career. In Paris, he echoed the Hanna Club line in insisting to Lincoln Steffens and his young bride Ella Winter that writing was only a matter of "utter honesty and hard labor." Anybody could write, he told Ella one evening in 1924, feigning a left to her jaw. "It's hell. It takes it all out of you. It nearly kills you but you can do it." Steffens decided that Ernest had left out one indispensable ingredient: genius.

Hemingway may have agreed privately; but publicly he continued to stress the rigors of the craft, and he did so more frequently as he grew older. "The hardest thing to do," he said in 1934, "is to write straight honest prose on human beings. First you have to know the subject, then you have to know how to write," and both took a lifetime to learn. By 1940, he told Charles Scribner, his writing had become a disease, a vice, and an obsession. It was a disease because he could not be happy without it, a vice because he enjoyed it, and an obsession since he aimed, beyond all conceivable fulfillment, to write better prose than anyone else had ever done. Nobody really knew or understood what he was trying to do, he observed about *The Old Man and the Sea* twelve years later. The secret of that book was that it was "poetry written into prose," and that, he added, was "the hardest of all things to do." Writing was a perpetual challenge to him, he observed; "it is more difficult than anything else that I have ever done—so I do it."

That last four-word phrase embodied Hemingway's capitulation to the work ethic. It was not enough that writing was difficult for him: it had to be *more* difficult than any other occupation at all before he could take proper satisfaction from it. Simply adding up the word count at the end of a productive day—and telling someone else about it—could bring him a surge of joy. Wrote 1641 words the day before yesterday, he boasted in September 1949, and another 1224 today. Yesterday itself, feeling virtuous, he'd spent fishing.

Ernest believed that you had to earn your time at play. As he became more successful, however, the hours spent hunting, fishing, watching bullfights, carousing, or womanizing sometimes lengthened into days or weeks. Then he invariably would return to his usual routine, full of shame and self-abasement, ready for the flagellation he felt he deserved for neglecting his work. But he never succeeded in satisfying his own standards of personal industry or any other facet of the strict code of conduct he fashioned for himself out of his Oak Park inheritance. "No one of us," he wrote after his 1954 brush with death in the African plane crashes, "lives by as rigid standards nor has as good ethics as we planned but an attempt is made."

xii

Mastery

The Divided Self

If a novelist is to be any good at all, Scott Fitzgerald believed, he must be several people rolled into one. But while such a writer might produce surpassingly good fiction, his personal life was almost certain to lack psychological integration. So it turned out for Fitzgerald's contemporary Ernest Hemingway, who was a man deeply divided against himself, with the most conspicuous split separating the writer, worker, and man of feeling on the one hand, from the adventurer, sportsman, and man of action on the other.

What he wanted, as Ernest spelled it out in *Green Hills of Africa*, was to have it both ways: "To write as well as I can and learn as I go along. At the same time I have my life which I enjoy and which is a damned good life." Here, as in dozens of passages, he drew the line between his two selves, one a writer who would get his reward after he was dead, the other a man who got "his everything" now. If he could not fish and hunt, he wrote Marjorie Kinnan Rawlings in 1936, he would probably go crazy with the strain of trying to write. Surely the sportsman was entitled to enjoy himself as long as the artist kept producing.

Reconciling the two existences sometimes proved very difficult. After several years away from serious fiction during World War II,

259

Ernest wrote Buck Lanham in April 1945 that he really didn't give a damn about writing. A life of action suited him far better. He was not satisfied to sit on the sidelines while the cavalcade rolled by. Writers in America, as Archibald MacLeish observed, were "supposed to be watchers," but Hemingway took part. "What he took part in was not the private history of Ernest Hemingway or the social history of Oak Park, Ill., or the intellectual history of a generation of his fellow countrymen. What he took part in was a public—even a universal—history of wars and animals and gigantic fish." The man of action in Hemingway derived a certain pleasure from defying public expectations. Nothing made him happier than earning the admiration of the professional warrior or hunter or fisherman who accepted him as an initiate and did not care or would not believe that he wrote books. At the same time, the artist in Hemingway insistently nudged him back to his desk, the only place where he could labor toward immortality. In *A Moveable Feast*, he combined the two images in presenting himself as he wished to be remembered—as a poor, hungry, and rugged young man who had been to war and liked to fish and ski and hike, but who was totally dedicated to the goal of whittling one true sentence at a time. "See him now in his café," as Alfred Kazin described Hemingway's self-portrait of the artist, "with his sweatshirt under his shirt, his blue-backed notebook to write in, his two pencils and his little pencil sharpener. . . . You think this is less of an American fable than Huck Finn on a raft, Ben Franklin waiting for his kite to be hit by lightning?"

The division between the writer and the sportsman, the man at work and the man at play, formed only part of a wider and more damaging fissure within Hemingway. This resulted, according to the argument of Irvin D. and Marilyn Yalom (the most persuasive of many psychological studies of Hemingway and his fiction), from Ernest's creation of, and attempt to live up to, an idealized self-image.

Children conjure up such images, the Yaloms argue, when they meet lack of acceptance from their parents. Regarding parents as omniscient, such youngsters conclude there must be something terribly wrong with themselves; so, instead of developing their genuine selves, they set about constructing idealized images. According to the Yaloms' theory, Hemingway was such a child, and built up an idealized image "crystallized around a search for mastery" which would prove his superiority to others. The ideal Hemingway was extremely virile, eternally faithful, absolutely courageous, and so strong as to be virtually impervious to the wounds of life. He was also a brilliant sportsman and consummate craftsman, possessed of wisdom beyond the ken of other men. Ernest sought to transfer to his idealized self those same marvelous attributes which, in a May 1950 letter, he assigned to his "God." That marvelous personage, he wrote, had painted many wonderful pictures and written some excellent books and fought Napoleon's most effective rearguard actions and cured yellow fever and sired Citation. He was the best god-damned God anyone had ever known. Above all, he was incredibly independent, sufficient unto himself. He was, in short, such a creature as never did or could live, and therein lay Hemingway's downfall. The godhood he aimed for eluded him forever—though not for lack of trying.

Omniscience and Invincibility

Fueled by a powerful will and body, Hemingway set out to achieve superhuman ends: not only to write better but to know more, to behave more courageously, to be more loyal, to demonstrate more skill ånd strength, to survive more terrible wounds, to sleep less, to endure more bitter cold, and to drink more than anyone else in the world.

Hemingway's ability to speak (or write) as from a trove of superior knowledge was acquired early. Even in his young manhood, in Paris, Ernest Walsh was inclined to conclude of him, *"This kid knows a few things"* and to suggest the dimensions of those things by listing Hemingway's fields of expertise:

> Papa soldier pugilist bullfighter
> Writer gourmet lionhead aesthete
> He's a big guy from near Chicago

Yet, as a young writer, Hemingway was keenly aware of what he had to learn. How could he hope to "write like Hardy and Hamsun when he only knew ten years of life?" He could not, nor could he become "a great writer" until he knew enough things. But, he added confidently,

"That would come. He knew." It was not formal education he was after, but knowledge itself. Indeed, like other self-taught men he tended to drive a wedge between the two: "It would have been useful to be educated but then maybe I wouldn't have had time to learn anything." And learn he did. As Cowley has observed, Hemingway "taught himself an effective knowledge of French, Spanish, Italian. He taught himself celestial navigation. And he turned . . . whatever sport he was studying into what would now be a university subject."

Whatever the subject, Ernest's overwhelming interest was in practical applications rather than theory. Very much in the American spirit of technological accomplishment, he wanted to know *how to*: how to write, most of all, but also how to fish and hunt and watch a bullfight and fight a war and eat and drink and make love. His early dispatches for the Toronto newspapers consistently reflect this fascination with how to do things. There are articles on how to shoplift (the store detectives were on to the candy-bag, umbrella, and baby-carriage tricks); how to fish for trout with worms (don't use the pale yellowish ones found under manure, never let your shadow fall over a hole where trout may be hiding); how to steer a Swiss *luge* (by dragging your left foot if it started to sheer off to the right and vice versa); how to plant *banderillos* in the shoulders of a charging bull (rise on your toes, bend forward, and just as the bull is about to hit you drop the darts evenly, one on each side, in the bull's hump just back of his horns); how to avoid mosquitoes (put a little oil of citronella on the mosquito netting that covers the front of your tent), fry fish (cook them over coals, not over a brightly burning fire), and bake pie crusts (take "a cup and a half of flour, one-half teaspoonful of salt," and so forth) while camping out; and how to survive if caught in an avalanche (kick off your skis, and swim in it as though you were in the water). On these various subjects—as on how to shoot a horse (*Esquire*, June 1935: "stand so close to him that you cannot miss and shoot him in the forehead at the exact point where a line drawn from his left ear to his right eye and another line drawn from his right ear to the left eye would intersect"), and how to fake injury or illness so as to avoid combat (*Across the River and into the Trees*: several ways mentioned, including the injection of paraffin under one's kneecap)—Hemingway played the role of a teacher of extraordinarily wide experience, one who could give proper instruction out of his own storehouse of personal knowledge. To son Patrick, away at prep school in the fall of 1942, Ernest discoursed on the secrets of successful football tackling. Open your arms wide before you make the tackle, he wrote, and then slam them together hard. Patrick should also learn to fall sideways so as to protect his testicles and should wear a jockstrap for the same reason. In August 1948 he wrote a long letter to Mary, supplying her with meticulously detailed directions for having her hair done. She should switch, he instructed, from her short-and-curly look to a long and sleek, Ann-Harding-blond hair style.

Since Ernest was forever expounding on how to do things, it was important that his listeners should know how to listen. There were times, naturally, when members of the audience tired of his "Old Master" posture. In the middle 1930s, for example, both John and Katy Dos Passos grew restive under the barrage of oracular pronouncements issuing from their old friend. Dos Passos went so far as to object in advance of publication to those parts of *Death in the Afternoon* "where Old Hem straps on the longwhite whiskers and gives the boys the low-down." Heeding the warning, Ernest cut down, he told Dos Passos, on some of the longer authorial intrusions. But his tutorial, just-listen-to-Papa attitude was hardening in those Key West years, and during the last two decades of his life very few of Ernest's close companions (John or Katy were no longer among these) would risk contradicting him.

Hemingway's determination to excel in whatever he undertook also drove him to take risks and engage in feats of bravado designed to demonstrate his nerve, his skill, and his strength. Not only did he test himself under combat conditions in several wars but also (so he told A. E. Hotchner) in one-to-one confrontations with animals. On meeting Hotchner in 1948, Hemingway talked about an act he was hoping to develop with two "cotsies," or five-year-old lions, who made up part of a circus visiting Havana. The climax of the act would come "when I lie down and both cotsies put their front feet on my chest. I started to practice this but got raked on the arm a couple of times gentling them." Working with the lions, Ernest said, took his "mind off things."

The everyday act of driving an automobile became, for Ernest and his companions, yet another test of nerve. *New York Times*man Herbert Matthews described the Hemingway of Spanish Civil War days as "a wizard with a car," but diplomat Claude Bowers, at about the same time, gave devout thanks for his survival after but one trip in Ernest's battered old Belgian Minerva. Bowers would undoubtedly have been even more terrified if he had gone along on the "chicken" rides that

Ernest and his friend Jane Mason used to take in Key West. First, they would fortify themselves with daiquiris, then head off cross-country in her sports car. They took turns driving, and whoever was driving could go anywhere he wished, on or off the road. The object was to see how long the passenger could last without crying, "Watch out!" Ernest usually won.

Hemingway's best-known display of skill and nerve, though, involved his shooting a cigarette out of the hand or mouth of an accomplice. It is amazing how many accomplices he found. During their boyhood in Horton Bay, Michigan, Ernest said that Bill Smith willingly let him shoot a cigarette out of his mouth. In the early 1950s Gianfranco Ivancich allowed him to shoot anything out of his hand at ten paces and his servant Roberto Herrera, Ernest maintained, permitted him to shoot a cigarette held in his mouth and then *cut off whatever was left* with a second shot. During the African safari of 1953, he put on a show for Masai natives shooting cigarettes out of hands, including those of white hunter Denis Zaphiro. At his birthday party in 1959, Antonio Ordóñez and the Maharajah of Cooch Behar bravely held their ground while Hemingway celebrated his sixty years by shooting cigarettes from between their lips.

As early as high school, he grasped the opportunity to display his unusual strength. In February of his senior year at Oak Park three girls were "flying to destruction" on a dumbwaiter in the school lunchroom when Ernest, realizing the danger, grabbed the rope, was jerked off his feet, and with his bare hands blocked the pulley at the top until four other boys ran to help him pull the girls to safety.

Twenty years later, in Spain, Sefton Delmer recalled, Ernest ostentatiously insisted on carrying duffle bags loaded with tinned food up seven flights of stairs, all by himself. Delmer and fellow correspondent Matthews had reason to be grateful for Hemingway's strength, though, when he saved their lives by pulling against the current of the Ebro River to keep their rowboat from striking the jagged remnants of a bombed-out bridge in November 1937. According to Lillian Hellman, Hemingway challenged Dashiell Hammett to repeat Ernest's trick of making a spoon bend between the muscles of his upper and lower arm, and was infuriated when Hammett refused to try. One day in 1944, drinking with John Steinbeck and John O'Hara at Tim Costello's Third Avenue bar in New York, Hemingway won a $50 bet by bending O'Hara's Irish blackthorn stick until it cracked.

Hemingway's eagerness to expose himself to stresses and strains, combined as it was with his native awkwardness and imperfect eyesight, helped make him vulnerable to a series of wounds and accidents.

The most famous of these wounds occurred in Italy in 1918, but many others followed. In 1928 he yanked on the chain in his Paris toilet, bringing the skylight crashing down to knock him silly; the gash over his right eye needed nine-stitches. In the spring of 1930 he required six more stitches to sew up his right index finger, cut clear to the bone while he was working out on a punching bag. And in Wyoming that summer, more stitches were needed to close a face wound he suffered when his horse bolted. Driving east that same fall he broke his right arm. In 1935 he shot himself in both legs while attempting to kill a shark. A London auto accident in 1944 (someone else was driving) hospitalized Ernest with a severe concussion and forty-seven stitches in his battered head. In 1950 he slipped and fell on the deck of the *Pilar*, banging his head against a metal clamp and opening a three-stitch cut in his head. Among his injuries in the African plane crashes of 1954 were a bad concussion, "a ruptured liver, spleen, and kidney, temporary loss of vision in the left eye, loss of hearing in the left ear, a crushed vertebra, a sprained right arm and shoulder, a sprained left leg, paralysis of the sphincter, and first degree burns on his face, arms, and head." The following month he foolishly tried to help fight a brushfire that sprang up near their camp at Shimoni, fell into the flames, and suffered still further burns to his legs, abdomen, chest, lips, left hand, and right forearm.

In letters and conversations, Ernest tended to exaggerate his unusual record of mishaps. Though he maintained that his wounding in World War I had disabused him of any sense of his own immortality, that wound—when allied with many other accidents—seemed to have the opposite effect. Having walked often in the shadow of death and survived, he adopted a stance of invincibility. Brendan Gill, after interviewing him for *The New Yorker* in 1947, entitled his account "Indestructible," for that was the impression Ernest conveyed. He could, so he came to believe, withstand the penalties nature exacted of lesser men.

Ernest brought an unusual store of energy to the business of living. It was almost, Buck Lanham remarked, as if "all his psychic adrenals had been stepped on in his infancy." He gloried in his capacity for endurance, and especially in his ability to function with very little sleep. Ted Brumback, a fellow reporter on the Kansas City *Star* in 1918, marveled at Ernest's ability to read and drink all night and get through his work the following day as if nothing had happened. He often heard the clock strike every hour and half-hour from midnight to daylight, Ernest asserted in response to a questionnaire in 1931. He averaged only two hours and thirty-two minutes of sleep a night for forty-two days during his son Patrick's illness in the spring of 1947, he wrote Lanham, and still felt fine. He had seen "all the sunrises" in his half a hundred years, he bragged to Lillian Ross in 1950.

Undoubtedly Hemingway did sleep less than most men. He was troubled by insomnia, he wrote, caused by lack of exercise, or two much thinking, or the pain of physical wounds. He was also subject throughout his life to nightmares that brought him awake sweating profusely. From the time as a boy when, after reading *Dracula*, he woke screaming, through the post-World War I period when terrifying visions of the terrain where he had been wounded came to him in his dreams, through the post-World War II period when two Seconal tablets would guarantee five hours of sleep but not prevent the occasional really good, sound, unimpeachable nightmare that made him change pajamas three times, Ernest was victimized by "the horrors" at night. Perhaps, he suggested in an April 1945 letter to Mary, he was paying at night for consciously shutting off the taproots of fear during the daytime. Whatever their origins, he tended to make a virtue of his nightmares as of his wounds. What could you expect, he asked scornfully, of a man like Peter Viertel who "by his own admission had only two sleepless nights in his entire life?"

By his own account, he was virtually impervious to cold as well. He ran into a blizzard while skiing in Austria, he wrote Harold Loeb in 1925, and had to rub his penis with snow to keep it from freezing. Then he skied five miles down the side of a glacier in under twelve minutes. Prior to the battle of Teruel in the Spanish war, Ilya Ehrenburg was startled to see Ernest in summer clothes. "You're crazy," Ehrenburg said. "It's deadly cold out there." Hemingway laughed and produced several flasks. "I've got my own central heating," he said, but in a dispatch for the North American Newspaper Alliance, he made rather more of his ordeal. He had survived "Siberian weather conditions," he wrote, "with two frozen fingers and eight hours non-consecutive sleep in the last seventy-two." When Lillian Ross first met Ernest in Idaho, he "was standing on hard-packed snow, in dry cold of ten degrees below zero, wearing bedroom slippers, no socks, Western trousers. . . ." Ross was absolutely freezing. Hemingway wasn't a bit cold, he told her.

By his own testimony and that of others, Ernest consumed vast quantities of liquor. During the 1930s his regular tab at Sloppy Joe's in Key West indicated an intake of about 125 drinks a month, exclusive of what he drank at home or at parties. In September 1945, prior to his marriage to Mary Welsh, he set himself a "non-drinking" routine which included two martinis before lunch, but not until after 12 noon, and three drinks in the evening, but not after dinner. He couldn't promise to stick to so strict a regimen, he told Mary, since a drink before you went to bed was a wonderful thing and there were other times a drink was good too, but for the moment it was helping his writing enormously. By the time of the African safari of 1953, the regimen had clearly broken down. White hunter Zaphiro reported that liquor consumption among the three of them—Zaphiro, Hemingway, and Mary—"ran to about two fifths of gin a day, not counting the gin and Campari at lunch and the case of wine a week for dinner."

Hemingway's drinking career began in an effort to show others that he could outdrink them. He and Bill Smith, when teen-agers, used to compete in chug-a-lugs from the hard-cider jug up in Michigan; the winner was the one who could take the longest slug and still stay reasonably coherent. As a young adult, Hemingway continued to look on drinking as a contest in which he was not about to be outdone. Donald Ogden Stewart, he write Dos Passos in April 1925, was now claiming to be a drinker, but they knew better. Remember, Ernest asked, how Don vomited all over Pamplona? Drinking beer with Hemingway in Paris, during 1929, Morley Callaghan soon discovered he was an unwitting competitor in a contest. Ernest would empty his glass in a few gulps, then challenge Callaghan to join him in another. Morley kept up with him for three rounds, then asked himself, "Why the hell am I doing this?" and quit. Before they left the bar, Ernest had accumulated a pile of seven saucers to Callaghan's three. Once, in Cuba, according to a letter to Charles Poore, Ernest and "the greatest Jai-Alai player in the world" embarked on a drinking bout, which ended after each man had consumed, standing up, sixteen double frozen daiquiris each containing four ounces of Bacardi rum. Then Ernest went home, read all night, and never felt better, he said.

But there was more to his fondness of liquor than the lure of competition. "I love getting drunk," he confided as early as 1923.

"Right from the start it is the best feeling." "Don't you drink?" he asked Ivan Kashkeen, in the mid-1930s, and went on to extol the virtues of alcohol: "When you work hard all day with your head and know you must work again the next day what else can change your ideas and make them run on a different plane like whiskey? When you are cold and wet what else can warm you? Before an attack who can say anything that gives you the momentary well being that rum does? I would as soon not eat at night as not to have red wine and water."

In the beginning, drinking brought him a sense of well-being and helped him relax from his labors. Then it became, as for Robert Jordan, a medicine designed to facilitate escape into a nostalgic past. One cup of absinthe in water, Jordan reflected, could take "the place . . . of all the things that he had enjoyed and forgotten and that came back to him when he tasted that opaque, bitter, tongue-numbing, stomach-warming, idea-changing liquid alchemy." Later Ernest used liquor as a specific against his lengthening spells of depression. Yet he always insisted that he should not be classified as a drunk or an alcoholic. "Rummies are rummies," he wrote in 1953, but he was different, because he had learned to drink "before he was 14" and had drunk ever since and loved to drink and could still write well. Would-be reformers he regarded as crashing bores. "God pity rummies, but God please save us from the ex-rummy and from all tracts, for or against, deliver me," he wrote in his "African Journal." Mary was alarmed by the quantity he drank, but did not want to nag or become a bore. As she pointed out, Papa hadn't married a policeman. In his last few years, though, when—as she observed—her husband derived almost as much nourishment from alcohol as from food, the pleasant medicine turned toxic.

One way or another, Hemingway was constantly testing himself against no ordinary standard of accomplishment, but against the standard of the master. The effort cost him a lot physically, for the prodigious drinking, like the series of accidents and the sleepless nights, sapped his vitality and undermined his health. It cost him artistically, since he was forever being distracted from his work to some other field of endeavor. And the process of pursuing mastery in one such field—that of gambling—probably cost him financially as well.

Ernie the Greek

One of the things wrong with Robert Cohn, in *The Sun Also Rises*, is that he does not know how to gamble. He usually wins his bets, but in the process manages to alienate almost everyone around him. While visiting New York, Cohn holds some good cards, wins several hundred dollars playing in a steep bridge game, and begins bragging about "how a man could always make a living at bridge if he were ever forced to." He wins a 100-peseta bet with Bill Gorton that Mike Campbell and Brett will not arrive as scheduled in Pamplona, but Gorton is provoked into the bet because of Cohn's arrogance in parading inside knowledge of their English companions' habits, and the wager costs Cohn any possibility of friendship with Bill. Later he stupidly proposes betting on the bullfights and then announces that he'll probably be bored by them.

There is a good deal of gambling in *The Sun Also Rises*. Harvey Stone wins 200 francs from Jake Barnes shaking poker dice, Bill and Jake and Robert match for drinks at Bayonne, Bill and Jake and Mike roll for them at Biarritz. Here as elsewhere the novel reflects the way it was, for there was a good deal of gambling in Hemingway's life as well.

Ernest had, by 1926, already acquired what he fancied to be expert knowledge of craps and roulette. He had spent a great deal of time following the races at Auteuil and Enghien ("It was not really racing," he admitted in *A Moveable Feast*. "It was gambling on horses, but we called it racing.") He had participated in long poker games at Schruns during the winter of 1924–25—on one memorable occasion drawing the ace of spades to fill a royal flush and winning 430,000 kronen. In "The Snows of Kilimanjaro," the writer Harry looked back nostalgically on the week in February 1925 when they had played poker at the Madlenerhaus, a chalet built into the side of the Kresperspitz, while a blizzard raged outside and finally Herr Walther Lent, the manager of the ski school, had "lost it all. Everything, the skischule money and all the season's profit and then his capital." There was always gambling then, Harry remembered. "When there was no snow you gambled and when there was too much you gambled. He thought of all the time in his life that he had spent gambling."

As with Harry, so with Hemingway—and if like his fictional

counterpart he felt a twinge of regret for the hours spent on gambling, that did not make him stop. Spurred by his competitive spirit, he liked to test his skill at shooting, whether for large stakes or small. One day in 1929 he challenged Morley Callaghan to a contest at a miniature shooting gallery in Chartres. "Whoever loses, pays," he said, and so he and Callaghan knocked down row after row of ducks and dolls set up so close that it was almost impossible to miss. Finally Callaghan's wife persuaded Morley that he should concede, to Ernest's obvious satisfaction. In Cuba after World War II he competed in live-pigeon shoots "for the large money" against such well-to-do opponents as Winston Guest, Tommy Shevlin, Thorwald Sanchez, and Pichon Aguilera, and such skillful ballplayer-nimrods as Brooklyn Dodgers Curt Davis, Billy Herman, Augie Galan, and Hugh Casey. It was a miserable spectator sport, Ernest admitted, but "with strong, really fast birds it is still the best participant sport for betting I know."

On a nonparticipant basis, Hemingway not only bet on the races but on boxing, a sport where he felt his own experience gave him an insider's edge, and on baseball. Though less than notably successful in these wagers, he insisted that gambling, like everything else worth doing at all, had to be done properly and professionally.

In Hemingway's formulation, the intelligent gambler had first to understand that most sporting events could be, and often were, fixed. He'd given up the races in France even though he was winning, he wrote in *A Moveable Feast*, because it took too much time and because eventually, he "knew too much about what went on at Enghien and at the flat racing tracks too." What went on, according to "My Old Man," was that the order of finish was sometimes determined before the race began. Similarly, in *A Farewell to Arms*, Frederic and Catherine go out to Milan's San Siro with an American named Meyers who has advance information about which horses to bet on. The whole business disgusts Catherine, who feels "much cleaner" after losing a bet on a horse Meyers wasn't backing.

The theme of the crooked fight, like that of the crooked race, crops up repeatedly in Hemingway's early fiction: in "A Matter of Colour," a 1916 high-school story; in "Fifty Grand," where Jack Brennan bets on himself to lose and must foul his opponent to win $50,000; in "The Killers," where Ole Andreson awaits the hired assassins who have apparently been sent by the mob to dispose of him as a double-crossing fighter; in *The Sun Also Rises*, where a Negro fighting in

Vienna can't collect his share of the purse after knocking out a white Austrian in violation of the prebout agreement.

In a 1923 feature for the Toronto *Star Weekly*, Hemingway explained that it was almost impossible to make any money dealing with the town's illegal but very active bookmakers, since they paid the parimutuel prices only up to a certain limit. No matter how long the odds at the track, you could not collect more than 15 to 1, or $30 on a $2 bet, in Toronto. In a poem called "The Sport of Kings," he told with wry humor the story of a plunger who reposed too much faith in a hot tip:

> The friend who calls up over the telephone.
> The horse that has been especially wired from Pimlico.
> The letting in of the friends in the office.
> The search for ready money.
> The study of the entries.
> The mysterious absence from the office.
> The time of suspense and waiting.
> The feeling of excitement among the friends in the office.
> The trip outside to buy a sporting extra.
> The search for the results.
> The sad return upstairs.
> The hope that the paper may have made a mistake.
> The feeling among the friends in the office that the paper is right.
> The attitude of the friends in the office.
> The feeling of remorse.
> The lightened pay envelope.

Both in his early fiction and journalism, Hemingway's message was that you really couldn't win, that the soundest policy (as he later expressed it) was "never to bet on an animal that could talk," except possibly oneself. Which having established he set out to ignore and contradict his own cautionary tales.

For if one understood what he was up against, if he was privy to *real* inside information, and if he was tremendously skillful, he might still defy the odds. From his correspondence, it is clear that Hemingway came to regard himself as just such a superior bettor: he got along well with both whores and gamblers, he wrote in 1952, on a comradely "thieves like us" basis. Yet in discussing his gambling exploits, he revealed himself as a rank amateur by bragging about his winnings, by refusing to acknowledge his losses, and—when he had indisputably lost—by invariably insisting that it was a good bet anyway.

Hemingway particularly liked to yarn about his victories to A. E. Hotchner, his companion in Hemhotch, Ltd., a partnership formed by the two men for the duration of the 1949 race meeting at Auteuil. In the early-1920s, he told Hotchner, he used to astound Evan Shipman and Harold Stearns, both track experts as well as writers, by his success at picking winners. His secret, he maintained, was to go down to the paddock between races and smell the horses; those that smelled good to him usually won. Unfortunately, Ernest added, his nose was no longer reliable by mid-decade when he and John Dos Passos pooled all their resources and bet them on the nose of a sweet-smelling horse who proceeded to fall at the first jump and send them home without a sou.

Mostly, though, Hemingway told Hotchner about his gambling triumphs, and these are recorded in *Papa Hemingway*. Among the triumphs were two killings he made on French racetracks, one in his youth and the other in his middle age. The first presumably occurred during the early days in Paris when he bet baby Bumby's milk money and everything he could borrow on a horse named Epinard which breezed home in the Prix Yacoulef at Deauville, paying 59 to 10 and supporting the Hemingways for six to eight months. The second came at Auteuil on December 21, 1949, when the Hemhotch syndicate found itself only slightly ahead with the meeting almost over and decided to bank its entire stake on a jumper called Bataclan II. This time, Hemingway persuaded the bartenders and waiters and even the men's room attendant at the posh Paris Ritz to join him in backing Bataclan, which ran a distant third up to the last jump when both the leading mounts fell and the horse came loping in a 232-to-10 winner, enriching Hemhotch, the hired help at the Ritz, and the merchants of Paris who swallowed up most of the winnings in a Christmas spending spree.

Only one boxing bet is mentioned by Hotchner. That was Ernest's supposedly betting $1000 on Ingemar Johansson, a 4-to-1 underdog, when he knocked out Floyd Patterson in 1959. According to Hotchner, Hemingway got Toots Shor to place the bet for him, and then received a cable from the restaurateur during the fiesta in Pamplona, reading, "Ernie, where shall I send the four thousand bucks, you bum?" It may be that Ernest constructed this tale out of his active imagination, and relayed it to Hotchner. A born story-teller with a flair for self-aggrandizement, he was every bit as capable of creating a winning bet

out of thin air as he was of making a losing bet disappear, a rabbit trick
he performed in connection with the Jack Dempsey-Georges Carpentier
fight in the spring of 1921. When the match was announced the previous fall, Ernest praised the Frenchman in an article for the Toronto *Star
Weekly* headlined, "Carpentier Sure to Give Dempsey Fight Worth
While." Dempsey was "over-rated," he wrote, and Carpentier had "a
most excellent chance to defeat" him. Then, obviously, he put his
money where his mouth was, for after the bout, his fiancée Hadley
Richardson sent Ernest a note commiserating with him for losing $50
on Carpentier. Four years later, however, he wrote Horace Liveright
that his book, *In Our Time*, had a good 3-to-1 chance of selling well,
because it could be read by anyone with a high-school education, and
added in support of his judgment that he had "never bet" on Carpentier or any other sentimental causes.

Hemingway expounded on boxing and betting most thoroughly in
his correspondence during the 1950s with Harvey Breit, a fellow fight
fan. In his opening letter to Breit, Ernest immediately began to establish
his credentials as an expert on the subject. He had, he claimed, seen
most of the great fighters of his day and had worked out with some of
them. As a "punk kid," he lied, he had sparred with Benny Leonard
and Eddie McGoorty. The new breed of heavyweights who could hit but
had not learned to box, like Joe Jouis and Rocky Marciano, might
impress Breit but could not inspire anyone who had seen such fighters
as Gene Tunney, Jack Johnson, Sam Langford, Jimmy McLarnin, Billy
Petrolle, Kid Chocolate, Harry Greb, Jack Bratton, Ted Kid Lewis,
Jimmy Clabby, Dave Shade, Mickey Walker, Pancho Villa, Jimmy
Wilde, Memphis Pat Moore, Young Stribling, Charles Ledoux, Johnny
Dundee, and Marcel Cerdan. The Cuban middleweight Kid Tunero, he
wrote, frequently came to the Finca Vigia for a meal and an evening of
watching old fights on 16mm. film, including Tony Zale versus Rocky
Graziano, Cerdan versus Zale, and Dempsey versus Tunney. Tunero,
who had fought four middleweight champions of the world and who at
forty had beaten Ezzard Charles (later to become heavyweight champion of the world) in his home town of Cincinnati—despite giving
Charles eighteen pounds in the weights—kept him posted on what was
going on in the boxing world. Long ago, he told Breit, he'd learned that
"Never Bet on Fights" was an excellent motto, yet he had lived and
written for over six months on what he'd made when "Gene" (Tunney)
whipped Dempsey the first time.

Having established his expertise, Ernest went on to propose a bet on Tiburio Mitri, an Italian middleweight from Trieste, who was much better, he asserted, than anyone in New York yet knew. The ideal bet, he wrote in April 1950, would be Mitri against Rocky Graziano, who looked to Hemingway—on the television fights—to have lost so much that his best punch was the one after the bell. In a straight fight with an honest referee, Mitri figured to ruin Graziano. When they matched Mitri with Jake LaMotta (not Graziano), Hemingway wrote Breit a strange letter on June 24, 1950, the first half explaining why it would be foolhardy to risk anything on the fight (you had to consider what percentage of the gate each man was getting, and whether thumbing and butting would be allowed) and the second half instructing Breit how much and when to bet on Mitri. A week later he sent along a check for $250. Breit was to put $200 on Mitri at the earliest odds (by fight time, Hemingway thought, the smart money might swing the odds in Mitri's favor) and bet the rest for himself or Hemingway later at his discretion. He was not trying to corrupt Breit or the *Times*, Ernest added. Harvey could pay him back whenever he could afford it.

Breit was unable to reimburse Hemingway out of winnings, for Mitri lost a unanimous decision to LaMotta. This outcome prompted a lengthy letter from Ernest, the burden of which was that though they'd lost, they hadn't been suckers at all and it was still a good bet. In fact, he insisted, if Mitri hadn't hurt his hand early in the bout, it would have been a wonderful bet.

Undaunted by the Mitri defeat, Hemingway continued to supply Breit with his predictions on boxing and baseball. In August 1951, for example, he made five sporting forecasts, each of which he supported with a wager of his own: Sandy Saddler over Willie Pep, Kid Gavilan over Billy Graham, Randy Turpin over Ray Robinson, the Brooklyn Dodgers to win the National League pennant, and the Cleveland Indians the American. A couple of months later, when all the results were in, he had won two of the five bets, on Gavilan and Saddler, and Gavilan had squeaked through on a split decision. But the Turpin bet had been a sound one, too, he insisted; if Turpin had not been knocked out, his youth and strength would have carried him on to defeat Robinson. As for the Indians and the Dodgers, neither team made it to the World Series.

Three years in a row, from 1950 through 1952, Hemingway bet on the National League entry to beat the New York Yankees in the

Series. Three times in a row he was wrong, but he was not about to admit his mistake. He'd lost some money betting on the Philadelphia Phillies in the first two games of the 1950 Series, he wrote Breit, but with Jim Konstanty and Robin Roberts pitching the Phillies were an awfully good bet. The Yankees won in four straight. In the fall of 1951, he backed the "miracle" New York Giants against the Yankees, and this time tended to blame the outcome on a possible fix. He did not like the "feel" of one game, Ernest wrote, though he'd only heard it on the radio and couldn't be sure. The Yankees won, four games to two. Let's not talk about the 1952 Series, he began a letter to Breit following the next year's matchup between the Yankees and the Brooklyn Dodgers. He had made a wonderful bet on the Dodgers, getting 2-to-1 odds, and if Jackie Robinson or Roy Campanella or Gil Hodges had hit at all, he would surely have cashed his ticket. The Yankees won, four games to three.

The image that emerges of Hemingway as gambler is that of a man given to somewhat foolish bets on underdogs, from Carpentier in 1921 to any team against the powerful Yankees of the early 1950s, and simultaneously determined to rationalize his losses as owing to injuries or bad breaks or the fix or other circumstances beyond his control. Above all, he felt compelled to play the expert, and even, when given the opportunity, to serve as mentor on gambling to those younger and less experienced than himself.

His first foray into advice on gambling was a letter-lecture on roulette sent to Dorothy Connable in February 1920. After explaining that roulette was almost invariably honest, inasmuch as the zero and double zero gave the house all the advantage it needed, he went on to suggest two systems he'd learned, he said, in the gambling hells of Europe.

The first, "scientific" way of playing was to watch the wheel carefully for a while, notice which numbers weren't winning, and then support one number that hadn't been up for a long time, on the mathematically dubious theory that since each number ought to come up once in every thirty-eight spins, if it hasn't come up for twenty or thirty times in a row, it ought to be due pretty soon. The second technique he recommended depended upon a principle exactly opposite from that of the first. Again, the player was to watch the wheel to see whether it was running to the low, middle, or high third (or group of twelve numbers), and then, if the low numbers had been coming up, for example, to bet on *them*—not the other two thirds. In a diagram he showed Dorothy how she could cover each of the numbers in the lowest twelve by betting as few as four chips, one each on, say, the 1-2-5-6 and 3-4-7-8 quarters, and one each on 9-10 and 11-12. When you were lucky and the low third kept coming up, he pointed out, you could win a lot of money with this system. Then he concluded with his only truly sensible remark: that in roulette, unlike craps or poker, there was no stigma attached to taking your winnings and quitting. When you get well ahead, he advised Miss Connable, just walk away from the wheel.

Despite the shortcomings of his roulette system, Ernest managed to run a stake of $6 up to $59, he reported, during the following summer in northern Michigan. This windfall came shortly after he'd been kicked out of the Hemingways' summer cottage, and saved him—he maintained in a letter to Edith Quinlan—from having to seek work at the cement plant in Petoskey. It probably also encouraged him in his inclination to play the role of the expert (in May 1920 he had discoursed on techniques at the crap table in the Toronto *Star Weekly*). Since he was not yet twenty-one when he wrote the Connable letter, it is obvious that this impulse was there from the first. But as he grew older, Hemingway lapsed still more often into the role of Ernie the Greek, master gambler. Stick around for another week, he told his brother Leicester in 1946, and he would enlighten him about women, reading and writing, and "how to pick them in the [jai alai] quinielas." Then, in 1950, he wrote Lillian Ross two letters on how to play poker. It was basically a matter of percentages, he instructed her, but there were also several thousand angles. For the purposes of teaching, he boiled the several thousand down to two basic rules. Neither of these dealt directly with the general considerations which, according to Albert H. Morehead's *The Complete Guide to Winning Poker*, apply to all forms of poker: namely, the ethics and etiquette of the game, the mathematics of the game, psychology and bluffing, position, money-management, and card memory and analysis. By way of contrast to the closely reasoned approach of Morehead or of any other book of advice on how to gamble, Hemingway's rules were crude and whimsical. One stated the obvious point that you should back your good cards for keeps when you held them and ride out your bad cards by staying out of the pot. The other rule was far more radical, and if practiced at the table would have led to a very lively game indeed. He advised Ross never to *call* a bet, but either to raise or fold.

What Hemingway aimed to create by dispensing knowledge about gambling that he did not possess was the illusion of mastery. He obviously admired Cayetano Ruiz, the gambler in his story, "The Gambler, the Nun, and the Radio." One of the more conspicuous heroes in Hemingway's fiction, the Mexican Ruiz clings to his personal code of right conduct under the severest pressures. He declines to tell the police the name of the man who shot him twice in a dispute over a card game. He refuses, despite excruciating pain, to complain about his wounds. Most important of all, he is a professional at his trade, possessing intelligence and nerve and the good hands he makes his living with. But Ruiz remains "a cheap card player" because he likes to gamble for large stakes and is basically unlucky. He has "passed at dice for three thousand dollars and crapped out for the six. With good dice. More than once." He has had bad luck for fifteen years, yet continues to practice his craft in hopes that his luck will one day change.

Luck determines the Mexican's fiancial situation, but he himself remains in control of the way he lives his life. He occupies a position poles removed from that of Robert Cohn, who is lucky but lacks dignity, who does not know when to keep his mouth shut, who boasts about his skill and falsely pretends to expertise. Ernest Hemingway would like to have behaved like Cayetano Ruiz. All too often, he found himself acting like Robert Cohn.

The Man Who Would Be King

The admirable Cayetano Ruiz is contrasted, within "The Gambler, the Nun, and the Radio," to Mr. Frazer, a writer who is also hospitalized and in pain but who cannot achieve the Mexican's stoical detachment. Like Hemingway himself when he was confined to a Billings hospital, Mr. Frazer's "nerves" went bad after five long weeks, and he required "a little spot of the giant killer" and the company of his radio to get through the sleepless nights. The contrast between Ruiz and Frazer is well summed up in Philip Young's distinction between the "code hero" in Hemingway's fiction, a man who confronts a difficult world cheerfully and bravely, and the "Hemingway hero," a protagonist modeled upon the author himself, who cannot adjust to that world without bemoaning his fate. The code hero, usually a foreigner like Ruiz or the bullfighter Pedro Romero in *The Sun Also Rises*, came to represent the ideal which Hemingway measured himself and others against, to their inevitable disadvantage.

Cautious about letting friend or lover come too close, he kept his distance by demanding of them an impossibly rigorous code of behavior and greeting their every deviation with an intolerance often conveyed by his sardonic wit. "None are to be found more clever than Ernie," ran the legend beneath his senior picture in the 1917 Oak Park high-school yearbook, and that must have pleased him, for he thought of himself then primarily as a funny writer. But from the beginning he salted his jokes with sarcasm at the expense of others. There was nearly always something mean in Ernest's wit, Donald Ogden Stewart decided. His wicked satirical gift, Cyril Connolly concluded, must have sprung from "something warped in his character." Ernest "could be terrifyingly witty," Dawn Powell remarked, whenever he chose to put people down.

Even as a lad, he poked fun at his father by calling him "the Great Physician" with mock reverence, and stigmatized his younger brother in a couplet, "Leicester Clarence/Pesters Parents." When a high-school teacher in Brooklyn wrote him in 1924, asking if he would share his writing secrets with his class, Ernest launched into an ironic description of "how" he'd written "The Undefeated." He'd got the idea, he asserted, while standing on the back platform of an AE bus just as it was passing the Bon Marché. Then he'd done the actual writing during the next few days in a series of cafés. Perhaps these hints might be useful in New York, if the pupils substituted the Fifth Avenue bus for the AE, Saks for the Bon Marché, and a drugstore for the café. In subsequent years he worked this acidulous vein to pillory the lazy and the phony and the pretentious and the cowardly and the inefficient and the shoddy and the solemn wherever he found them, and he found them everywhere, even among those with whom he seemed to enjoy the best possible relationships. In 1950, for example, when his publisher and friend Charles Scribner asked him if he'd brought along some letters Scribner had written him, Hemingway replied, "I carry them every place I go, Charlie, together with a copy of the poems of Robert Browning."

He not only deflated individuals but entire nationalities. In *The Sun Also Rises*, he jested at moralistic middle-class American views of expatriation, yet he partially shared those views, and reserved his deepest scorn for American poseurs, "the oldest scum, the thickest scum, and the scummiest scum" of Greenwich Village transplanted to the Latin Quarter, where they pursued a bohemian existence while pretending to be artists. By 1929 he was ready to abandon Paris as a nasty place inhabited by these pretenders, along with hard-faced lesbians and fairies, in favor of fishing the Caribbean off Key West with a group of friends, barefoot and black from the sun, with the champagne cooling astern in a sack full of ice.

By that time, too, he had grown weary of the French passion for the franc. "Liberté, Venalité, et Stupidité" predominated not only among the French military (as Colonel Cantwell reflected) but in daily life as well. Parisian cab drivers bullied and swindled their passengers into giving tips of more than double the fare. To become "A Friend of France" meant first that you had to die, for otherwise the French would not commit themselves so far, and, second, that you had "either spent much money for France, obtained much money for France, or simply sucked after certain people long enough to get the Legion of Honor. In the last case they call you a Friend of France in much smaller type."

The Italians he characterized in 1925 as even "worse crooks" than the French. He belittled their mercurial political enthusiasms, and could not for many years forgive the country where he had been wounded for selling out, so soon after the Treaty of Versailles, to the false cause of fascism. After falling in love with Adriana Ivancich and Venice in the late 1940s, he modified this view. "If you want to travel gaily," he wrote in 1960, "and I do, travel with good Italians."

With most other nationalities, though, his biases held firm. Encountering traveling "Belgiums" in 1948, he tried to describe to Mary Hemingway what they smelled like: a combination of traitorous King, toe jam, unwashed navels, sweaty old bicycle saddles, and paving stones, with a touch of leek soup and boiling parsnips thrown in. The English had their own peculiar and undesirable odor, too, but at least you could escape "when your nose was deep in a tall glass of dry sparkling cider from Devon." Ernest also twitted the English for their exotic language. He could, he wrote, "read and write Canadian clearly and had a smattering of Scottish and a few words of New Zealand." He could understand Australian well enough to play poker and order drinks and shove his way into a bar, and South African he dominated "as a spoken tongue almost as well as Basque." But English, over the telephone or—worse—over the radio telephone, was just "a glorious mystery." In addition, he attacked the British for their military arrogance and incompetence, most notably in *Across the River and into the Trees.*

For all her failings, Great Britain deserved more respect than Rumania, "the one country that no one in Europe takes seriously." "Sometimes the allies are useful," he commented. "Sometimes they are Rumania." Among the neutrals, the Swiss were depicted in Hemingway's gallery of national portraiture as careful and calculating. A Swiss would not marry, he maintained, until his intended bride had her original teeth replaced with store teeth because the girl's father, not her husband, should have to pay for them. And a Swiss hotel keeper would "raise prices with the easy grace of a Pullman car poker shark backing a pat full house. . . ."

Though he respected them as soldiers, Germans seemed to Hemingway overinquisitive, like the maître d'hôtel in *The Sun Also Rises.* Or they were excessively rude: like the husband in the railroad car who assures his wife, struck on the head by a heavy rucksack he has pulled from the luggage rack, that she has not been hurt, and another traveling German who gorges himself in the dining car alone and returns "an hour and a half later bearing a very beery breath and parts of rolls stuffed with bits of cheese" for his wife's dinner. These two male chauvinists he depicted in dispatches to the Toronto papers, along with the portrait of German tourists traveling in packs so that you could not walk through the Black Forest without encountering groups of six or eight, "their heads shaved, their knees bare, cock feathers in their hats, sauerkraut on their breath, the wanderlust in their eyes and a collection of aluminum cooking utensils clashing against their legs."

With Spaniards alone among Europeans, his humor turned mellow instead of vituperative. The Madrid hotel manager in *The Fifth Column*, for example, speaks in an amusing pidgin English about the shortcomings of his electrician. "Is bright," he insists. "But the drink. Always the drink. Then rapidly the failing to concentrate upon electricity." And in *Death in the Afternoon*, Ernest was amused by a lapse of courage in the bullfighter El Gallo which he would have condemned in anyone less theatrically brilliant or honest. Gallo was constantly giving farewell performances in the bull ring, but none equaled his "first formal permanent farewell" in Sevilla. Full of emotion, he dedicated what was supposedly the last bull of his life to, successively, his old friend Señor Fulano, to another old friend in the stands, and to the retired bullfighter Algabeño, in each case making the dedication with a rhetorical flourish. Then he spun on his heel, walked toward the bull, took a close look at him and turned to his brother, Joselito: "Kill him for me, José. Take him for me. I don't like the way he looks at me."

Spain was different, since it was the one country where he'd "never felt like a foreigner." But what he asked of people, whatever their nationality, is suggested by a conversation in *Across the River and into the Trees*, where Renata and her Colonel Cantwell discuss the merits of the restaurateur and hotel-owner Cipriani. "Cipriani is very intelligent," Renata observes. "He's more than that," the colonel replies. "He's able." Toward those who were not and did not make themselves able, Hemingway refused to be tolerant. He extended no mercy to those who slowed down or could not stay the course. For the mature Hemingway, there were simply no excuses. "If you're any damned good at all," he told his brother, "*everything* is your own damned fault."

"I'm the judge I'd like to appear before after I'm dead," he told José Luis Castillo-Puche in Madrid one day in 1959. If so, he'd be facing the sternest of final judges, for the Hemingway who was intolerant of the failings of others despised them in himself. His first wife, Hadley, once remarked to him, half in jest, that she thought he would like to be a king, with all the powers and denominations thereunto appending. Ernest replied in full seriousness that yes, he would like to be a king, a response which gave her the eerie feeling that she was "sleeping with Napoleon Bonaparte." Her observation struck exactly the right note, for it was a Napoleon, a king not by birth but by achievement, a master among men possessed of surpassing knowledge and skill, that Hemingway in his intense ambition was forever striving to become.

xiii

Death

That Old Whore

Several of the premature obituaries which Hemingway read after the near-fatal African plane crashes of 1954 emphasized that he had been seeking death all his life. But, he objected, could "one imagine that if a man sought death all of his life he could not have found her before the age of fifty-four?" Death was the easiest thing to find that he could think of; you could find her in the home or on the highway, in a bottle or a bathtub.

In letters and conversations, as the pronouns above suggest, Ernest tended to personify death, and thus to suggest an intimacy between them. Death, he wrote to Lillian Ross in 1950, had been his girl and his enemy and his horse and his hounds and his hawk and his little brother. Colonel Cantwell, in *Across the River and into the Trees*, transformed the little brother into the man with the scythe, "old brother death." But most often Hemingway characterized death as a whore—either "a beautiful harlot who could put you soundly to sleep" and so must be cagily avoided, or "the oldest whore in Havana," whom he knew very well and would be glad to have a drink with, but not to go upstairs with. Eventually such an assignation would be unavoidable ("Now sleeps he with that old whore death who yesterday denied her thrice," begins the long poem to Mary he wrote during World War II.)

Though he would not court the harlot, he kept on sociable terms with her, and in his prose examined her visage keenly and relentlessly.

The most remarkable thing about Hemingway's writing on death was his fascination with its grislier aspects. In "A Natural History of the Dead," for example, he adopted the objective tone of the naturalist while examining, in the most minute and terrible detail, the decomposition of the Italian dead after the Austrian offensive of June 1918. "Until the dead are buried," he observed, "They change somewhat in appearance each day. The color change in Caucasian races is from white to yellow, to yellow-green, to black. If left long enough in the heat the flesh comes to resemble coal-tar, especially where it has been broken or torn, and it has quite a visible tarlike iridescence. The dead grow larger each day until sometimes they become quite too big for their uniforms, filling these until they seem blown tight enough to burst. The individual members may increase in girth to an unbelievable extent and faces fill as taut and globular as balloons." Similarly, in inveighing against the Italian war on Ethiopia in January 1936, Ernest chose to write about the five birds of prey which flourished in East Africa and prospered particularly during Mussolini's war. Perhaps it was not so bad when up to five hundred of these birds feasted upon a *dead* Ethiopian, but these carrion birds would "hit a wounded man, lying in the open, as quickly as they will a dead man. I have seen them leave nothing of a zebra but the bones and a greasy black circle covered with feathers twenty minutes from the time the animal was killed provided the belly skin was slit open so they could get an opening." This was a feature of the war, he wrote, which Il Duce would "do well to keep censored out of his newspapers."

Hemingway partially justified his fascination with the macabre as a requirement of art. The dedicated artist, he decided early in his career, must study as intimately as possible the face of that "old whore death." During a trip to Spain in the mid-1920s, for example, Ernest criticized Robert McAlmon for turning his head away from the maggot-eaten corpse of a dog. He advised "a detached and scientific attitude," McAlmon wrote. "He tenderly explained that we of our generation must inure ourselves to the sight of pain and grim reality. I recalled that Ezra Pound had talked once of Hemingway's 'self-hardening process.' " Ten years later, lunching with Stephen Spender during the Spanish Civil War, Ernest said that he had cured Martha Gellhorn of her squeamishness by taking her to the Madrid morgue each morning after the fascist shellings. He then drew from his pocket a sheaf of photographs depicting wartime atrocities and advised Spender to inspect them closely. The British poet, he'd decided, was far too squeamish himself.

Ernest's obsession with the subject cannot be entirely accounted for either by antiwar sentiments or by artistic convictions, however. Allowing these motives their full measure of influence, there still remained in his make-up a detectable streak of morbidity. How else can one explain "An Alpine Idyll," a relatively pointless tale in which an ignorant Austrian peasant stashes his frozen wife in the woodshed and hangs a lantern from her mouth all winter while he cuts wood? What function is served by the gallows humor of Philip Rawlings in *The Fifth Column*, when he talks about propping up a corpse in a chair and sticking a lit cigarette in its mouth? To what other cause can one attribute Hemingway's vivid re-creation, in *Green Hills of Africa*, of the "comic" death of the hyena—"the classic hyena, that hit too far back while running, would circle madly, snapping and tearing at himself until he pulled his own intestines out, and then stood there, jerking them out and eating them with relish"? If Hemingway did not actually court his own end, the death of man or beast was to him an eternally engrossing subject. At the bullfights, when a bull could not be properly killed with a sword, the procedure was to kill the bull back of the horns with the short knife, or *puntillo*. "I love to see the *puntillo* used," Hemingway wrote. "It is exactly like turning off an electric light bulb."

Hemingway's fiction alone, Cyril Connolly wrote in his July 1961 tribute, supported the assertion that "he must have had from boyhood a preoccupation with death and violence, an imagination drawn irresistibly towards the macabre." Certainly his best and most famous stories were "based, almost without exception, on the relationship between man and death, the confrontation of man's nobility and courage with the ineluctable adversary." Ole Andreson lies in his rooming house bed awaiting his certain murder as a horrified Nick decides to leave town; Francis Macomber's jealous anger turns to courage and when he goes in pursuit of the wounded buffalo, his wife guns him down; Harry casts off his rotting body and soul and is borne on fanciful wings to the peak of Kilimanjaro; the old man cherishes another brandy at the clean, well-lighted café as an alternative to killing himself.

What is true of the stories applies to Hemingway's novels as well. "Death," as Vance Bourjaily commented, "was a country he knew how to hunt, and from which he brought back the great trophies which are his major books." Only in his first novel, *The Sun Also Rises*, does death take a temporary holiday, though even there the specter of mortality hovers over the wounded survivors of the war and the bullfighters in the ring. In 1927, the year after the publication of this novel, Ernest wrote Wyndham Lewis that he expected there would be less bloodshed in his future work. Yet in each subsequent novel the death of the protagonist or of his loved one forms the climactic event. Catherine Barkley dies in childbirth, Robert Jordan faces down the enemy and the savage god within, Harry Morgan bleeds away his life on the deck of the *Queen Conch*, Colonel Cantwell suffers a fatal heart attack, Santiago loses his beloved marlin to the sharks, and Thomas Hudson is "probably going to die"—so Hemingway said—of the gunshot wounds he suffers while chasing German submarines.

What interested Hemingway most was the question of how to die. Dying itself was easy, for it meant "no more worries." But a man had a duty to lose his life "intelligently, the way you would sell a position you were defending, if you could not hold it, as expensively as possible, trying to make it the most expensive position that was ever sold." A man should not submit too easily, go too gently.

Thoughts on Taking One's Life

In their early teens, Ernest Hemingway and his sister Marcelline loved reading Robert Louis Stevenson, "especially one of his lesser-known volumes" which included the story, "The Suicide Club." When he was sixteen, he wrote a three-inch account for the school newspaper of an attempted suicide by drowning. A few months earlier, he published his first story, "Judgment of Manitou," in the school literary magazine. The story ends when a northwoodsman, caught in a bear trap, reaches for his own rifle to commit suicide. Other tales of a similar sort coursed through his youthful mind: "Mancelona. Rainy night. Tough looking lumberjack. Young Indian girl. Kills self and girl." Suicide, very nearly an obsession with the young Hemingway, continued to fascinate him all his life.

In talking and writing to others, he frequently brought up the question of self-destruction. Lying wounded in World War I, he contemplated taking his life. On the eve of his wedding to Hadley Richardson in 1921, he suffered one of the recurrent attacks of depression (or "black ass," as he later called it) that plagued his final years. "What's this?" Hadley wrote her fiancé. "Not truly so low as to crave mortage are you?" (*Mortage* in their argot equaled death, as *eatage* meant food.) Unhappy in Canada two years later, Ernest wrote Gertrude Stein and others that he understood for the first time how a man might commit suicide to escape the impossible tangle of things to do piled up ahead of him. Disturbed by the breakup of his marriage in 1926, he seriously considered suicide and contemplated various ways of doing it. About the best way, he wrote, "unless you could arrange to die . . . while asleep, would be to go off a liner at night. That way there could be no doubt about the thing going through and it does not seem a nasty death. There would be only the moment of taking the jump and it is very easy for me to take almost any sort of jump."

Ernest's mind led him to such speculations time and again, both before, and especially after, his father killed himself in December 1928. Out West in 1932 the vibrantly alive Hemingway startled his hunting companions by proclaiming that he would not hesitate to kill himself if "it came to that." Outraged at the reception of his work by the critics, he threatened, in 1935, to take a Tommy gun and open up in the *New Republic* offices in order to give "shitdom" a few martyrs and include himself after he'd wiped out the others. It would be a "big disgust," he wrote Archibald MacLeish the next year, when the time came to shoot himself. In 1939 he proposed a suicide pact to Clara Spiegel; if either of them was tempted, he should first let the other one know. At about the same time, he carefully explained to Martha Gellhorn how it was possible to kill oneself with a shotgun, springing the trigger with his toe. Upset about his passion for Adriana Ivancich in 1950, he wrote Lillian Ross that he had dived deep down into the Gulf Stream's warm waters one summer's day and almost decided to stay down there. In 1954, after being mobbed by a crowd in Cuneo, he told A. E. Hotchner that he should have stayed in "the second kite" (airplane) as it crashed and burned in Africa. Weeks later, he wrote Buck Lanham from shipboard that he'd been staring at the wake of the ship and found it very appealing. But Buck took most such remarks as barracks talk, for they'd often discussed the topic of suicide and agreed on two basic conclusions. The first was that a man had the right to control his own life and death. The second was that he should not take his own life unless conditions became truly intolerable.

Despite his occasional flirtations with the dark lady, Ernest was essentially prejudiced against suicide. He'd known too many people for whom talk of self-destruction represented "something . . . banal." In an early poem he pilloried those denizens of Montparnasse who threatened the act but were unsuccessful in completing it. There were "never any suicides in the quarter among people one knows," he wrote. A Chinese boy kills himself, or a Norwegian boy kills himself, or a model kills herself, and they were all very dead. But "Sweet oil, the white of eggs, mustard and water soapsuds and stomach pumps rescue the people one knows," so that every afternoon they "can be found at the café." In *The Torrents of Spring*, he chose a mocking tone in reproducing the ruminations of the obtuse Yogi Johnson: "What black thoughts he had been thinking! He had been on the verge of suicide. Self-destruction. Killing himself. Here in this beanery. What a mistake that would have been. He knew now. What a botch he might have made of life. Killing himself."

In *Islands in the Stream*, his last long fiction, Hemingway once more poked macabre fun at a yearner after oblivion. The Bimini bartender, Mr. Bobby, tells the story of a tourist from New York who used to drink a good part of the day and was forever talking about how he was going to kill himself. The constable warned him it was illegal, but the fellow they called "Suicides" kept talking about it and finally the other customers started encouraging him and eventually, after an extended binge, he dove off the dock into the channel and hit his head on some old concrete and drowned. The regulars at the bar concluded that Suicides must have been crazy, and sure enough, they found out that he "suffered from a thing called Mechanic's Depressive."

One thing emphatically *not* worth committing suicide about, Hemingway believed, was the loss of money. In Paris for three weeks at the bottom of the Depression (February 1934), he devoutly wished he were somewhere other than that gloomy city: "This old friend shot himself. That old friend took an overdose of something. That old friend went back to New York and jumped out of, or rather fell from, a high window. . . . All of the old friends have lost their money. All of the old friends are very discouraged. Few of the old friends are healthy. Me, I like it better out on the ranch, or in Piggott, Arkansas, in the fall, or in Key West, and very much better, say, at the Dry Tortugas."

His deepest scorn was reserved for those rich who, upon the collapse of the stock market, decided that life was no longer worth living. In his near-proletarian novel, *To Have and Have Not*, he catalogued their means of escape:

> Some made the long drop from the apartment or the office window; some took it quietly in two-car garages with the motor running; some used the native tradition of the Colt or Smith and Wesson; those well-constructed implements that end insomnia, terminate remorse, cure cancer, avoid bankruptcy, and blast an exit from intolerable positions by the pressure of a finger; those admirable American instruments so easily carried, so sure of effect, so well designed to end the American dream when it becomes a nightmare, their only drawback the mess they leave for relatives to clean up.

Among the men who would soon take their own lives in one of these ways was Henry Carpenter, an unemployed, unmarried thirty-six-year-old homosexual with charm and a Harvard M.A., whose monthly income had been reduced through unwise investments to $200 a month. "The money on which it was not worth while for him to live," the novelist commented by way of pointing the moral, "was one hundred and seventy dollars more a month than the fisherman Albert Tracy had been supporting his family on at the time of his death [not by suicide] three days before."

The fictional Carpenter, to Ernest's way of thinking, was a weakling who was prepared to yield to death without a struggle. When he learned, in 1939, of the suicide of Frank Tinker, an Arkansan who had fought with the Loyalists in Spain, Ernest said he would have tried to talk Tinker out of it if he'd had the chance. The important thing, he wrote Hadley at the time, was not to get so discouraged that you'd take the easy way out, as both her father and his father had done. It was mostly a matter of strength of mind and character, he told Lillian Ross in 1950. Boxers used to go twenty rounds; pitchers used to pitch double headers. We might have gained something in speed, but we'd lost plenty in stamina and confidence. What Ernest couldn't understand was how a writer like Thomas Heggen, who had made some money with his play *Mister Roberts*, could decide to kill himself. Pretty soon, he predicted, little children would be hanging themselves because they were "not yet President."

As far as his own case was concerned, there were at least three good reasons why Ernest repeatedly talked himself out of suicide: The first was that he had his work to do, and only those who endured could finish their work. "Survival, with honor," he said in his *Paris Review* interview, "is as difficult as ever and as all important to a writer. Those who do not last are always more beloved since no one has to see them in their long, dull, unrelenting, no-quarter-given-and-no-quarter-received, fights that they make to do something as they believe it should be done before they die."

Second, he repudiated self-destruction because in his good moods he took enormous pleasure in living. "The real reason for not committing suicide," he wrote Isidor Schneider in October 1926, "is because you always know how swell life gets again after the hell is over." One of the most favorably depicted people in *A Moveable Feast* is the "lovely painter," Jules Pascin, a man who knew how to enjoy life. Later he hanged himself, but when Hemingway knew him he lived with zest and infectious good humor. "They say the seeds of what we will do are in all of us," Hemingway commented about Pascin, "but it always seemed to me that in those who make jokes in life the seeds are covered with better soil and with a higher grade of manure."

Here, he gave overt expression to a point of view already implicit in his fiction; there the good characters are cheerful and the bad ones are sad. Robert Jordan observes Pablo's sadness with alarm: "That's the sadness they get before they quit or before they betray. That is the sadness that comes before the sell-out." Colonel Cantwell knows his heart will betray him soon, but in the meantime will not cultivate his sorrow. "No horse named Morbid," he reminds himself, "ever won a race." In exasperation, he sends his driver Jackson out on the town in Venice: "I'm tired of seeing you, because you worry and you don't have fun. For Christ sake have yourself some fun."

Hemingway himself did have fun, and he communicated to others his *joie de vivre*. Dorothy Connable, remembering the young Hemingway of 1920 in Toronto, stressed that he had been "very handsome, very charming, very considerate, very gentle, but mostly, I think, just very gay." And Hotchner, on first encountering the middle-aged Hemingway in 1948, felt he had "never seen anyone with such an aura of fun and well-being. He radiated it and everyone in the [Floridita] responded." As Mary Hemingway has remarked, until his final illness her husband had an almost limitless "capacity for gaiety and fun and enjoying whatever he was doing, with no evident second thoughts or afterthoughts or strings attached." For Ernest as for Pascin the highs alternated with lows, but when he was happy he was gloriously happy.

The third reason why he postponed his own suicide for so long was that it would serve as a bad example to the children. It was this thought, he told Lillian Ross, that brought him kicking and gasping to the surface of the inviting Gulf Stream waters in August 1950. And in *Islands in the Stream*, Thomas Hudson argues that his friend, the writer Roger Davis, shouldn't kill himself because "it would be a hell of an example for the boys." Roger isn't so sure: "when you get into that business that far you don't think much about examples." But Hemingway himself thought about them, since his own father had set him the example of self-destruction. In a sense, each of his arguments against suicide stand as mute accusations of Dr. C. E. Hemingway, who killed himself because he'd lost most of his money, his pride in his work, his capacity to enjoy life, and his good health. But Ernest was disinclined to allow his father the benefit of any of these excuses. In his son's judgment, Ed Hemingway's suicide was the natural consequence of knuckling under for too long to Grace Hall Hemingway, his dominating wife. His father had killed himself, he believed, out of weakness—and that Ernest could not bring himself to accept.

Grace and Ed Hemingway

By the force of her powerful personality, Grace Hemingway ruled the roost, both at the house on Kenilworth Avenue in Oak Park and at Windemere in northern Michigan. In doing so, she emulated the pattern of matriarchy which had been established by both of Ernest's grandmothers. Leicester Hemingway describes his (and Ernest's) paternal grandmother, Adelaide Hemingway, as a "dedicated intense woman who absolutely" controlled her family of six children, while on the other side of the family Caroline Hancock Hall also "dictated the lives of her husband and two children." Grandmother Hall virtually forbade her daughter Grace the use of the kitchen. "Run along, dear," she'd say. "Don't soil your hands with cooking." Left to her own devices, Grace expended her remarkable store of energy on mastering the high-wheel bicycle (a daring adventure for a girl in Victorian times) and on developing her good contralto voice. So talented was Ernest's mother, in fact, that she spent a year in New York studying under the well-known Madame Capriani and made her singing debut at Madison Square Garden. This early taste of musical success gave her an advantage over the husband she returned to Oak Park to marry. But for marriage and motherhood, she could and did claim, she might have made a brilliant career. "You know, dear," she told her daughter Marcelline, "Schumann-Heink is now taking the place I might have had in opera."

Possibly as a consequence, Grace Hemingway quite refused to do the chores expected of her. Except for singing lullabies and breast-feeding, she lacked both talent and inclination for domestic tasks. She "abhorred didies, deficient manners, stomach upsets, house-cleaning, and cooking," Leicester wrote. Since she and Dr. Hemingway produced six children, this meant that a succession of nurses and mother's helpers, maids and cooks paraded through the family home. It also meant that Ed Hemingway, in addition to conducting his medical practice, took on additional domestic duties. In the midst of making his rounds, Ernest's neighbor and friend Lew Clarahan recalled, Dr. Hemingway would call home and tell Grace or whoever answered that it was time to put the roast in. Mrs. Hemingway "couldn't have cared less about housekeeping," said Clarahan. As a schoolboy Ernie lost a valuable fountain pen; three years later it turned up behind the sofa. Furthermore, Leicester observed, when family crises threatened, his mother rushed to her room, drew the shades—her eyes were unusually sensitive to light—and declared she had a sick headache. There were, by his account, hundreds of such crises while the children were growing up. (In "The Last Good Country," a Nick Adams story unpublished at Ernest's death, Nick's mother succumbs to a "sick headache" when the game wardens come looking for her son.)

Grace Hemingway found time, however, to pursue her musical interests. In the family's massive thirty-by-thirty-foot music room, built to her specifications, she gave voice and piano lessons to her own children, regular pupils, the children's choir of the Third Congregational Church, and even the maids. She also tried to organize a family quartet with her husband, Marcelline, and Ernest, but Dr. Hemingway's cornet had a way of slipping off key, and Ernie showed no particular flair for the cello, his assigned instrument. Up in Michigan, in 1919, she arranged to have a cottage built for her exclusive occupancy. She and her husband, she confided to Marcelline, "frequently got on each other's nerves." As for her offspring, "I love you all," she explained, "but I have to have a rest from you all now and then if I am to go on living." For such respite, she would move into her cottage a day or more at a time, "miles away from anyone." Sometimes, Marcelline remembers, "she'd invite the rest of us over for a picnic."

Five feet seven inches tall and disinclined to curb her tendency to put on weight, Mrs. Hemingway in later life presented an imposing appearance. "She wore long skirts before the New Look," Otto Mc-Feeley, a veteran Oak Park newspaperman, wrote of her in 1948, "and always recalled to me . . . the Dowager Queen of England who also [was] very unfashionable." She carried considerable weight in Oak Park cultural circles, as much in her own right as because she was the mother of a famous author. After middle age, she turned from music to art, and while in her seventies drove "all over the country painting landscapes." She traveled in a Ford because the steering wheel sloped at just the right angle for her easel, and so she could paint without hoisting her considerable girth out of the car. McFeeley, who viewed an exhibition at the Oak Park Art League in the summer of 1948, was less than enchanted with her work. "Most of the painters confine their efforts to landscapes," he wrote. "Those most expert sometimes paint a cow knee-deep in a pool. Mrs. H. exhibited one painting, offered at $500. It was an isle with palms, in a sea that must have been the Dead Sea. There were no ripples or waves. The title was, believe it or not, 'The Birthplace of Jesus Christ.' "

But McFeeley also recognized what others have since come to see, that Grace Hemingway was "responsible for Ernest." From her he inherited his immense energy, his forceful personality, and his creative drive. Their views on what constituted art, however, could not possibly have been more widely divergent. When he sent several copies of *in our time*, his first slim book of sketches, home from Paris, she and Dr. Hemingway sent them right back. Her reaction to subsequent books was hardly more favorable. "Honestly, Marce," she complained to her daughter after glancing through *The Sun Also Rises*, "with the whole world full of beauty, why does he have to pick out thoughts and words from the gutter?" For her own part, she told an interviewer from the Oak Park *News* in 1927, she deplored the pessimism of "these young writers" and preferred to depict scenes which reflected her belief that "God's in his heaven, all's right with the world." As late as 1940 she wrote Ernest that she hoped that *For Whom the Bell Tolls*, the novel then in press, might contain something "constructive." Perhaps it would, her son wrote back mildly, but he continued to seethe over what he regarded as a deficiency of loyalty on her part.

Ernest also rebelled against his mother's attempt to run his life as she had run his father's. When he came home from World War I, she treated him, he felt, like an irresponsible child. In the spring of 1919 he dated a girl named Kathryn Longwell, and in a gesture of gallantry presented her with his Italian officer's cloak. Outraged, Grace Hemingway demanded that he get it back. The next two summers Ernest spent much of his time at Windemere, fishing with some of his wartime friends—a practice which led to the maternal edict, in July 1920, that he'd have to quite sponging off his family. After that blowup, Ernest rarely mentioned his mother without insisting on how much he hated her.

Often this declaration disturbed sensitive listeners, but Ernest would only repeat, "It's all right, it's only the truth, I really do hate her." From the earliest days of his friendship with Buck Lanham, he invariably referred to his mother as "that bitch. He must have told me a thousand times," Lanham added, "how much he hated her and in how many ways." If his mother could be "crossed" with Madame Chautard, his harridan of a landlady in Paris during the 1920s, Ernest hypothesized in 1944, the result would certainly win the blue ribbon at the all-time, all-comers, international bitch show. When Grace Hemingway died in 1951, having lived more than eighty years, Ernest declined to go back to Oak Park for the funeral. Part of the reason was that he had already made that journey twenty-three years earlier after the death of his father—a death for which he held both his parents responsible.

To the best of his ability, Dr. Ed Hemingway played the role of the stern Victorian father. He did not approve of smoking and regarded with scorn any besotted soul who used alcoholic beverages. In conversation, even mild oaths were taboo, and the subject of sex was best ignored altogether. Dr. Ed had been taught at then straitlaced Oberlin College that card-playing, dancing, and gambling were wrong. Any idleness, in fact, he regarded as an invitation to the devil, and so he constantly urged his children to be up and doing. Dr. Hemingway was also a stickler for personal cleanliness and hygiene, and strongly opposed new styles of dress or grooming.

But Ernest's father failed in his attempt to transplant Victorian standards into the twentieth century. In some instances the children got the better of him, as on the issue of bobbed hair. One dinner hour, Marcelline writes in her memoir, Dr. Hemingway "announced triumphantly that the hospital staff had agreed to fire any nurse who was found with bobbed hair." His moment of moral victory was short-lived, however, for his daughter Madelaine (Sunny) was sitting at the table, and she had cut her hair a week earlier. Teasingly, Sunny challenged him to repeat that he would throw out any daughter of his who violated his prescription against bobbed hair and drew forth the assertion that "short hair is unwomanly and I won't have it in my house" before letting him know that she'd cut her own hair a week before and he'd never noticed it. Daddy, Marcelline reported, tried to speak but "just sputtered."

At other times Mrs. Hemingway—whose views were by no means as rigid as her husband's—intervened and had her way with him, as on the question of whether Marcelline and Ernest should learn to dance. The impetus was Marcelline's, who was tearful about not knowing the dance steps all her school friends knew. Grace Hemingway took her daughter's case to Dr. Hemingway and as usual won her point. The children were duly enrolled in Miss Marybelle Ingram's dancing classes, and as a further humiliation Daddy was assigned to drive them to the Colonial Club for their lessons, muttering all the while, "Leads to hell and damnation—don't know what the world is coming to—it's all your mother's idea."

Mother prevailed on this relatively trivial issue, just as she settled more important ones. Throughout his young manhood, for example, Ed Hemingway had wanted to be a medical missionary like his brother Will. According to Leicester, he had opportunities to serve in Guam and in Greenland. Alternatively, Dr. Hemingway, an avid outdoorsman, planned to move to Nevada as an escape from city life. But Grace said no to both proposals, and so he stayed in Oak Park, where, besides building up a private practice, he served as medical examiner for several insurance companies, as head of the obstetrical department at Oak Park Hospital, and as something less than the head of his household.

In the mid-1920s the fabric of Dr. Hemingway's life began to unravel. Though Leicester, the youngest of their six children, was just beginning his school days in 1923, the doctor and Grace began to lay plans for retirement in Florida. With some apprehension, he took and passed the exams which qualified him to practice in that state. Then most of the family's savings were invested, unwisely, in Florida real estate. The Hemingways plunged too late; the land boom in Florida was over. High payments on their real estate continued, while the land itself steadily dwindled in value. The family's financial troubles were intensified when Dr. Hemingway fell ill in 1927 and was forced to cut down on his practice.

The major medical problem was diabetes, and in frustration Dr. Hemingway went on a strict diet to control his level of blood sugar. "I've never been sick," he raged. "I can't be sick. There's too much to do." But diabetes, in combination with angina pectoris, rapidly took its toll, so that by April 1928, when Dr. and Mrs. Hemingway visited Ernest and his new wife Pauline in Key West, the doctor's hair and beard had turned gray and his neck had grown scrawny underneath his wing collar. Ernest could not help resenting the contrast between his emaciated appearance and the blooming good health his mother seemed to enjoy. His father's physical decline was accompanied by a psychological one. The illness had transformed him, according to Marcelline, "from his high-strung, active, determined, cheerful self . . . to an irritable, suspicious person." He doubted other people's motives and began to spend long hours behind closed doors in his office. Distrustful, he locked his bureau drawers and his clothes closet. He refused to let anyone else drive the car.

Troubled about his father's failing health, Ernest paid a visit to the family homestead—his first in five years—in October 1928, and he was again struck by Dr. Hemingway's depressed spirits and gray complexion. Though failing fast, the doctor continued to drive himself to the limit of his energies. On the morning of December 6, 1928, he went his medical rounds as usual before coming home at noon for a nap. Then he retired to his bedroom, put his father's old Smith and Wesson .32 revolver behind his right ear, and pulled the trigger.

Generalizing from his own experience, Sigmund Freud wrote in 1908 that the death of a father constituted the most important event in any man's life. If that was true of Ernest Hemingway, he did his best to conceal the depth of his feelings. A month after the suicide, he wrote Guy Hickok, who was in Paris, a half-serious, half-comic note explaining that though he knew the Brooklyn *Eagle* had been sold and Guy might soon find himself without a job, Ernest would be unable, just at present, to take over the maintenance of Hickok's family. Guy could count on him for next year probably, but this year what with his father shooting himself and not leaving much money and one thing and another he was very busy. His old man, he wrote Waldo Peirce, had shot himself, a hell of a lonely way to die. On the other hand, he himself was busy shooting snipe, which made very good eating.

Such mordant flippancy concealed a deep resentment about his father's suicide. In a passage excised from *Green Hills of Africa*, Ernest located the source of that resentment: "My father was a coward. He shot himself without necessity." Ten years later, what he left out of the book emerged in long wartime conversations with Buck Lanham. "Despite his protestations to the contrary," Lanham recalled, "I don't think Ernest had one goddamned bit of respect for his father. Whenever we talked about him, his father came through as a weakling and the suicide as an act of cowardice." Hemingway would probably have accepted and condoned his father's killing his mother, Lanham thought, but he could not approve the suicide as a means of escape from her. "It wasn't suicide *qua* suicide that got to Ernest, but suicide in the sense of a guy running out of a fight."

Lanham's view is supported by Hemingway's fiction, particularly by the close-to-autobiographical Nick Adams stories. Whenever there is a direct confrontation between Nick's parents in these stories, it is the mother who dominates. But even where Dr. Adams is depicted apart from his wife, he emerges as less than admirable. He shows a trace of cowardice in "The Doctor and the Doctor's Wife" when he backs down from a fight with a tough half-breed. Nick sees that happen, and he also hears his father talking nonsense in "Indian Camp," the first story in *In Our Time*. Here Dr. Adams proceeds with seeming cold-blooded efficiency to perform a Caesarean section on an Indian woman. Nick is present, and his father takes the occasion as a chance to instruct the terrified boy in the triviality of pain. No anesthetic is available, but it does not matter, Dr. Adams explains. He does not hear the screams "because they are not important." Four men hold the Indian woman down while he operates, and when it is over, Dr. Adams expands upon his accomplishment. "That's one for the medical journal, George. . . . Doing a Caesarean with a jack-knife and sewing it up with nine-foot, tapered gut leaders." But Nick's Uncle George is unimpressed: "Oh, you're a great man, all right." And the doctor's next, offhand, bedside-manner remark, "Ought to have a look at the proud father. They're usually the worst sufferers in these little affairs," reveals his insensitivity, for the Indian father has slit his throat rather than to endure the screams which were not important enough for Dr. Adams to hear.

There is no concrete evidence to prove that Dr. Hemingway ever delivered a baby under such circumstances, or that he refused to fight a belligerent half-breed, but in "Fathers and Sons," the last of Hemingway's forty-nine collected stories, Dr. Adams clearly takes on the lineaments of Ernest's father. In the story, Nick has grown up and is talking with his own son about his youth. Nostalgically, he remembers his father's magnificent shooting eye and the hunting they had done together. "His father came back to him in the fall of the year," he recalls, "or in the early spring when there had been jacksnipe on the prairie, or when he saw shocks of corn, or when he saw a lake, or if he ever saw a horse and buggy, or when he saw, or heard, wild geese, or in a duck blind. . . . His father was with him, suddenly, in deserted orchards and in new-plowed fields, in thickets, on small hills, or when going through dead grass, whenever splitting wood or hauling water, by grist mills, cider mills and dams and always with open fires." But these were the outdoor memories of an adolescent; from the age of fifteen, Nick realizes, "he had shared nothing" with his father. In his priggish attitude toward sex, Dr. Adams had failed to supply his son with important information. In his miserliness, even during those earliest, happiest days, he had caused Nick to rebel against him:

> Nick loved his father but hated the smell of him and once when he had to wear a suit of his father's underwear that had gotten too small for his father it made him feel sick and he took it off and put it under two stones in the creek and said that he had lost it. . . . When Nick came home from fishing without it and said he lost it he was whipped for lying.
>
> Afterwards he had sat inside the woodshed with the door open, his shotgun loaded and cocked, looking across at his father sitting on the screen porch reading the paper, and thought, "I can blow him to hell. I can kill him."

In this instance Nick's experience and Ernest's run parallel, for he told Bill Smith in 1917 that after his father had punished him he sometimes sat in the open door of the tool shed up in Michigan, aiming his loaded shotgun at Dr. Hemingway's head. Nick's son, who has heard none of this, is distressed that he has never been taken to "pray at the tomb of his grandfather." "We live in a different part of the country," Nick offers in explanation, but the boy is persistent. At the very end of the story, Nick apparently relents, but in a tone full of irony. "We'll have to go," Nick said. "I can see we'll have to go."

They will not go, for reasons that the reader has come to understand, but which Nick will not tell his young son: because his grandfather was a coward who let his wife rule him and finally shot himself. At one time, Ernest contemplated writing a novel about his father killing himself and why. But too many people were still alive, he said, and the novel—part of which would have been "wonderful"—went unwritten. The fact is, however, that Ernest did tell part of that story, under camouflage, in two other books. One of these, oddly enough, is *The Old Man and the Sea*, which is more about fathers and sons than has been usually detected. In that novel the boy Manolo constantly compares his own father unfavorably to Santiago. He does not like his father to wake him up, Manolo tells the old fisherman, because it makes him feel inferior. Santiago says he understands. His father, who is also a fisherman, never lets him help with the gear and the bait, but as Santiago observes, he and Manolo "are different. . . . I let you carry things when you were five years old." Manolo's father thinks George Sisler was the greatest baseball manager, but Santiago disabuses the boy of that notion. His father only thinks that, he tells the boy, because Sisler came to Cuba so many times. "If Durocher had continued to come here each year your father would think him the greatest manager." Once Manolo had fished with Santiago, but his father ordered him to stay away from the old man's unlucky boat. "He hasn't much faith," as the boy says. No, Santiago replies, "But we have. Haven't we?"

In Santiago's encouragement of Manolo's filial impieties, as in his longing for the boy's companionship during his three-day fight with the marlin, Hemingway conveyed the loneliness of the old man. As for the boy's feelings, the novel, as Carlos Baker has pointed out, is partly about the "love of a son for an adopted father." The boy Manolo, had he been free to do so, would surely have cast off his own father entirely to be with Santiago. In yet another novel with a foreign setting, the Sierra de Guadarrama of Spain, Ernest Hemingway created another character who achieves an inner dignity by choosing, in a moment of sorest need, to repudiate his father's example.

A Novel about How to Die

For Whom the Bell Tolls traces the painful education, telescoped into three short days, of its protagonist Robert Jordan. From Maria, he learns what it is to love. From Pilar and Anselmo, he learns what it is to belong to a family. Finally he learns in triumph how to die, the most difficult lesson of all and one which he must master on his own.

The novel stands as an in-depth study of death, a theme reflected not only in its title but in Hemingway's alternate title, "The Undiscovered Country" from whose bourn no traveler returns. Early in *For Whom the Bell Tolls*, Pilar "reads" Jordan's imminent death in his palm; after that, the issue becomes not whether Jordan will die, but how. To understand the point, Hemingway continually presents his protagonist, the Spanish literature teacher from Montana who has come to fight for the Loyalists as a demolition expert, with examples of the way others have faced death.

This is one function served by Pilar's long and detailed account of how the mob, led by Pablo, massacred the fascists of their village. Some die well, some do not. Don Benito, the mayor, takes his blows and his fall into oblivion without comment. The brave Don Ricardo defies his persecutors, cursing and spitting at them before they club him to death. The cowardly Don Faustino, on the other hand, dies in humiliation, begging for mercy on his knees, and his example turns the mob ugly and robs the succeeding fascists—even relatively good men like Don Guillermo—of the chance "to be killed quickly and with dignity."

In another scene, El Sordo's last hopeless battle against the fascists, Hemingway once more draws a distinction between dying well and dying badly. Trapped atop a hill, with a superior force surrounding him below and airplanes bringing certain death from above, El Sordo does not fear death, though he hates to give up the joys of living. He fights to the end, firing in futility at the death-dealing planes. El Sordo's dignity and bravery are contrasted here with the prideful stupidity of the fascist Captain Mora, who is tricked into believing that all the Loyalists atop the hill have been killed and so presents himself as a target for Sordo's guns.

The kind of death most meticulously explored in the novel is death by suicide: appropriately enough, for at the end Jordan will face, and conquer, the temptation to take his own life. In the abstract, and under the extraordinary pressures of war, Hemingway makes no brief against self-destruction. Maria asks Jordan to teach her how to use a pistol, so that "either one of us could shoot the other and himself, or herself, if one were wounded and it were necessary to avoid capture." She has already had instruction from Pilar on how to cut the carotid artery with a razor blade in the event of capture, and though she's prepared to use the razor blade if need be, she would rather have Jordan shoot her. He promises to do so, though troubled by her matter-of-fact willingness to embrace death.

In the cynical Russian journalist Karkov, he encounters a similar attitude. Karkov has been ordered to poison three wounded Russians and obliterate all evidence of their nationality, in case the fascists take Madrid. But it "isn't so simple just suddenly to poison people," Jordan objects. "Oh, yes it is," Karkov replies, "when you carry it always for your own use"; and he shows Jordan the double suicide kit he carries, one poison capsule in his cigarette case, the other under his lapel, where he could bite and swallow it even if bound. Karkov is no defeatist, he insists, he has simply prepared himself against the possibility of capture.

But it is another Russian, Kashkin, whose situation most closely matches Jordan's. Also a bomb expert, he works with the guerrillas in blowing up trains; then, when he is wounded and faces capture, he persuades Jordan to shoot him and take him out of his misery. Earlier Kashkin had grown "jumpy" in combat, and extracted a fatalistic promise from Pablo to kill him if wounded. Jordan understands that you "can't have people around doing this sort of work and talking like that." So he rejects out of hand Pablo's suggestion, early in the book, that he might require a similar service:

> "And you," Pablo said. "If you are wounded in such a thing as this bridge, you would be willing to be left behind?"
> "Listen," Robert Jordan said and, leaning forward, he dipped himself another cup of the red wine. "Listen to me clearly. If ever I should have any little favors to ask of any man, I will ask him at the time."

At the end, of course, Jordan *is* wounded and cannot escape the fascist troops, but, unlike Kashkin, he turns down Agustín's well-intentioned offer to kill him. That, he knows, would be equivalent to committing suicide, and he has his own reasons for not taking that step—reasons stemming from a family heritage which parallels Hemingway's own.

While the origins of Jake Barnes and Frederic Henry, the protagonists of Hemingway's first two novels, are left purposely indistinct, Robert Jordan's background is far more clearly sketched. He is the grandson of a cavalry officer in the Civil War and the Indian wars who fought bravely and who with his tales had started Robert reading and studying about war when he was only a boy. In Ernest's case, both grandparents had fought for the Union. Grandfather Hall, an English immigrant, carried a Confederate Minié-ball in his body to the end of his days, and indignantly refused a government pension from his adopted country for his service in the war. But it was Grandfather Hemingway, a pillar of the G.A.R. and speechmaker in the schools on Decoration Day, who awoke Ernest's abiding interest in war with a combination of patriotic rhetoric and irreverent war stories.

Jordan's parents are obviously modeled on Dr. and Mrs. Hemingway. His father, like Hemingway's, shot himself with a Smith and Wesson Civil War pistol, and without undergoing the intolerable wartime circumstances that make it possible for Jordan to contemplate the act more or less dispassionately. Maria, Karkov, Kashkin are all faced with the certainty of torture if captured—but Jordan's father had died without that excuse. Under questioning from Pilar, Jordan allows her to think that his father, as a Republican in the United States, faced the same fate that confronted Republicans in Spain:

> "And is thy father still active in the Republic?" Pilar asked.
> "No. He is dead."
> "Can one ask how he died?"
> "He shot himself."
> "To avoid being tortured?" the woman asked.
> "Yes," Robert Jordan said. "To avoid being tortured."

Then Maria looks at him with tears in her eyes, for her own father could not obtain a weapon and so was subjected to brutal physical torture by the fascists. "I am very glad," she says, "that your father had the good fortune to obtain a weapon." Yes, Jordan responds, "it was pretty lucky." Then, to drop a subject which he never brings up again except in dialogue with himself, "Should we talk about something else?"

Jordan is ashamed of his father "because if he wasn't a coward he would have stood up to that woman and not let her bully him." On the eve of the climactic morning when the bridge must be blown, his mind takes him back to memories of his grandfather and his father. Suppose, he thinks, that the four years of the Civil War and then the Indian fighting had used up his grandfather's supply of courage and so he had none left to bequeath and made a *cobarde* out of his father the way second-generation bullfighters almost always were. But that speculation leads him to a topic he would rather ignore. It was pleasant thinking of his grandfather, but "thinking of his father had thrown him off. He understood his father and he forgave him everything and he pitied him but he was ashamed of him." You'd "have to be awfully occupied with yourself," he thinks, "to do a thing like that."

Yet on the next day, as Robert Jordan lies in excruciating pain, it is the memory of his father's cowardice and his grandfather's courage which steels him against taking his own life. Soon, he knows, the fascist troops will come bringing certain death, and before he will succumb Jordan is determined to put up a battle with his submachine gun. Maybe, he thinks, he can hold up the fascists a while and help Maria and Pilar and the others escape. But mostly he is motivated against suicide by his father's bad example: "Oh, let them come, he said. I don't want to do that business that my father did. I will do it all right but I'd much prefer not to have to. I'm against that . . . The pain had started suddenly with the swelling after he had moved and he said, Maybe I'll just do it now. I guess I'm not awfully good at pain. Listen, if I do that now you wouldn't misunderstand, would you? *Who are you talking to?* Nobody, he said. Grandfather, I guess. No. Nobody."

But if not his grandfather, then it is Jordan whom Jordan must prove himself to. So he fights back the agony and lasts until the fascist lieutenant rides into range and he can start the fire-fight which will relieve all his pain and enable him to take death, like El Sordo, "as an aspirin."

The Final Torture

Shortly after Ernest's father died, a package arrived in Key West containing the revolver with which Dr. Hemingway had shot himself, along with a moldy chocolate cake and several paintings Mrs. Hemingway wanted her son to sell for her in Paris. Publicly, Ernest maintained that sending him the suicide weapon had been his mother's own idea, and that her gesture signified a willingness for him to go and do likewise. But in fact he had asked for the gun himself, as—he said—a historical keepsake. Perhaps he wanted to have the weapon around as a warning against following his father's example; if so, the talisman failed to work its magic. Shortly after dawn on the morning of July 2, 1961, he stole downstairs in his Ketchum, Idaho, home, loaded his double-barreled Boss shotgun, pressed it against his forehead, and tripped both barrels.

It was not his first attempt at suicide. In the last years of his life, as A. E. Hotchner's chilling account suggests, Ernest suffered a series of blows to his mental and physical health which left him "intent on destroying himself." His system never totally recovered from the African plane crashes of 1954. He suffered from high blood pressure. He was overweight. His liver had been damaged by years of drinking too much. There were signs of incipient diabetes. Serious as his physical decline was, however, Hemingway's worst troubles were psychological.

As early as the mid-1920s, Ernest had been subject to spells of depression. ("I've never seen a man," MacLeish said of him even then, "go through the floor of despair as he did.") By the late 1950s such spells became more frequent and more severe. Characteristically, Ernest's handwriting seemed to signal periods of depression by sloping downward on the page from left to right. In his final years, as his depressive phase deepened and came to dominate his personality, the angle of his handwriting sloped ever more sharply down.

Like his father before him, he became suspicious of others' motives. The authorities, he thought, were out to get him. The IRS, he was certain, was determined to make him poor, and would probably arrest him for not withholding taxes from the wages he paid his household help. The FBI and immigration agents, he believed, were ready to clap him in jail for encouraging the emigration of Valerie Danby-Smith from

Ireland. Lawsuits, he felt sure, would descend upon him if he published *A Moveable Feast*. Even his old friend Bill Davis, he was convinced, planned to kill him in a trumped-up "automobile accident." After a lifetime of exorcising real demons, Hemingway succumbed to a succession of imaginary ones.

In the construction of his idealized self, courage ranked as one of the three virtues Ernest valued above all others. Tourists came snooping around the Finca Vigia, he observed in July 1954, as if to discover some all-embracing secret about him. But there was no secret except working hard and paying all debts and not being spooked, no secret except courage and commitment and industry. In the end, all three eluded him.

The keeping of commitments, a powerful theme in much of Hemingway's fiction, emerges with particular emphasis in two of his last novels. Colonel Cantwell, dying of a heart attack, cannot help reflecting on what he has left undone. He has shot enough ducks for the boy and his wife at the Gritti Palace to eat, but not enough for them to make a quilt with the feathers. He has neglected to give the dog Bobby the sausage he bought for him. He has not provided the old boatman with a new engine for his boat. Almost with his last breath, he arranges to send Renata his shotguns and her painting, but he leaves the last letter to her unwritten. As his life ebbs away, he regrets promises unkept and debts unpaid. Thomas Hudson, perhaps, is better off. He faces his last hours without his sons, his love, or his honor, but at least he can do his duty: what he said he'd do. Yet neither of these Hemingway heroes can resist touching the wound they'd inflicted on themselves many years before by abandoning their first and truest love. The same wound festered in their creator. He would do his best, he promised Buck Lanham, to do whatever he said he would do and to keep doing it until he died. But as a fallible man, he could not be certain he would keep all commitments he made to other people, and especially to women.

Hemingway at least had his work to fall back on and think well of himself for. Or so he did until the mind went blank and the pencil did not feel right in the hand. During the last year of his life, he complained bitterly—to Hotchner; to his personal physician, Dr. George Saviers; to old hunting companions like Pappy Arnold and Chuck Atkinson—that the words simply wouldn't come. Perhaps this was the turn of the rack that pushed his torture beyond the bearing. Perhaps, as the poet Richmond Lattimore expressed it, he'd "lost youth lost art and mumbled till he knew/he mumbled, and so drew the trigger." Perhaps what he had accomplished—one of the enduring literary accomplishments of the twentieth century—could offer no solace to a man who could think only of what he could no longer do.

"I keep thinking," Ernest's son Jack remarked of his father, "what a wonderful old man he would have made if he had learned how." That was one lesson which Hemingway was unwilling to master. As he put it himself very early, "a long life deprives man of his optimism." It was much better "to die in all the happy period of unillusioned youth, to go out in a blaze of light, than to have your body worn out and old and illusions shattered." But in his last months that is precisely what happened. Leslie Fiedler and Seymour Betsky, visiting him at Ketchum in November 1960, were struck by how frail and uncertain the once powerful frame had become. To Michael Bessie, who saw him in April 1961, Ernest looked like "a wounded animal who should be allowed to go off and die as he chose." In his last letter to Lanham, he summoned up a trace of bravado. Sent from the Mayo Clinic, the body of the letter was dictated and dull, but at the bottom, in pencil, Ernest scrawled a final brave message to his old comrade-in-arms. Buck, he wrote, should stop sweating him out. The only things to sweat out were flying weather and the common cold.

That scribble served as a gallant confession that Ernest had made up his mind, that conditions had finally become intolerable enough to warrant suicide. In time, his bodily ills might have become ameliorated, but the illusions were beyond recovery. Even as a boy, his sister Marcelline wrote, he "didn't like anyone to disapprove of him, in any way at any time." But for the mature man, who had four wives and drank too much and sweated away his nightmares and needed others more than he would admit, the most damning disapproval came from within. All his life long he had driven other people away. But the irremediable separation came when Ernest's idealized self crumbled before his eyes, and he was left in desolation to confront his real and far from despicable but all too weak and human self. Aboard the *Liberté*, in October 1959, he wrote poignantly from the depths of depression to Bill Davis, the very man who, in his delusions, he thought was trying to kill him. He had never "missed people so much" before, Ernest said. In the past, he had always been rather "relieved to leave people," but no longer. Now he felt very much like someone whose twin brother had died.

ACKNOWLEDGMENTS AND SOURCES

This book could not have been written without the generous assistance of two men. Malcolm Cowley encouraged the project from its early stages on, and with that same perception and tact that emanates from his own writing guided the manuscript through two difficult revisions. He also made available some valuable and previously unconsulted letters about Hemingway from Nathan Asch, Otto McFeeley, and Evan Shipman. In *Ernest Hemingway: A Life Story*, Carlos Baker cleared away the tangled underbrush of lies and half-truths to establish the basic facts of Hemingway's life. For anyone seeking to understand that life, his biography is an indispensable source. Baker read this book in draft form, and his acute eye helped clear the finished project of a number of errors. With quite extraordinary hospitality toward aftercomers, he also allowed me to consult letters and interview notes in his own office files, files which turned up a great many quotations and observations Baker cut for reasons of length during the excision of more than five hundred pages from his definitive life of Hemingway.

A block away from that office lies the great trove of Hemingway letters at Princeton University's Firestone Library, where I worked during the summer of 1972. Other letters were examined during visits to the Library of Congress, the Clifton Waller Barrett Library at the University of Virginia, the McKeldin Library at the University of Maryland, the Humanities Research Center at the University of Texas in Austin, the Berg Collection at the New York Public Library, the Oral History Research Office of the Butler Library at Columbia University, and Yale's Beinecke Library. Those who kindly sent copies of Hemingway correspondence include the Lilly Library at Indiana University, the Cornell University Library, the Library of the College of Physicians of Philadelphia, and the University of Florida Library.

The catalogues of such dealers as Charles Hamilton Autographs and Sotheby Parke Bernet proved particularly useful, since these catalogues often printed Hemingway letters, many of which were in turn reproduced in *Hemingway at Auction: 1930–1973*, compiled by Matthew J. Bruccoli and C. E. Frazer Clark, Jr. As a consequence, I have been able to capture much of the flavor of Hemingway's lively epistolary style through full and direct quotation.

Bruccoli and Clark also gathered a number of the friends of Hemingway's boyhood and youth—among them Lewis Clarahan, Raymond George, William D. Horne, Mrs. Carl Kesler, and Frederick W. Spiegel —for a conference during the 1971 Modern Language Association meeting in Chicago. This group interview provided an impetus to this book, as did subsequent talks with Baker, Cowley, Mary Hemingway, C. T. Lanham, William W. Seward, Jr., Stephen Spender, and Donald Ogden Stewart. No full-scale attempt has been made to retrace Baker's steps by conducting world-wide interviews. I have profited substantially, however, from the recent work along these lines of Patrick Hynan and Donald St. John. In editing "Hemingway—A Portrait in Sound," four long-playing sides of reminiscence and commentary by Morley Callaghan, Cowley, A. E. Hotchner, Archibald MacLeish, Hadley Mowrer, and others for broadcast on CBC radio in 1970, Hynan accomplished one of the most interesting and intelligent jobs of research yet done on Hemingway. St. John's medium, in which he is equally expert, is the intimate personal interview, as with Dorothy Connable, Leicester Hemingway, and William B. Smith, for example. These interviews have usually appeared in the pages of the *Connecticut Review*.

My graduate students have often supplied me with insights into Hemingway's work during seminars these past five years. Deserving special mention are Jacqueline Chapman, P. A. Parrington-Jackson, and C. S. Waddington at the University of Leeds, and Nigel Cutting,

Joan Detz, Arthur Maurice, Paula Rankin, Frank Sersanti, Joy Spaugh, Jan Van Horn, Suzanne West, and Brad Wilson at the College of William and Mary. William and Mary supported this undertaking through one summer and one semester-long research grant; the American Philosophical Society also contributed toward a summer's research. I have willingly played student to the instruction of my wife, Janet Donaldson, because of her gift for detecting the arch, the vague, and the questionable in my prose.

Without launching into an exhaustive bibliographical exercise, it is difficult to indicate the extent of my indebtedness to what has been written, especially during the last ten years, about Ernest Hemingway and his work. Among the best critical books are Baker's *Hemingway: The Writer as Artist*, Jackson J. Benson's *Hemingway: The Writer's Art of Self-Defense*, Charles A. Fenton's *The Apprenticeship of Ernest Hemingway: The Early Years*, Sheldon Norman Grebstein's *Hemingway's Craft*, Richard B. Hovey's *Hemingway: The Inward Terrain*, Earl Rovit's *Ernest Hemingway*, Robert O. Stephens's *Hemingway's Nonfiction: The Public Voice*, Delbert E. Wylder's *Hemingway's Heroes*, and Philip Young's *Ernest Hemingway: A Reconsideration*. The best biographical sources have included Morley Callaghan's *That Summer in Paris*, Malcolm Cowley's *A Second Flowering*, John Dos Passos's *The Best Times*, F. Scott Fitzgerald's *The Crack-Up* and *The Letters of F. Scott Fitzgerald*, Arnold Gingrich's *Nothing But People*, Leicester Hemingway's *My Brother, Ernest Hemingway*, A. E. Hotchner's *Papa Hemingway*, Nicholas Joost's *Ernest Hemingway and the Little Magazines: The Paris Years*, James McLendon's *Papa: Hemingway in Key West*, Constance Cappell Montgomery's *Hemingway in Michigan*, Lillian Ross's *Portrait of Hemingway*, Marcelline Hemingway Sanford's *At the Hemingways*, and Bertram D. Sarason's *Hemingway and the Sun Set*. Two other publications demand special acknowledgment: Bruccoli and Clark's *Fitzgerald/Hemingway Annual*, ongoing since 1969, and Audre Hanneman's *Ernest Hemingway: A Comprehensive Bibliography*, published in 1967 with a supplement in 1975. I cannot even begin here to enumerate the hundreds of magazine and periodical articles which have played a role in shaping this book. They are acknowledged in the notes below.

The notes do not give page references for quotations from the writings of Ernest Hemingway which have been collected in book form as part of his established canon. There are three exceptions to this rule:

first, those fragmentary stories and sketches first printed in *The Nick Adams Stories*; second, the stories that appeared between book covers for the first time in *The Fifth Column and Four Stories of the Spanish Civil War*, and third, the magazine articles and newspaper dispatches assembled in *Byline: Ernest Hemingway* and *The Wild Years*.

Scott Donaldson
June 1976
Williamsburg, Virginia

NOTES

Introduction

xi *"in your novels"* A. E. Hotchner, *Papa Hemingway* (New York: Random House, 1966), p. 199. (Hereafter Hotchner.)

xi *"I do not believe . . .* Evan Shipman to Malcolm Cowley, 1 April 1948.

xi *The nonfiction is* See Robert O. Stephens, *Hemingway's Nonfiction: The Public Voice* (Chapel Hill: University of North Carolina Press, 1968). (Hereafter Stephens.)

xii *"deficiency . . . mind"* Lionel Trilling, "Contemporary American Literature and Its Relation to Ideas," *American Quarterly*, 1 (Fall 1949), 208.

xii *"lack(ed) all mentality"* Ben Hecht, interview for Popular Arts Project, Third Series, Vol. III, "Motion Pictures," No. 1 (1960), Oral History Archives, Columbia University, 769–70.

xii *style . . . simpler* Wright Morris, "One Law for the Lion," *Partisan Review*, 28 (September–November 1961), 551.

xii *not to think . . . trauma* Robert Evans, "Hemingway and the Pale Cast of Thought," *American Literature*, 38 (May 1966), 161–76.

xiii *Big Thinking* EH, introduction to *Kiki's Memoirs* (Paris: Edward W. Titus, 1930), pp. 9–14.

xiii *adjective . . . "simple."* Margaret Anderson, *My Thirty Years' War*, quoted by Arthur Dewing, "The Mistake about Hemingway," *North American Review*, 232 (October 1931), 364.

xiii *chose "complicated"* Malcolm Cowley, quoted by Denis Brian, "The Importance of Knowing Ernest," *Esquire* (February 1972), p. 101.

xiii *"titan of ego"*   James Gray, *John Steinbeck* (Minneapolis: University of Minnesota Press, 1971), p. 5.

xiii *"mind . . . observation"*   Allen Tate, "Random Thoughts on the Twenties," *Minnesota Review*, 1 (Fall 1960), 56.

xiii–xiv *"There must be/Moments . . ."*   Archibald MacLeish, "Poet" (for Ernest Hemingway), in *Songs for Eve* (Boston: Houghton Mifflin, 1954), p. 51.

i. Fame

THE WRITER AS CELEBRITY

1 *Vatican and Kremlin*   Philip Young, "The End of Compendium Reviewing," *Three Bags Full* (New York: Harcourt Brace Jovanovich, 1973), p. 51. (Hereafter Young.)

2 *"tremendous physical presence"*   Archibald MacLeish, on "Hemingway—A Portrait in Sound," ed. Patrick Hynan (broadcast on radio by Canadian Broadcasting Corporation, 26 May 1970), CBC Recording T–56820–3, Side One. (Hereafter CBC.)

2 *power of projecting himself*   Malcolm Cowley, "Hemingway: The Old Lion," *A Second Flowering* (New York: Viking, 1973), p. 223. (Hereafter Cowley.)

2 *mentioned . . . The Trapeze,*   Matthew J. Bruccoli, ed., *Ernest Hemingway's Apprenticeship: Oak Park, 1916–1917* (Washington, D.C.: NCR Microcard Editions, 1971), p. xiv. (Hereafter *Oak Park*.)

2 *"had a peculiar . . . fatal quality"*   Morley Callaghan, *That Summer in Paris* (New York: Coward-McCann, 1963), p. 26. (Hereafter Callaghan.)

2 first *genuine celebrity*   John Raeburn, "Ernest Hemingway: The Public Writer as Popular Culture," *Journal of Popular Culture*, 8 (Summer 1974), 91–98.

3 *Hemingway's treatment by Hollywood*   Frank M. Laurence, "Hollywood Publicity and Hemingway's Popular Reputation," *Journal of Popular Culture*, 6 (Summer 1972), 20–31.

4 *autograph seekers*   Ben Finney, *Feet First* (New York: Crown, 1971), p. 195.

5 *intimacy with . . . columnists*   John O'Hara, *Sweet and Sour* (New York: Random House, 1954), pp. 40–42.

5 *"pretty picturesque*   John Crosby, *With Love and Loathing* (New York: McGraw-Hill, 1963), p. 13.

THE PENALTIES OF FAME

6 *". . . nothing to do with literature*   Emilio Cecchi, quoted by Harry Levin, "Observations on the Style of Ernest Hemingway," *Contexts of Criticism* (Cambridge: Harvard University Press, 1957), p. 237.

6 *wait until . . . success* EH to Arnold Gingrich, 18 October 1934.

6 *". . . the writer's personality* Earl Rovit, *Ernest Hemingway* (New York, Twayne, 1963), p. 26. (Hereafter Rovit.)

7 *"that Baudelaire parked the lobster* EH, "American Bohemians in Paris a Weird Lot," Toronto *Star Weekly* (25 March 1922), p. 15.

7 *evening with Eric Knight . . . couldn't stop.* EH to Eric Knight, 10 October 1931.

8 *"worst invented character"* Edmund Wilson, "Hemingway: Gauge of Morale," in *Ernest Hemingway: The Man and His Work*, ed. John K. M. McCaffery (Cleveland and New York: World, 1950), p. 245. (Hereafter Wilson.)

8 *lure to impostors* EH to Charles Ritz, 22 February 1952.

9 *The most persistent . . . impostor* Robert Daley, *The Swords of Spain* (New York: Dial Press, 1966), pp. 132–35.

9 *nearly crushed by a crowd* Carlos Baker, *Ernest Hemingway: A Life Story* (New York: Scribner's, 1969), p. 524. (Hereafter Baker.)

9 *"to hell with" publicity* Baker, pp. 525–29.

9 fame "over a weekend" EH to Harvey Breit, 8 July 1950.

9 *"Never again" . . . interrupt* EH, "A Situation Report," *Look* (4 September 1956), pp. 23–31.

9 *public fool* Stanley Kauffmann, "Before and After Papa," the *New Republic* (10 June 1967), p. 18.

9 *". . . not the same you"* Gertrude Stein, quoted by Earl Fendelman, "Happy Birthday, Gertrude Stein," *American Quarterly*, 27 (March 1975), 100.

9 *Dante . . . a lesson* EH to John Dos Passos, 17 September 1949.

ii. Money

PREOCCUPATION WITH THE DOLLAR

10 *. . . catalogue of subjects* Baker, p. 161.

11–13 *young Canadians cultivated . . . afford to be a communist.* J. Herbert Cranston, *Ink on My Fingers* (Toronto: Ryerson Press, 1953), p. 107 (hereafter Cranston). Some of Hemingway's dispatches to the Toronto papers are collected in *Byline: Ernest Hemingway* (hereafter *Byline*), ed. William White (New York: Scribner's, 1967), and in *The Wild Years: Ernest Hemingway* (hereafter *Wild Years*), ed. Gene Z. Hanrahan (New York: Dell, 1962).

11 *stay in Germany . . . free.* Leicester Hemingway, *My Brother, Ernest Hemingway* (Cleveland: World, 1962), p. 80. (Hereafter Leicester.)

12 *bitterest tragedies* EH to Owen Wister, 1 March 1929.

14 *". . . paved with easy money"* Leicester, pp. 40–41.

14 *allowance of a penny* Marcelline Hemingway Sanford, *At the Hemingways: A Family Portrait* (Boston: Atlantic-Little, Brown, 1962), pp. 129–31. (Hereafter Marcelline.)

14 *Dr. Hemingway first wrote . . . letters* Leicester, pp. 64–70.

15 *mother's love . . . bank account* Baker, p. 72.

OFFERS REFUSED AND ACCEPTED

16 *Captain Gamble drove* William Dodge Horne to Scott Donaldson, 25 October 1972.

16 *"men loved him"* Mrs. William C. Stanfield, Jr., to Scott Donaldson, 18 November 1972.

16 *smoothed out all the bad* EH to James Gamble, 12 December 1923.

16 *proposal . . . difficult to refuse* Baker, pp. 54–55.

17 *"slip on the dock"* Jack Buck, interview with Mrs. William O. Stanfield, Jr., 27 May 1957.

17 *Gamble an intimate note . . . "chief."* EH to James Gamble, 3 March 1919.

18 *Gamble had another suggestion . . . do him good.* James Gamble to EH, 10 April 1919.

18 *But two years later . . . one more time.* Baker, p. 77.

18 *they must keep in touch* EH to James Gamble, 12 December 1923.

18 *Gamble . . . "recognized the greatness"* William Dodge Horne to Scott Donaldson, 25 October 1972.

19 *income . . . drastically reduced.* Hadley Mowrer, CBC, Side One.

20 *"even though . . . the balls."* EH to Harold Loeb, 27 February 1925.

20 *Stewart . . . sent . . . "enormous" check* EH to Harold Loeb, 5 January 1925.

20 *"I liked him"* Donald St. John, "Interview with Donald Ogden Stewart," in *Hemingway and the Sun Set*, ed. Bertram D. Sarason (Washington, D.C.: NCR Microcard Editions, 1972), p. 200. (Hereafter *Sun Set*.)

20 *"a Tom Sawyerish way"* Kathleen Cannell to Carlos Baker, 13 October 1965.

20 *one such touch* Kathleen Cannell, "Scenes with a Hero," in *Sun Set*, p. 147.

20 *"a bad man to lend"* Morrill Cody, quoted by Ted Stranger, "Hemingway Remembered at Paris Reunion," Newport News (Va.) *Daily Press* (23 July 1972).

20 *quarrels over money* Baker, pp. 135–36; EH to Ernest Walsh, 19 April 1925.

21 *"he paid them off* Virgil Thomson, quoted by Oscar Levant, *The Memoirs of an American* (New York: Putnam, 1965), p. 224.

THE MORALITY OF COMPENSATION

21 *Emerson puzzled* *Selections from Ralph Waldo Emerson*, ed. Stephen E. Whicher (Boston: Houghton Mifflin, 1957), pp. 14–15.

21 *essay on "The Tragic" . . . cannot rise."* Ralph Waldo Emerson, "The Tragic," *Dial*, 4 (April 1844), 515–21.

21–22 *"For each extatic instant* Poem 125, *The Poems of Emily Dickinson*, ed. Thomas H. Johnson (Cambridge: Harvard University Press, 1958), I, 89–90.

23 *Cowley and his wife* Malcolm Cowley, *Exile's Return* (New York: Viking, 1951), pp. 79–81.

23–24 *bargains . . . at Schruns . . . eat and drink.* Baker, p. 134.

24 *"nearly all loafers* EH, "American Bohemians in Paris a Weird Lot," Toronto *Star Weekly* (25 March 1922), p. 15.

26 *"a sturdy moral backbone"* Carlos Baker, *Hemingway: The Writer as Artist* (Princeton, N.J.: Princeton University Press, 1963), pp. 82–83, 92.

32 *"Everything was . . . changed . . . about money."* Donald Ogden Stewart to Carlos Baker, 20 February 1951, 2 March 1962.

32 *protagonist . . . never called Jake* Philip Young, CBC, Side Two.

AN ANGEL NAMED GUS

33 *The understanding was* Archibald MacLeish to Carlos Baker, 31 January 1965.

33 *Murphy also deposited* Baker, p. 174.

33 *"actual cash-support"* Baker, p. 178.

33–34 *Gus Pfeiffer . . . generous . . . Hemingways in style.* Baker, pp. 183–86, 210, 221, 226; James McLendon, *Papa: Hemingway in Key West* (Miami, Florida: E. A. Seemann, 1972), p. 76 (hereafter McLendon); Kenneth W. Rendell, Inc. "Catalogue 37" (1969), Items 75 and 76, "Catalogue 38" (1969), Items 51 and 52; John Dos Passos, *The Best Times: An Informal Memoir* (New York: New American Library, 1966), p. 204 (hereafter Dos Passos).

35 *"a special and private . . . analysis"* Philip Young, *Ernest Hemingway: A Reconsideration* (New York: Harcourt, Brace and World, 1966), p. 75.

35 *helped . . . pay his taxes* McLendon, p. 201.

35 *the house . . . remained hers* McLendon, p. 207.

36 *Dr. Hemingway finally asked* Leicester, pp. 110–11.

36 *Wister responded* EH to Owen Wister, 1 March 1929.

36 *To his mother* Baker, p. 200.

37 pp. 36–37, *he set up a . . . trust fund* Leicester, p. 129.

37 *Once he had revolted* Jackson J. Benson, *Hemingway Notes* (Spring 1974), p. 5.

THE ARTIST AS BUSINESSMAN

38 *he made a secret agreement* Baker, p. 97.

38 *"That . . . action seared* Hadley Mowrer file, Carlos Baker's office.

38 *jump their . . . lease* Baker, p. 122.

38 *The whole world . . . "crooked"* EH to Bill Smith, 17 February 1925.

38 *Grabbing off writers . . . get them drunk.* EH to Horace Liveright, 21 June 1925.

39 *"He and I are . . . thick"* F. Scott Fitzgerald to Maxwell Perkins, c. 20 December 1925, c. 19 January 1926.

39 *He had "known all along"* EH to F. Scott Fitzgerald, 31 December 1925, quoted by Arthur Mizener, *The Far Side of Paradise* (Boston: Houghton Mifflin, 1949), p. 213. (Hereafter Mizener.)

39 *a brash letter* EH to Horace Liveright, 7 December 1925.

40 *"Really, old top"* Horace Liveright to EH, 30 December 1925.

40 *in 1927 he flirted* EH to Eric S. Pinker, 23 September 1927.

40 *What was he . . . to do* EH to Sir Hugh Walpole, 10 December 1929?.

41 *Gingrich . . . first-name basis* EH to Arnold Gingrich, 24 May 1933.

41 *Ernest played the editor* John Dos Passos, "Old Hem Was a Sport," *Sports Illustrated* (29 June 1964), p. 66.

41 *After Dave Smart* Arnold Gingrich, *Nothing But People* (New York: Crown, 1971), p. 87. (Hereafter Gingrich.)

41 *two rules . . . as guidelines . . . give nothing away.* Leicester, p. 132.

41 *". . . The hell with the honor"* EH to "Dear Jack," 7 March 1949, reproduced in *Hemingway at Auction*, comp. Matthew J. Bruccoli and C. E. Frazer Clark, Jr. (Detroit: Gale Research, 1973), p. 141. (Hereafter *Auction.*)

41 *"first serial rights* Hotchner, p. 24.

42 *a story . . . for* True EH to Peter Barrett, 7 December 1951 and 16 December 1951, reproduced in Charles Hamilton Autographs "Catalogue 78," Items 195 and 196, p. 35.

42 *ultimate magazine price* Guinness Book of Records, eds. Norris and Ross McWhirter (Enfield, England: Guinness, 1970), p. 92.

42 *he'd been burned* EH to Guy Hickok, 5 December 1930.

42 *may have dickered* Joseph Losey to Ralph Ingersoll, 24 March 1939.

42 *"bloody wonderful" sale . . . New York.* Baker, p. 354.

iii. Money (Continued)

MONUMENTAL GENEROSITY

43 *Hemingway befuddled*   Nelson Algren, *Notes From a Sea Diary: Hemingway All the Way* (New York: Putnam, 1965), pp. 250–51. (Hereafter Algren.)

44 *He loaned Hickok*   Guy Hickok to EH, 1 June 1931, 30 May 1938.

44 *Ernest sent Dos Passos*   Baker, p. 241.

44 *writer Ned Calmer*   Ned Calmer to Carlos Baker, 18 February 1963; EH to Ned Calmer, 8 May 1936.

44 *his house . . . Dawn Powell.*   Dawn Powell to Carlos Baker, 4 June 1965.

44 *beneficiaries . . . Ezra Pound . . . glory."*   Harold M. Hurwitz, "Hemingway's Tutor, Ezra Pound," *Modern Fiction Studies*, 17 (Winter 1971–1972), 469–82; Baker, pp. 681, 696.

44 *turned down . . . venture*   EH to George S. Albee, 31 January 1934.

45 *Quintanilla . . . exhibition*   Leicester, p. 179.

45 *Hemingway contributed . . . $40,000*   Cyril Connolly, "Death of a Titan: Hemingway's Moments of Truth," (London) *Sunday Times* (9 July 1961), p. 27. (Hereafter Connolly.)

45 *"he supported . . . refugees*   Malcolm Cowley, CBC, Side Three.

45 *To Margaret Anderson*   EH to Solita Solano, 26 January 1941.

45 *he lent . . . Milton Wolff*   Baker, p. 631.

45 *prefaces . . . Gustav Regler.*   Baker, p. 348.

46 *check . . . to Vittorini*   Baker, p. 649.

46 *stipend . . . to Juanito Quintana*   Hotchner, p. 129; Leah Rice Koontz, " 'Montoya' Remembers *The Sun Also Rises*," in *Sun Set*, p. 210.

46 *Tom Bennett . . . money*   Leicester, pp. 217–18.

46 *$85 . . . to a farmer*   Baker, p. 354.

46 *pound notes . . . to Jimmy*   Baker, pp. 391–92.

46 *bulls for a bellhop*   Hotchner, pp. 182–83.

46 *term at the Sorbonne*   Hotchner, p. 213.

46 *How . . . explain his decision*   Young, "Hemingway and Me: A Rather Long Story," pp. 23–24.

46 *"the International Whore"*   Scott Donaldson, interview with C. T. Lanham, 5 April 1974.

46 *a young Frenchman*   Malcolm Cowley, CBC, Side Four.

47 *enjoyed his bursts of generosity*   Leicester, p. 94.

47 *gave Gianfranco the manuscript*   EH to Hans Hinrichs, 20 October 1952.

47 *Mayito Menocal . . . ostracized*   Baker, p. 381.
48 *"You can have true affection"*   Hotchner, p. 88.
48 *Don't people . . . always give*   EH to Carlos Baker, 3 October 1951.
48 *". . . old Chinese principle"*   Baker, p. 534.
48 *". . . materialistic mystic."*   Andrew Turnbull, *Scott Fitzgerald* (New York: Scribner's, 1962), p. 168. (Hereafter Turnbull.)
48 *resented . . . divorce*   Mario G. Menocal to Carlos Baker, 13 November 1964; EH to Archibald MacLeish, May 1943; Hotchner, p. 125.
49 *apparently argued*   EH to Mary Hemingway, 18 September 1950, undated.
49 *he urged . . . Hadley . . . Bumby working.*   EH to Hadley Mowrer, 8 April 1942, 12 June 1942.
49 *broke with Dos Passos*   EH to John Dos Passos, 1938.
49–50 *quarreled with MacLeish . . . money.*   EH to Archibald MacLeish, c. July 1938.
50 *MacLeish wrote back*   Archibald MacLeish to EH, 6 August 1938.
50 *repair the breach*   EH to Archibald MacLeish, 4 April 1943.

MONEY CORRUPTS

50 *"You seen a lot . . . airplanes."*   Ezra Pound to EH, 28 November 1936, in *The Letters of Ezra Pound: 1907–1941*, ed. D. D. Paige (New York: Harcourt, Brace, 1950), p. 283.
51 *"the only people*   EH, "Wings Always Over Africa: An Ornithological Letter," *Esquire* (January 1936), in *Byline*, p. 234.
51 *Chinese custom of "squeeze"*   EH, "Hemingway Interviewed by Ralph Ingersoll," *PM* (9 June 1941) in *Byline*, p. 312.
52 *Money . . . the ruination*   Baker, p. 203.
53 *"There are bullfighters*   Hotchner, p. 141.

MOVEABLE DISGUST

54 *people . . . nicer . . . broke."*   EH to Owen Wister, 30 June 1932.
54 *". . . wealthy bore."*   EH, "African Journal," *Sports Illustrated* (December 1971–January 1972), Part Three, unnumbered pages. (Hereafter "African Journal.")
54 *As fishing companions*   EH, "Out in the Stream: A Cuban Letter, *Esquire* (August 1934), in *Byline*, p. 177.
54 *articles . . . Vanderbilt*   EH to Arnold Gingrich, 19 December 1933.
55 GUEST: *. . . few million."*   Nita Jensen Houk to Carlos Baker, undated.

55 *any other foreign country.* EH to C. T. Lanham, 23 December 1946.

55 *"All of Ernest's friends* Mario G. Menocal to Carlos Baker, 18 November 1970.

55 *embraced . . . Bellville's offer* EH to Rupert Bellville, 17 February 1954, 29 March 1954.

55–56 *". . . not a snob . . . indictment."* Mario G. Menocal to Carlos Baker, 16 November 1964.

56 *yarn . . . pigeons* Hotchner, p. 45.

57 *hungry artist"* Leo Hamalian, "Hemingway as Hunger Artist," *The Literary Review,* 16 (Fall 1972), 5–13.

58 *". . . a quart of blood—* Archibald MacLeish to Carlos Baker, 28 June 1965.

58 *". . . phobia about losing . . . money."* John Hess, "Jack Hemingway Remembers His Father," *National Wildlife* (February 1961), p. 15.

59 *note . . . with figures.* Baker, p. 560.

iv. Sport

HEMINGWAY AS WALTER MITTY

60 *forty-three of . . . forty-nine* Stewart Rodnon, "Sports, Sporting Codes, and Sportsmanship in the Work of Ring Lardner, James T. Farrell, Ernest Hemingway, and William Faulkner," Ph.D. dissertation, New York University (1961), p. 94.

60 *football . . . baseball* EH to Harvey Breit, Spring 1950.

61 *Ernest would . . . catch* Donald St. John, "Interview with Hemingway's 'Bill Gorton'," in *Sun Set,* p. 171.

61 *"I pitch like a hen"* Leicester, p. 31.

61 *stumbling over . . . feet* Baker, p. 26.

61 *Two understanding . . . teachers* Charles A. Fenton, *The Apprenticeship of Ernest Hemingway* (New York: Farrar, Straus and Young, 1954), p. 6. (Hereafter Fenton.)

61 *lightweight team.* Marcelline, p. 136.

61 *managed . . . two games* Otto McFeeley to Malcolm Cowley, 2 July 1948.

61 *Philip M. White* Philip White, quoted in Otto McFeeley to Malcolm Cowley, 19 July 1948.

61 *William C. Phelps* William Phelps, quoted in Otto McFeeley to Malcolm Cowley, 19 July 1948.

61–62 *challenged Mike Burke . . . high spirits.* Baker, p. 431.

62 *"While in Oak Park high* "War Hero Returns," Oak Park (High School) *Trapeze* (21 March 1919), p. 3.

62 *"You are to remember*   Ford Madox Ford, quoted in Bernard J. Poli, *Ford Madox Ford and the Transatlantic Review* (Syracuse, N.Y.: Syracuse University Press, 1967), p. 13.

62 *"born on the wrong side*   Archibald MacLeish, CBC, Side Three.

BOXING AND BRAWLING

63 *injured his eye*   William Dodge Horne to Harold Loeb, 31 August 1961.

63 *inaccurate information . . . gladiators.*   Baker, pp. 21–23; Marcelline, p. 137.

63 *diminutive . . . Galantière*   Baker, p. 84.

64 *Loeb . . . bouts*   Harold Loeb, "Hemingway's Bitterness," in *Sun Set*, pp. 114–15.

64 *demeaning ritual . . . you have."*   Callaghan, pp. 99–101.

64 *Callaghan in a corner*   Callaghan, p. 104.

64 *notorious encounter*   Baker, p. 202.

64 *lectured Fitzgerald*   EH to Scott Fitzgerald, Spring 1929.

65 *ring in back yard*   McLendon, p. 150.

65 *$250 challenge*   Baker, p. 274.

65 *terrified . . . Braden*   Spruille Braden, *Diplomats and Demagogues* (New Rochelle: Arlington House, 1971), p. 283.

65 *slugging . . . McAlmon*   EH to Ernest Walsh, 1 February 1926.

65 *obligation not to fight*   EH to Carlos Baker, 29 April 1951.

65–66 *(Toby) and Betty Bruce . . . companions.*   Carlos Baker, interview with the Bruces, 22 March 1965.

66 *Leo Fitzpatrick*   Baker, p. 36.

66 *myopic James Joyce*   Wright Morris, "One Law for the Lion," *Partisan Review*, 28 (September–November 1961), 543.

66 *rich American bastards*   Carlos Baker, interview with Mary Hemingway, 3 August 1964.

66 *hit him, "automatically."*   EH to Carlos Baker, 29 April 1951.

66 *Smith . . . altercation*   Chard Powers Smith to EH, 1 January 1927; EH to Chard Powers Smith, undated (may never have been sent).

66 *threatened . . . Mencken's office*   "The Reminiscences of August Mencken," Vol. I (1958), Oral History Archives, Columbia University, p. 43.

66–67 *Fenton . . . enclosed place.*   EH to Charles A. Fenton, 13 July 1943.

67 *"totally humiliated"*   McLendon, p. 186.

67 *flattened . . . Knapp*   Baker, p. 273.

67 *Stevens . . . provoked a fight*   Baker, pp. 285–86.

67 *Grant . . . complained*   Baker, p. 410–11.

67 *Saroyan . . . brawl*   Baker, p. 442.

67 *insults at . . . Boyer*   Baker, pp. 458–59.

67 *". . . Hem . . . nasty"*   Scott Donaldson, interview with C. T. Lanham, 5 April 1974.

67–68 *walking over the shards . . . imperviousness*   Baker, p. 71.

68 *"he had all the lingo*   Callaghan, p. 124.

68 *Martha Gellhorn . . . singles*   EH to Lillian Ross, 2 July 1948.

68 *"pig ball" . . . ever managed to do.*   EH, "African Journal," Part Three.

68–69 *". . . high sense of craft . . . learn his trade."*   Charles A. Fenton, "No Money for the Kingbird: Hemingway's Prizefight Stories," *American Quarterly*, 4 (Winter 1952), 339–50.

OUTDOORSMAN: TYRO TO TUTOR

69 *firearms . . . "Ernest . . . when 2½*   Hotchner, p. 16.

69 *proper care . . . of guns.*   Marcelline, p. 79.

69 *Agassiz Society lessons*   Leicester, p. 32.

69 *Ed Hemingway stressed*   Marcelline, pp. 32–33.

70 *wounded bird*   Marcelline, p. 23.

70 *wild life for . . . sustenance*   Baker, pp. 9–10.

70 *A porcupine had stung*   Marcelline, p. 81.

70 *smuggled brook trout*   Marcelline, p. 41.

70 *"an occasional grouse*   Marcelline, p. 82.

70 *"Shoot the birds!"*   Y. K. Smith to Malcolm Cowley, 1948.

71 *"You can remember*   EH, "Remembering Shooting-Flying: A Key West Letter," *Esquire* (February 1935), in *Byline*, pp. 186–91.

71 *He liked to shoot*   EH to Janet Flanner, 8 April 1933.

72 *If he had not spent*   Richard Drinnon, "In the American Heartland: Hemingway and Death," *Psychoanalytic Review*, 52 (Summer 1965), 28–29.

72 *Fishing . . . war*   EH to Archibald MacLeish, c. September 1928.

72 *the best thing*   EH to Waldo Peirce, 17 June 1928.

72 *"the Black*   EH, "On Writing," *The Nick Adams Stories* (New York: Scribner's, 1972), p. 234. (Hereafter *Adams Stories*.)

72 *horsing a . . . trout*   EH, "The Last Good Country," *Adams Stories*, p. 111.

72 *deep blue river*   EH, "The Great Blue River," *Holiday* (July 1949), in *Byline*, p. 404.

72 *took "great pleasure*   EH, "On the Blue Water: A Gulf Stream Letter," *Esquire* (April 1956), in *Byline*, p. 243.

72 *"To stay in places*   Baker, p. 261. Hemingway cut this passage out of *Death in the Afternoon*.

73 *"had . . . fondness . . . for the earth*   EH to Maxwell Perkins, quoted by C. Hugh Holman, "Hemingway and *Vanity Fair*," *Carolina Quarterly*, 8 (Summer 1956), 31–37.

74 *Wright Morris . . . concludes . . . Wilderness."*   Wright Morris,

"One Law for the Lion," *Partisan Review*, 28 (September–November 1961), 548–51.

75   *"Maggots of life"*   EH, unpublished poem, c. 1921.

75   *nothing but . . . prairie*   EH to Carlos Baker, 29 April 1951.

75   *"move . . . further"*   EH, "Remembering Shooting-Flying: A Key West Letter," *Esquire* (February 1935), in *Byline*, p. 188.

75   *Nick . . . escaping*   EH, "The Last Good Country," *Adams Stories*, p. 89.

75   *"the last free place*   Stephens, p. 176.

75   *places . . . overrun*   EH, "A Visit with Hemingway," *Look* (4 September 1956), p. 24.

76   *"mystical countries"*   EH, "African Journal," Part One.

76   *attempted "to do country*   EH to Edward O'Brien, c. 1924, in *Auction*, p. 243.

76   *lessons . . . Cézanne.*   Emily Stipes Watts, *Ernest Hemingway and the Arts* (Urbana: University of Illinois Press, 1971), pp. 29–42.

77   *felt for his wounds*   EH, "African Journal," Part Two.

77   *"all real hunters*   Quoted by Patrick Hemingway, "My Papa, Papa," *Playboy* (December 1968), p. 198.

78   *unshared by . . . Pound*   Ezra Pound to EH, 28 November 1936, in *The Letters of Ezra Pound*, p. 283.

78   *not interested in . . . bears.*   EH to Marjorie Kinnan Rawlings, 16 August 1936.

78   *always plenty of danger.*   EH, "On the Blue Water: A Gulf Stream Letter," *Esquire* (April 1936), in *Byline*, p. 238.

78   *"Fighting . . . big fish*   EH, "The Great Blue River, *Holiday* (July 1949), in *Byline*, pp. 412–13.

79   *The moose*   EH, "A Paris Letter," *Esquire* (February 1934), in *Byline*, p. 154.

79   *too big to eat.*   EH, "On Writing," *Adams Stories*, p. 240.

79   *fish . . . were wasted.*   EH to Harvey Breit, 7 September 1952.

79   *". . . to kill cleanly"*   EH to Peter Barrett, 27 January 1950, in Charles Hamilton Autographs Catalogue #78 (13 June 1974), Item 189, p. 34.

80   *". . . two ways to murder*   EH, "Shootism versus Sport: The Second Tanganyika Letter," *Esquire* (June 1934), in *Byline*, pp. 162–63.

80   *". . . tackle made now . . . sweat much."*   EH, "The Great Blue River," *Holiday* (July 1949), in *Byline*, pp. 411–12.

80   *". . . due for . . . housecleaning*   Kip Farrington, "Remembering Great Men and Great Fish," *Field and Stream* (April 1971), p. 165.

81   *"In the ethics*   EH, "Notes on Dangerous Game: The Third Tanganyika Letter," *Esquire* (July 1934), in *Byline*, p. 167.

81   *"meat fisherman"*   Arnold Gingrich, "Horsing Them in with Hemingway," *Playboy* (September 1965), p. 123.

82   *Atlantic sailfishing*   McLendon, pp. 112–13.

82   *unmutilated tuna . . . slow-moving fish.*   Leicester, p. 182.

82 *Ernest's theory* Kip Farrington, *Fishing the Atlantic: Offshore and On* (New York: Coward-McCann, 1949), p. 11.

82 *hammerhead shark* Bror von Blixen-Finecke, *African Hunter* (New York: Knopf, 1938), pp. 195–96.

82 *double on grouse* *The Dialogues of Archibald MacLeish and Mark Van Doren,* ed. Warren V. Bush (New York: Dutton, 1964), p. 85.

82–83 *one hungover dawn . . . rifle held between his legs."* John Dos Passos, "Old Hem Was a Sport," *Sports Illustrated* (29 June 1964), pp. 66–67.

83 *shot . . . blue heron . . . $15 fine* Marcelline, pp. 100–102.

83 *Key West appealed* John Dos Passos, "Old Hem Was a Sport," *Sports Illustrated* (29 June 1964), p. 60.

83 *tyro . . . tutor* Rovit, pp. 53–77.

84 *"Papa got me started"* H. S. [Horace Sutton], "Bumby at Fifty," *Saturday Review/World* (23 February 1974), p. 38.

84 *"nothing . . . wasted . . . there either."* John Hess, "Jack Hemingway Remembers His Father," *National Wildlife* (February 1971), pp. 13–14.

84 *"even sports . . . education." One . . . skill.* Patrick Hemingway, "My Papa, Papa," *Playboy* (December 1968), p. 198.

85 *". . . slightly murderous."* EH, "African Journal," Part Two.

85 *"never wound . . . and leave* Mary Hemingway, "An American Appreciation: Ernest's Idaho and Mine," *World* (7 November 1972), p. 36.

AFICIONADO AND TEACHER

86 *Reardon . . . noted . . . "super-geniuses."* John Reardon, "Hemingway's Esthetic and Ethical Sportsmen," *University Review* (Kansas City), 34 (October 1967), 13–23.

88 *no sadist* EH to Bill Smith, 14 February 1925.

91 *". . . makes Ernest . . . passionate . . . knows not"* Eric Sevareid, *This Is Eric Sevareid* (New York: McGraw-Hill, 1964), p. 299.

91 *Peter Buckley visiting* A. E. Hotchner, CBC, Side Two.

v. Politics

"SOME SORT OF Y.M.C.A. SHOW"

93 *the great book* Cyril Connolly, *New Statesman and Nation* (16 October 1937), p. 606.

93 *labeled Mussolini* Baker, p. 103.

93 *Roosevelt-Hoover* Baker, p. 231.

94 *"lucrative profession"* EH, "The Friend of Spain: A Spanish Letter," *Esquire* (January 1934), in *Byline*, p. 146.

94 *Italians . . . "the best people"* EH to Ernest Walsh, c. August 1925.

94 *Henry Ford.* EH to Owen Wister, 30 June 1932.

95 *distaste for communism* EH to Ivan Kashkeen, 19 August 1935, in "Letters of Ernest Hemingway to Soviet Writers," *Soviet Literature,* 11 (1962), 161.

95 *message . . . Dos Passos* EH to John Dos Passos, 30 May 1932.

95 *"make . . . a nice career"* EH, "Old Newsman Writes: A Letter from Cuba," *Esquire* (December 1934), in *Byline*, pp. 183–85.

95 *"Everyone tries* EH to Ivan Kashkeen, 19 August 1935, in "Letters of Ernest Hemingway to Soviet Writers," *Soviet Literature,* 11 (1962), 161.

96 *"malady of power"* EH, "The Malady of Power: A Second Serious Letter," *Esquire* (November 1935), in *Byline*, p. 227.

96 *stay out of . . . war . . . not have to fight."* EH, "A Paris Letter," *Esquire* (February 1934), in *Byline*, pp. 157–58; EH, "Notes on the Next War: A Serious Topical Letter," *Esquire* (September 1935), in *Byline*, p. 205; EH, "The Malady of Power: A Second Serious Letter," *Esquire* (November 1935), in *Byline*, p. 228.

97 *Rexford Tugwell* Baker, p. 297.

97 *communism out of . . . system* EH to F. Scott Fitzgerald, 12 April 1931.

97 *Paul Romaine . . . let alone a revolution?"* EH to Paul Romaine, 6 July 1932, 9 August 1932.

97 *no economic system* EH to Owen Wister, 30 June 1932.

97–98 *law of history* EH, "Old Newsman Writes: A Letter from Cuba," *Esquire* (December 1934), in *Byline*, p. 180.

98 *Dos Passos . . . scheme . . . happily occupied.* EH to John Dos Passos, c. 1933.

COURTSHIP BY THE *MASSES*

99 *"the thinnest . . . red lines"* Baker, pp. 276–82.

99–100 *hurricane struck* David Sanders, "Ernest Hemingway's Spanish Civil War Experience," *American Quarterly*, 12 (Summer 1960), 135–36.

100 *Ambulance Committee* Carlos Baker, "The Spanish Tragedy," *Hemingway: The Writer as Artist*, pp. 229–30.

100 *$13,000 budget* Baker, p. 621.

100–101 *New York Times review* J.T.M. [John T. McManus], review of *The Spanish Earth*, *The New York Times* (21 August 1937), p. 7.

101 *communion . . . with . . . land* EH, "The American Dead in Spain," quoted in Joseph North, *No Men Are Strangers* (New York: International Publishers, 1958), pp. 146–47 (hereafter North); Allen Guttman, "'Mechanized Doom': Ernest Hemingway and the Spanish Civil War," *Massachusetts Review*, 1 (May 1960), 541–61.

101 *Roosevelt's "Harvardian" manner* Baker, p. 315.

101 *"like a whirlwind"* F. Scott Fitzgerald to Maxwell Perkins, before 19 July 1937, in *The Letters of F. Scott Fitzgerald*, ed. Andrew Turnbull (New York: Scribner's, 1963), p. 274. (Hereafter *Letters FSF*.)

101–102 *only public speech . . . dashed offstage.* Whit Burnett, *The Literary Life and the Hell with It* (New York: Harper, 1939), pp. 173–76.

102 *speech "was responsible* Baker, p. 335.

102 *"anti-war . . . correspondent."* Baker, p. 300.

102 *grisly vignettes* Richard Freedman, "Hemingway's Spanish Civil War Dispatches," *Texas Studies in Literature and Language*, 1 (Summer 1959), 175.

102 *strongest political statements* Baker, pp. 331–32.

103 *Mike Gold* Review quoted by Herbert Solow, "Substitution at Left Tackle: Hemingway for Dos Passos," *Partisan Review*, 4 (April 1938), 62.

103 *Robert Forsythe* Baker, pp. 279–80; "Robert Forsythe" [Kyle Crichton], "In This Corner, Mr. Hemingway," *New Masses* (27 November 1934), p. 26.

103 *Hunting . . . Hicks* Granville Hicks, review of *Green Hills of Africa*, *New Masses* (19 November 1935), p. 23.

103 *Hicks hailed* Granville Hicks, quoted in David Sanders, "Ernest Hemingway's Spanish Civil War Experience," *American Quarterly*, 12 (Summer 1960), 136.

104 *suppress the novel* Van Wyck Brooks, Archibald MacLeish, and Thornton Wilder, "Questions for Catholic Church Leaders," *Nation* (23 July 1938), p. 96.

104 *Edwin Berry Burgum* Edwin Berry Burgum, review of *The Fifth Column and the First Forty Nine Stories*, *New Masses* (22 November 1938), pp. 21–24.

104 *Herbert Solow* Herbert Solow, "Substitution at Left Tackle: Hemingway for Dos Passos," *Partisan Review*, 4 (April 1938), 62–64.

104 *book about Kahle* Baker, p. 310.

104 *Lukacz . . . girls* Hugh Thomas, *The Spanish Civil War* (New York: Harper, 161), p. 388.

105 *Mikhail Koltsov* Baker, p. 306.

105 *Robles . . . executed* Baker, pp. 305–306.

105 *Arnold Gingrich* Gingrich, p. 145.

TWO VIOLENT HEROES

106 *Lionel Trilling* Lionel Trilling, "Hemingway and His Critics," *Partisan Review*, 6 (Winter 1939), 52, 60.

106 *promotion drive*   John Unrue, "Hemingway and the *New Masses*," *Fitzgerald/Hemingway Annual: 1969* (Washington, D.C.: NCR Microcard Editions, 1970), pp. 131–40.

106 *Samuel Putnam*   Quoted in *Auction*, p. 192.

106 *Philip Rahv*   Philip Rahv, "The Social Muse and the Great Kudu," *Partisan Review*, 4 (December 1937), 62–64.

107 *Edgar Johnson*   Edgar Johnson, "Farewell the Separate Peace," *Sewanee Review*, 48 (July–September 1940), 289–300.

108 *Sinclair Lewis*   Sinclair Lewis, review of *To Have and Have Not*, *Newsweek* (18 October 1937), p. 34.

109 *"the decline . . . individual"*   Baker, p. 287.

109 *Charles Poore*   EH to Charles Poore, 23 January 1953, in *Auction*, p. 167.

112 *Edmund Wilson*   Edmund Wilson, "Hemingway and the Wars," *Nation* (10 December 1938), pp. 628, 630.

112 *". . . most unsatisfactory*   Quoted by Carlos Baker, "The Spanish Tragedy," *Ernest Hemingway: Critiques of Four Major Novels* (New York: Scribner's, 1962), p. 114. (Hereafter *Critiques*.)

THE BELL TOLLS

112 *". . . first communion."*   "The Spanish Tragedy," *Critiques*, p. 118.

112 *"I like Communists*   North, *Strangers*, pp. 142–45.

112 *Jim . . . Lardner*   Vincent Sheean, *Not Peace But a Sword* (New York: Doubleday, Doran, 1939), p. 248.

113 *"The Denunciation" . . . friend*   EH, *The Fifth Column and Four Stories of the Spanish Civil War* (New York: Bantam, 1970), pp. 139–52. (Hereafter *Stories Spanish.*)

113 *"Under the Ridge"*   EH, "Under the Ridge," *Stories Spanish*, pp. 201–15.

113 *"Night Before Battle"*   EH, "Night Before Battle," *Stories Spanish*, pp. 165–200.

113–14 *"Butterfly . . . Marseilles."*   EH, "The Butterfly and the Tank," *Stories Spanish*, pp. 153–64.

114 *cacophony . . . criticism.*   Baker, pp. 356–57.

117 *"always . . . vomit*   Baker, p. 347.

118 *"the idiocy . . . stupidity*   EH, "War Writers on Democracy," *Life* (24 June 1940), p. 8.

119 *Alvah Bessie*   Alvah Bessie, review of *For Whom the Bell Tolls*, *New Masses* (5 November 1940), pp. 25–29.

119–20 *metaphor . . . flask.*   For calling the exchange of gifts motif to my attention, I am indebted to Arthur Maurice, graduate student of English at William and Mary, 1974–75.

IN DISPRAISE OF GOVERNMENT

121 *relations . . . Russia.* Matthew Josephson, *Infidel in the Temple* (New York: Knopf, 1967), p. 477.

121 *"anti-alien"* EH, form letter for American Committee for Protection of Foreign Born, 16 January 1940.

121 *varieties . . . breed* EH to Harvey Breit, 20 April 1950.

122 *After Debs* EH to Lillian Ross, 28 July 1948.

122 *(HUAC . . . contempt* EH to C. T. Lanham, 27 November 1947.

122 *Senator Joseph McCarthy* EH, "The Christmas Gift," *Look* (20 May 1954), in *Byline*, p. 450; EH, "African Journal," Part Three.

122 *Batista . . . looted* Baker, p. 543.

122 *killed his dog* Baker, p. 538.

122–23 *country . . . atrocious . . . Cuba.* EH to Patrick Hemingway, 24 November 1958.

123 *"had no consistent . . . ideas."* Carlos Baker, interview with John Dos Passos, 28 May 1962.

123 *Nixon . . . ascendancy* EH to C. T. Lanham, 17 April 1953.

124 *Adams . . . "poison."* Henry Adams, *The Education of Henry Adams* (New York: Random House, 1931), p. 418.

124 *no freedom* EH to Patrick Hemingway, 24 November 1958.

124 *Christopher Caudwell* "Christopher Caudwell" [Christopher St. John Sprigg], *Romance and Realism: A Study of English Bourgeois Literature*, ed. Samuel Hynes (Princeton, N.J.: Princeton University Press, 1970), pp. 116–18.

vi. War

WAR LOVER AND HATER

125 *hired a taxicab* Baker, p. 40.

125 *ambulance service* Malcolm Cowley, *Exile's Return*, pp. 38–39, 43.

125 *canister exploded* Baker, pp. 44–45.

126 *private pilgrimage . . . the same.* EH to William Dodge Horne, 17 July 1923.

126 *not "destroyed"* EH to Carlos Baker, 8 January 1953.

129 *"Soldiers pitch* EH, "Champs d'Honneur," *Three Stories and Ten Poems* (Paris: Contact Publishing Co., 1923), unnumbered pages.

130 *King and country* EH, "To Good Guys Dead," unpublished poem, c. 1921.

130 *introduction . . . 1948*   EH, *A Farewell to Arms* (New York: Scribner's, 1948), p. x.

130 *.only World War II*   Quoted in Malcolm Cowley, "A Portrait of Mister Papa," *Life* (10 January 1949), p. 89.

131 *loved the 4th Infantry*   EH to Charles Poore, 16 March 1953.

131 *days . . . happiest*   Baker, p. 424.

131 *son Jack*   EH to Hadley Mowrer, 28 November 1942.

131 *case of Patrick*   EH to Patrick Hemingway, 24 November 1951.

131 *Korea*   EH to Harvey Breit, 30 June 1950; EH to Lillian Ross, 12 July 1950.

131 *terrible sin*   EH to Lillian Ross, 13 August 1950.

131 *"I love combat"*   Baker, p. 408.

132 *war . . . best subject*   EH to F. Scott Fitzgerald, 15 December 1925.

132 *novels . . . distrust*   Archibald MacLeish, "Post-War Writers and Pre-War Readers," *New Republic* (10 June 1940), pp. 789–90; EH, "War Writers on Democracy," *Life* (24 June 1940), p. 8.

132 *Wolff . . . "dry*   Baker, p. 357.

132 *"they" would deny*   Quoted in Irvin D. and Marilyn Yalom, "Ernest Hemingway—A Psychiatric View," *Archives of General Psychology*, 24 (June 1971), 488.

133 *medals . . . in a drawer*   Hotchner, p. 103.

133 *wound stripes*   Leicester, pp. 51–52.

TESTS OF BRAVERY

133 *". . . dangerous terrain*   Carlos Baker, telephone interview with Jimmy Cannon, 11 October 1960.

133 *Mussolini . . . dueling*   EH, "Mussolini, Europe's Prize Bluffer, More Like Bottomley than Napoleon," Toronto *Daily Star* (27 January 1923), p. 11.

133 *danger . . . purify*   Baker, p. 217.

133 *fellow correspondent*   Baker, p. 423.

134 *shells . . . Hotel Florida*   Claude G. Bowers, *My Mission in Spain* (New York: Simon & Schuster, 1954), pp. 372–73.

134 *88 shell*   Baker, p. 427.

134 *monumental calm*   Baker, p. 438.

134 *"what it meant to be . . . a coward."*   Baker, p. 252.

134 *breaking point*   Baker, p. 434.

134 *"Learning to suspend*   *Men at War* (New York: Crown, 1942), ed. and introd. EH, p. xxvii.

134 *"Fuck you*   EH to C. T. Lanham, 31 January 1945.

135 *concentrate rigidly*   Peter Wykeham-Barnes, CBC, Side Two.

135 *sick to his stomach*   EH to David Garnett, 1 November 1938.

135 *". . . . stupidity . . . "prickling* EH, "African Journal," Part 3.

135 *". . . capacity for fear* EH, "Nobody Ever Dies," *Cosmopolitan* (March 1939), pp. 28–31, 74–76.

135 *Harold Loeb* Harold Loeb, "Ernest Hemingway: A Life Story" (review of Carlos Baker's biography), *Southern Review*, 5 (Summer 1969), 1219.

135 *"fraid . . .* Baker, p. 16.

135 *dark was peopled* F. Scott Fitzgerald, *The Crack-Up* ed. Edmund Wilson (New York: New Directions, 1945), p. 174. (Hereafter *Crack-Up*.)

135–36 *Nick . . . fearful . . . at that age.* EH, "Three Shots," *Adams Stories*, pp. 13–15.

137 *"Night Before Landing" . . . combat.* EH, "Night Before Landing," *Adams Stories*, pp. 141–42.

137 *phobia about snakes)* EH, *Green Hills of Africa* (New York: Scribner's, 1935), pp. 58–59.

137 *Stein . . . "yellow."* Baker, p. 307.

137–38 *Faulkner roused . . . as a writer."* Baker, pp. 461, 647; EH to C. T. Lanham, 24–25 May 1947; C. T. Lanham to William Faulkner, 24 June 1947; William Faulkner to C. T. Lanham, 28 June 1947; Scott Donaldson, interview with C. T. Lanham, 5 April 1974.

138 *lacked . . . self-confidence.* Baker, p. 420.

138 *"they" . . . accuse* EH to Carlos Baker, 3 November 1952.

138–39 *letter . . . Ross . . . eighteen men.* EH to Lillian Ross, 18 September 1945.

MILES GLORIOSUS

139 *miles gloriosus* Kermit Vanderbilt, "The Last Words of Ernest Hemingway," *Nation* (25 October 1965), pp. 284–85.

139 *". . . twenty-eight bullets* Leicester, p. 53.

139 *Trapeze . . . Arditi* Leicester, pp. 54–56.

140 *infantry officer* Stewart F. Sanderson, *Ernest Hemingway* (Edinburgh and London: Oliver & Boyd, 1961), p. 17. (Hereafter Sanderson.)

140 *machine guns . . . urine.* Baker, p. 512–13.

140 *Pauline believed* Baker, p. 621.

140 *Ingersoll . . . stories . . . own purposes.* Taylor Alderman, review of R. Sturgis Ingersoll, *Recollections of a Philadelphian at Eighty*, *Hemingway Notes*, 2 (Fall 1972), 21.

140 *career as braggart* Baker, pp. 405, 426, 455–56, 474, 638.

141 *A week before* Baker, pp. 408–14.

141–42 *accusations against . . . out of trouble.* Baker, pp. 428–30.

142 *told Dorman-O'Gowan* EH to E. E. Dorman-O'Gowan, 21 May 1950.

142 *told Lanham*   EH to C. T. Lanham, 24 May 1948.
142 *told Charles Poore*   EH to Charles Poore, 3 April 1953, in *Auction*, p. 171.
142 *home a hero*   EH to C. T. Lanham, 17 October 1944.
143 *Fifty years from now*   EH to C. T. Lanham, 24 May 1948.
143 *variance . . . truth*   C. T. Lanham to Carlos Baker, 23 August 1965.
143 *self-aggrandizement.*   Carlos Baker, interview with Martha Gellhorn, 30 April 1963; Scott Donaldson, interview with C. T. Lanham, 5 April 1974.

vii. Love

FIRST LOVES

144 *"about time"*   Marcelline, p. 144.
145 *madly in love*   EH to Bill Smith, December 1918.
145 *send him . . . bed.*   Marcelline, p. 188.
145 *if Ag came back*   Scott Donaldson, interview with Ella Winter, 14 October 1972.
145 *Kathryn Longwell*   Baker, p. 59.
145 *Grace Quinlan*   Baker, p. 65.
145 *Irene Goldstein . . . apartment.*   Irene Gordon to Carlos Baker, 12 March 1962.
146 *Katy Smith . . . few months.*   EH, "Summer People," *Adams Stories*, pp. 217–28; EH to C. T. Lanham, 24 November 1948; Hadley Richardson to EH, 22 June 1921.
146 *Hadley . . . pregnant . . . rest of the family.*   Gertrude Stein, *The Autobiography of Alice B. Toklas* (New York: Harcourt, Brace, 1933), pp. 261–71 (hereafter Stein); Guy Hickok, quoted in Lincoln Steffens, *The Autobiography of Lincoln Steffens* (New York: Harcourt, Brace, 1931), p. 835 (hereafter Steffens); EH to William Dodge Horne, 17 July 1923.
147 *Twice . . . loans.*   Baker, pp. 155–57.
147 *Hadley . . . affair*   Young, "The End of Compendium Reviewing," p. 40.

NOT GETTING OVER HADLEY

148 *son of a bitch.*   EH to F. Scott Fitzgerald, September 1926, December 1926.
148 *Donald Ogden Stewart*   Scott Donaldson, interview with Donald Ogden Stewart, 27 September 1972.
148 *go to Hell*   Baker, p. 176.
148 *". . . immoral life."*   Baker, p. 182.

148 *". . . stuffy Oak Park*   Carlos Baker, interview with Isabelle Godolphin, 22 October 1964.

148 *Jack . . . Mary*   Denis Brian, "The Importance of Knowing Ernest," *Esquire* (February 1972), pp. 168–69.

149 *Faulkner remarked*   Joseph Blotner, *Faulkner: A Biography* (New York: Random House, 1974), p. 1790.

150 *Even an unsympathetic*   David J. Gordon, "Some Recent Novels: Connoisseurs of Chaos," *Yale Review*, 60 (1971), 429.

150 *Ernest's reminiscence . . . sin."*   EH, "African Journal," Part Three.

FREDERIC HENRY, SELFISH LOVER

151 *"fully idyllic"*   Wilson, "Hemingway: Gauge of Morale," p. 242.

151 *". . . Paolo and Francesca . . . heroic scale.*   Robert Morss Lovett, "Ernest Hemingway," *English Journal*, 21 (October 1932), 615.

151–52 A Farewell . . . *"immoral book."*   Baker, p. 338.

152 *responsible . . . narrator."*   Quoted in Arthur L. Scott, "In Defense of Robert Cohn," *College English*, 18 (March 1957), 309.

162 *Holden . . . "insincerity"*   Delbert E. Wylder, *Hemingway's Heroes* (Albuquerque: University of New Mexico Press, 1969), p. 67, calls attention to Holden Caufield's reservations in his chapter on *"A Farewell to Arms*: The Guilt-Ridden Anti-Hero"; other critics who have detected noteworthy faults in Frederic include Jackson J. Benson, *Hemingway: The Writer's Art of Self-Defense* (Minneapolis: University of Minnesota Press, 1969, hereafter Benson), and Richard B. Hovey, *Hemingway: The Inward Terrain* (Seattle: University of Washington Press, 1968).

162 *E. M. Halliday*   E. M. Halliday, "Hemingway's Narrative Perspective," *Sewanee Review*, 60 (Spring 1952), 211.

THE LAST THREE WIVES

163 *admired Hadley*   EH to Hadley Mowrer, 26 July 1939.

163 *"stinko . . . lonely"*   EH to Hadley Mowrer, 1 December 1939.

163 *"Miss . . . Kat."*   EH to Hadley Mowrer, 25 July 1942, 25 November 1943.

164 *"She undervalued . . . remorse."*   Shelley Cohen, "Hemingway Papers . . ." AP dispatch, 12 July 1975.

164 *sexual reasons . . . birth-control devices.*   Baker, p. 491.

164 *cobra.*   Martha Gellhorn to Carlos Baker, n.d.

164 *"biggest mistake"*   EH to C. T. Lanham, 23 July 1945.

165 *five months*   EH to Dawn Powell, 31 January 1944.

165 *sharp tongue*   Carlos Baker, interview with Gustavo Durán, 19 February 1962.

165 *noisy . . . companions*   Ellis O. Briggs to Carlos Baker, 27 February 1964.

165 *". . . stand me up"*   Baker, p. 444.

165 *openly cuckolded*   Donald St. John, "Leicester Hemingway, Chief of State," *Connecticut Review*, 3 (April 1970), 16.

165 *virulently ambitious*   EH to Archibald MacLeish, 5 October 1952.

165 *new woman . . . book"*   Callaghan, p. 161.

166 *side of his foot*   EH to Mary Welsh, 23 September 1945.

166 *less than smooth.*   EH to Patrick Hemingway, 21 January 1946; EH to C. T. Lanham, 20 January 1946, 21 February 1946.

166 *bitter altercation*   Baker, p. 454.

166 *multitude of roles—*   Scott Donaldson, interview with William W. Seward, Jr., 17 April 1972.

166 *an appreciation*   EH, "A Situation Report," *Look* (4 September 1956), in *Byline*, pp. 473–74.

166–67 *"wonderful . . . forgetting . . . forgave you, too."*   EH, "African Journal," Part Two.

167 *acquire . . . wives.*   Mary Hemingway to EH, November 1952.

167 *Adriana . . . chaperoned*   Baker, p. 477.

167 *heart . . . target*   EH to A. E. Hotchner, 2 January 1950.

167 *heated correspondence*   EH to Adriana Ivancich, 17 April 1950, 27 June 1950.

167 *Mary . . . anger.*   EH to Lillian Ross, 5 October 1950.

167 cosa sagrada   EH to Adriana Ivancich, 13 February 1954.

167 *young woman . . . made no play*   EH to Robert M. Brown, 25 May 1956.

168 *Irish girl*   José Luis Castillo-Puche, *Hemingway in Spain* (Garden City, N.Y.: Doubleday, 1974), pp. 184, 191. (Hereafter Castillo-Puche.)

168 *warm Valerie*   Scott Donaldson, interview with C. T. Lanham, 5 April 1974.

168 *tuition . . . expenses*   EH to A. E. Hotchner, 25 October 1960.

168 *a letter . . . beginning with A.*   EH to Valerie Danby-Smith, 25 October 1960.

168 *treat Mary . . . badly.*   Scott Donaldson, interview with Carlos Baker, 25, May 1972.

169 *lucky . . . Mary.*   EH to John Dos Passos, 17 September 1949.

"GETTING CONNECTED UP."

170 *D. H. Lawrence . . . a trap.*   D. H. Lawrence, *"In Our Time*: A Review," in *Hemingway: A Collection of Critical Essays*, ed. Robert P. Weeks (Englewood Cliffs, N.J.: Prentice-Hall, 1962), pp. 93–94.

170 *passage . . . cut*   Sheldon Norman Grebstein, *Hemingway's*

Craft (Carbondale: Southern Illinois University Press, 1973), pp. 214–15. (Hereafter Grebstein.)

170 *firing babysitter . . . "or get hurt."* McLendon, p. 182.

170 *loss of manhood.* EH to Arthur Mizener, 22 April 1950; EH to Adriana Ivancich, 20 September 1955.

171 *"seen enough fights* EH, "The Last Good Country," *Adams Stories*, p. 85.

171 *"the impossible . . . woman* Dolores Barracano Schmidt, "The Great American Bitch," *College English*, 32 (1971), 900.

171 *Margot . . . succumb* Tom Burnam, "Primitivism and Masculinity in the Work of Ernest Hemingway," *Modern Fiction Studies*, 1 (August 1955), 23–24.

172 *Pete . . . wimmins is difficult."* Scott Donaldson, interview with C. T. Lanham, 5 April 1974.

172 *secret places . . . the way.* EH, unpublished poem to Mary, 13 October 1950.

173 *curing "all loneliness."* Baker, p. 398.

173 *very touching."* Archibald MacLeish, CBC, Side One.

173 *two against . . . others.* EH to Pauline Pfeiffer, 3 December 1926.

173 Who's Who *Who's Who* questionnaire, dated 13 January 1928.

173 *Christmas holidays* McLendon, p. 198.

173–74 *Erich Fromm . . . remain two."* Erich Fromm, *The Art of Loving* (New York: Harper, 1956).

viii. Sex

GREAT LOVER . . .

175 *"had the clap"* Scott Donaldson, interview with C. T. Lanham, 5 April 1974.

175 *reform school* EH to Arthur Mizener, 1 June 1950.

175–76 *fictional Alice . . . Billings, Montana.* EH, "Saturday Night at the Whorehouse in Billings, Montana," *Ernest Hemingway Reading*, Caedmon Recording TC118, Side Two.

176 *Ernest blushing* Baker, p. 43.

176 *introduction to* Kiki EH, introduction to *Kiki's Memoirs*, pp. 9–14.

176 *Xenophobia . . . her return.* EH to Lillian Ross, 6 May 1950; EH to A. E. Hotchner, 11 October 1949.

176 *never . . . prostitute.* Mario G. Menocal to Carlos Baker, 18 November 1970.

176 *never . . . asked* Scott Donaldson, interview with Ella Winter, 14 October 1972.

176 *Thornton Wilder* Malcolm Cowley to Scott Donaldson, 19 September 1975.

177 *saltpeter* Edmund Wilson, *The Twenties* (New York: Farrar, Straus and Giroux, 175), p. 346.

177 *sex-sedating nuts* Scott Donaldson, interview with Stephen Spender, 14 April 1975.

171 *"bum" . . . Kinsey.* EH to C. T. Lanham, 25 August 1948.

177 *bedroom accomplishments.* Scott Donaldson, interview with C. T. Lanham, 5 April 1974.

177 *two emotions* Mario G. Menocal to Carlos Baker, 16 November 1964.

177 *attempts . . . to seduce* Baker, p. 650.

177 *Mata Hari.* Donald St. John, "Leicester Hemingway, Chief of State," *Connecticut Review*, 3 (April 1970), 12.

177 *Legs Diamond.* Hotchner, pp. 33–34.

178 *safari . . . girl* Baker, p. 659.

178 *offer to finance* Alden Whitman, "Hemingway Letters Reproach Critics," *The New York Times* (9 March 1972), p. 36.

178 *passionate innkeepers* EH, "African Journal," Part Two; Baker, pp. 55–56.

178 *a famous French writer* EH to Charles Poore, 4 August 1949.

178 *Kate "slut"* EH, "Summer People," *Adams Stories*, pp. 227–28.

178 *After intercourse* EH to George S. Albee, 7 May 1931.

178 *pleasure . . . Wolff* Baker, pp. 319–20.

178 *"an amateur pimp"* Scott Donaldson, interview with C. T. Lanham, 5 April 1974.

. . . OR SEXUAL PURITAN

179 *"a bit priggish"* Donald St. John, "Interview with Donald Ogden Stewart," in *Sun Set*, p. 205.

179 *"a Puritan."* Harold Loeb, "Hemingway's Bitterness," in *Sun Set*, p. 123.

179 *came home disgusted* Max Eastman, *Great Companions* (New York: Farrar, Straus and Cudahy, 1959), p. 50.

179 *wasting of time* Quoted in *Crack-Up*, p. 25.

180 *number of orgasms* Baker, p. 205.

180 *strawberries* Baker, pp. 628–29.

180 *disapproved . . . promiscuity* See Sheldon Norman Grebstein, "Sex, Hemingway, and the Critics," *The Humanist*, 21 (July–August 1961), 212–18.

181 *homosexuals . . . talented.* Baker, p. 240.

THE MINCING GENTRY

182 *"utterly charming* EH, "Queer Mixture of Aristocrats, Profiteers, Sheep and Wolves at the Hotels of Switzerland," Toronto *Star Weekly* (4 March 1922), p. 3, in *The Wild Years*, p. 164.

182 *Lord Curzon* Quoted in Nicholas Joost, *Ernest Hemingway and the Little Magazines* (Barre, Mass.: Barre Publishers, 1968), p. 56. (Hereafter Joost.)

184 *band . . . of fairies* EH to Harold Loeb, 21 June 1925.

185 *Sloppy Joe's* McLendon, p. 153.

185 *Sidney Franklin* Denis Brian, "The Importance of Knowing Ernest," *Esquire* (February 1972), pp. 165–66.

185 *Tennessee Williams* Baker, p. 545.

185 *beat up McAlmon* Baker, p. 206.

186 *Eastman . . . review* Max Eastman, "Bull in the Afternoon," *The New Republic* (7 June 1933), pp. 94–97.

186 *responses . . . MacLeish* Archibald MacLeish to the editor of *The New Republic*, 7 June 1933.

186 *Friedrich proposed* Otto Friedrich, "Ernest Hemingway: Joy Through Strength," *American Scholar*, 26 (Autumn 1957), 527.

186 *Galantière wondered . . . fire?* Carlos Baker, interview with Lewis Galantière, 13 January 1964.

187 *nasty questions* Quoted in Baker, p. 242.

187 *"conviction . . . gentle . . . puritanical* Max Eastman to the editor of *The New Republic*, 15 June 1933.

187 *ensuing contretemps* Baker, pp. 317–18.

188 *"This Englishman* EH to Charles Poore, 23–28 February 1953, in *Auction*, p. 170.

THE *MACHO* AND MIDWESTERNER

188 *the* macho Octavio Paz, "Mexican Masks," *Labyrinth of Solitude* (New York: Grove Press, 1961), pp. 29–42.

189 *"the shyest man"* Yousuf Karsh, *Karsh Portfolio* (London: Nelson, 1967), pp. 81–83.

189 *"Miss Dietrich . . . Garbo* EH, reply to questionnaire, *Transition*, No. 27 (April–May 1938), p. 237.

189–90 *". . . twins . . . everything alike."* Marcelline, pp. 61–62.

ix. *Friendship*

A GIFT FOR FRIENDSHIP

191–92 *semifictional fragment . . . "any joke."* EH, "On Writing," *Adams Stories*, p. 234.

192 *"Women . . . important*   Donald St. John, "Interview with Donald Ogden Stewart," in *Sun Set*, p. 194.

192 *". . . immense charm" . . . had to say.*   Cowley, p. 225.

192 *"get right into . . . heart*   Hadley Mowrer, CBC, Side Two.

192 *"but . . . tan . . . sunbathers*   Baker, p. 49.

192–93 *relationship . . . Stewart . . . end of that.*   Donald Ogden Stewart, "Recollections of Fitzgerald and Hemingway," *Fitzgerald/Hemingway Annual: 1971* (Washington, D.C.: NCR Microcard Editions, 1972), pp. 180–83; Matthew J. Bruccoli, "Donald Ogden Stewart: An Interview," *Fitzgerald/Hemingway Annual: 1973* (Washington, D.C.: NCR Microcard Editions, 1974), pp. 83–85; Scott Donaldson, interview with Donald Ogden Stewart, 27 September 1972.

193–94 *Tate . . . convert*   Allen Tate, "Random Thoughts on the Twenties," *Minnesota Review*, 1 (Fall 1960), 52.

194 *Evan Shipman . . . Miró's painting*   Evan Shipman to Malcolm Cowley, 1 April 1948.

"THE CAREER, THE CAREER"

194 *conscious careerist"*   Nathan Asch to Malcolm Cowley, 23 March 1948.

194–95 *Pound . . . introduced*   Joost, p. 9.

195 *". . . helping hand*   Turnbull, p. 346.

195 *". . . good rations."*   Sherwood Anderson, *Memoirs* (New York: Harcourt, Brace, 1942), p. 473. (Hereafter Anderson.)

195 *". . . a big dog . . . Anderson."*   Archibald MacLeish, CBC, Side One.

196 *". . . kill . . . father."*   Morley Callaghan, CBC, Side One.

196 *breaking the news . . . satire.*   EH to Sherwood Anderson, 21 May 1926.

196 *". . . Literature . . . bigger*   Anderson, *Memoirs*, p. 475.

196 *motivation . . . best*   EH, "The Art of the Short Story," unpublished article, p. 11.

196 *clever . . . annihilation."*   Wright Morris, "One Law for the Lion," *Partisan Review*, 28 (September–November 1961), 545.

196 *"and not . . . good description."*   Baker, p. 87.

196–97 *". . . the career"*   Stein, pp. 261–71.

197 *". . . break . . . friendships*   EH to W. O. Rogers, 29 July 1948, in Gotham Book Mart & Gallery, Inc. catalogue.

197 *Ford . . . "The best writer"*   Quoted in *The Left Bank Revisited*, ed. Hugh Ford (University Park: Pennsylvania State University Press, 1972), pp. 241–42.

197 *fat, asthmatic*   Baker, pp. 123–24.

198 *". . . Eliot . . . sausage*   Baker, p. 135.

198 *"Pay for . . . drinks"*   Baker, p. 136.

198–99 *letters . . . O'Brien . . . "The Killers."*   EH to Edward

O'Brien, 21 May 1923, later 1923, 12 September 1924, 3 October 1924.

198 *"Fifty Grand"* EH to Edward O'Brien, 31 August 1927.

199–200 *Hemingway . . . Wister . . . friendship.* See Ben Merchant Vorpahl, "Ernest Hemingway and Owen Wister: Finding the Lost Generation," *Library Chronicle* (University of Pennsylvania), 36 (Spring 1970), 126–37; EH to Owen Wister, 24 June 1929.

200 *thoroughly ashamed* EH to Harold Loeb, June 1925.

200 *favor . . . dead.* Robert M. Coates to Malcolm Cowley, 8 August 1966.

201 *"a dangerous friend"* *Sun Set*, p. 72.

SCOTT VERSUS ERNEST

201 *". . . brilliant future."* F. Scott Fitzgerald to Maxwell Perkins, before 18 October 1924, *Letters FSF*, p. 167.

201 *dedication to . . . craft* Nancy Milford, *Zelda* (New York: Harper & Row, 1970), p. 115. (Hereafter Milford).

201 *admiring . . . the man* Turnbull, p. 159.

202 *Glenway Wescott* Glenway Wescott, "The Moral of F. Scott Fitzgerald," in *Crack-Up*, pp. 324–25.

202 *". . . charming fellow"* F. Scott Fitzgerald to Maxwell Perkins, 22 April 1925, *Letters FSF*, p. 200.

202 *advised Perkins* F. Scott Fitzgerald to Maxwell Perkins, c. 30 December 1925, c. 19 January 1926, *Letters FSF*, pp. 217–20.

202 *". . . minimum of changes"* F. Scott Fitzgerald to Maxwell Perkins, c. 26 June 1926, *Letters FSF*, p. 228.

203 *Fitzgerald . . . changes* Philip Young and Charles W. Mann, "Fitzgerald's *Sun Also Rises*: Notes and Comments," and F. Scott Fitzgerald, "Letter to Ernest Hemingway," *Fitzgerald/Hemingway Annual: 1970* (Washington, D.C.: NCR Microcard Editions, 1970), pp. 1–13.

203 *Farewell . . . nine pages* F. Scott Fitzgerald, critique of *A Farewell to Arms*, unpublished manuscript.

204 *a lousy critic . . . before."* EH to Charles Poore, 23 January 1953, in *Auction*, p. 169; EH to Arthur Mizener, 2 January 1951, in *Auction*, p. 175.

204 *Scott . . . minimized* F. Scott Fitzgerald to John O'Hara, 25 July 1936, *Letters FSF*, p. 559.

204–205 *"For God's sakes* F. Scott Fitzgerald to EH, 10 May 1934, *Letters FSF*, p. 334.

205 *genuine tenderness* F. Scott Fitzgerald to EH, November 1927, *Letters FSF*, p. 328; EH to F. Scott Fitzgerald, 31 March 1927.

205 *Reading List.* *Crack-Up*, p. 176.

205 *scatological satire . . . was dead."* Philip Young, "Scott Fitzgerald on His Thirtieth Birthday Sends a Small Gift to Ernest Hemingway," *Modern Fiction Studies*, 14 (Summer 1968), 229–30.

205 *"used B.V.D.'s*   F. Scott Fitzgerald to EH, December 1927, *Letters FSF*, pp. 328–29.

206 *long "set-piece . . . mounts."*   Turnbull, p. 188.

206 *"182,000 bits"*   EH to F. Scott Fitzgerald, 1927.

206 *version of Heaven*   EH to F. Scott Fitzgerald, 1 July 1925.

207 *man named Johnston*   F. Scott Fitzgerald to EH, 30 November 1925, *Letters FSF*, p. 321.

208 *Zelda . . . Ernest.*   Milford, pp. 116–17, 153; Sara Mayfield, *Exiles from Paradise: Zelda and Scott Fitzgerald* (New York: Delacorte Press, 1971), p. 218 (hereafter Mayfield); F. Scott Fitzgerald to Maxwell Perkins, c. 14 May 1932, *Letters FSF*, p. 253; EH to Arthur Mizener, 4 April 1950, in *Auction*, p. 174.

208 *"you two take . . . emotional states."*   The Papers of Christian Gauss, ed. K. G. Jackson and Hiram Haydn (New York: Random House, 1957), p. 218.

208–209 *Stein . . . "flame"*   Turnbull, pp. 189–90; EH to F. Scott Fitzgerald, spring 1929.

209 *"I was silent*   Quoted in Tony Buttitta, *After the Good Gay Times* (New York: Viking, 1974), p. 118.

209 *Perkins . . . complaint*   F. Scott Fitzgerald to Maxwell Perkins, 25 September 1933, *Letters FSF*, p. 257.

209 *". . . out of print*   F. Scott Fitzgerald to Maxwell Perkins, 24 December 1938, *Letters FSF*, p. 280.

209 *". . . steep trajectory"*   EH to Arthur Mizener, 6 July 1949, in *Auction*, p. 174.

209 *". . . writing unnecessary."*   Quoted in Mizener, p. 305.

209 *literally terrified*   Lillian Hellman, *An Unfinished Woman* (Boston: Little, Brown, 1969), pp. 66–69. (Hereafter Hellman.)

209 *". . . authority of failure*   Crack-Up, p. 181.

210 *"I am a plodder*   Quoted in Turnbull, p. 238.

210 *"artistic conscience"*   Crack-Up, p. 79.

210 *". . . stick hardened*   F. Scott Fitzgerald to Maxwell Perkins, c. 1 September 1930, *Letters FSF*, p. 247.

210 *somebody's hero*   EH to Arthur Mizener, 4 January 1951, in *Auction*, p. 175.

210 *novel . . . "Philippe*   F. Scott Fitzgerald, "Philippe, Count of Darkness," *Redbook* (October 1934, June 1935, August 1935, November 1941).

211 *"walk . . . cleats"*   Crack-Up, p. 147.

211 *"half bait*   Quoted in Mizener, p. 247.

211 *"Forget . . . tragedy"*   Quoted in Mizener, pp. 259–60.

211 *". . . growing up . . . old."*   Quoted in Mizener, p. 74.

211 *travel to Cuba*   Quoted in Turnbull, p. 277.

212 *open season*   EH to Maxwell Perkins, 17 February 1936.

212 *rhetorically asked*   EH to Arthur Mizener, 4 January 1951, in *Auction*, p. 175.

212 *"Somehow I love* F. Scott Fitzgerald to Maxwell Perkins, 19 September 1936, *Letters FSF*, pp. 293–94.

212 *joke . . . on Ernest* Andrew Turnbull, *Thomas Wolfe* (New York: Scribner's, 1967), p. 243.

213 *". . . megalomania* F. Scott Fitzgerald to Beatrice Dance, 15 September 1936, *Letters FSF*, p. 564.

213 *". . . adoring . . . obsessed."* Edmund Wilson, *The Twenties*, p. 94.

213 *"how superior* F. Scott Fitzgerald to Zelda Fitzgerald, 28 September 1940, *Letters FSF*, p. 145.

213 *congratulations* F. Scott Fitzgerald to EH, *Crack-Up*, pp. 284–85.

213 *". . . come up fighting* Arthur Mizener to EH, 16 July 1949.

213–14 *Mizener . . . Hemingway . . . big leagues."* EH to Arthur Mizener, 4 April 1950, 12 May 1950, 1 June 1950, 6 June 1950, 2 January 1951, 4 January 1951, in *Auction*, pp. 174–75.

214 *"Most Pleasant Trips"* *Crack-Up*, p. 224.

214 *"slick drive* F. Scott Fitzgerald to Gertrude Stein, June 1925, *Letters FSF*, p. 503.

214 *". . . piercing jabs* Mayfield, p. 93.

214–15 *"I'm sorry for you . . . an author."* F. Scott Fitzgerald to EH, December 1926, 23 December 1926, *Letters FSF*, pp. 324–25.

A SMALL CLUB FOR THE FAITHFUL

215 *Y. K. Smith . . . dispute* Baker, pp. 81–82, 88; EH to Howell Jenkins, 20 March 1922, 15 August 1925.

216 *one-eyed Portuguese* Baker, p. 495.

216 *". . . impossible friend"* Baker, pp. 261–62.

216 *every dull bastard* EH to Waldo Peirce, 26 May 1934.

216 *"a con man"* Gingrich, p. 87.

216 *". . . mean or nasty"* Donald St. John, "Leicester Hemingway, Chief of State," *Connecticut Review*, 3 (April 1970), p. 12.

216 *treat a fly* Leicester, p. 204.

216 *"turned on . . . friends."* Milford, p. 116.

216 *subscription* EH to Archibald MacLeish, n.d.

217 *trust nobody* EH to C. T. Lanham, 2 March 1945?

217 *praise him* EH to Carlos Baker, 30 June 1951.

217 *hat at the bust* John Dos Passos, "Old Hem Was a Sport," *Sports Illustrated* (29 June 1964), p. 67.

217 *loyalty . . . Ward* Hotchner, p. 43.

217 *liar . . . oath.* EH to Lillian Ross, 1 November 1950.

217 *"would have killed him"* Denis Brian, "The Importance of Knowing Ernest," *Esquire* (February 1972), p. 170.

217–18 *The "sads" . . . life.* See Ted R. Spivey, "Hemingway's

Pursuit of Happiness on the Open Road," *Emory University Quarterly*, 11 (December 1955), 240–53.

218 *". . . the good fight*   Quoted in Sanderson, p. 4.
218 *too strong a feeling*   EH to C. T. Lanham, 31 January 1945?
218 *". . . most compassionate*   C. T. Lanham file, Carlos Baker's office.

219 *Durán . . . insult.*   Gustavo Durán file, Carlos Baker's office; Baker, pp. 378–79, 448, 629.

220 *gift of mimicry*   Edmund Wilson, "An Effort at Self-Revelation," *The New Yorker* (2 January 1971), p. 60.

220 *". . . cry . . . drunk*   Baker, pp. 120–21.

220 *"a son of a bitch*   William W. Seward, Jr., *My Friend, Ernest Hemingway* (New York: A. S. Barnes, 1969), p. 56.

220 *"cross-grained*   Archibald MacLeish, CBC, Side Two.

220 *"perhaps the nicest man"*   Quoted in Mary Hemingway, "Department of Amplification," *The New Yorker* (16 March 1963), p. 163.

220 *on his guard*   Rovit, pp. 22–23.

220 *best . . . friend*   Scott Donaldson, interview with Carlos Baker, 25 May 1972.

220 *"There seemed to be . . . reserve."*   Archibald MacLeish, CBC, Side Two.

221 *"a psychological device*   Leicester, p. 117.

221 *"some person . . . details.' "*   Mario G. Menocal, Jr. to Carlos Baker, 18 November 1970.

221 *run errands*   EH to A. E. Hotchner, 7 December 1950, 16 June 1959.

221 *"Yes, Papa"*   Baker, p. 382.
221 *"very little depth*   Baker, p. 544.
221 *pallbearers*   Baker, p. 668.

x. Religion

OAK PARK PIETY

222 *prayer service*   Marcelline, pp. 14–15.
222 *friend . . . Moody*   Marcelline, p. 18.
222–23 *brief biography*   Constance Cappel Montgomery, *Hemingway in Michigan* (New York: Fleet, 1966), pp. 31–32. (Hereafter Montgomery.)
223 *Dr. C. E. Hemingway . . . sorry for him.*   Baker, pp. 9, 31.
223 *more a Tom Sawyer*   EH to Lillian Ross, 16 June 1950; Carlos Baker to C. T. Lanham, 16 December 1956.
223 *flowing kimono*   Dorothy Powell Vandercook, "Pictures with a Past," *Saturday Evening Post* (21 November 1953), p. 17.

223 *Plymouth League* Marcelline, pp. 147–48.
223 *Lloyd Harter* Baker, p. 29.
223–24 *Dr. William E. Barton* ... *"all time.* Marcelline, p. 148.
224 *"Christer element"* EH to Charles Fenton, 22 June 1952.
224 *"The age* ... *demanded."* EH, "The Age Demanded," *The Collected Poems of Ernest Hemingway* ("Originally Published in Paris": The Library of Living Poetry, 1960), unnumbered pages. Pirated edition. (Hereafter *Collected Poems.*)
224 *"* ... *'rules'* ... *impossible"* See Richard C. Gerhardt, "Denial and Affirmation of Values in the Fiction of Ernest Hemingway," Ph.D. dissertation, Michigan State University (1969), pp. 75–78.

CONVERT TO CATHOLICISM?

225 *anointing* Baker, p. 45.
225 *scared as hell became a Catholic* EH to Guy Hickok, 20 August 1932.
225 *Agnes* ... *religion* Mrs. William C. Stanfield, Jr., to Scott Donaldson, 18 November 1972.
225 *married* ... *Methodist* Montgomery, p. 185.
225 *son* ... *Episcopal* Baker, p. 126.
226 *"* ... *Catholic husband"* Baker, p. 175
226 *"If* ... *anything"* EH to Ernest Walsh and Ethel Moorhead, 2 January 1926, in *Auction*, p. 236.
226 *reunion* ... *priest* Baker, pp. 183–84.
226 *a Dominican father* Baker, p. 185.
226 *"wolf a Wafer* F. Scott Fitzgerald to Ernest Hemingway, c. July 1928.
226 *Mass be said* Marcelline, pp. 232–33.
226 *Dr. Hemingway* ... *purgatory* Leicester, p. 111.
226 *Saint-Sulpice* Andre Le Vot, "Fitzgerald in Paris," *Fitzgerald/Hemingway Annual: 1973* (Washington, D.C.: NCR Microcard Editions, 1973), p. 62.
226 *round-trip drive* Baker, p. 231.
226 *sending* ... *$25* Baker, p. 614.
227 *"* ... *a million seeds."* Baker, p. 220.
227 *Angrily* ... *proposed* ... *encyclicals.* EH to Guy Hickok, 15 July 1931?
227 *Church* ... *fascist salute* Baker, p. 333.
227 *Franco* ... *not bomb children.* EH, "The Cardinal Picks a Winner," *Ken* (5 May 1938), p. 38; Gingrich, p. 148.
227 *foxholes* ... *chaplain* ... *pray for him* EH to E. E. Dorman-O'Gowan, 10 July 1950; Baker, p. 435.
228 *"Schloss Hemingstein* Baker, p. 439–40.
228 *Two letters* EH to Mary Welsh, 4 September 1945, 29 September 1945.

228 *"... better Catholic."*   Hotchner, p. 130.
228 *Fraser Drew ... "hardened"*   Baker, p. 530.
228 *praying . . . sexual adventure.*   EH to Grace Quinlan, 30 September 1920.
228 *"... prayer" ... impotence.*   Hotchner, p. 51.
229 *praying for himself*   EH to Robert M. Brown, 14 July 1954; EH to Thomas J. Welsh, 19 June 1945.

SUPERSTITIONS AND RITUALS

230 *Cooper ... "belief."*   Baker, pp. 542–43.
230 *not actually ... Catholic*   Montgomery, p. 189.
230 *Christmas card*   EH to Rev. Dr. William S. Boice, December 195?.
230 *Betty Bruce*   Carlos Baker, interview with the Bruces, 22 March 1965.
230 *"... like horoscopes*   Quoted in Brad Reynolds, "Afternoon with Mary Hemingway," *America* (25 March 1972), p. 320.
230 *"... medieval peasant."*   Baker, p. 433.
230 *bad luck ... Sunday.*   Hotchner, p. 201.
230–31 *moonstruck*   EH to Grace Quinlan, 8 August 1920.
231 *"Hemingway's Death."*   Baker, p. 229.
231 *a red stone . . . champagne cork*   Leicester, pp. 239–40; Carlos Baker, interview with Lael Tucker Wertenbaker, 7 January 1966; Hotchner, p. 59.
231–32 *horse chestnut ... ring.*   Hotchner, p. 299.
232 *knocking . . . wood*   EH, "Night Before Battle," *Stories Spanish*, p. 173; Castillo-Puche, p. 56; Baker, p. 433.
232 *smelled ... doom.*   Baker, pp. 406–407, 434.
232 *Dietrich . . . astrology*   Denis Brian, "The Importance of Knowing Ernest," *Esquire* (February 1972), p. 99.
232 *". . . simple truth"*   Alan Lebowitz, "Hemingway in Our Time," *Yale Review*, 58 (March 1969), 322.
234 *existentialist . . . chaos.*   See John Killinger, *Hemingway and the Dead Gods* (Lexington: University of Kentucky Press, 1960); Cleanth Brooks, "Man on His Moral Uppers," *The Hidden God* (New Haven: Yale University Press, 1963), p. 10; John Clellon Holmes, "Existentialism and the Novel: Notes and Questions," *Chicago Review*, 13 (Summer 1959), 146.
234 *". . . evil spirits."*   Malcolm Cowley, Introduction, *The Portable Hemingway* (New York: Viking, 1944), pp. 13–14.

A RELIGIOUS WRITER

235 *"... Ten Commandments*   Quoted in Algren, p. 207.
236 *Catholic . . . unfavorably.*   Malcolm Cowley to Robert M. Brown, 30 August 1954.

236 *Sister Florence* Baker, p. 218.
236 *Lord's Prayer . . . cider.* Donald St. John, "Interview with Hemingway's 'Bill Gorton'," in *Sun Set*, p. 172.
236–37 *In 1927 . . . my shepherd* EH, "Neo-Thomist Poem," *Collected Poems*; Baker, pp. 595–96.
237 *"Trilogies* Quoted in Dos Passos, p. 202.
237 *marauding lion* EH, "African Journal," Part One.
237 *"A Divine Gesture"* EH, "A Divine Gesture," *The Double-Dealer* (May 1922), pp. 267–68.
237 *cynical view . . . "yellowed out"* EH to John Dos Passos, 26 March 1932.
238 *blasphemy . . . heresy* EH to Robert M. Brown, 22 July 1956.

AFFIRMATIONS

239 *Santiago . . . inundated* See Joseph Waldmeir, "Confiteor Hominem: Ernest Hemingway's Religion of Man," *Papers of the Michigan Academy of Science, Arts, and Letters*, 42 (1956), 349–56.
240 *". . . radical holiness"* Nathan A. Scott, Jr., *Ernest Hemingway: A Critical Essay* (Grand Rapids, Mich.: William B. Eerdmans, 1966), pp. 10–21, 29, 40.

xi. Art

FORGING A STYLE

241 *"Artist, art* Baker, p. 85.
241–42 *". . . old prose* Quoted in Alden Whitman, "Hemingway Letters Reproach Critics," *The New York Times* (9 March 1972), p. 36.
242 *at least two styles* See John McCormick, *The Middle Distance: A Comparative History of American Imaginative Literature: 1919–1932* (New York: Free Press, 1971), pp. 48–49.
242 *wiry . . . sentences* Dos Passos, pp. 141–42.
242 *". . . pebbles . . . brook."* Quoted in Philip Young, *Ernest Hemingway* (Minneapolis: University of Minnesota Press, 1959), p. 32.
243 *Basic English* See Harry Levin, "Observations on the Style of Ernest Hemingway," *Kenyon Review*, 13 (Autumn 1951), 581–609.

ICEBERGS AND SWORDS

244 *". . . hands off."* Thornton Wilder to EH, 22 November 1926.
245 *drastically reduced* See Fenton, pp. 231–36.

245 *Did you know* EH to John Robben, 6 December 1951.

246 *irony . . . functions* See Benson, pp. 114–28.

246 *". . . refinement"* Quoted in Thomas Neal Hagood, "Elements of Humor in Ernest Hemingway," Ph.D. dissertation, Louisiana State University (1969), p. 89.

247 *antiliterary* Daniel Fuchs, "Ernest Hemingway, Literary Critic," *American Literature*, 36 (January 1965), 433.

247 *Henry James . . . a fake?* EH to Waldo Peirce, late December 1927.

247 *Eliot . . . Pound.* EH to Harvey Breit, 9 July 1950.

247–48 *Hemingway instructed . . . exercise."* EH, "Monologue to the Maestro: A High Seas Letter," *Esquire* (October 1935), in *Byline*, p. 219.

248 *". . . father is dying* Callaghan, p. 30.

248 *". . . blacksmith or anybody* Quoted in Kyle Crichton, *Total Recoil* (Garden City, N.Y.: Doubleday, 1960), pp. 160–61.

248 *Isidor Schneider* EH to Isidor Schneider, 18–19–20 January 1927, in *Auction*, p. 117.

248 *". . . shit detector.* George Plimpton, interview with Ernest Hemingway, *Writers at Work*, Second Series (New York: Viking, 1963), p. 239. (Hereafter Plimpton.)

249 *". . . real old man* Sanderson, p. 114.

249 *"The Lottery"* EH to Lillian Ross, 28 July 1948.

249 *lectured Fitzgerald* Turnbull, p. 244.

249 *"The only writing* EH, "On Writing," *Adams Stories*, pp. 237–38.

249 *"You invent* Quoted in Hotchner, p. 103.

249 *Sevastapol* EH to Charles Poore, 23 January 1953.

249 *a "superliar"* Baker, pp. 505–506.

249–50 *"From things . . . immortality."* Plimpton, p. 239.

CRITICS AND COMPETITORS

250 *eleven critics* Joost, pp. 88–89.

250 *doggerel . . . decay."* EH, "Valentine" (For a Mr. Lee Wilson Dodd and Any of His Friends Who Want It), *Little Review*, 12 (May 1929), 42.

250 *writers of the past* EH, "Monologue to the Maestro," *Esquire* (October 1935) Maestro: A High Seas Letter," *Esquire* (October 1935), in *Byline*, pp. 218–19.

251 *Nobel . . . speech* *The New York Times* (11 December 1964), p. 5.

251 *champion of the world.* EH to Lillian Ross, 6 May 1950.

251 *Nathan Asch* Nathan Asch to Malcolm Cowley, 23 March 1948.

251 *Joseph M. Hopkins* EH to Joseph M. Hopkins, 6 December 1935, 15 December 1935, in *Auction*, p. 211.

251 *J. D. Salinger* Baker, p. 420; J. D. Salinger to EH, 27 July 1946.

251 *"writing Irish"* EH to Robert M. Brown, 22 July 1956.

251 *Sinclair Lewis.* See Stephens, *Hemingway's Nonfiction: The Public Voice* (Chapel Hill: University of North Carolina Press, 1968), pp. 123–24.

251–53 *Faulkner . . . Hemingway . . . Dr. Faulkner."* Henry Strater, "Hemingway," *Art in America*, 44 (1961), 84–85; EH to Harvey Breit, 27 June 1952, 29 June 1952; EH, "The Art of the Short Story," unpublished manuscript, p. 8; Baker, pp. 503–504, 532; Leicester, p. 277; EH to "Mr. Rider," 29 July 1956, in *Auction*, p. 83; Joseph Blotner, *Faulkner: A Biography* (New York: Random House, 1974), pp. 1266, 1334, 1428–1429, 1560, 1586.

THE WORK ETHIC

253 *repudiated . . . values* Malcolm Cowley, *Exile's Return*, p. 9.

253 *unsound . . . conceptions* EH to Mary Welsh, c. 3 September 1945.

253–54 *". . . essentially moral . . . "morality" "* D. H. Lawrence, *Studies in Classic American Literature*, in *The Shock of Recognition*, ed. Edmund Wilson (New York: Modern Library, 1955), p. 1070.

254 *James T. Farrell* James T. Farrell, "The Sun Also Rises," *The New York Times*, Book Review (1 August 1943).

254 *"awful . . . remorse* Baker, p. 605.

254–55 *Hanna Club . . . afterwards."* EH, "Mr. Quayle Rouses Hanna Club," Oak Park (High School) *The Trapeze* (17 February 1916) and EH, "Problems of Boyhood Discussed at Hanna Club," Oak Park (High School) *The Trapeze* (9 March 1916), in *Oak Park*, pp. 13, 17.

255 *scheme . . . Orient* Marcelline, pp. 203–204.

255 *son married* Marcelline, p. 210.

255 *". . . always at work."* Quoted in Cowley, p. 61.

255 *eight hours a day.* EH to F. Scott Fitzgerald, September 1928.

255 *". . . respectable aspect."* Martha Gellhorn to Carlos Baker, 13 June 1966.

255–56 *writing . . . tropics* Mary Hemingway, "Life with Papa: A Portrait of Ernest Hemingway," *Flair* (Jaunary 1961), pp. 29, 116.

256 *regular . . . routine.* See Stephens, pp. 218–21.

256 *"I have every word* Max Eastman to Charles A. Fenton, 3 February 1952.

256 *"When . . . talking"* Quoted in Grebstein, p. 96.

256 *". . . work is in his head."* Quoted in Cranston, p. 189.

257 *Steffens . . . labor."*   Quoted in Malcolm Cowley, p. 61.
257 *"The hardest thing*   EH, "Old Newsman Writes: A Letter from Cuba," *Esquire* (December 1934), in *Byline*, pp. 183–84.
257 *a disease*   Baker, p. 347.
257 *"poetry . . . into prose"*   Baker, p. 656.
257 *perpetual challenge*   EH to Ivan Kashkeen, 19 August 1935, "Letters of Ernest Hemingway to Soviet Writers," *Soviet Literature*, 11 (1962), 162.
257 *word count*   EH to John Dos Passos, 17 September 1949.
258 *". . . rigid standards*   EH, "The Christmas Gift," *Look* (20 May 1954), in *Byline*, p. 461.

xii. Mastery

THE DIVIDED SELF

259 *If a novelist*   *Crack-Up*, p. 117.
259 *fish and hunt*   EH to Marjorie Kinnan Rawlings, 16 August 1936.
259 *Reconciling*   Baker, p. 609.
260 *damn about writing.*   EH to C. T. Lanham, April 1945.
260 *". . . watchers . . . fish."*   Archibald MacLeish, "His Mirror Was Danger," *Life* (14 July 1961), p. 71.
260 *". . . American fable*   Alfred Kazin, "Hemingway as His Own Fable," *Atlantic Monthly* (June 1964), p. 56.
260 *idealized self-image . . . others.*   Irvin D. and Marilyn Yalom, "Ernest Hemingway—A Psychiatric View," *Archives of General Psychiatry*, 24 (June 1971), pp. 485–94.
261 *his "God."*   EH to Arthur Mizener, 12 May 1950.

OMNISCIENCE AND INVINCIBILITY

261 "This kid   Ernest Walsh, "Ernest Hemingway," *This Quarter*, 1 (Autumn–Winter 1925–1926), p. 67.
261–62 *". . . Hardy and Hamsun*   EH, "Summer People," *Adams Stories*, p. 219.
262 *drive a wedge*   EH to Monique de Beaumont, 31 August 1959, in *Auction*, p. 227.
262 *"taught himself . . . subject."*   Malcolm Cowley, CBC, Side Two.
262 how to   See Cowley, p. 50.
262 *dispatches . . . Toronto*   EH, "Store Thieves Use Three Tricks," Toronto *Star Weekly* (3 April 1920), in *Wild Years*, pp. 60–61; EH,

"Fishing for Trout in a Sporting Way," Toronto *Star Weekly* (24 April 1920), in *Wild Years*, pp. 246–49; EH, "Flivver, Canoe, Pram and Taxi Combined Is the Luge, the Joy of Everybody in Switzerland," Toronto *Star Weekly*), in *Wild Years*, pp. 166–67; EH, "Bullfighting Is Not a Sport—It Is a Tragedy," Toronto *Star Weekly* (20 October 1923), in *Wild Years*, p. 228; EH, "When You Camp Out Do It Right," Toronto *Star Weekly* (26 June 1920), in *Wild Years*, pp. 266–67; EH, "Skier's Only Escape from Alpine Avalanches Is to Swim," Toronto *Star Weekly* (12 January 1964), in *Wild Years*, p. 273.

262 *shoot a horse* EH, "On Being Shot Again: A Gulf Stream Letter," *Esquire* (June 1935), in *Byline*, p. 198.

262–63 *football tackling.* EH to Patrick Hemingway, 7 October 1942.

263 *her hair done* EH to Mary Hemingway, August 1948.

263 *Dos Passos . . . restive* Dos Passos, p. 211; John Dos Passos to EH, February 1932, in *The Fourteenth Chronicle*, ed. Townsend Ludington (Boston: Gambit, 1973), pp. 402–403.

263 *"cotsies"* Hotchner, pp. 15, 22–23.

263 *driving* Herbert L. Matthews, *A World in Revolution* (New York: Scribner's, 1971), p. 24; "The Reminiscences of Claude G. Bowers" (1957), Oral History Archives, Columbia University; Leicester, pp. 119–20.

264 *shooting . . . cigarettes* Baker, pp. 471, 515; EH to Philip Percival, 14 September 1955; EH to Harvey Breit, 6 February 1951; Hotchner, p. 219.

264 *dumbwaiter* "Three Girls Rescued," Oak Park (High School) *Trapeze* (9 June 1917), p. 7.

264 *duffle bags* Baker, p. 621.

264 *saved their lives* Herbert L. Matthews, *The Education of a Correspondent* (New York: Harcourt, Brace, 1946), p. 138.

264 *spoon bend . . . try.* Hellman, pp. 71–72.

264 *O'Hara's . . . blackthorn* Baker, pp. 387, 649.

265 *wounds . . . forearm.* Baker, pp. 45, 189–90, 391, 484–85, 522–23; EH to Waldo Peirce, 1 June 1930; EH to F. Scott Fitzgerald, 12 April 1931.

265 *". . . psychic adrenals* Carlos Baker, interview with C. T. Lanham, 16 August 1963.

266 *Ted Brumback* Baker, p. 52.

266 *a questionnaire* EH to Dr. Israel Bram, 9 December 1931.

266 *forty-two days* EH to C. T. Lanham, 24 May 1947.

266 *"all the sunrises"* Quoted in Lillian Ross, *Portrait of Hemingway* (New York: Simon & Schuster, 1961), p. 42. (Hereafter Ross.)

266 *insomnia* EH to F. Scott Fitzgerald, 21 December 1935.

266 Dracula Marcelline, p. 100.

266 *two Seconal* EH to Lillian Ross, 20 September 1950.

266 *change pajamas* EH to Carlos Baker, 24 April 1951.

266 *taproots of fear* EH to Mary Welsh, 10 April 1945.

266 *Peter Viertel*   Hotchner, p. 123.
266 *penis . . . snow*   EH to Harold Loeb, 27 February 1925.
266 *battle of Teruel . . . ordeal.*   Ilya Ehrenburg, *Memoirs: 1921–1941* (Cleveland: World, 1964), pp. 387–88; Stanley Weintraub, *The Last Great Cause* (New York: Weybright and Talley, 1968), p. 202.
266–67 *". . . bedroom slippers*   Ross, p. 12.
267 *regular tab*   McLendon, p. 148.
267 *"non-drinking" routine*   EH to Mary Welsh, 18 September 1945.

267 *regimen*   Denis Zaphiro and Worth Bingham, "Hemingway's Last Safari," *Rogue* (February 1967), p. 20.

267 *chug-a-lugs*   Donald St. John, "Interview with Hemingway's 'Bill Gorton'," in *Sun Set*, p. 167.

267 *Stewart . . . drinker*   EH to John Dos Passos, 22 April 1925.
267 *beer . . . contest.*   Callaghan, p. 96.
267 *double frozen daiquiris*   EH to Charles Poore, 30 January 1953, in *Auction*, p. 168.
267 *"I love . . . drunk"*   Baker, p. 121.
268 *"Don't you drink?"*   EH to Ivan Kashkeen, 19 August 1935, in "Letters of Ernest Hemingway to Soviet Writers," *Soviet Literature*, 11 (November 1962), 158–67.

268 *"Rummies are*   Alden Whitman, "Hemingway Letters Reproach Critics," *The New York Times* (9 March 1972), p. 37.

268 *"God pity*   EH, "African Journal," Part Two.
268 *did not . . . nag*   Hotchner, p. 188; Castillo-Puche, p. 275.

ERNIE THE GREEK

269 *kronen.*   Baker, p. 140.
270 *shooting gallery*   Callaghan, p. 236.
270 *". . . large money"*   EH, "The Great Blue River," *Holiday* (July 1949), in *Byline*, pp. 403–404.
270 *"A Matter of Colour"*   Montgomery, pp. 47–49.
271 *bookmakers*   EH, "Toronto is Biggest Betting Place in North America—10,000 People Bet $100,000 on Horses Every Day," Toronto *Star Weekly* (29 December 1923), in *Wild Years*, pp. 62–68.
271 *"The Sport of Kings . . . envelope."*   EH, "The Sport of Kings," Toronto *Star Weekly* (24 November 1923), p. 17.
271 *". . . animal . . . talk"*   Hotchner, p. 217.
271 *"thieves like us"*   EH to Harvey Breit, 20 July 1952.
272 *smell the horses*   Hotchner, pp. 39–46.
272 *Prix Yacoulef*   Hotchner, p. 38.
272 *Bataclan II.*   Hotchner, pp. 58–63; Baker, p. 480.
272 *Ingemar Johansson*   Hotchner, p. 217.
273 *Dempsey was "over-rated"*   EH, "Carpentier Sure to Give

Dempsey Fight Worth While," Toronto *Star Weekly* (30 October 1920), p. 3.

273   *losing $50*   Hadley Richardson to EH, 2 July 1921.

273   *"never bet on Carpentier*   EH to Horace Liveright, 31 March 1925.

273   *boxing . . . credentials . . . first time*   EH to Harvey Breit, 20 April 1950, 1 May 1950, 18 March 1955.

273   *Kid Tunero*   EH to Harvey Breit, 24 June 1950.

273   *"Never Bet on Fights"*   EH to Harvey Breit, 20 April 1950, 8 July 1950.

274   *Mitri . . . Graziano*   EH to Harvey Breit, 24 April 1950.

274   *strange letter . . . Mitri.*   EH to Harvey Breit, 24 June 1950.

274   *check . . . $250.*   EH to Harvey Breit, 30 June 1950.

274   *still . . . a wonderful bet.*   EH to Harvey Breit, 17 July 1950, 23 October 1951.

274   *five . . . forecasts . . . Series*   EH to Harvey Breit, 27 August 1951, 23 October 1951.

274–75   *beat . . . Yankees*   EH to Harvey Breit, 6 October 1950, 23 October 1951, 13 October 1952.

275–76   *letter-lecture . . . roulette . . . wheel.*   EH to Dorothy Connable, 16 February 1920.

276   *run a stake . . . in Petoskey.*   Montgomery, p. 185.

276   *crap table*   EH, "Galloping Dominoes, alias African," Toronto *Star Weekly* (22 May 1920), p. 21.

276   *"how to pick them*   Leicester, p. 269.

276   *poker . . . angles.*   EH to Lillian Ross, 20 September 1950, 5 October 1950.

276   *Morehead's . . . poker*   Albert H. Morehead, *The Complete Guide to Winning Poker* (New York: Simon & Schuster, 1967), p. 54.

THE MAN WHO WOULD BE KING

278   *"None . . . more clever*   Daniel P. Reichard, "None Are More Clever Than Ernie," *English Journal*, 58 (May 1969), 668–72.

278   *something mean*   Quoted in *Sun Set*, p. 70.

278   *"something warped*   Connolly, p. 27.

278   *father . . . brother*   Marcelline, p. 127.

278   *"how" . . . "The Undefeated"*   EH to Henry Goodman, 16 January 1924.

278   *poems . . . Browning."*   Quoted in Ross, p. 62.

278–79   *"the oldest . . . scum"*   EH, "American Bohemians in Paris a Weird Lot," Toronto *Star Weekly* (25 March 1922), in *Byline*, p. 23.

279   *abandon Paris*   EH to Thornton Wilder, 26 May 1929.

279   *Parisian cab drivers*   EH, "French Politeness," Toronto *Star Weekly* (15 April 1922), p. 29.

279 *"A Friend of France"* EH, "The Friend of Spain: A Spanish Letter," *Esquire* (January 1934), in *Byline*, p. 645.

279 *Italians* Steffens, p. 836; EH, "Picked Sharpshooters Patrol Genoa Streets," Toronto *Daily Star* (13 April 1922), in *Wild Years*, pp. 183–84; EH, "The Dangerous Summer," *Life* (5 September 1960), p. 85.

279 *"Belgiums"* EH to Mary Hemingway, 20 November 1948.

279 *exotic language.* EH, "London Fights the Robots," *Collier's* (19 August 1944), in *Byline*, pp. 361–62.

280 *Rumania . . . seriously."* EH, "King Business in Europe Isn't What It Used to Be," Toronto *Star Weekly* (15 September 1923), in *Wild Years*, pp. 158–59; EH, "Notes on the Next War: A Serious topical Letter," *Esquire* (September 1935), in *Byline*, p. 211.

280 *Swiss . . . full house. . . ."* EH to William C. Lengel, n.d.; EH, "Tourists Are Scarce at the Swiss Resorts," Toronto *Star Weekly* (4 February 1922), in *Wild Years*, p. 120.

280 *Germans . . . dinner.* EH, "Hubby Dines First, Wife Gets Crumbs," Toronto *Daily Star* (30 September 1922), in *Wild Years*, p. 103; EH, "Once Over Permit Obstacle, Fishing in Baden Perfect," Toronto *Daily Star* (2 September 1922), in *Wild Years*, pp. 120–21.

281 *own . . . fault"* Quoted in Leicester, p. 82.

281 *"I'm the judge* Quoted Castillo-Puche, p. 23.

281 *like to be king* Hadley Mowrer file, Carlos Baker's office.

xiii. Death

THAT OLD WHORE

282 *"one . . . sought death* EH, "The Christmas Gift," *Look* (20 May 1954), in *Byline*, p. 460.

282 *girl . . . enemy* EH to Lillian Ross, 20 September 1950.

282 *"the oldest whore* Baker, p. 432.

283 *five birds* EH, "Wings Always Over Africa: An Ornithological Letter," *Esquire* (January 1936), in *Byline*, pp. 230–31.

283 *maggot-eaten corpse* Robert McAlmon, *McAlmon and the Lost Generation: A Self-Portrait*, ed. Robert E. Knoll (Lincoln: University of Nebraska Press, 1962), p. 230.

283–84 *Madrid morgue* Scott Donaldson, interview with Stephen Spender, 24 April 1975.

284 *puntillo.* EH, "The Soul of Spain," *Collected Poems*.

284 *preoccupation with death* Connolly, p. 27.

284 *"Death . . . country* Quoted in Edward L. Galligan, "Hemingway's Staying Power," *Massachusetts Review*, 8 (Summer 1967), 436–37.

284 *less bloodshed* EH to Wyndham Lewis, 24 October 1927.

284 *Dying . . . "intelligent* Quoted Rovit, p. 29.

THOUGHTS ON TAKING ONE'S LIFE

285 *"The Suicide Club."* Marcelline, p. 133.

285 *first story* Reprinted in Montgomery, pp. 44–45.

285 *Tough . . . lumberjack."* Baker, p. 25.

285–86 *Lying wounded* Baker, p. 45.

286 *mortage* Hadley Richardson to EH, 8 July 1921.

286 *Unhappy in Canada* EH to Gertrude Stein, 11 October 1923; Baker, p. 119.

286 *"unless . . . off a liner* Baker, p. 167.

286 *startled . . . companions* McLendon, pp. 92–93.

286 *Tommy gun* EH to John Dos Passos, 17 December 1935.

286 *"big disgust" . . . himself.* EH to Archibald MacLeish, 26 September 1936; Baker, p. 293.

286 *suicide pact* Baker, p. 344.

286 *dived deep* EH to Lillian Ross, 24 August 1950; Baker, pp. 485–86, 651.

286 *"the second kite"* Hotchner, p. 109.

286 *barracks talk* Scott Donaldson, interview with C. T. Lanham, 5 April 1974.

287 *early poem . . . café."* EH, "Montparnasse," *Collected Poems.*

287 *"This old friend* EH, "A Paris Letter," *Esquire* (February 1934), in *Byline*, p. 155.

288 *Frank Tinker . . . chance.* Baker, p. 627.

288 *lost . . . stamina* EH to Lillian Ross, 27 April 1950.

289 *"Survival* Plimpton, p. 237.

289 *"The real reason . . . over."* EH to Isidor Schneider, early October 1926, in *Auction*, p. 116.

289 *"very . . . gay"* Donald St. John, "Hemingway and the Girl Who Could Skate," *Connecticut Review*, 2 (October 1968), 11.

289 *aura of fun* Hotchner, p. 6.

289–90 *limitless "capacity* Mary Hemingway, "Department of Amplification," *The New Yorker* (16 March 1963), p. 163.

GRACE AND ED HEMINGWAY

290 *pattern of matriarchy* Hugh MacLennan, "Hemingway, Hunter and the Hunted," Montreal *Star* (21 September 1963), p. 4.

290 *grandmothers.* Leicester, p. 19.

290 *"Run along* Marcelline, p. 54.

291 *marriage . . . career . . . opera."* Montgomery, pp. 22, 81.

291 *"abhorred didies* Leicester, p. 22.

291 *roast . . . fountain pen* Lewis Clarahan, at Hemingway Conference, Modern Language Association meeting, Chicago, 28 December 1971.

291 *sick headache.* Leicester, p. 42.
291 *family . . . cornet* Marcelline, p. 66.
291 *cottage* Marcelline, pp. 194–95; Baker, p. 62.
292 *imposing appearance.* Donald St. John, "Hemingway and the Girl Who Could Skate," *Connecticut Review*, 2 (October 1968), 13.
292 *"She . . . long skirts . . . exhibited* Otto McFeeley to Malcolm Cowley, 1 July 1948, 6 July 1948.
292 *"Honestly, Marce"* Marcelline, pp. 240–41.
292 *deplored . . . "young writers"* Baker, pp. 188–89.
293 *"constructive."* Baker, p. 349.
293 *gallantry* Baker, p. 59.
293 *"that bitch.* C. T. Lanham to Carlos Baker, 7 December 1966.
293 *blue ribbon* Baker, p. 418.
293 *stern . . . father.* Marcelline, p. 39.
293 *bobbed hair.* Marcelline, pp. 206–207.
294 *dance steps* Marcelline, pp. 140–43.
294 *missionary . . . escape* Leicester, p. 21.
295 *"I've never been sick"* Marcelline, pp. 224–26.
295 *neck . . . scrawny* Baker, p. 193.
295 *illness . . . transformed . . . car.* Marcelline, pp. 118–19.
295 *pulled the trigger.* Baker, pp. 198–99.
295 *Sigmund Freud* Quoted in *Harper's* (May 1975), p. 9.
295–96 *Hickok . . . note . . . busy.* EH to Guy Hickok, 9 January 1929.
296 *lonely . . . snipe* EH to Waldo Peirce, 4 January 1929.
296 *passage excised* Baker, p. 609.
296 *respect . . . father.* C. T. Lanham to Carlos Baker, 7 December 1966.
297 *experience . . . parallel* Baker, p. 31.
298 *too many people* EH to Carlos Baker, 11 June 1953.
298 *"love of a son* *The Writer as Artist*, p. 305.

A NOVEL ABOUT HOW TO DIE

299 *in-depth . . . death* See Donald J. Greiner, "The Education of Robert Jordan: Death with Dignity," *Hemingway Notes*, 1 (Fall 1971), 14–20.
301 *Minié-ball* Marcelline, p. 7.
301 *pillar . . . G.A.R.* Marcelline, p. 170.

THE FINAL TORTURE

303 *revolver . . . cake* Dos Passos, p. 210; Baker, p. 200.
303 *shotgun . . . barrels.* Baker, pp. 563–64.
303 *"intent* A. E. Hotchner, CBC, Side Four.

303　*("I've never seen . . . floor of despair*　Archibald MacLeish, CBC, Side Two.

304　*snooping . . . secret*　EH to Robert M. Brown, 14 July 1954.

304　*fallible man*　EH to C. T. Lanham, 23 July 1945.

304　*words . . . wouldn't come.*　EH to A. E. Hotchner, 8 September 1960; Carlos Baker, interview with Lloyd Arnold, 20 July 1964; Carlos Baker, interview with Chuck Atkinson, 2 August 1964.

304–305　*"lost youth*　Richmond Lattimore, "Old Hemingway," *Kenyon Review*, 26 (Autumn 1964), 674.

305　*"what . . . wonderful old man*　Quoted in Denis Brian, "The Importance of Knowing Ernest," *Esquire* (February 1972), p. 168.

305　*"to die . . . youth*　Baker, p. 52.

305　*Fiedler . . . Betsky*　Leslie Fiedler, "An Almost Imaginary Interview: Hemingway in Ketchum," *Partisan Review*, 24 (Summer 1962), 395–405; Seymour Betsky, "A Last Visit," *Saturday Review* (29 July 1961), p. 22.

305　*"a wounded animal*　Quoted in Reynolds Price, "For Ernest Hemingway," *New American Review*, 14 (1972), 50.

305　*sweat out*　Scott Donaldson, interview with C. T. Lanham, 5 April 1974.

305　*Even as a boy*　Marcelline Sanford, CBC, Side Two.

305　*twin brother*　EH to Nathan (Bill) Davis, 28 October 1959, in *Auction*, p. 121.

INDEX